Japan's Ultra-Right

JAPANESE SOCIETY SERIES
General Editor: Yoshio Sugimoto

A Social History of Science and Technology in Contemporary Japan, Volume 4
Shigeru Nakayama and Hitoshi Yoshioka

Scams and Sweeteners: A Sociology of Fraud
Masahiro Ogino

Toyota's Assembly Line: A View from the Factory Floor
Ryoji Ihara

Village Life in Modern Japan: An Environmental Perspective
Akira Furukawa

Social Welfare in Japan: Principles and Applications
Kojun Furukawa

Escape from Work: Freelancing Youth and the Challenge to Corporate Japan
Reiko Kosugi

Japan's Whaling: The Politics of Culture in Historical Perspective
Hiroyuki Watanabe

Gender Gymnastics: Performing and Consuming Japan's Takarazuka Revue
Leonie R. Stickland

Poverty and Social Welfare in Japan
Masami Iwata and Akihiko Nishizawa

The Modern Japanese Family: Its Rise and Fall
Chizuko Ueno

Widows of Japan: An Anthropological Perspective
Deborah McDowell Aoki

In Pursuit of the Seikatsusha:
A Genealogy of the Autonomous Citizen in Japan
Masako Amano

Demographic Change and Inequality in Japan
Sawako Shirahase

The Origins of Japanese Credentialism
Ikuo Amano

Pop Culture and the Everyday in Japan: Sociological Perspectives
Katsuya Minamida and Izumi Tsuji

Japanese Perceptions of Foreigners
Shunsuke Tanabe

Migrant Workers in Contemporary Japan:
An Institutional Perspective on Transnational Employment
Kiyoto Tanno

The Boundaries of 'the Japanese', Volume 1:
Okinawa 1868–1972 – Inclusion and Exclusion
Eiji Oguma

International Migrants in Japan: Contributions in an Era of Population Decline
Yoshitaka Ishikawa

Globalizing Japan: Striving to Engage the World
Ross Mouer

Beyond Fukushima: Toward a Post-Nuclear Society
Koichi Hasegawa

Japan's Ultra-Right
Naoto Higuchi

Japan's Ultra-Right

By

Naoto Higuchi

Translated by
Teresa Castelvetere

Trans Pacific Press

Melbourne

First published in Japanese in 2014 by the University of Nagoya Press as
NIHON-GATA HAIGAI-SHUGI by Naoto Higuchi
Copyright © 2014 HIGUCHI Naoto
All rights reserved.
Originally published in Japan.
English translation rights arranged with The University of Nagoya Press
Through THE SAKAI AGENCY.

This English language edition published in 2016 by
Trans Pacific Press, PO Box 164, Balwyn North, Victoria 3104, Australia
Telephone: +61-(0)3-9859-1112 Fax: +61-(0)3-8611-7989
Email: tpp.mail@gmail.com
Web: http://www.transpacificpress.com

Designed and set by Digital Environs, Melbourne, Australia.

Distributors

Australia and New Zealand
James Bennett Pty Ltd
Locked Bag 537
Frenchs Forest NSW 2086
Australia
Telephone: +61-(0)2-8988-5000
Fax: +61-(0)2-8988-5031
Email: info@bennett.com.au
Web: www.bennett.com.au

USA and Canada
International Specialized Book
Services (ISBS)
920 NE 58th Avenue, Suite 300
Portland, Oregon 97213-3786
USA
Telephone: 1-800-944-6190
Fax: 1-503-280-8832
Email: orders@isbs.com
Web: http://www.isbs.com

Asia and the Pacific
Kinokuniya Company Ltd.
Head office:
3-7-10 Shimomeguro
Meguro-ku
Tokyo 153-8504
Japan
Telephone: +81-(0)3-6910-0531
Fax: +81-(0)3-6420-1362
Email: bkimp@kinokuniya.co.jp
Web: www.kinokuniya.co.jp
Asia-Pacific office:
Kinokuniya Book Stores of Singapore Pte., Ltd.
391B Orchard Road #13-06/07/08
Ngee Ann City Tower B
Singapore 238874
Telephone: +65-6276-5558
Fax: +65-6276-5570
Email: SSO@kinokuniya.co.jp

ISSN   1443-9670 (Japanese Society Series)

ISBN   978-1-920901-68-4

Contents

Figures

Tables

Acknowledgements

I must confess that I had long had no more than a passing interest in East Asia. This was because while conducting fieldwork on migration from South America to Japan I had superficially thought that there was little connection between this and the experiences of *Zainichi* Koreans. It was while I was in the Netherlands in 2009 that I realized the importance of looking at East Asia, and that this was essential beyond the concerns of my own research. At that time, I was spending my sabbatical year at Utrecht University analyzing the support base of then Governor of Tokyo, Shintarō Ishihara, who was seen as the epitome of the Japanese ultra-right politician.

I would like to express my gratitude to Marcel Lubbers, who reminded me of the East Asian context in comparisons of the support bases for Wilders, the head of the Dutch extreme right Party for Freedom, and Ishihara. When he pointed out the significance of nationalism in explaining the support for Ishihara, a map of East Asia stretching from China to Japan came clearly to my mind. It was just like the tea and madeleines in *In Search of Lost Time.*

To me it was obvious that nationalism was the most important factor in the explanation of Ishihara's support, but this was not what a scholar of Western Europe saw when he looked at the data. Because anti-immigrant sentiment is most closely related to support for European ultra-right parties, he found it unusual that nationalism stood out as the analysis result. I had mechanically tried to apply Western European results, thinking that the ultra-right is the same everywhere, but it is impossible not to consider that Japan is deeply embedded in East Asia. During the interviews that I conducted following my return to Japan, I sometimes felt embarrassed about communicating with ultra-right activists, a sentiment shared by many researchers who work on ultra-right movements. I conducted all the interviews and prepared the data in the Appendix, but the research behind this book was a collaborative effort, and it is the product of the following projects:

- Grant-in-Aid for Scientific Research Support, 'Changes of Government and Social Movements: What is the Impact of DPJ Government on Social Movements? (2010–2013, with Nanako Inaba, Ki-young Shin, Woncheol Sung, Ryosuke Takaki, Shun Harada and Mitsuru Matsutani.) Ki-young also taught me the South Korean perspective regarding international relations in East Asia.
- Grant-in-Aid for Scientific Research, 'East Asian Geopolitics and Social Upheaval: Towards a Japanese Version of Transnational Social Movement Research,' (2012–2013, with Ki-young Shin, Woncheol Sung, Mizuho Tsuchino and Mitsuru Matsutani.
- Grant-in-Aid for Scientific Research, 'Action Research Towards Post-Multicultural Symbiosis Migration Research,' (2009–2011, with Nanako Inaba, Sachi Takaya, Yasuhiko Hikichi and Satoru Furuya).
- Grant-in-Aid for Scientific Research, 'Analysis of the Socio-economic Status of Foreigners in Japan,' (2012–2014, with Nanako Inaba, Yukiko Omagari, Itaru Kaji and Sachi Takaya).
- Nomura Foundation Grant, 'The Foreigner Problem in Japan and Politics: Why are Voting Rights for Foreign Residents Only a Problem in Japan?'

I acknowledge a Grant-in-Aid for Publication of Scientific Research Results bestowed by the Japan Society for the Promotion of Science (JSPS) in support of the translation and publication of this volume.

Prologue

In the second half of the 2000s, surprise greeted street demonstrations in Japan calling for the expulsion of foreigners. While Japan is known as a country that is closed to migrants, organized nativist movements had not been seen before. Why then has this kind of movement sprung forth at this time? Journalism and research to date have abounded with interpretations relying on stereotyped phrases. Since the end of the 1990s, Japan has experienced the loss of the stable social structure that it had enjoyed during the period of long-term high economic growth and also rising 'anxiety (*fuan*)' brought about by the fluidization of the economy under globalization and the long-term economic slump. The worst manifestation of this anxiety is the rise of nativism which attacks vulnerable people. Youths with nowhere to go, who have embraced nativism, turn their situation into a hatred of foreigners and take to marching through cities calling for their expulsion – or, so the argument goes.

This kind of argument, however, relies on a considerable number of unverified premises which although essential to its own thesis cannot withstand academic scrutiny. At a glance, explanations that focus on grievance or anxiety appear to be reasonable and based on common knowledge. Since those taking part in nativist movements would, in fact, not have any reason to do so if they did not harbor some form of grievance, it seems intuitive to conclude that this is a core factor. But is this kind of explanation really sufficient?

The aim of this book is to analyze Japan's nativist movement with considerable reference to Western European research on the radical right. My interviews with activists within nativist movements, including *Zainichi tokken o yurusanai shimin no kai* (Association of Citizens against the Special Privileges of *Zainichi*, hereafter *Zaitokukai*), provide the basis for elucidating the appearance of what I call 'Japanese-style xenophobia'.

Zaitokukai was established in 2007 and, with a membership of over 15,000 by March 2016, it is the largest and also the most well-known nativist group.[1] *Zaitokukai* has introduced scenes of 'ordinary youths' mobilized on the streets of Japan hurling abusive hate speech at ethnic minorities, primarily *Zainichi* Koreans.[2] The resulting media coverage has put *Zaitokukai* activities in the spotlight (Yasuda 2012a) and led to regulations surrounding hate speech being discussed in the Diet and also in newspaper editorials (Arita 2013).

I started researching nativism after having worked on an analysis of the support for the writer and well-known politician, Shintarō Ishihara, whom I regard as a Japanese-style far-right-winger (Higuchi and Matsutani 2016; Matsutani et al. 2006). *Zaitokukai's* direct action was not the initial impetus for the research on nativist movements contained in the following chapters; it has grown out of a research interest in voting rights for foreign residents, which I had already been pursuing intermittently for over ten years. Voting rights for foreign residents became a focal issue following the 2009 change of government from the Liberal Democratic Party to the Democratic Party, but its politicization proceeded in a manner unthinkable in other countries. As will be seen in Chapter 7, Japanese-style nativism can be understood by focussing on this distinctiveness.

In the second half of the 2000s, there were claims about the 'dangers of voting rights for foreign residents' and many people began to believe the idea that Japan would be taken over by foreign powers if these rights were to become a reality. Surprisingly, the LDP, which had had a long run in power in Japanese politics, also saw this red herring as credible, and sent its delegates to Yonaguni Island on the Taiwan–Japan border (*Jiyū Minshutō Seimu Chōsakai Yonagunichō Chōsadan* 2010). There is no need to attempt to establish whether there is any empirical basis for this anxiety; the following mock phone-in radio program exchange should put this anxiety into perspective.

> Q: If voting rights for foreign residents were to be enacted, close to a million votes would suddenly exert their influence on Japanese politics. Since there was so much anxiety as a result of voices saying that China and South Korea had designs on our border zones, we felt compelled to send a Commission of Enquiry to Yonaguni Island.
> A: I sympathize with your patriotic spirit, and I have been waiting for your call to understand why you feel an unavoidable sense of anxiety!

Q: There are fears about China and South Korea holding casting votes on issues related to intervention in our domestic affairs. What would we do if China wanted the United States military to leave Japan and sent large numbers of its people with permanent residence in Japan to cities where these bases are located, thus seizing the casting vote and bringing about the election of a group of citizens who oppose the bases?

A: I find it unimaginable that, as a professional electoral group that has been in power for a very long time, you have expressed this view. Let us assume that a candidate backed by China were to run in the city of Nago, where the relocation of American bases is a prominent issue. In this situation, if patriots, just like all of you listeners, were merely to reveal the fact that the candidate in question was a 'stooge of the Chinese government', the election would become a conflict between the Japanese and Chinese people, and the electorate would surely show the common sense that one would expect. Consequently, that other country's expectations would backfire completely, and without any effort on your part you would be able to control the election. Do you think that Japan would be incapable of dealing with even the sort of crude tactics that you fear?

Q: We have actually seen it. In Japan's border town of Yonaguni, members of the local assembly have been elected by roughly 130 votes. If people from China were to migrate to Yonaguni as a group, wouldn't it be a simple matter for them to seize control of the assembly?

A: The reason why it is possible to win an election by several hundred votes lies in the fact that this is an underpopulated area, which is suffering population decline. Do you think that people who have lived in a country for so long that they have acquired permanent residency status would intentionally pick up and move *en masse* to an underpopulated area? Would the Chinese government fork out thirty thousand US dollars a year, behind the scenes, to fund the lifestyles of its expatriate permanent residents in Japan? If 150 people were to make this move, it would cost that government 4.5 million USD a year. And the ultimate result and reason for doing this would be to bring about the election of a single member of a local assembly in one election held once every four years. Why on earth would the Chinese government think of such an absurd way of spending their money? In normal thinking, the outcome sought by migrants from other countries would not be interference in domestic affairs but relief from depopulation.

Q: But, I think that politicians ought to draw up countermeasures with every possible risk in mind.
A: You are quite correct in what you say. However, that being the case, debating preparations for a response to aliens landing from space could be seen as a more realistic possibility than the issue of voting rights for foreign residents. Listening to the discussion up to this point, as a politician, I find everyone's powers of imagination truly laudable. You display an aptitude as writers of fantasy rather than as politicians. It is still not too late; I encourage you, as a group, to make a career move and try to win a Nobel Prize for your country.

The theme of anxiety is commonly present in society, and feeling a temptation to link anxiety and nativism is understandable. Is it, however, also the case that the leaders of the major political parties, having become anxious about their inability to bear life in opposition, are now captive to these sorts of wild ideas?[3] Anxiety-based explanations are easy to understand and seem to accord with common sense but, from the viewpoint of sociology, must be viewed with considerable reservations. By citing this sort of main cause, we are telling a routine type of story and, paradoxically, this even leads us to feel more relaxed. The reason for intentionally citing the preceding extreme example was to show the irrational outcomes of anxiety-based explanations and to urge a reconsideration of these.

What then, aside from anxiety, should we focus on? In order to position the issue within a broader framework, this work uses the previously mentioned concept of Japanese-style nativism. Here nativism refers to 'an ideology, which holds that states should be inhabited exclusively by members of the native group ('the nation') and that non-native elements (persons and ideas) are fundamentally threatening to the homogeneous nation-states' (Mudde 2007: 19). In reality, however, not all non-native groups are seen as threats; there are variations depending on the country and time. The targets of nativism in Japan are resident Koreans and, to a lesser extent, Chinese; groups that would, for example, have been most unlikely targets in the Western European context in recent years. Conversely, while it is Muslims who have been the targets of exclusion in Europe in recent years, Japanese nativist movements do not even seem to acknowledge the existence of resident Muslims.[4]

These sorts of discrepancies cannot be explained either in terms of population size or the socioeconomic status of groups; another analytical framework is needed. In the search for this framework, this work will adopt a policy of disentangling the background factors in nativism by focussing on the most unreasonable aspects of nativist logic. Examples such as the nonsensical Swiss adoption of a referendum vote on the issue of banning minarets and the exaggerated French focus on the extremely small number of Muslim women who wear the burka illustrate the characteristics of Western European nativism (Kallis 2013). Conversely, the striking features of Japanese-style nativism are to be found in examples such as, the previously cited, illogical reactions to voting rights for foreign residents and to issues relating to various East Asian countries.

This book regards these sorts of reactions, all of which form the backdrop to 'the geopolitical structure of East Asia', as the characteristics of Japanese-style nativism.[5] Following the end of the 19th century, East Asia was polarized into 'empires' and 'colonies', and problems continue to surround the issue of colonial settlements, including the post-World War Two reparations issue. Furthermore, even after the end of the 1990s, a Cold War structure still remained in East Asia, and yet China, Japan and Korea – which had all been either 'empires' or 'colonies' – were now leading world economies and had become equal economic players. Moreover, as a result of diplomatic difficulties, which render it unable to form an intra-regional organization such as the EU or ASEAN, East Asia possesses distinct characteristics which are not found in other areas. Its structure is reflected, in a warped manner, by hatred towards culturally-similar neighboring countries. In terms of its links with an insistence on 'the abolition of special privileges for resident Koreans', Japanese-style nativism is extremely political in nature.

Japan's *Zainichi* Korean community reflects the divided nature of the Korean Peninsula, and experiences the impact of East Asian geopolitical influences as a community of two distinct parts. This has been symbolized in the conflict between its two organizations: the South Korean group, Association of Koreans in Japan (hereafter *Mindan*), and the North Korean group, General Association of Koreans in Japan (hereafter *Sōren*). While most of the *Zainichi* Koreans in Japan hold South Korean nationality, there are also a number with North Korean nationality. As used here, North Korean nationality certainly does not imply that they all possess North Korean nationality. There are some North Koreans who identify with North Korea but also others who do not. In the immediate post-war period, these Koreans living in Japan were recorded as North Koreans under the alien registration system. Since then, some have taken South Korean nationality and some, given the inability to acquire Japanese nationality, have continued on as North Korean nationals. Since Japan does not recognize North Korea as a country, people with North Korean nationality have been placed in a situation close to statelessness. As we will see in Chapter 8, this separation of the north and south as well as the unhappy state of Japan–Korea relations have prescribed Japanese government policy towards Koreans living in Japan.

In an attempt to develop and substantiate this claim, the first half of this book includes an analysis focussing on the microstructural basis for movement participation. There is a theoretical conflict between the variables of 'grievance' and 'resources' in relation to movement participation. I rely on an explanation that focuses on the 'resources' variable to verify one of my assertions, and this gives rise to conflict with the often-cited 'grievance' variable. The concept of resources is a common one for anyone with even a passing acquaintance with social movement research, and since the 1970s this concept has been built into the paradigm of resource mobilization theory. I have deliberately mentioned the concept of resources because it is clear that the emergence of unreasonable aspects in the existing discourse around nativist movements is linked to the fact that the resources variable has been ignored.

The discussion of 'East Asian geopolitics' is, by contrast, not sufficiently developed in this book. I will, however, look at accounts of movement participation and also at policies concerning non-Japanese to highlight the fact that there is an inseparable link between Japanese-style nativism and East Asian geopolitics.[6] The following discussion sets out the framework and methodology of this argument. I think that by relying on the data I will be able to show that Japanese-style nativism is an unwanted child of East Asian geopolitics and not the product of a migration problem.

Introduction: Questions about Japanese-style Nativism

The sudden rise to power of Japanese-style nativism

From the right wing to nativism

Although Japan has had a right wing since the dawn of its modernization, it has not had an acknowledged far right or, indeed, a social movement publicly touting nativism as its stance. In Japan, the well-known image of the right wing is of groups engaged in public oratory in black propaganda trucks with loud music blaring. The established right wing has not had nativism as a core aspect, and researchers have seen the ideology of the post-war Japanese right wing as authoritarian traditionalism, symbolized by the Emperor System and anti-communism (Hori, 1993).[1] The answer to the question whether or not the right wing is nativist should correctly be that while it is extremely nativist, *Zainichi* Koreans have not been a major issue for the established right wing.[2]

None of this is to suggest that nativism is new to Japan; the Japanese government has been pursuing nativist policies throughout the whole of the post-war period. If not for the existence of external pressures in the form of international treaties, there would not have been any revisions of these policies (Hiroshi Tanaka, 1995).[3] These nativist policies include the imposition of 'sanctions' targeting *Sōren* and related bodies, after the 1980s, ostensibly for having relationships with North Korea. The exclusion of students of Korean high schools from tuition subsidies, which became a problem under the DPJ administration, is just one such case. In this sense, it really ought to be affirmed that 'most of the assertions and behavior of *Zaitokukai* rather than being "new" are, in reality, merely adaptations of what the Japanese government and mass media have been saying all along' (Chong 2013b: 9).[4]

However, perhaps the present-day nativist movement could be called the first instance of organized action with the principal aim of excluding foreigners, in Japan.[5] There have certainly been attacks on the North Korea-affiliated *Sōren* by the right wing and also violence by right-wing students against students at Korean schools (Ozawa, 1974; *Zainichi chōsenjin no jinken o mamoru kai*, 1977; *Zainichi kankoku seinen dōmei chūō honbu*, 1970). Attacks which involved tearing the national Korean dress worn as school uniforms, problematized in the 1980s and 1990s, also bear a strong resemblance to present-day nativism (Han 2006; Kim 2008), but these cannot be said to have been organized harassment. In contrast to these earlier events, what emerged in the late 2000s was a nativist movement which explicitly targeted resident foreigners. This movement differed considerably from previous movements both in terms of its social base and its style. 'Cadres' of old right-wing movements lurk on the margins of civil society, but *Zaitokukai* draws practically all of its members from amongst 'ordinary' people with jobs. It also differs from the established right wing in that its assertions showcase its nativism, which is embodied in its opinions on 'Korean special privileges'.

The three sources of the nativist movement and their backgrounds

Japan's nativist movement has three sources: part of the established right wing; historical revisionist citizens' groups; and the internet right wing. Firstly, in the early 1990s, a segment of the new right wing established the League of National Socialists (*Kokka shakaishugisha dōmei*) and held a rally in Ueno Park calling for the expulsion of Iranians.[6] In 2004, this group established the NPO for the Eradication of Crime by Foreigners (*Gaikokujin hanzai tsuihō undō*), which acted as a faction of the right wing.[7] Right wingers involved in anti-China movements, such as those related to the 'free Tibet movement', also displayed their nativism by establishing a group which aimed at the restoration of Japan's sovereignty.[8] Although these right wingers are small in terms of the numbers involved, they are important for the vital know-how, in areas such as street oratory, that they have provided to the movement.

Secondly, there is a movement which writes revisionist school history textbooks (Japan Society for History Textbook Reform (hereafter *Tsukurukai*)) that came into being in the 1990s, whose theme was appropriated by nativist groups.[9] It can, in fact, be said that

Japanese nativism is a variant of historical revisionism, rather than of the 'anti-foreigner' emphasis seen in Western Europe (see Chapter 6). The historical revisionist movement which appeared in the 1990s itself began to wane as a result of internal disputes within *Tsukurukai* following the unexpectedly low selection rate for revisionist textbooks. The important point is, however, that the revisionism of *Tsukurukai* was transformed into nativism and inherited by the nativist movement.

Thirdly, *Zaitokukai*, the largest group within the nativist movement, is characterized by its organizational style that has managed to mobilize the previously unorganized internet right wing. People who read and post right-wing content on the internet are referred to as the internet right wing, and practically all of the members of *Zaitokukai* – membership and activists – have been recruited via the internet. As will be seen in Chapter 5, *Zaitokukai* surpasses left-wing citizens' groups in terms of its 'mobilizing technologies' on the internet (Oliver and Marwell, 1992), particularly its ability to speak through videos; the left wing trails behind in this area.

In short, the present-day nativist movement has managed to acquire: know-how from right-wing veterans; the idea of nativism from historical revisionism; and mobilization potential from the internet right wingers. Although the nucleus of the nativist movement is made up of a youth layer with no experience of movements – just like Makoto Sakurai, the founder of *Zaitokukai* who was born in the 1970s, it has made use of its existing base. It has also been able to grow rapidly through the development of new mobilization techniques that utilize the internet.[10]

Zaitokukai was established in January 2007, but interest in the movement has fluctuated considerably. Figure 0.1 gives a numerical representation of the changes in *Zaitokukai* membership numbers. The trigger for a relatively sustained increase in popularity was provided by the Spring 2009 demonstrations harassing an irregular Filipino migrant family in the city of Warabi who applied for Special Permission to Stay in Japan. Membership of the group increased rapidly from this time, and *Zaitokukai* came to be acknowledged as the representative organization of the nativist movement. One of the characteristics of *Zaitokukai*'s action policy may have been a lack of planning, as a result of which ideas were acted on just as they occurred, but it was deliberate in its methods for acquiring members. These methods were linked to an extreme approach envisaged as useful in expanding the membership, but the harassment demonstrations in Warabi exposed their manifest ineffectiveness as all they had succeeded in doing was giving *Zaitokukai* a resoundingly bad name. That is, when activists were arrested at harassment events aimed at Kyoto Daiichi Korean Elementary School and at teachers' labor unions there was no accompanying increase in membership numbers.[11] Membership numbers saw another temporary rapid rise in June 2013 when hate speech was problematized in the political arena following the rise of the anti-racism movement. A further rise was recorded in October 2014 following a meeting between Makoto Sakurai, the *Zaitokukai* Chairman, and Tōru Hashimoto, Mayor of Osaka and one of the most famous populist politicians. Thereafter, however, this growth soon declined and there is a strong likelihood that social control measures, such as arrests, and also the rise of anti-racism movements will cause the stagnation of the *Zaitokukai* movement.[12] It may also be possible to predict that if hate speech were legally restricted, the vigor of the movement would be even further diminished.[13]

Why was *Zaitokukai* able to expand its influence so rapidly in the first place? In other words, what makes it possible to carry out 'stunts' such as urging on elusive internet users and getting them to believe the lie of 'special privileges for *Zainichi* Koreans'? Observers and analysts are just as 'oblivious' to the reasons for the rise and fall of the nativist movement as the people engaged in it; meanwhile, explanations based on speculation and guessing abound. The Prologue raised doubts concerning explanations regarding 'anxiety', but there are a very large number of other unexplained points of issue surrounding Japan's nativist movement. Practically none of the basic questions surrounding the movement have been clarified: who, when, where, what, how do they mobilize; who supports them; and who do they view as hostile? The following section sets out the order in which arguments will be developed in this book in an attempt to understand this phenomenon.

Who rushes to join nativist movements?

Kōichi Yasuda's 'The Internet and Patriotism'

Mention of the internet right wing rapidly provokes stereotypes. That is, it is made up of people who lead unfulfilled lives bereft of social connections and filled with a sense of alienation and

Figure 0.1 Changes in Zaitokukai membership numbers

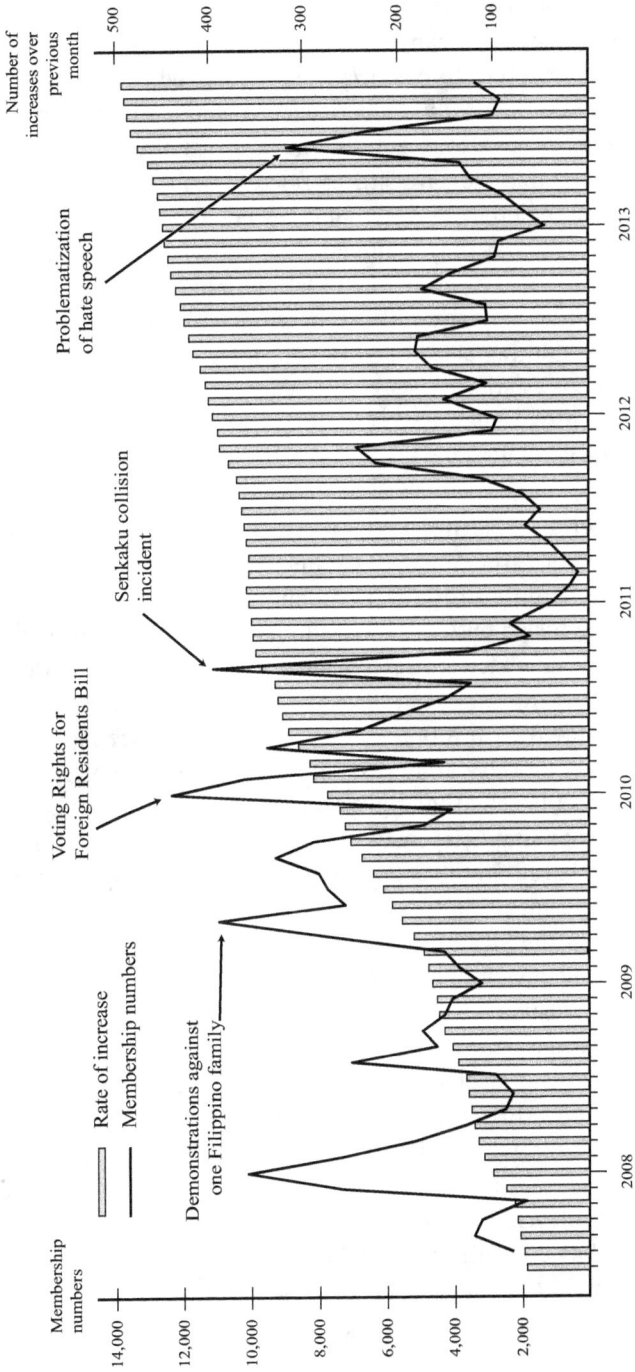

Membership numbers

Rate of increase

Membership numbers

Demonstrations against one Filippino family

Voting Rights for Foreign Residents Bill

Senkaku collision incident

Problematization of hate speech

Number of increases over previous month

Source: Compiled using Makoto Sakurai's blog (http://ameblo.jp/doranpo01/page-1.html#main).

grievance. Most of these people, who are male, find that the internet is a place where they can dispel their accumulated gloom, and they devote themselves to bashing the 'enemy' which is made up of Korea, China and *Zainichi* Koreans. When there is any news at all this group is the first to react – so much so that it seems unavoidable to conclude that they are sitting glued to their computers waiting for just these opportunities – and they demonstrate a peculiar zeal in posting disparaging comments linking any topic whatsoever to 'Korea, China, or *Zainichi* Koreans'. We want to nod in agreement with this kind of image of the right wing: with leisure time to spare they have nothing else to do but pour their zeal into these sorts of unproductive actions.

The 2000s, when nativist comments began to saturate the internet, were also a period beset with the problems of Japan's declining economic standing, increasing irregular employment and growing disparities and poverty. As awareness of the increase in both the degree of social exclusion and the number of people suffering from it grows, arguments about the socially excluded searching for an outlet seem intuitive. And it is as a result of this that thinking which seeks to explain the origins and expansion of the nativist movement in terms of grievance, anxiety and class has put down firm roots. However, as we will see in Chapter 1, grievance, anxiety and class do not suffice as explanations of the support bases of far-right political parties in other countries. This type of simplistic image of supporters compels a large-scale revision, based on the accumulation of a solid body of empirical research results.

What is the situation in Japan? I will attempt to verify the validity of conventional explanations by examining the arguments of Kōichi Yasuda – a freelance journalist and author of *The Internet and Patriotism*, the definitive work on a range of subjects related to the nativist movement. Yasuda's work differs from other books on the topic which serve up baseless ideas; it is not at all a book that has been written in an off-hand and careless manner. My judgement, on the basis of my own fieldwork experience, is that Yasuda's efforts in collecting data have been very thorough and that he has carefully included data even on people who are not mentioned in the book. Yasuda's interpretation struck readers as authentic because it was based on commonsensical and simple assumptions constructed on the basis of the picture that emerged from the data that he had collected. I would like to consider Yasuda's arguments on a somewhat abstract level while also raising questions for the present study and indicating the problematic issues in his work.

Firstly, regarding the question 'Who are the supporters of the nativist movement?' Yasuda says, 'practically all of the members of *Zaitokukai* whom I met were temporary workers and most were economically insecure' (Yasuda, 2012c: 87). It was not just their economic conditions that were bad, many were also in a bad place emotionally; Yasuda describes them, below, as 'stressed people'.

> Although I may be misunderstood in saying this, in the present state of affairs it was not at all unusual that they were exclusively 'stressed people' ... They, themselves, seemed to be suffering over just how to control their overwhelming levels of anxiety, grievance and resentment. (Yasuda, 2012d: 7)

Participants in nativist movements, especially *Zaitokukai* demonstrations or propaganda activities on the street, will include a certain percentage of people who could be seen as experiencing difficulties with ordinary social life. There are also undoubtedly a certain proportion of people who are poor at communicating. Whilst acknowledging this, it would, however, be unreasonable to see the movement as being made up *exclusively* of 'stressed people'. From the point of view of social movement studies, the organization of these movements and their ability to carry out external activities are not simple matters. If *Zaitokukai* were, in fact, to be made up exclusively of 'stressed people', then it would have to be rated as an outstanding organization in terms of its success in the social disciplining of people on the fringes of society – although its objectives and actions are of the worst kind.

In reality, the nativist movement is made up of a decidedly varied range of supporters, and if we focus solely on 'stressed people' we will miss a considerable number of things. From the outset, *Zaitokukai* has financed its office and the expenses to cover its actions from donations. But it is difficult to imagine that 'stressed people' would be able to sympathize with *Zaitokukai* and contribute at levels sufficient to support the organization. This serves as further proof of the diversity of people within *Zaitokukai*. It also provides an adequate rebuttal of Yasuda's specific statement that all of its supporters are 'stressed people'. However, Yasuda does not tell us the number of people included in his data collection activities or whether he identified how many of them were from lower economic classes or had emotional difficulties. Let us now examine the validity of Yasuda's statement by considering the actual people who appear in his book and newspaper articles.[14]

We have information regarding the attributes of thirty-eight of the people who appear in Yasuda's various works, and this can be found in Table 0.1. Combining my own information and interview data with that included in Yasuda's works, we can specify the socioeconomic backgrounds of twenty-three of these people, and only seven of them could be identified as 'stressed people'.[15] Most of these are connected with the 'Team Kansai' group who, with their multiple arrests and immersion in youth gang culture, form a unique group within the nativist movement.[16] If we exclude this group, only a low proportion can explicitly be called 'stressed people', and the actual situation appears consistent with Yasuda's assertion that 'most are temporary workers'. Some of the people in the bottom half of Table 0.1 have also been referred to in the media, but as Kashiwazaki (2011) says, we can consider the middle classes to be the best represented.

Rebellion by lonely singles?

As we have seen in the preceding section, supporters of nativist movements experience diverse socioeconomic circumstances, and we cannot be prescriptive in saying that they are all drawn from the ranks of 'stressed people' (see Chapter 2). There is, however, one thing that can be said in connection to their socioeconomic characteristics: there has been a preponderance of unmarried men in nativist movements. It is easy to take this fact and paint a picture of 'a group of men unpopular with women' who being 'dissatisfied with their actual offline lives' join nativist movements, which they think will address their resentment, and gain satisfaction from wining the approval of those around them.[17] In fact, Yasuda (2012a: 42) gives an insinuating portrayal of the head of *Zaitokukai*'s Information Bureau as 'Single: appears to not even have a lover'. He also makes the following direct statement.

Zaitokukai members who are married and have their own families are few, and the leaders are practically all single. Since they have no family and are isolated in the communities where they live, it is inevitable that they should start identifying with the nation. (Yasuda, 2012c: 90)

This displays significant prejudice against single people but even leaving this to one side, the statement contains considerable leaps in logic. To begin with, having no family and no points of contact with the community in which one lives and identifying with the nation are logically separate matters; to link them abruptly in this manner is unreasonable. In addition, the fact that single people have low levels of contact within their communities is nothing new. If Yasuda's premise were correct, then single people would always 'have started identifying with the nation'. If we were to develop this idea as a general proposition, the social trend towards not marrying and marrying late would necessarily result in an increase in people 'identifying with the nation'. If we go on to extrapolate from this, we would be facing the strange theory that the shift to the right in recent years is caused by the increase in single people and also that this trend will be continuing into the future. In terms of *Zaitokukai*, Yasuda's proposition seems to have some credibility at first glance. However, if subjected to serious scrutiny it would ultimately be exposed as lacking general applicability.

This might be countered with the argument that individualization is increasing, as seen in the decline in community organizations and in membership of labor unions, leading to the dilution of social relations for single people. However, as has been noted regarding the influence of urbanization on social relations, the view that social relations have been 'disorganized' sits alongside the view that they have been 'reorganized'. In empirical research, there has been support for the view that whilst some social relations are lost others are constructed anew in response to changes in the environment (Fischer, 1982, 1984; Wellman 1979). In the case of the internet also, rather than seeing it as having resulted in isolated individuals shut away in their own rooms, it is more appropriate to see the result as a rearrangement of social relations (Fischer 1995; Rainie and Wellman 2012; Wellman and Gulia 1999). Even if Yasuda's argument were not based on this kind of opinion, it could only stand up to scrutiny once the mechanism linking this 'disorganizing' with nationalism has been made clear.

Table 0.1: Activists who appear in various publications

No.	Age	Area	Education	Occupation	Source
1	38	Kanto	Ph.D.	Engineer	Yasuda 2012a: 54
2	49	Kanto	University	Editor	Yasuda 2012a: 40
3	29	Kyushu	University	Office worker	Yasuda 2012a: 60
4	late 30s	Hokkaido	University	Self-employed	Yasuda 2012a: 77–8
5	27	Tohoku	University	Bank clerk	Yasuda 2012a: 84–91
6	25	Tokyo	University	—	Yasuda 2012a: 154
7	58	Kansai	University	Self-employed	Yasuda 2012a: 339–40
8	57	Kansai	University	Employer	Yasuda 2012a: 226–7
9	44	Tohoku	University	Veterinarian	Yasuda 2012b: 293–4
10	62	Tokyo	University dropout	Construction worker	Yasuda 2012a: 145–8
11	34	Kanto	University dropout	Administrative scrivener	Yasuda 2012a: 178–9
12	28	Chugoku	University student	Private school teacher	Yasuda 2013a:10–19
13	39	Kyushu	Vocational school	Mechanic	Yasuda 2012a: 69
14	32	Kansai	Vocational school	Delivery worker	Yasuda 2012a: 314–8
15	35	Kansai	Vocational school dropout	Self-employed	Yasuda 2012a: 332–5 Asahi 2010.12.30
16	39	Kanto	High school	Part-time public servant	Yasuda 2012a: 16–30
17	40	Kansai	High school	Mechanic	Yasuda 2012a: 118–27
18	47	Kansai	High school	Bar owner	Yasuda 2012a: 118–42
19	36	Tokyo	High school	—	Yasuda 2012a: 163–4
20	mid 40s	Kanto	High school	Self-employed	Yasuda 2012a: 173
21	27	Tokyo	High school	—	Yasuda 2012a: 178–81
22	42	Kansai	High school	Realtor	Yasuda 2012a: 118–31
23	21	Kansai	High school	Fish monger	Yasuda 2012a: 118–41
24	24	Kansai	High school	Gardener	Yasuda 2012a: 118–38
25	35	Kansai	High school dropout	Nailist	Yasuda 2012a: 118–42
26	42	Kansai	High school dropout	Construction worker	Yasuda 2012a: 118–34

27	14	Tohoku	Junior high school student	—	Yasuda 2012a: 82–3
28	54	Kyushu	—	Beautician	Yasuda 2012a: 58–9
29	32	Kyushu	—	Farmer	Yasuda 2012a: 67
30	28	Hokkaido	—	Office worker	Yasuda 2012a: 73
31	41	Tohoku	—	Truck driver	Yasuda 2012a: 85
32	30s	Tohoku	—	Office worker	Yasuda 2012a: 85–6
33	30s	Western Japan	—	Self-employed	Yasuda 2012a: 264
34	40s	Western Japan	—	Office worker	Yasuda 2012a: 280–1
35	30s	Kansai	—	Office worker	Yasuda 2012a: 337–8
36	32	Okinawa	—	Part timer	Yasuda 2012b: 291
37	50s	Okinawa	—	Self-employed	Yasuda 2012b: 291–2
38	25	Tokyo	—	Precariat	Yasuda 2013a: 31–4
39	31	Chubu	Post-graduate	Engineer	Asahi 2010.3.17
40	34	Shikoku	University	Self-employed	Asahi 2010.3.17
41	20	Chugoku	University student	Student	Mainichi 2013.6.13
42	19	Kanto	University student	Student	Asahi 2010.3.15
43	18	Kansai	High school dropout	Precariat	Sankei 2013.5.13
44	49	Kanto	—	Manager	Asahi 2010.3.15
45	54	Kanto	—	Administrative scrivener	Asahi 2010.3.1
46	45	—	—	Office worker	Asahi 2010.3.17
47	25	Kansai	—	Unemployed	Asahi 2010.5.3
48	34	Kansai	—	Self-employed	Yomiuri 2010.9.6
49	40s	Kanto	—	Office worker	Nishinihon 2013.4.7
50	39	Kanto	—	Office worker	Asahi 2013.4.28
51	20s	Kanto	—	Office worker	Asahi 2013.5.3
52	25	Kanto	—	Office worker	Japan Times 2013.5.23
53	26	Kansai	—	Driver	Mainichi 2013.6.14
54	26	Kansai	—	Office worker	Mainichi 2013.6.25
55	27	Kansai	—	Office worker	Mainichi 2013.6.25
56	28	Kanto	—	Office worker	Kyodo News 2013.7.3
57	33	Kansai	—	Office worker	Yomiuri 2013.7.3
58	20s	Tokyo	—	Student	Yomiuri 2013.7.3
59	41	Chubu	—	Nurse	Chunichi 2013.7.16

How then are we to understand this situation? A different sociological explanation for why there are so many single people in nativist movements could be made as follows. Firstly, it is generally single people who have abundant time resources. This is not only a matter of having time for the movement but also time to spend on the internet, which is the point of contact for nativist movements. Furthermore, having a family acts as a brake on radicalization and is a restraining factor when it comes to direct action in terms of participation in the movement. In short, the likelihood of people with families encountering hate web pages is reduced, and even if they show some interest in this sort of thing, they would be exposed to other people's views such as 'What kind of rubbish are you talking about?' Even if they did want to join a movement, they would not have time or it is likely that they would abandon the idea on being met with comments such as, 'Stop that silly rubbish' (Klandermans and Oegema 1987; McAdam 1986; McAdam and Paulsen 1993; Oegema and Klandermans 1994; and Wiltfang and McAdam 1991).

In short, let us assume that, apart from their family configurations, 'A, married,' and 'B, unmarried and living away from home,' find themselves in the same circumstances – including the degree to which they 'identify with the nation'. In contrast to B, who comes home from work and spends three hours in front of his computer surfing the internet, A spends only fifteen minutes taking care of essential business online. In this alone, their relative likelihoods of coming into contact with nativist information differ considerably. Also, even if A were to become absorbed in a nativist movement video and then talk passionately to his family about it, he may well regain a balanced view after being laughed down. In addition, since A needs to spend his days off with his family, he will not be able to take part in any propaganda activities on the streets either. Compared with B, A has considerably more obstacles to overcome in order to be able to participate in the movement.

This is an extremely standard way of thinking in micromobilization theory, which analyzes the process by which individuals come to participate in movements. The Information Bureau Chief mentioned above says, 'I probably *wouldn't be able* to take part in this kind of movement if I were married' (Yasuda 2012a: 42, author's emphasis). In short, it could be said that while it is possible to explain the situation in terms of 'being able to because one is single', Yasuda misleads the reader by depending solely on the view that single equals isolated.

Why do people rush to nativist movements?

Can 'craving recognition' and 'venting anger' explain participation?

Views positing grievance and anxiety as the factors that bring about the movement, such as 'Isolated and insecure people are drawn into easy nationalism' (Yasuda 2011b: 47), dominated former social movement research (Buechler 2004). Before I examine these classical theories in Chapter 2, this section will examine 'craving recognition' and 'venting anger' which are the keywords symbolizing Yasuda's argument. When describing activists, Yasuda uses the contrast between 'anxiety and grievance felt in daily life' (2012a: 314) and 'being able to find a circle of friends' (2012a: 87) as a sort of basic decryption code. What links the two are the terms craving recognition and venting anger; the craving of recognition by people who are anxious and dissatisfied is satisfied by encountering a circle of friends in *Zaitokukai*, and they give vent to their anger when they shout on the streets. Thus they are all depicted using this *basso continuo*.

Even if we leave aside this theoretical problem with the argument, it is necessary to examine whether 'craving recognition' and 'venting anger' can be given as causes of participation in the movement. When participating in a movement there is the initial participation stage and the subsequent continuation stage, and the primary factors which prescribe these two are not necessarily the same (McAdam 1986). Citing an interview with a former member, Yasuda implies that he probably 'plunged into *Zaitokukai*' because the street was a place where he could win recognition and give vent to his anger.

Once, when we were out on the streets, someone suddenly started bothering us. I found myself shouting 'Get him out of here!' and all my mates around me backed me up. I had a pleasant feeling when I called out my suggestion loudly and a sense of security that my mates were protecting me. My absorption in *Zaitokukai*, even though it only lasted a short time, was because of these feelings. (Yasuda 2012a: 332–3)

Even if this had been the explanation for the continuing stage (why he kept going), it does not explain the participation stage (why he joined). Yasuda says that the general reason for joining the movement was a lack of acknowledgment, '[They] joined *Zaitokukai* precisely because they were types that were ignored in the communities where they lived' (Yasuda 2012a: 337). Was it, however, the case that the former member quoted above participated *because* he thought that his craving for recognition would be satisfied and that he would vent his anger on the streets, and did he become absorbed *because* he won recognition, as he had anticipated? This was not the case, and as we can see by reading his own explanation, he won 'recognition' as a result of having participated. Even if we make a provisional guess that 'recognition' and 'venting anger' were the heart's desire of *Zaitokukai* members, this only makes sense if they are thought of as outcomes of and not reasons for participating in the movement. Yasuda's work contains many similar examples of the confusion of cause and effect, and these mislead the reader.

Generally, the costs associated with initial recruitment are higher than those of continued participation.[18] Consequently, it is not 'recognition' after one has joined that is theoretically important, but an elucidation of the course and motives leading to participation, but Yasuda's writing is extremely thin on these points. An abdication of explanation is the only way to describe Yasuda's statement that, 'The only place that they finally found, in searching for somewhere to go with the anxiety and grievance that they feel in their daily lives, was, *by chance*, the battlefield called patriotism' (Yasuda 2012a: 313 author's emphasis). If it really were 'by chance' that people became involved with *Zaitokukai*, then its rise and fall would simply be a function of the total amount of 'the anxiety and grievance that they feel in their daily lives'. The reasons why this is not the explanation for movement participation will be discussed in detail from Chapter 2 onwards.

Non-ideological activists?

The political ideology of participants in movements is another important factor. However, when explaining nativist movements, the focus has been exclusively on the vague concepts of grievance and anxiety rather than on the ideological background of activists. This is the basic tenor of newspaper articles, and, as we see below, Yasuda is also similarly sceptical about ideology-based explanations.

I hesitate to talk about *Zaitokukai* in the context of right wing or conservatives, or populist factions and nationalism. In brief, it is doubtful just how meaningful it would be to talk about *Zaitokukai* in a political context. (Kimura, Sono and Yasuda 2013: 12)

Existing right wingers also make the same criticisms. According to this view, the activities of *Zaitokukai* are a form of bullying and, lacking any ideology, the group cannot be called right wing. However, as is clear in European research, ideologies of the ultra-right are considerably diverse (Mudde 2000), [19] and they share practically no common traits apart from nationalism and nativism (Mudde 2007). Nativist movements that are frank about their hatred of 'anti-Japanese powers' and 'foreigners resident in Japan', when compared with other countries, fit unmistakably within the ultra-right category.[20] Rather than lacking any ideology, it would be more appropriate to think of them as 'attempting to construct a 'new' conservative image which differs from the one that has existed to date' (Kinoshita 2010:17). This is likely to be simply a case of new participants in the movement finding the reactionary stance of the established right wing, with its central focus on obeying the emperor, 'uninteresting because it is too old-fashioned'.[21]

What do we lose when we ignore the ideological aspect? Let us conduct a concrete examination of Yasuda's writing. In Yasuda's reportage, his depiction of the outward appearance provides a useful device for the reader in imagining the scene. As someone who knows practically all of the people who appear in *The Internet and Patriotism,* I acknowledge that he is generally precise in describing their outward characteristics although he shuns painting an overly favorable picture of people who have been cooperative. However, as a researcher myself, I can only imagine that Yasuda may have misheard something important or forgot to mention it when writing; he should have paid attention to the ideological basis of activists. The following quote illustrates this point.

What drew my attention was a lone woman participating in the street activities. She was a twenty-nine year old office lady who had come along looking rather rough, in a pair of jeans and a T-shirt with a red and white border. The appearance of her shoulder blade-length hair blowing in the wind highlighted the disparity between her and the somewhat unrefined male participants. With traces of childhood in her two big round eyes, there would be nothing strange in using the expression 'a maiden' to describe her appearance. (Yasuda 2012a: 60)

It seems that this 'twenty-nine year old office lady' rushed to join the movement after viewing the video of *Zaitokukai*'s 'Deport the Calderon Family Demonstration'. However, what I thought was important during my interview with her, was not her outward appearance of being 'a maiden' but the fact that she had been reading the right-wing magazine, *Seiron*, since her schooldays (Higuchi 2012m). Yasuda comments on the T-shirt with a border that she was wearing and makes no mention of the fact that since her schooldays she has been passionately reading a magazine of conservative criticism (it is likely that he did not hear this). It is not that Yasuda did not ask anything about activists' ideological backgrounds, and there are passages where he touches on it. For example, as seen below, *Zaitokukai*'s Deputy President for the Hokkaido region is introduced as having been raised in an extremely unusual family background.

Fujita says that, in an era before the spread of the internet, he felt 'the loneliness of not being able to share my anger with anyone'. He was raised in a conservative household. His father, in particular, sternly admonished him to 'be aware of himself as Japanese'. This was a father who immediately sank to a kneeling position on the floor when the emperor's image appeared on the television. Fujita had had the *Imperial Rescript on Education* drummed into him when he was in junior high school and he could recite it from memory. (Yasuda 2012a: 77–8)

This sort of right-wing ideological background is, however, given scant treatment in Yasuda's writings; the Deputy President quoted above is instead treated as an example of the feelings of 'loneliness' felt by participants.[22] The ideological background of activists is an indispensable factor in explaining movement participation. This point will be discussed in detail in Chapters 2 and 3, but Yasuda rejects 'right-wing and conservative' viewpoints and, consequently, ends up trying to force an explanation in terms of grievance and anxiety. Because, despite having spent considerable time on painstakingly amassing an extensive collection of materials, Yasuda summed everything up in a simple story of the 'loneliness' of 'stressed people', he ended up letting what could have been an abundance of findings escape his attention.

On Korean 'special privileges'

Making grievance and anxiety in daily life explanatory factors for the rise of the movement gives rise to yet another point of dispute that is difficult to understand. Namely, why is it that cries for the expulsion of *Zainichi* Koreans have arisen at this point in time?[23] Nativism is a phenomenon that can be widely observed throughout the world, and in countries with large numbers of migrants, such as those in North America and Western Europe, this is also the subject of a correspondingly substantial amount of research. We will sort through this existing research in Chapter 1, but even with the help of the lessons gleaned from this research we are unable to explain adequately one of the special characteristics observed in the Japanese case: why have *Zainichi* Koreans, who have a long history of living in Japan, become the targets of expulsion (see Chapter 2)?[24] The general view in English language research on Japanese right wingers argues that there is a possibility that the increase in the number of foreign workers will give rise to a nativist right wing in the future (Szymkowiak and Steinhoff 1995). This point will be discussed in detail in Chapter 8; however, the group that has come to be targeted by nativist movements is not newcomer foreigners, but *Zainichi* Koreans – a group with a low probability of being targeted in this way in any other country.

The repeal of the *Special Immigration Control Act*, which applies mainly to *Zainichi* Koreans, is *Zaitokukai*'s goal.[25] Special permanent residency, the issuing of subsidies to Korean schools, favorable welfare provisions and the system of aliases (use of Japanese names) are thought to constitute 'special privileges for Korean residents'.[26] However, suggesting that these are 'special privileges' is evidence of ignorance; even the system of aliases, which came about as a result of discrimination that did not allow people to use their real (Korean) names, is considered a 'special privilege'. There is no space for discussing the stupidity of the manner in which 'special privileges' are perceived, nor is there any value in examining it.[27] Also, while special permanent residence rights may be comparatively new, having been legislated in 1991, they had been customary social practice for quite some time before that.

Why is it that so many people, nevertheless, now believe in the existence of 'special privileges'? There are broadly two possible answers to this, aside from the 'difficulty living in-society' hypothesis, which we have already repudiated. One level of argument concerns individual reception: people who become internet right wingers swallow baseless information because they have low levels of media literacy. Alternatively, because they do not know what to do with their grievance and anxiety they end up believing misinformation to be true. The second argument concerns society as a whole: because prejudice against *Zainichi* Koreans has penetrated the whole of Japanese society, and has not been limited to the nativist movement, 'special privileges' are merely an extreme form of expression rather than an exception. Or, then again, the increasing severity of social exclusion, as seen in the increase in irregular employment, has led to people in strong positions bullying the weak. This simplistic and overly awkward argument is, on the contrary, more likely to hinder any clarification of the matter. Although I also explain things on the level of both individual and society, my analysis will follow the course set out below.

Firstly, there will be as detailed an analysis as possible of the process by which activists perceive the 'special privileges for resident Koreans' frame (see Figure 3.1 for an explanatory schema) and also of its foundation. The use of the term process here indicates a long-term view, including political interests and ideological formation from infancy, with the ideological foundations of nativism as the object of the examination. There is no doubting that activists in nativist movements display a striking lack of any realistic judgement on the subject of 'special privileges for resident Koreans'. However, what needs to be done is not to link this with vague notions of grievance and anxiety but to make clear precisely those cognitive processes that have arisen in each individual activist. To this end, I will start with a consideration of the basis on which they accepted 'special privileges for resident Koreans' in their most recent encounter with the idea (Chapter 3). In addition, I will analyze the resonance between an activist's ideology and the 'special privileges for resident Koreans' frame as well as the process by which this is accepted (Chapter 4). Moreover, as the internet plays a decisive role in the process by which activists encounter 'special privileges for resident Koreans', Chapter 5 will elucidate how the internet works as a mechanism of persuasion.

Secondly, I will analyze the background that gives rise to the 'special privileges for *Zainichi* Koreans' frame. 'Special privileges for *Zainichi* Koreans' is the principal issue for the nativist movement, but this focus did not emerge from a vacuum. There are certain kinds of political conditions that form the background to the appearance of the term 'special privileges for *Zainichi* Koreans', and rather than focussing on this side issue of 'special privileges for *Zainichi* Koreans' what is required is a consideration of the more comprehensive ideology that lies at its core. Unless we do this, we can only dream of elucidating the main social causes that account for its prominence.

The first thing that we need to do in order to achieve this is to make clear the relationship between existing conservative power and the nativist movement (Chapter 6). What is meant by relationships in this context is not links between people but connections in the discourse. In the opening paragraph of this work, it was pointed out that the claims of the nativist movement were nothing more than re-workings of what had already been said by the existing political powers. In addition, the discourse of the nativist movement faithfully reflects the changes that have occurred in the right-wing world of criticism, which appeared after the end of the Cold War, particularly at the beginning of the 2000s. The imaginary enemy for the conservatives at the time of the Cold War was without doubt the Soviet Union and the Communist bloc. Meanwhile, from the second half of the 1990s, it is neighboring East Asian countries in the form of 'anti-Japanese' powers that have crystallized as the enemy, and this tendency has been spurred on throughout the 2000s. This makes it clear that unless we establish the links with the nature of conservative power, there can be no real understanding.

Following this (Chapter 7), there will be a discussion, based on the case of voting rights for foreign residents and also of how we can link 'the foreigner problem' and 'East Asian geopolitics'. Discussions of 'internationally accepted common practice' concerning voting rights for foreign residents have been based on a premise that sees the political integration of migrants who settle permanently as essential to a healthy democracy. Japan's problem of voting rights for foreign residents was, to word it differently, one link in the colonial settlement between Japan and Korea, which ought to have been resolved at a much earlier date. Voting rights for foreign residents, which should be a problem of the political integration of migrants, has, in conjunction with the wild ideas that we saw being linked to security threats in the Prologue, become a problem of East Asian geopolitics.

Following the steps set out above, we will finally be able to explain the principal reasons why *Zainichi* Koreans have become the targets of expulsion (Chapter 8). As one group of foreign nationals, *Zainichi* Koreans have acquired various rights, but they have meanwhile also come to be treated as 'past nationals = people from the old colonies' (Higuchi 2001). Whilst being considered 'past nationals' has, on the one hand, been a primary factor in promoting policy, this has been influenced by the changes in the relationship between Japan and East Asian countries (see Chapter 6). Namely, there is as yet still no colonial settlement and, with the current Japanese Prime Minister, Shinzō Abe, giving his support to historical revisionism, people from former colonies are getting caught up in the conflict with neighboring countries. What the nativist movement looks at are not flesh and blood figures but phantoms in the form of neighboring countries, an approach that churns out hate against *Zainichi* Koreans.

From 'normal pathology' to 'pathological normalcy'

In this book, I have criticized 'simplistic and naïve understandings of nativist movements' and 'reducing the problem to psychological distress'. Following a detailed discussion, I have also suggested the questions that we need to ask. If we isolate the nativist movement – specifically *Zaitokukai* – from other groups, arguing that we are dealing with strange people and strange behavior, then we will lose sight of the main issue surrounding Japan's ultra-right. If we explain participation in the movement in terms of the socio-psychological primary cause of 'being stressed' this will result in the erroneous diagnosis that economic stagnation and the dismantling of society produced the nativist movement. If we ignore the political character of the nativist movement, we will be unable to detect the points of contact between the existing right wing, the conservative powers and the nativist movement. This would end up reducing the problem to 'pathological behavior by pathological people' and this is not consistent with reality.[28]

This problem is not limited to Yasuda alone; similar arguments are found over and over again in newspapers and ordinary magazines, and researchers are also repeating the same mistakes (see Chapter 2). Surely a careful analysis that cuts through the guesswork and predictions is necessary precisely because the nativist movement has many characteristics that have emerged in recent years, which are not found in other groups. The minimum requirements in achieving this are: (1) not speculating but doing properly conducted empirical research; (2) broadly examining all possible theoretical frameworks; (3) using comparisons with similar precedents in other countries to bring characteristics to the fore; and (4) making clear which features have their origins in the particular circumstances of Japanese history. Regrettably, as far as I can see, arguments surrounding nativism have been accumulating without a single one of these requirements having been met.

In order to meet these objectives this book will apply the following two premises. Firstly, the nativist movement has to date been treated as 'normal pathology' but here it will be regarded as 'pathological normalcy' (Mudde 2010, 2013). Traditionally, the ultra-right has been treated as 'abnormal' and as being outside normal democracy. It has come to be seen as a manifestation of the crisis that accompanies social changes such as globalization, the risk society, post-Fordism and post-industrial society. However, there is research which casts doubt on the empirical basis of this view and which, while seeing ultra-right movements as pathological phenomena, regards them as one part of normal democracy. This book learns from these studies. I will attempt, as far as possible, to explain that the founding of the nativist movement on the basis of the lie about 'special privileges for *Zainichi* Koreans' is also logical and not simply an illogical pathology.[29]

This book, which must carry out its analysis on the basis of these premises, will adopt both positivist and constructivist perspectives. When looking at the behavior of people who attack 'special privileges for *Zainichi* Koreans' simply pointing out that these privileges do not exist will only lead to the conclusion that they are foolish people who believe in imaginary things. A constructivist approach is needed to understand the process by which activists come to accept that 'special privileges for *Zainichi* Koreans' are real. The aim of this book is to give a multifaceted explanation of the nativist movement which has arisen in present-day Japan. Consequently, I see methodology as 'a matter of choosing the appropriate means for a desired goal' (Beck 2000: 211) and of adopting these means pragmatically in a manner that accords with each respective setting.

1 Who Supports the Ultra-Right and Why?

Ultra-right research in Western Europe

The first step in looking at Japan's nativist movement needs to be a review of the examples of ultra-right political parties and nativist movements in other countries. This section will outline the findings about support for these parties in other countries and the following chapter will look at supporters of nativist movements. To begin with, who supports nativist forces and why? Little is known about the answer to this question in the case of Japan and yet it is the pivotal question for this chapter. Not only is empirical research in Japan still in the beginning stages but there is also too little information available in Japanese regarding the situation in other countries, principally Western Europe, where there is a robust body of research.

This chapter will address these questions by examining the knowledge gleaned from substantive investigations of support for ultra-right political parties. The questions 'who and why' tend to be understood with reference to a fixed image of supporters: 'young male, with no college education, working in a blue-collar job in the private sector, and living in an urban environment' (Immerfall 1998: 250). This kind of 'because the disadvantaged are dissatisfied' stereotype is repeated again and again in Japan, but reality is not that simple. The rise of ultra-right political parties has led to a large volume of research, and the methods of analysis have become quite sophisticated. The unit of analysis has also expanded from one public opinion poll in one country to a very large scale which uses data from several countries over a period of time. This has provided a clearer picture of both the support base and logic of the ultra-right, enabling us to move away from a static image of them. What follows is a consolidation of the critical findings in the research literature on the Japanese nativist movement.[1]

Research on emergence of the ultra-right

The term ultra-right (extreme right, far right or radical right) political party is frequently used in the media and in academia in Western Europe, but there are no parties that profess themselves to be 'ultra-right'. These ultra-right political parties differ somewhat from one another, and their policies and support bases also change over time (Ignazi 2003). It is, however, possible to extract some common factors such as the nature of the support for these political parties, and this is what we will be considering here. The strength of ultra-right political parties also varies considerably depending on the country and the point in time, but these variables – which are influenced by other primary factors aside from voters, such as the relationship between the electoral system and political parties as well as policy distance – will not be dealt with here.[2] Any explanation of the phenomenon of the drift to the right by existing political parties, which is often referred to in the case of Japan, is also outside the direct scope of this chapter. Furthermore, the explanatory factors for the rise of the ultra-right are often classified into demand (voters) and supply (political structure and party organizations), but in this section demand will be restricted to the 'who and why' of support. Within these limitations, I would like to examine the explanatory power of four related theories: 'losers of modernization' theory; competition theory; protest party theory; and rational choice theory.[3]

'Losers of modernization' theory

In the early period, 'losers of modernization' theory was both the mainstream approach to research on, and the most popular understanding of, the ultra-right. It argues that grievances on the part of people experiencing downward mobility because of social changes fuel the growth of the ultra-right. In other words, the rise of ultra-right political parties in several Western European countries following the 1980s was not a matter of chance. It was the crisis in the Keynesian welfare state and the fall in the value of unskilled and semi-skilled workers accompanying this crisis that produced 'losers of modernization'. There was an increase in the stratum of people whose living standards had declined or stagnated due to the economic changes that followed the period of economic growth – the increase in migrant workers, offshore production in developing countries and the dysfunction of the welfare state (Kriesi 1999: 401–3). This is viewed as having led to a loss of confidence in governments that have been unable to respond effectively and also to the rise of the ultra-right as the group that has organized this anger most successfully. In short, the uncertainty unleashed by changes in the social structure led to psychological strain, and people voted for the ultra-right who they thought would resolve matters (Betz and Immerfall 1998: 7–8).

What then is this uncertainty that produces psychological strain? It should be understood not simply as a function of the economic situation but as the combination of two elements: the disorganization of society and relative deprivation (Rydgren 2007: 248). Let us borrow the language of class theory to describe how this leads to support for the ultra-right. Following the 1970s, society fragmented, individualization progressed, traditional social bonds stagnated, and various subcultures and milieux collapsed (Kriesi 1999). Stable identities changed and tended to become more context-dependent: for example, gender, ethnicity, sexual orientation, and lifestyle. In addition, individuals had also begun to shoulder greater levels of risk (Betz 1994: 29–33). The result of this was conflict between the winners who had been able to adapt to modernization and the losers who had not.[4] The losers lack adequate resources for adapting to change or even the confidence to face a globalizing and increasingly complex society. Consequently, losers suffer from anxiety and end up becoming pessimistic about their future lives (Mileti and Plomb 2007: 27). In the face of this, the ultra-right offers a solution that is both simple and easy to understand, and it secures supporters from the groups most seriously affected by the losses brought about by change (Betz 1994: 176).

The losers, with their lower levels of education and unskilled jobs, were beneficiaries of the post-war period of economic growth, but these lower levels of schooling have limited their opportunities to develop a liberal consciousness through education, and they thus continue to hold authoritarian attitudes (Kriesi 1999). In the past, these people were integrated into social democratic parties; they were social democratic in economic matters but conservative on social issues and it is this latter aspect that intersects with the ultra-right. Instead of being integrated into society on the basis of class, as they were once, people like this now espouse the nationalism touted by the ultra-right.[5] Arguments about support for the ultra-right that are based on the social foundation of 'losers of modernization' split into two analytical angles: 'interest politics' and 'identity politics'. The 'losers of modernization' hypothesis looks at support for the ultra-right as 'identity politics' and explains it using psychological variables such as 'anxiety' and 'frustration' rather than politico-economic interests.

Why has it been exclusively the ultra-right that has mobilized anxiety and linked it to support for its organizations? The 'migrant problem' was not a major topic for the pre-1980s ultra-right. However, the ultra-right of the following period made free use of nationalistic rhetoric and succeeded in appealing emotionally to ordinary people as the party that would resolve their frustrations, anxiety and disillusionment (Ebata 1997). It has been argued that acceptance of ultra-right conspiracy theories results from self-defense mechanisms of suppressing one's emotions, facing stress, preserving one's self-respect and justifying one's failures (Ebata 1997: 23–4). This is a kind of scapegoat theory: politically and economically oppressed people attempt to improve their own standing by targeting those who are even weaker than themselves. The idea is that when foreigners, in particular, are targeted one can gain self-respect as an individual by drawing on the self-respect felt as a nation.

Competition theory

The 'migrant problem' continued to be the most important issue for the ultra-right after the 1990s. Instead of the 'losers of modernization' theory's concern with extensive structural changes, competition theory focused on the 'migrant problem' and provided an explanatory schema based on the migrant variable (Rydgren 2007: 250).[6] Ethnic competition theory sees intergroup economic, political, and cultural competition for scarce resources as the background to ethnic conflict. It places greatest importance on the labor market, stressing that the ethnic division of labor lies behind conflict. This is based on the assumption that competition between ethnic groups over jobs produces mutual enmity and that this gives rise to collective action. If it were possible to isolate separate stable niches for each group then this competition would not arise, but the overlapping of niches, as a result of the influx of new groups and the mobility of particular groups, leads to the outbreak of competition (Olzak and Nagel 1986; Olzak 1992).

Western European research, rather than measuring the levels and actual state of 'competition' attributes the outbreak of competition to increases in the numbers of migrants, refugees and asylum seekers. Since the competition that results from these influxes has an impact not only on the labor market but also on welfare provision and even marriage (Rydgren 2007: 250), it could be possible to establish the premise that influxes in themselves produce competition. This would allow the following sorts of predictions using competition theory. Firstly, there is considerable support for the ultra-right in areas with a large population of migrants, refugees and asylum seekers and also in areas where there has been a rapid increase in their numbers. Secondly, there is considerable support for the ultra-right in areas where competition is likely to break out; namely, areas where the unemployment rate is high. Thirdly, supporters of the ultra-right tend to be concentrated amongst those most affected by competition; that is, people in lower social strata are more likely to vote for the ultra-right (Lubbers, Gijsberts and Scheepers 2002: 352). Blue-collar workers and the unemployed are particular supporters of ultra-right political parties but, according to competition theory, there are two main reasons for this support. The first, material threat (Mughan and Paxton 2006), says that it is not just the labor market but also retired people who are exposed to competition in the area of social security. The second holds that blue-collar workers and those with low levels of education, who hold on to authoritarian attitudes, feel that the influx of migrants is posing a cultural threat and also that their own culture is in crisis.

Protest vote theory

Unlike both 'losers of modernization' theory and competition theory, protest vote theory and rational choice theory (which will be examined in the next section) do not assume a fixed demographic basis. The basic theory, in which the ultra-right wins support because people who are disillusioned with the state of politics see it as being different from the established parties, has been repeated over again. There is consequently a tendency to see votes supporting the ultra-right, *a priori*, as protest votes, but this merely leads to the tautology that 'they are protest votes because they are given to protest political parties'(Van der Brug, Fennema and Tillie 2000: 82). There is a sense that the concept of protest votes has been used without an adequate examination of what it means (Van der Brug and Fennema 2003: 56–7). In order to elucidate this concept, let us begin by defining a protest vote as 'a vote primarily cast to scare the elites that is not policy driven' (Van der Brug and Fennema 2003: 57–8). This definition is based on the following two premises.

The first premise is declining political trust. People with low levels of political trust are looking for an alternative to the established political parties and, in order to punish political elites, they cast their votes for the ultra-right which loathes the elites (Van der Brug, Fennema and Tillie 2005: 541). While they could equally abstain from voting or cast a blank vote as a means of expressing political distrust, they do not; instead, they direct their votes to a political party that can be seen as being free from vested interests.[7] However, there is no equivalence between the fact that someone who votes for the ultra-right feels a high degree of political distrust and the fact this is a protest vote. In Western Europe, ultra-right parties are stigmatized by other political parties as being dangerous entities within the political system. Consequently, even if the ultra-right were to win seats, they would not, with a few exceptions, become the ruling party. In short, supporters of the ultra-right fall into a state of distrusting politics because the party that they support will be in opposition forever; political distrust is not the cause of support for the ultra-right but its result. This renders the interpretation that protest votes exist because of low levels of political trust untenable.

Consequently, an essential condition of the second premise is that the aim of a protest vote for the ultra-right is not to support its policies but to scare the political elites. If people were to vote for the ultra-right because they sympathized with its ideology – even if they felt strong political distrust, then that would be normal voting practice and it would be inappropriate to refer to it as a protest vote. Votes for the ultra-right can only be seen as protest votes when the aim of voting is to cast a vote for a party other than the established political parties. In fact, the ultra-right makes considerable use of populism as a political technique by portraying itself as an outsider in the political system (Mudde 2007: 111–2). Alternatively, it emphasizes leadership as a means of differentiating itself from other political parties.[8] This is interpreted as a case of ultra-right parties winning large numbers of protest votes by adopting political techniques that differ from those of the established political parties.

To take this argument a step further, given that support for the ultra-right is the result of its exclusion from other political parties, if it were to become a mainstream political party – by, for example, winning power – it would lose this support. Arguments regarding disillusionment with established political parties could have some explanatory force in the case of the temporary rise of ultra-right political parties (Rydgren 2007: 251). However, despite the repeated process of alliances and ruptures that actual ultra-right parties undergo, they have put down stable roots in Western European politics (Rydgren 2007: 251; Eatwell 2003: 52), and it is the political context in which the ultra-right finds itself that influences changes in the effectiveness of protest vote theory.

Rational choice theory

Unlike the case of other theories mentioned so far, the advocates of rational choice theory have produced only a few of the works that make explicit use of this theory (Van der Brug, Fennema and Tillie 2000; Van der Brug and Fennema 2003; Van der Brug, Fennema and Tillie 2005). From a rational choice theory stance, voters vote for the ultra-right because they expect to be able to gain some benefit from the government (Spanje and Van der Brug 2009: 356). Most researchers do not want to see votes for the ultra-right in this light, and this is why rational choice theory is unpopular in research on the ultra-right (Van der Brug 2003: 93), but it opens up further possibilities by introducing theoretical variation. Firstly, rational choice theory provides an antithetical image of voters to that of the emotional and illogical voters assumed by 'losers of modernization' theory. This application of a logical–illogical continuum when looking at votes for the ultra-right places competition theory and protest vote theory somewhere between two poles on the continuum. This allows us to see support for the ultra-right as a response to the threats presupposed under competition theory simultaneously as an illogical and also a logical response to circumstances. Similarly, both the idea of protest votes and, most certainly, the act of logically determining the best political party as a declaration of one's protest intentions could be perceived to be illogical emotional responses.

Secondly, while 'losers of modernization' theory has as its premise a link between specific attributes and voting behavior, rational choice theory explains voting behavior not as an attribute but in terms of preferences regarding ideologies, policies and issues. These differing viewpoints reflect changes in overall voting behavior. In a 1960s analysis of eight European countries, more than twenty per cent of voting behavior could be explained by demographic variables (Franklin et al. 2009: 386). With the subsequent decline of cleavage politics the explanatory power of demographic variables has fallen to less than ten per cent. This decline is thought to have been offset by policy voting (Van der Brug and Fennema 2003: 66); that is, voters now choose political parties whose policies reflect their own preferences rather than voting on the basis of personal attributes. A set of demographic variables is discernible in the ultra-right vote, but does the policy vote argument really apply? The introduction of rational choice theory enriches our investigations by broadening the field of analysis concerning the voting behavior of supporters of the ultra-right.

According to the assumptions of rational choice theory, ultra-right voters make the same rational decisions as other voters. This view is based on the realization that it is not exclusively ultra-right voters whose voting behavior is motivated by specific reasons (such as expressions of anger and protest) (Van der Brug, Fennema and Tillie 2000: 78). In short, voters vote for the ultra-right either because they think that their own ideology belongs on the ultra-right or because they value the policies of the ultra-right. The premise is thus that the usual relationships of the electoral market are at play, with voters voting for ultra-right political parties because the policies that they supply meet voter demands.

Empirical studies of support for the ultra-right

The relation to attributes

Gender

We know that, apart from a small number of exceptions, ultra-right political parties have been strongly supported by men rather than women (de Buijn and Veenbrink 2012; Fontana, Sidler and Hardmeier 2006: Rippl and Seipel 1999; Mudde 2007: 111–2). The ratio of men and women voting for the ultra-right is roughly two to one, and the explanations given for this disparity are as follows. Firstly, in general and not just in the case of the ultra-right, women dislike politically extreme positions and tend to be concentrated near the middle. There is also the argument that the ultra-right's patriarchal values do not appeal to women. However, simply saying that women do not support the ultra-right because they do not have an ultra-right ideology does not explain the gender disparity (Mudde 2007: 113). Another argument is that women do not support new parties because they have a low level of interest in politics, but given that there tends to be a high rate of female support for green parties this argument also seems to lack any empirical basis (Betz 1994: 143). Rather than looking at consciousness, what is needed as a priority, is a consideration of differing socioeconomic conditions based on gender.

The relationship between work and gender is often cited as a cause of the preponderance of male support for the ultra-right. The majority of ultra-right supporters are in the workforce but women are less likely to be in work than men (Betz 1994: 144–5). There is also a higher ratio of men to women in blue-collar manufacturing industries, which form the base of ultra-right support. Women's high rates of employment in service industries and the public sector can also be seen as an explanation for why they do not become supporters of the ultra-right. Similarly, the fact that a high proportion of women have some connection with religion and a high proportion of ultra-right supporters do not belong to any church (Lubbers, Gijsberts and Scheepers 2002) could also explain why women do not support the ultra-right (Betz 1994: 145). Whilst people with strong religious beliefs have conservative political attitudes, they tend to vote for Christian democrats, in line with the wishes of the church (Billiet 1995; Lubbers and Scheepers 2000: 81). It is also possible to argue that because women live longer than men many of them are elderly and continue to vote for established political parties (Gidengil et al. 2005).

However, even if we control for these variables, the results of multivariate analysis show that there are significant gender differences amongst supporters of the ultra-right (Givens 2004: 49–50; Arzheimer and Carter 2006: 428). Even when comparisons are made of men and women in the same occupation, women do not support the ultra-right to the same extent as men. To begin with, the occupational disparities between women are not as considerable as those found between men (Coffé 2012). This is why existing research attempts to explain the gender gap with reference to differences in political consciousness rather than attributes as such. That is to say, the fact that women are not conservative with regard to cultural issues means that they are effective in curtailing support for the ultra-right (Gidengil et al. 2006: 1145–6). We are, however, unable to completely explain the gender gap as it persists even after having incorporated this consciousness variable (Givens 2004). [9]

Age

Most studies have referred to the fact that the young display a strong tendency to vote for the ultra-right. [10] There are works that explain this using 'losers of modernization' theory (Betz 1990), but it can mostly be explained using age and cohort effects. If we consider the age effect, it is the young who become supporters of not only the ultra-right but also emerging political parties such as green parties. Because the young do not have the same level of connection as their parents' generation to existing parties they are also not resistant to new parties, making it easier for them to vote for the ultra-right (Betz 1994: 147–8; Givens 2005: 60). Even when the political consciousness of older people aligns closely to that of the ultra-right, they do not vote for the ultra-right because they have always voted for the existing parties (Billiet and de Witte 1995: 193). However, generational disparity is not as clear-cut as gender disparity, and support for the ultra-right is spreading comparatively significantly across the generations (Givens 2005: 60).

Taking a long-term view shows the need to consider cohort effects. [11] That is, rather than saying that people vote for the ultra-right because they are young, it is more a case of those who voted for the ultra-right when they were young being likely to continue to support it into the future. In fact, the core support for the British National Party (BNP) is not amongst youth under twenty-five but amongst older age groups (Cutts, Ford and Goodwin 2011: 427; Goodwin et al. 2010: 199). This is because those who were raised in the period of political conflict over the migrant problem support the BNP, while the youth who have internalized multiculturalism do not (Ford and Goodwin 2010: 8). However, ultra-right political parties have expanded their power and stabilized support throughout Western Europe since the 1990s. It could also be hypothesized that, in the future, today's youth will continue to support the ultra-right as they enter middle and old age and that this combined with the support of youth in the future will lead to a further expansion in the power of ultra-right parties.

Education and occupation

Education and occupation will be discussed together because they are both closely related to socioeconomic status. In terms of links with occupation, in the past it was the self-employed who provided the support base for fascism (Fromm 1941), but recent ultra-right political parties can be characterized as working class parties (Arzheimer 2012). That is to say, in addition to the blue-collar workers from manufacturing industry, who make up the core support base for ultra-right political parties, their supporters include the self-employed, the unemployed and retirees. Although ultra-right political parties espouse right-wing authoritarian issues, their support base consists of an amalgamation of a class of farmers and the self-employed who support capitalism (believe in self-help and economic liberalism) and the working classes who are welfare chauvinists (opposition to welfare cuts and supporters of the exclusion of foreigners from welfare) (Ivarsflaten 2005; Kitschelt 1995). While both groups share an authoritarian emphasis on 'law and order' their support bases change along with changes in policy emphasis. Most of the ultra-right political parties that have been around since before the 1980s used to espouse economic liberalism but, following their adoption of an anti-migrant platform in the1980s, they now have a support base with an increasingly 'proletarian character' (Betz 1994: 161).

When it comes to education, people with a low level of education will generally support the ultra-right (Lubbers, Gijsberts and Scheepers 2002: 364; Lubbers and Scheepers 2000). As the people in this group are also the most authoritarian, the education effect increases when issues have a connection with authoritarianism (Ivarsflaten and Stubager 2012). In other words, as the migrant problem – which is seen as problematic by authoritarian people – gains prominence as an issue more people with a low level of education will support the ultra-right.

At the same time, however, education is also related to the willingness to pay the costs of political participation: the least educated are not the most likely to vote for the ultra-right. This is borne out by the results of a large-scale survey in which people with a mid-range education were the greatest supporters of the ultra-right (Rydgren 2008: 755; Bornschier and Kriesi 2012; Lubbers, Scheepers and Billet 2000; Arzheimer and Carter 2006). The results vary depending on whether or not abstentions, more frequently engaged in by the lower educated, are included in the analysis of votes. People who have a low level of education and are economically insecure – despite being ideologically close to the moderate right wing or the ultra-right – do not bother turning out to vote as their interest in politics is low (Bornschier and Kriesi 2012). This is why people with the lowest levels of education are overrepresented in abstention from voting rather than voting for the ultra-right. The very act of voting is an active declaration of one's intentions, with costs attached. Therefore, it is inaccurate to expect that the lower educated will support the ultra-right because they are in distress; rather, they should be seen as not having the leeway to be interested in politics.

Demographic variables

Of the four theories considered above, 'losers of modernization' theory and competition theory assumed a link between demographic variables and support for the ultra-right. Competition theory is applied in cases where ultra-right political parties adopt certain socioeconomic interests, while the 'losers of modernization' theory is used to explain irrational support, such as resolving the frustrations of the lower classes. At first glance, 'losers of modernization' theory explains the relationship between demographic variables and support for the ultra-right parties well: the lower classes vote for them.[12] However, the explanatory power of education and occupation is not sufficiently strong to enable us to say that they support the 'losers of modernization' theory.[13]

Thus, even taking into account all of the literature cited in this chapter, demographic variables can explain only three to nine per cent of voting behavior with regard to the ultra-right.[14] Since even adding gender – with its significant disparities – does not alter the result, the explanatory power of occupation, education and age will be lower still. Van der Brug and Fennema (2003: 69) found that the role played by sociological variables in explaining support was lower for ultra-right political parties than for other political parties.

In short, even if arguments about 'losers of modernization' and 'people exposed to competition' are partially relevant, it seems exaggerated to view them as the cause of the rise of ultra-right political parties.[15] Regarding supporters of the ultra-right as 'losers of modernization' and 'a class exposed to competition' cannot explain the situation after the 2000s in which some ultra-right parties have won over twenty per cent of the vote at elections. The strength of ultra-right political parties is, rather, that they gain support far more broadly than just from 'losers', and this is also where their potential resides for expanding their strength as a party (Flecker, Hentges and Balazs 2007). It is, in fact, voters with anti-immigrant sentiments and a sense of grievance with politics who – without any regard whatsoever to social class and age – vote most often for the ultra-right (Kessler and Freeman 2005). This means that, even if 'losers of modernization' theory and competition theory may be partially supported, they can explain no more than merely peripheral elements connected with votes for the ultra-right.

Furthermore, psychological stress which is yet another assumption in the 'losers of modernization' theory cannot be an explanatory factor for support for the ultra-right. There are, on the one hand, a large number of survey results saying that most of the people who vote for the ultra-right have weak links with religion and labor unions and live isolated lives in cities (Eatwell 2003: 53). It is not, however, the case that isolated people, who are unable to endure their psychological stress, vote for the ultra-right because they seek to return to the nation (Lubbers and Scheepers 2000: 81–2). It is, rather, the fact that they do not join existing organizations that leaves them without any consciousness of conforming to traditional norms, and it is this aspect that removes any resistance to supporting the ultra-right. If people do not follow the directives of either religion or labor unions but choose a political party that is close to their own preferences, it is not appropriate to call this anomie.[16] Furthermore, the results of recent large-scale data analyses have also rejected the view that socially isolated people vote for the ultra-right (Zhirkov 2014; Rydgren 2009). It may, therefore, be necessary to re-examine the social isolation thesis too.

An examination of competition theory

Efforts to test competition theory, using factors other than demographic variables, have revealed only weak support for the theory (Bowyer 2008; Rydgren 2007: 250). For example, Rydgren's analysis of seven Western European countries found that competition theory was only supported in Denmark and the Netherlands (2008: 757). This is partly because of the variations in the explanatory powers of the different variables used to test competition theory. Of these variables, the percentage of migrants in the population shows a steady link with support for the ultra-right; people living in areas where the proportion of migrants in the population is high are likely to support the ultra-right (Lubbers, Scheepers and Billet 2000: 376; Lubbers, Gijsberts and Scheepers 2002: 364; Rink, Phalet and Swyngedouw 2009; Norris 2005: 182).[17] Ivarsflaten (2008) showed that immigration restrictions alone – from amongst economic grievances, political grievances and immigration restrictions – were linked to support for ultra-right political parties in all of the seven countries analyzed. In the Flanders research, four per cent of all voters voted on the basis of immigration policy, but this rose to thirty-three per cent amongst ultra-right voters (Swyngedouw 1998: 226).

However, economic competition, which should be at the core of competition theory, does not produce the expected results. Cutts and colleagues concluded that the main reason why blue-collar and economically insecure people voted for the BNP was hostility towards migrants, which is in keeping with the forecasts of competition theory (Cutts, Ford and Goodwin 2011: 433). Nevertheless, if we limit our examination to the results from countries other than Britain, it is difficult to hypothesize a direct causal link in the form of economic competition → hostility towards migrants → support for the ultra-right.[18] In Flanders, there was no link between unemployment rates and support for the ultra-right (Lubbers, Scheepers and Billet 2000). A look at research results from the other areas shows that it is not simply a case of voters in areas with high unemployment rates supporting the ultra-right (Knigge 1998; Lubbers and Scheepers 2000: 77; Kessler and Freeman 2005: 280; Lubbers, Gijsberts and Scheepers 2002: 364). In an analysis of five of the countries in Rydgren's analysis, there was a link between cultural competition and support for the ultra-right, but in the area of economic competition only Austria showed a link between support for the ultra-right and work, while only in Switzerland and Norway was support linked to welfare (Oesch 2008). In Australian surveys also, results show that cultural competition is linked to votes for the ultra-right, but economic competition has no direct effect (Mughan and Paxton 2006: 354).

One image that emerges from summarizing these results is a highly utilitarian image of supporters of the ultra-right. To begin with, things do not progress in the following manner: class of unemployed → intensification of the struggle for resources → hostility towards migrants → support for the ultra-right. In areas with high unemployment rates, votes are not given to the ultra-right but to political parties from whose economic policies people can hope to gain something. Of the works quoted in this book, this sort of voter pragmatism is most noticeable in Arzheimer's article (2009: 273) which includes the largest-scale data analysis. According to Arzheimer, the three factors – immigration, unemployment and welfare provision – do not necessarily encourage votes for the ultra-right. It is only when both the immigration and unemployment rates are high and welfare provision is low, or when the immigration rate is low and welfare provision is abundant – in short, when there is an overlapping of factors in economic competition and people feel that their interests have been infringed – that they vote for the ultra-right.

By contrast, we can see a clear tendency for cultural, rather than economic, competition to be linked with votes for the ultra-right, as shown in the Australian case cited above. It was issues in the socio-cultural sphere, such as immigration, that consolidated a support base for the ultra-right amongst the self-employed and blue-collar workers, groups with conflicting economic interests (Ivarsflaten 2008). In Europe, the idea of a cultural threat is not associated with migrants in general but rather with hostility towards Islam. In the Flanders region, there was a clear link between the rate of immigration from Islamic countries and support for the ultra-right, but there was no major link with any other migrant group (Coffé, Heyndels and Vermeir 2007: 150). In Britain also, the proportion of votes for ultra-right political parties is high amongst people living in areas where there are large numbers of Muslims (Ford and Goodwin 2010: 19; Goodwin 2008a).[19]

An examination of protest vote theory

According to Mayer and Perineau, the results of the 1988 French Presidential election can be interpreted as a representative example of the accumulation of protest votes. Amongst those who voted for Le Pen – who won an unexpected number of votes – a mere twenty-eight per cent wanted him to become President. Even in the ranks of people who endorse the National Front's immigration policies, over forty per cent think that their measures for resolving these problems are non-existent. That is to say, they did not vote for Le Pen because they expected him to be President and his policies to be realized. The authors argue that these votes were protests against migrants and crime, the political elite and all political parties (Mayer and Perineau 1992: 133–4).[20]

Significant doubts have been raised, however, regarding the validity of this view. As we saw in the preceding section, because the votes of people with low levels of political trust cannot be regarded as protest votes, the examination of protest vote theory requires a two-stage process. Firstly, we need to recognize the nature of the voting behavior that has been called protest votes in previous research. Secondly, we need to look only at those votes that are consistent with protest votes, as defined in the previous stage, to determine the extent to which protest vote theory explains voting behavior.

Regarding the first of these stages, there are many survey results that say that the stronger a person's sense of political distrust, the more likely they are to vote for the ultra-right (Lubbers, Gijsberts and Scheepers 2002: 365). As mentioned previously, however, it is difficult, simply on this basis, to be clear about whether political distrust is a cause or effect of support for the right. Similarly, given that ultra-right supporters who feel political discontent are also staunch supporters of anti-migrant policies, it would be unreasonable to regard their vote for the ultra-right as a protest vote in the same sense as a blank ballot (Kessler and Freeman 2005: 273). That is to say, they vote for the ultra-right because they feel political distrust towards politics which will not resolve the 'migrant problem'. Alternatively, they can be interpreted as descending into political distrust because the policies that they wish to see will not be implemented even if they vote for the ultra-right. The suggestion that people vote for ideologically distant ultra-right parties as a protest does not hold because these voters actually do support some elements of ultra-right ideologies (Lubbers and Scheepers 2000: 82).

In reality, in countries where the ultra-right has become part of a ruling coalition or where governments have adopted its policies, levels of political grievance amongst supporters of the ultra-right are low (Norris 2005: 163–4). In countries where the ultra-right is consistently excluded from government, its supporters' levels of political grievance rise. This means that the political grievance felt by supporters of the ultra-right is not anger at the lack of a political outlet but anger that arises from not seeing one's own ideas reflected in politics. Rather than irrational grievance, we really ought to call this purposive rational grievance. It is not the case that support for the ultra-right results from grievance; since even supporting the ultra-right yields no gains it is possible to interpret grievance not as a cause but as an effect.

Now we consider the second stage in the process of examining protest vote theory. The results show that, of seven anti-immigrant political parties, only *Centrumdemocraten* in the Netherlands won protest votes (Van der Brug et al. 2000: 91–3). That is, one third of the people who voted for *Centrumdemocraten* acknowledge themselves to be far left, meaning that the ultra-right collected the protest votes of the far left. In Arzheimer's analysis also, ultra-right political parties are seen as being supported by only a certain social and ideological stratum; they are not seen as broadly providing a receptacle for collecting political distrust (Arzheimer 2009: 267). Looking at other analyses also shows that the argument that the ultra-right gains prominence because it collects protest votes does not have strong explanatory powers (de Weerdt et al. 2007: 74).[21]

On a related matter, it is also doubtful that some ultra-right political parties collect protest votes because of their charismatic leadership (Van der Brug and Mughan 2007). In their analysis of ultra-right political parties in the Netherlands, Van der Brug and Mughan examined whether or not three charismatic leaders influenced voting behavior and they were unable to see any party leader effect on the results. One of the three leaders, Pim Fortuyn, was assassinated just before the 2002 general election. His party, List Pim Fortuyn, achieved dramatic success, but even this was not due to the Fortuyn effect. It was as a result of the way in which Fortuyn had led the debate on migration issues that the party increased its votes; they gained votes because of their policies.

An examination of rational choice theory

The basis for examining the validity of rational choice theory is testing whether supporters of the ultra-right decide their voting behavior on the same (rational) basis as other voters. To begin with, is a preference for ultra-right political parties different from preferences for other parties? In the results from a survey of sixty-three political parties (ten of these ultra-right political parties) from eight polities, there were no significant disparities between ultra-right and other political parties (Van der Brug and Fennema 2003: 64). There is a tendency to regard ultra-right political parties as unique entities that are different from ordinary political parties, but voters see them as being no different from the other parties. They do not exist to resolve anxiety and grievance, nor as receptacles for protest votes.

The only point of difference with other parties is the degree of emphasis placed on the immigration issue, and as a consequence it has been argued that, rather than ultra-right parties, it would be more appropriate to call them anti-immigrant parties (Fennema 1997; Van der Brug and Fennema 2003: 69). The increase in support for ultra-right political parties as a consequence of their anti-immigration policies has been looked at in analyses of the election, mentioned above, in which List Pim Fortuyn made great advances. The Cox and Snell values regarding the votes for List Pim Fortuyn were as follows: attributes alone 0.07, attributes plus political distrust 0.13, and attributes plus political distrust plus policy preferences 0.33 (Van der Brug 2003: 96). This result suggests the possibility that List Pim Fortuyn collected some protest votes but, more than this, it can be interpreted as a result indicating support for the party's anti-immigration policies.

However, because policy preferences and voting behavior are rather similar variables, these strong links between them could be seen as a matter of course. In short, we cannot sweep away the tautological nature of rational choice theory: 'anti-immigration voters vote for anti-immigration parties'. This serves as a denial of the idea that 'even people who are not anti-immigration vote for anti-immigration parties' (protest votes), but it does not provide a fundamental answer to the question 'Why do people support ultra-right political parties?' In order to answer this, we need to connect the very formation of and variations in anti-immigrant sentiments with research on support for the ultra-right.

The 'normalization' of research into ultra-right parties

Few studies have completely rejected the four hypotheses examined in this chapter (Goodwin 2011). We could, thus, say that they all reflect one aspect of reality, but there are problems when it comes to a question of which hypothesis has the power to explain and to what extent. To begin with, the explanatory power of demographic variables has been declining due to the breakdown of political cleavage. Knutsen (2006) regards the rise of green and ultra-right parties as a reflection of new political cleavages because they are supported by the upper and the lower classes respectively. However, the explanatory power of attributes is not strong enough to say that ultra-right political parties have risen to prominence because 'losers of modernization' support them. Ultra-right political parties and other political parties display no fundamental differences when it comes to their links with attributes. It was not because ultra-right political parties appealed to 'losers of modernization' that they expanded their support but because they converted anti-immigrant sentiments, which proliferate in various strata of society, into votes (Eatwell and Goodwin 2010; Merkl 2004). In this sense, one can even say that ultra-right political parties are the more 'modern' political parties as they win or lose on the basis of their 'policies' more so than established parties (Van der Brug and Fennema 2003: 66).

In the case of competition theory also, we can regard support for the ultra-right as being based on rational decisions, at least with regard to economic competition. It is not that these voters regard the influx of migrants and economic competition in the same light; they choose parties that call for the exclusion of migrants, on the basis of their own situation and interests. One irrational aspect that we glimpsed in this regard was the support for the ultra-right brought about by cultural competition of the sort that shows hostility towards Muslim migrants.

If we leave aside this kind of exception, what becomes apparent from a review of the literature is a shift towards a research trend that treats ultra-right political parties not as unique entities but in the same manner as other political parties. We could also say that ultra-right political parties have, as mentioned in the Introduction, become established as 'pathological normalcy' (Mudde 2010, 2013). Protest vote theory may also appear to have credibility in explaining individual cases, but when it comes to analyses of large-scale data, differences with other political parties disappear. The same result also occurs with rational choice theory. Rather than being a problem of analytical methods, this is likely to be a result of the fact that ultra-right political parties have not been seen as unique entities to the extent imagined by the media, politicians and researchers.

Western European studies began by viewing ultra-right political parties and their supporters as abnormal, a view embodied in 'losers of modernization' theory. However, as the appearance of rational choice theory shows, there has been an increasingly powerful view that we cannot analyze ultra-right political parties and their supporters in terms of pathology. In short, a paradigm

Figure 1.1   The positioning of four theories

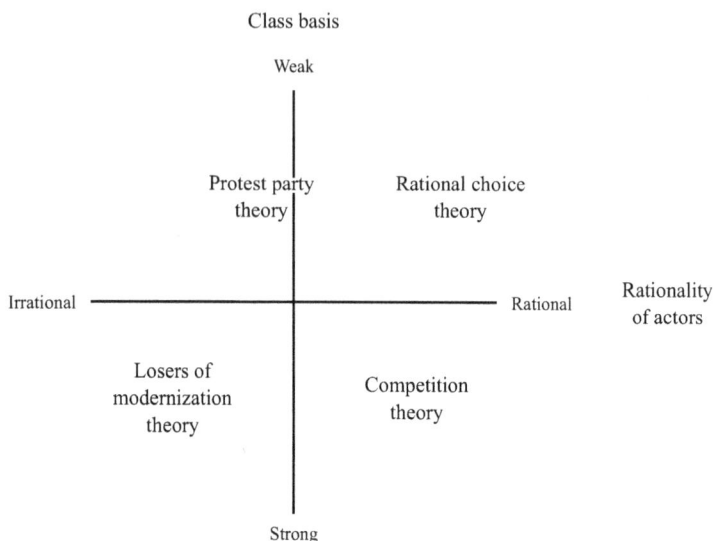

```
                         Class basis

                            Weak

                              |
                              |
                              |
            Protest party     |     Rational choice
              theory          |          theory
                              |
                                                                    Rationality
  Irrational ─────────────────┼──────────────── Rational          of actors
                              |
            Losers of         |
          modernization       |     Competition
             theory           |        theory
                              |
                              |
                              |

                            Strong
```

shift has been occurring away from the dominance of the lower left quadrant of Figure 1.1 towards the upper right, which is based on an accumulation of empirical evidence. To return to the question of this book, 'normalcy', which does not see either the supporters or the office bearers of ultra-right political parties as being unique, has numerous implications for an analysis of Japan. In our study of ultra-right politician Shintarō Ishihara's support base, we found 'normal support' in which Ishihara embodies the voters' ideologies (Matsutani et al. 2006). Quite similar results are found in the case of another ultra-right politician, Tōru Hashimoto (Matsutani 2011, 2012; Sakamoto 2012). If we look at these kinds of empirical studies, there are similarities between Japanese supporters of the ultra-right and those in Western Europe, and we see that we cannot link the ultra-right and deprivation *a priori*.

As a final point, however, it is necessary to indicate the pitfalls produced by this kind of normalization of ultra-right studies in connection with 'pathological normalcy' (Mudde 2010, 2013). The immigration problem is a matter of major concern for supporters of the ultra-right, and they choose who to vote for after rational consideration (Van der Brug and Fennema 2003: 69); this is why we can regard it as 'normal' voting behavior. However, this viewpoint ignores questions concerning pathological aspects: why have migrants been turned into a problem and what lies at the basis of this? If we do not ask these kinds of questions, we inevitably end up justifying exclusionism because 'voters wish to see immigration policies of expulsion and parties must reflect this'. There is, therefore, a critical need to delve into the source of cultural competition and make clear what lies behind the current hostility towards Muslims. In the context of studying Japan's ultra-right movement, it is necessary to make clear what underpins the enmity that it harbors towards various neighboring countries in East Asia. Chapter 8 deals with this in detail.

2 Can Grievance and Anxiety Explain Nativist Movements?

Grievance and anxiety within social movement research

If there were no grievances, then people would not take part in social movements. Listening to participants in social movements one is bound to hear them talk about some grievance or other. This is why it is easy to conclude that 'participants in social movements have this or that grievance' and that 'grievance is the cause of movements'. As an extension of this, it is then also a simple matter to extrapolate the anxiety felt by large numbers of people in the background to this grievance. Structural problems exist in all societies as do people who feel anxieties as a result. Increasing levels of irregular employment, Japan's economic collapse, the dismantling of communities … it is the anxiety resulting from these developments that spurs people on to aggressive actions and drives them towards the nativist movement – or so it is claimed.

The considerable deficiencies in the simplistic and naïve arguments about anxiety forming the background to the movement were discussed in the Introduction. For our purposes, 'anxiety' will be defined as psychological strain which is not directly linked with the issues taken up by the nativist movement. 'Grievance' is used to indicate psychological strain which is directly concerned with the issues taken up by the movement. In the context of this book, the 'difficulties of daily life' are anxieties and 'hostility towards *Zainichi* Koreans' is a grievance. Anxiety links general mental health problems and movement participation, while grievance looks at the linkages between actual issues and movement participation.

Grievance is an indispensible factor in social movements, but it is no more than just one of many factors (Jenkins 1985; McCarthy and Zald 1987: 18; Oberschall 1993: 19). The argument that grievance naturally produces social movements ignores the resource mobilization dimension that is essential to social movements. The kinds of grievance and anxiety that could lead to social movements exist in all places and at all times, but if these really were the causes, then movements would be far more widespread in society.[1] In reality, this is not the case, and grievance and anxiety have nothing to do with the emergence of movements (McCarthy and Zald 1987: 18). There are many processes on the road from grievance to movement and, in fact, the links between grievances and movements are not as strong as is commonly thought. Anxiety is an even vaguer concept that must first undergo a process of transformation to become a concrete grievance, making the distance between it and an actual movement even larger.

Nevertheless, there is no end of people who link the nativist movement with anxiety and smugly talk about the difficulties of young people's lives.[2] This chapter will examine the connections between grievance, anxiety and the nativist movement and will attempt to clarify the problems with the views that insist on causal links, by making use of theories that have historically underpinned social movement research. In classical theories, grievance and anxiety were held to be the primary causes of social movements, but following the 1970s these theories were criticized and social movement research underwent a major transformation. Accordingly, parts two and three of this chapter will examine the connections between grievance, anxiety and the rise of the nativist movement, referring once again to the validity of 'losers of modernization' theory and competition theory.

Looked at empirically, there are periods when levels of anxiety rise in society as a whole but we do not see repeated outbreaks of social movements at these times. Empirical research regarding strikes rules out the view that they occur with increased frequency during recessions, pointing out instead the importance of an organizational base, especially for labor unions (Shorter and Tilly 1974; Snyder and Tilly 1972). Similarly, in empirical terms, the view that it is people feeling high levels of anxiety who participate in social movements is mistaken (Opp 1988). Even in the case of grievance, there is no clear connection between it and objective conditions; the simplistic cause and effect relationship, along the lines of a worsening of conditions → an exacerbation of grievance → social movement, does not hold true. Grievance itself is not a given; a subjective process needs to occur in which movements problematize particular issues in order for grievance to be 'constructed' amongst individual people (Buechler

2004; Klandermans 1992; Klandermans, Roefs and Olivier 2001; Klandermans, van der Toorn and van Stekelenburg 2008).

What then is necessary for a nativist movement to appear? Social movements do not spring spontaneously from nowhere; they are built on a distinct base. The aim of this chapter is to examine existing research on the role of ideology and subculture, from the viewpoint of the base on which a social movement is built, and to connect this with the discussion that will follow Chapter 3.

Mass society theory and nativist movements

Classical theories of social movements viewed participation in these movements as irrational and pathological behavior (Gusfield 1994). Mass society theory, with its use of the 'anxiety' felt by individuals to explain the appearance of movements, is representative of these theories. This kind of argument, which explains the appearance of social movements using irrational psychological conditions, held a dominant place in sociology from the time of nineteenth-century crowd behavior theory (Le Bon 1895; Tarde 1901) until the arrival of the theory of collective behavior (Smelser 1963; Turner and Killian 1972).[3]

The distinctiveness of mass society theory arises, above all, from the fact that it emerged at a time when conditions threw up the serious task of explaining Nazism. Why had the totalitarianism of the Nazis been supported? Mass society theory is no different from other conventional theories in its adoption of the schema that, at that time, 'anxiety broke out in mass society' and 'social movements were the outlet for resolving that anxiety'. It does not, however, engage in simple psychological reductionism; totalitarianism is explained via the connections with the anxiety produced by social disintegration accompanying mass society. Elucidating this anxiety is the principal preoccupation of mass society theory, and it did this by adopting the following logical outline (Arendt 1968; Kornhauser 1959; Selznick 1970).

Totalitarianism rises to prominence not by ideological polarization but rather as a consequence of the collapse of ideology. According to Arendt, 'totalitarian movements are mass organizations of atomized, isolated individuals' (Arendt 1968: 323). They 'recruited their members from this mass of apparently indifferent people whom all other parties had given up as too apathetic or too stupid for their attention' (Arendt 1968: 311). Why is it that the masses, who were supposed to be apathetic, were mobilized by the totalitarian movement? The premise is that intermediary groups were weakened by social changes, in the form of an influx of people into cities and rapid industrialization, in conditions where there were no substitute groups or norms (Kornhauser 1959). To begin with, the word masses designates alienated people who have lost the place that they ought to occupy in the social structure and who whilst being in society are not members of society. The masses are amorphous in their stance as they bear no responsibility for maintaining existing values nor do they have any stable group affiliations. Alienated masses make anxiety-laden efforts to find a way back to status and to a sense of relationship with society. This is, however, enforced by urgent psychological pressures and, as a consequence, they end up being integrated into a substitute community, most explicitly revealed in totalitarianism (Selznick 1970: 263–4).

At a glance, mass society theory appears plausible but it has been criticized by resource mobilization theory, which will be referred to later, for its lack of an empirical base (Costain 1992; Jenkins 1985; McAdam 1982). Even after having been rejected by empirical social movement studies, the ghost of mass society theory continued to make repeated appearances in the area of social criticism.[4] In fact, a 'modern Japanese version of mass society theory' is also being applied to ultra-right movements including nativism. In this connection, I would now like to examine Oguma and Ueno's (2003) *Iyashi no nashonarizumu* (Comforting Nationalism) and Takahara's (2006) *Fuangata nashonarizumu no jidai* (The Age of Anxiety Nationalism).[5] Both authors use the term 'fluidization' to express the trait that has characterized Japan following the 1990s, and argue that this has brought about anxiety. That is to say, the historical revisionist group '*Tsukurukai* is the manifestation of the fluidization phenomenon within the conservative movement' (Oguma and Ueno 2003: 4). According to Takahara (2006: 38–9), 'it is clear that 'social fluidization' is an unavoidable global trend at this point in time'. And, thus, 'people are kicked out of the world of predictability and stability for their future lives as guaranteed by solid organization' (Takahara 2006: 38–9).

As a result, people begin to suffer from anxiety, which in turn drives the development of ultra-right movements. In other words, 'they gather together, each one of them an "ordinary citizen", bringing their own individual anxiety with them and this is how right-wing groups that embrace the violence of exclusion are formed' (Oguma and Ueno 2003: 220). Moreover, this must be understood as a phenomenon with no links to political ideology. Takahara asserts that, 'A sentiment tinged with individualized nationalism is neither an issue of national pride nor one to do with history. Rather, it is a sense of uncertainty about the future that accompanies the fluidization of society and the proliferation of consumerism' (2006: 140–1). Consequently, 'there cannot be any sense in focusing on "hatred towards Korea and China" or on "right-wing sentiments"' (Takahara 2006: 96–7).

It is unclear whether either Oguma or Takahara consulted mass society theory or not, but their arguments do resemble it. What is intended, however, by the key concept of 'fluidization' is not clear. Their arguments cannot stand as sociological arguments unless we specify the cause and effect relationships behind fluidization → anxiety → social movement participation, therefore, it is necessary to elaborate on and examine them. When we do this, we see that their arguments refer to the anxiety that accompanies the fluidization of the labor market – globalization, economic insecurity caused by prolonged recession, and an increase in irregular employment. If we follow this argument, we can interpret it as saying that 'people who are susceptible to anxiety as a result of fluidization' feel a *vague* anxiety and they become the supporters of the nativist movement.

Who can we say feels this anxiety or, alternatively, who can we say does not? Firstly, since there is no data for measuring or comparing 'anxiety' itself, we need to think about members of the nativist movement in connection with the social stratum that is most susceptible to feeling anxiety. On this basis, we could say that those most likely to feel anxiety would be the class of people with low levels of education and poor future prospects, or the class in insecure employment. I will use data from interviews with thirty-four nativist movement activists to address these questions. Interview participants are active members, and the data reveals the characteristics of the movement's cadre (of twenty-five *Zaitokukai* members interviewed, four were not part of the cadre) (see Appendix).

There are almost no other empirical surveys in this area. The thirty-four interviewees, listed in Table 2.1, break down into seven high school graduates, three from vocational schools and twenty-four university educated (these figures include some who have

Table 2.1: Backgrounds of nativist movement activists

Education		Occupation		Form of employment	
Graduated from high school	7	White collar	22	Regular	30
Dropped out of or graduated from technical school	3	Self-employed	4	Irregular	2
Enrolled in, dropped out of or graduated from university	24	Blue collar	6	Student	2
		Student	2		
Total	34		34		34

suspended their studies and some still studying). As a whole, their levels of education are decidedly not low.[6] In terms of occupation, there were two still attending university, twenty-two white-collar and six blue-collar workers and four retirees doing the same work as before their retirement. There were also only two people in irregular employment. Even though the tendency was for mainly white-collar workers with high levels of education to show a willingness to be interviewed, it would be difficult to claim that Sakurai, the founder of *Zaitokukai*, as a high school graduate in irregular employment is representative of all members.

Looking at previous research, we see that Oguma bases himself on Ueno's fieldwork when he says that *Tsukurukai* is 'clearly a middle class, urban movement' (Oguma and Ueno 2003: 190).[7] According to Daisuke Tsuji's (2008, 2009, 2011) internet survey, a high proportion of the people who had internet right-winger tendencies had not graduated from high school, however, this was no different from the proportion who had graduated from university. Since the levels of education of the participants of this survey were generally high, the internet right wingers in Tsuji's survey had levels of education that were higher than those found in society in general.

Given that I interviewed only thirty-four activists and Tsuji surveyed only thirty-one, it is not possible to conclude that the supporters of the nativist movement are primarily middle class. Even so, if we also take into account the arguments in the Introduction, it cannot be called a movement whose supporters are mainly from the lower classes, and it would be a further mistake to see participants in the movement as sharing the common denominator of unfortunate circumstances.[8] Whilst I am not arguing that there are no activists who find themselves in unfortunate circumstances, can we really go so far as to say that it was anxiety caused by misfortune that led to an accumulation of grievances, which in turn led to participation in the movement? On this point, after stating that 'the rise of conservative movements kept pace with the economic collapse of "Japan, the advanced country"' Yasuda (2012a: 354) says the following.

> People with resentments against society. People angered by injustice. People suffering from an inferiority complex. People who want a circle of friends. People looking for a place to escape to. People who cannot find a place to go back to. *Zaitokukai* is a magnet for these sorts of people. (Yasuda 2012a: 355)

However, if we look at each individual person's story as we attempt to determine to what extent there is a connection between economic collapse and activists' motives, we find that Yasuda's argument lacks the ability to persuade. Firstly, 'resentments against society' and 'anger at injustice' can be seen in practically all social movements, and there is no need to make special mention of them in connection with *Zaitokukai*. Next, even if it were true that 'most are workers in irregular employment' (Yasuda 2012c: 87), there are numerous questionable points regarding whether they would have 'inferiority complexes' because of this socioeconomic status. The problem for some people who appear in Yasuda's writings, such as an 'apprentice gardener', was not his education or his occupation but the fact that he had an Iranian mother. As for 'wanting a circle of friends', it is natural to gain a sense of fulfillment when acting together with fellow members, a feature common to most social movements. The 'loneliness' of the Hokkaido Deputy Chairman to which Yasuda refers has its origins in the fact that he cannot share his right-wing ideology with anyone, it is not based on a pre-existing desire for a circle of friends. In the case also of 'a fish shop assistant' it was the 'stylishness' of the leader of Team Kansai that attracted him, and it would be unreasonable to see his occupation as having any links with this.

Reading the pathology of the individual that forms the background to social pathology as alienation is a beguiling argument, but it loses its persuasive powers once individual cases are looked at in detail. Even if we limit ourselves to the three people just mentioned it is doubtful that they would share 'anxiety' as a factor in common. This weakness is not just an issue with Yasuda's work, it permeates mass society theory which fails to elucidate what it means by the conditions of alienation that it hypothesizes (Goodwin, Jasper and Polleta 2000: 67).

Competition theory and the nativist movement

To what extent can a competition theory point of view explain the reasons why *Zainichi* Koreans have become the target for the nativist movement? Various factors lie behind anti-migrant feelings, but we will now examine the direct 'grievances' related to competition theory.[9] The perception that migrants become a threat to the majority host society because of cultural, economic and political competition is the source of the 'grievance' referred to here. Competition theory hypothesizes a process in which there is recognition of the existence of foreigners in one's daily life → this is perceived as a threat to oneself → grievance → movement participation. The argument that competition heightens grievance is too naïve: we need to bear in mind the dimension of grievance in which 'competition' is a post hoc construction designed to increase grievance. That is to say, Muslims in Western Europe are not regarded with hostility because there are problems with them; it is the fact that they are viewed with hostility that becomes the cause of various problems (Sunier and Ginkel 2006), and it is this sort of viewpoint that is essential. In this chapter, however, let us, for the present, simply accept that 'competition' is a reality and consider how it actually applies to *Zainichi* Koreans.[10]

Firstly, cultural competition refers to a state of affairs in which a migrant group, with a different culture from that of the host society, continues to preserve its culture and this comes to be seen as a threat by the latter. Most migration scholars will regard *Zainichi* Koreans as a highly assimilated group like white ethnics in the United States.[11] Previously, Gordon has drawn a distinction between cultural assimilation, which concerns individual behavior, and structural assimilation, on the level of social groups, and then analyzed the changes in migrant groups (Gordon 1964). If we adopt this distinction, we see that *Zainichi* Koreans have already achieved high levels of assimilation, as might be expected, on the cultural assimilation side – such as language and daily customs, and also in terms of structural assimilation given that most are married to

Japanese nationals.[12] The numbers of *Zainichi* Koreans with foreign nationality who are special permanent residents is also declining annually by about 10,000 a year.[13] In this sense, even if 'cultural competition' with *Zainichi* Koreans had existed temporarily in the past, it is growing weaker year by year. Present-day *Zainichi* Koreans are in a state akin to what Gans has previously called symbolic ethnicity (Gans 1979, 1994), and it is difficult to fathom how one could find any basis for exclusion.[14]

   Zaitokukai gives 'preferential welfare treatment' as one of the 'zainichi special privileges'. As Table 2.2 shows, the proportion of *Zainichi* Koreans and other foreign residents receiving welfare is, as is claimed, high.[15] However, the idea that an administration which does not recognize welfare as a right for foreign residents would give 'special treatment' to *Zainichi* Koreans flies completely in the face of reality.[16] Why is there a high proportion of *Zainichi* Koreans receiving welfare in the first place? To begin with, there are many elderly recipients who cannot receive the public pension because they were not able to join the national pension scheme until Japan ratified the 'Convention Relating to the Status of Refugees'. Nor were there any transitional compensation measures for foreign residents.[17] Secondly, this is also a demographic issue. The number of younger *Zainichi* Koreans counted as South or North Korean nationals falls with declining age because of the high rates of acquisition of Japanese nationality or marriage to a Japanese person. As a result, there was an apparent rise in the proportion of *Zainichi* Koreans receiving welfare when recipients were divided by 'nationality'. Thirdly, the fact that *Zainichi* Koreans experience higher unemployment rates than Japanese also illustrates that poverty has assumed an invisible existence.[18]

   There is a considerable 'negative legacy from the past'–quality to this kind of poverty as it is brought about by discrimination when looking for work and exclusion from social security amongst the older generations, while the youth are achieving some upward mobility. This is illustrated by Figure 2.1, which shows the gap in white-collar employment rates between North and South Korean nationals and Japanese nationals by age group.[19] It has not been easy for *Zainichi* Koreans to find white-collar positions; they have faced employment discrimination from the large companies and the doors to becoming public sector employees have also largely been closed to them. However, the disparity in Figure 2.1, which reaches the

Table 2.2: *Realities of welfare for foreigners*

	Japan wide		South & North Korea		China		Philippines		Vietnam		Brazil	
	No. of hhs	(%)	No. of hhs	(%)	No. of hhs	(%)	No. of hhs	(%)	No. of hhs	(%)	No. of hhs	(%)
Estimated proportion of recipients	—	(1.6)	—	(8.0)	—	(3.0)	—	(7.2)	—	(9.2)	—	(1.7)
Eligibility criteria												
Elderly	639,760	(43.5)	14,940	(51.9)	543	(12.2)	20	(0.4)	72	(11.1)	124	(8.1)
Child benefit	106,060	(7.2)	1,876	(6.5)	819	(18.4)	3,606	(73.6)	209	(32.1)	397	(25.9)
Disability	158,490	(10.8)	2,883	(10.0)	372	(8.4)	62	(1.3)	43	(6.6)	83	(5.4)
Illness	296,310	(20.1)	5,321	(18.5)	1,434	(32.3)	323	(6.6)	98	(15.1)	262	(17.1)
Other	271,610	(18.4)	3,776	(13.1)	1,275	(28.7)	891	(18.2)	229	(35.2)	666	(43.5)
Total	1,472,230	(100.0)	28,796	(100.0)	4,443	(100.0)	4,902	(100.0)	651	(100.0)	1,532	(100.0)

Note: hhs = households.

Sources: For Japanese nationals – *Social Welfare Administrative Work Reports*, Statistics and Information Department, Minister's Secretariat, Ministry of Health, Labor and Welfare. Data for foreign nationals was compiled using *Foreign Residents Statistics*, 2012 and the simultaneous nationwide basic survey of welfare recipients for the 2011 fiscal year.

Figure 2.1 Proportion of white-collar jobs by date of birth (2005)

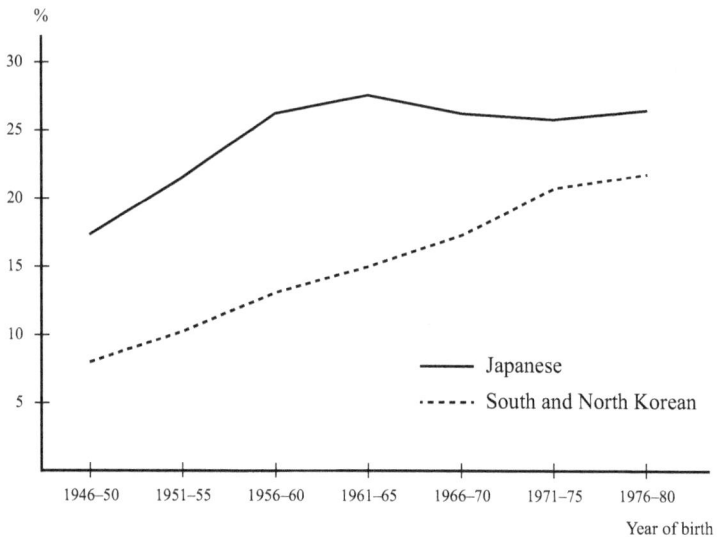

Source: User-defined aggregation of national census.

maximum of over ten points, eases in the case of youth, falling to as low as five points for those born in the 1970s.[20] In short, almost all of the causes of the welfare phenomenon are also accounted for by past exclusionary policies and poverty – we are nearing the resolution of the problem. Consequently, the eruption of welfare chauvinism at this point in time is at odds with the empirical data.

According to segmented labor market theory, which explains the relation between competition and hostility in the labor market, the market is divided along ethnic lines. In this segmented labor market, the ethnic division of labor gives rise to competition and hostility between groups (Bonacich 1972).[21] Ethnic conflicts are, however, less likely to happen if the segregation of ethnic niches in the labor market continues. Reduced segregation, caused by such conditions as the influx of a specific migrant group will conversely heighten hostility between ethnic groups.[22]

The characteristics of the labor market are clear concerning *Zainichi* Koreans. As Figure 2.2 shows, they have the highest rate amongst all nationality groups of running ethnic businesses.[23] This is a product of historical conditions in which employment discrimination left them with no choice but to set up their own businesses, but *Zainichi* Koreans can also be seen as having been

Figure 2.2 Business engagement ratios by nationality (2000)

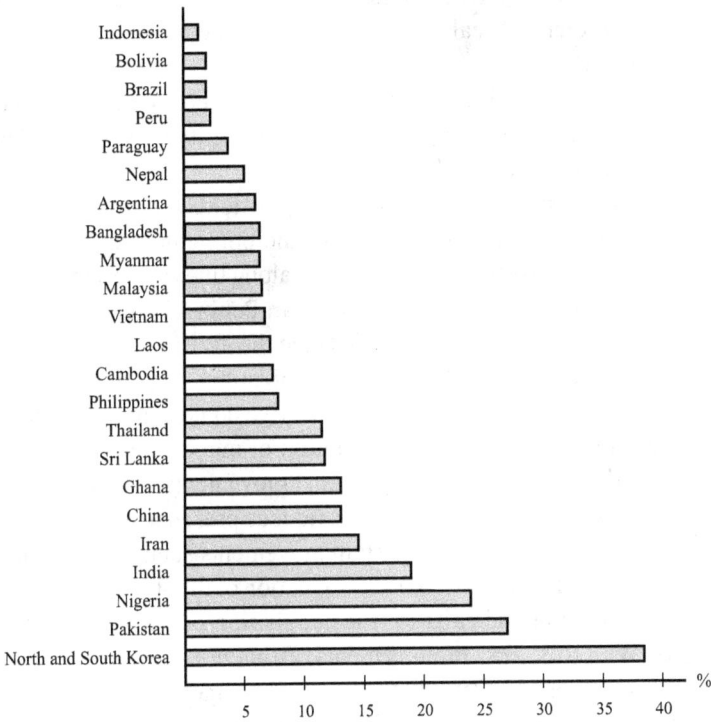

Source: Bureau of Statistics, Ministry of Internal Affairs and Communications 2004.

able to improve their lot as a group because they expanded into the independent business sector (Higuchi 2012y). In the case of *Zainichi* Koreans, therefore, competition for jobs does not lead to hostility.

Would it be possible perhaps to apply middleman minority theory to explain hostility towards a self-employed class? The middleman minority is made up of intermediaries who are located in a position between the dominant and inferior groups in society, and most middlemen have the inferior groups as their clients (Bonacich 1973; Bonacich and Modello 1980). Given the preponderance of independent businessmen amongst *Zainichi* Koreans, they do have the characteristics of a middleman minority, but they do not have inferior groups as their clients. The middleman minority attracts hostility because the groups in an inferior position see themselves as being looked down on and exploited by it. This aspect cannot be applied to *Zainichi* Koreans who do not have newcomers as their customers. It is also improbable to suggest that the class of Japanese in insecure employment would regard *Zainichi* Koreans as being superior to them.[24] Reality belies this idea; the only concerns that are likely to view *Zainichi* Korean businesses with hostility are *panchiko* parlours. Because the nature of this condemnation is not economic but political[25] it cannot explain hostility towards *Zainichi* Koreans in the labor market.

Finally, we come to 'political competition'. *Zainichi* Koreans enthusiastically carried out left-wing and ethnic movements, from the immediate post-war until the 1950s, along lines prescribed by the Cold War and the division of the Korean Peninsula into north and south (Park 1989; Sugimoto 1981). Once the division into north and south became fixed, the two large organizations *Mindan* and *Sōren* worked in cooperation with their respective home countries, but the period after the 1970s saw the eruption of movements demanding social and economic rights.[26] Citizens' movements, independent of *Mindan* and *Sōren*, were also a conspicuous presence in this period; citizens' groups initiated important movements such as the Hitachi employment discrimination trial, a rejection of the standard practice of fingerprinting and calls for the acquisition of municipal voting rights. With this array of movements, *Zainichi* Koreans, unlike the old Chinese community, which had hardly engaged in any political activity, can be said to have been a politically active group.[27]

The influence of ethnic bodies has been waning over the years. In addition to the fact that the number of people with North or South Korean nationality who hold special permanent residence is declining annually, there has also been a growing loss of interest in ethnic bodies. Meanwhile, a decline in *Mindan*'s ability to organize is likely to be another background factor explaining why the municipal voting rights movement has been unable to achieve the sort of broad appeal displayed by the 1980s Fingerprinting Refusal Movement. Fingerprinting refusal was not an initiative of ethnic bodies, but once underway *Mindan* became involved with the result that tens of thousands of people refused to be fingerprinted. Whilst the Fingerprinting Refusal Movement mobilized large numbers of Korean and Japanese supporters, the municipal voting rights movement has been suffering from a lack of mass mobilization. Although there had temporarily been some political disagreement, this has been declining in extent since the 1990s. It may be objected that voting rights for foreign residents is of an entirely different order of importance given that it is connected with national sovereignty but, as Chapter 7 shows, there is the hard fact that in other countries these rights have come into being without becoming political problems. The problem is not the nature of the 'welfare' and 'voting rights' issues; the problem lies with the manner in which the people who overreact to these issues construct their understanding of them.

An alternative explanation

Post hoc construction of the 'foreigner problem'

In terms of 'objective' indicators, not only can competition theory be used to explain just a limited number of factors but even these are tending to disappear as the years go by, and this is the background against which the nativist movement has emerged. Table 2.3, which shows the degree of interaction that activists have with foreigners, drives home the fact that competition theory cannot serve as an explanation. Three of the thirty-four activists harbored negative feelings on the basis of direct contact with foreigners. Twelve activists had had some interactions but these had no relationship with nativism, and nineteen – the vast majority – had had no interaction. There is practically no link between activists' experiences of contact with foreigners and the nativist movement; most were not even conscious of foreigners. The following statements by two *Zaitokukai* leaders show that, until they came into contact with *Zainichi* Koreans at work after graduating from university, they had not even been aware of the existence of this group.

> I first became aware of Koreans when I was around twenty-two or twenty-three. I'd had no idea before then that there were so many Koreans in Japan. I hadn't been interested either – in Korea. Maybe if you asked most Japanese people, 'Were you interested in Korea ten years ago?' I think that they would all say that they know about Korea because there is a Korea boom now. (Mr I, *Zaitokukai*, male, thirties)
>
> When I was asked, in 2006, what image I had of Korea, my answer was along the lines of 'Korea? Its capital is Seoul; it's reasonably good at baseball; it's a so-called neighboring country; what else is there'? (Mr S, *Zaitokukai*, male, thirties)

Table 2.3: Contact with foreigners and its influence

Contact with foreigners	Impact	How contact occurred
Some 15	Negative 3	*Zainichi* Koreans in the community Rising numbers of foreign workers in the area Chinese people in casual workplace
	No impact 12	
None 19		
Total 34		

When asked about their impetus for joining the nativist movement, merely six activists named 'the foreigner problem'. However, three of them had been connected with right-wing activities since the 1990s or earlier, and they had switched to nativism from there. Reports about the Filipino family touched on in the Introduction, who sought Special Permission to Stay, provided the impetus for two of the remaining activists, with only one activist giving direct contact with a *Zainichi* Korean as their motive for joining. In theoretical terms, this sort of contact with and awareness of foreigners has been seen as an issue that lies between contact theory and competition theory (Allport 1954, Olzak 1992). Contact theory argues that even when the number of foreigners is increasing, xenophobic feelings are suppressed if face-to-face relations are established. Thus, lack of contact may have led the activists in this book to be attracted to nativism.[28] Competition theory regards an awareness of increasing numbers of foreigners as being linked to nativism. However, as Table 2.4 shows, the very existence of foreigners is not acknowledged as meaningful by activists; both contact and competition are circumstances outside of their awareness.

Let us turn now to the factors that are commonly shared by activists. As Table 2.4 shows, eleven gave reasons for joining that were connected with South Korea, North Korea and China, but if we also include historical revisionism – which is intimately connected with Japan's neighboring countries – the number who gave matters connected with East Asia rises to nineteen. Seven people gave right-wing and conservative concerns as their motives, and the remaining two happened to see a critique of *Sōka Gakkai* in a video. What this tells us is that cognitive mobilization is at work; issues other than the 'foreigner problem' serve as the entry point to contact with the nativist movement, and it is then that 'special privileges for *Zainichi*

Table 2.4: Events leading to nativist movement membership

Classification	Actual motive	No. of people	
'Foreigner problem'	Foreign workers	2	
	Special Permission to Stay in Japan for a Filipino family	2	6
	Voting rights for foreign residents	1	
	Problems in area with concentrations of *Zainichi* Korean residents	1	
South Korea	Sport (Soccer World Cup, Olympics)	2	2
North Korea	Abduction issue	4	4
China	Senkaku issue	1	
	Anti-Japanese demonstrations in China	1	5
	Tianemen Square incident	1	
	Beijing Olympics Torch Relay	2	
History	Historical revisionism	8	8
Other	Human Rights Law	1	
	Critical of *Sōka Gakkai*	2	
	Totsuka Yacht School sympathizer	1	
	Start of Democratic Party period of government	2	9
	Admiration for the ultra-right	2	
	Recruited by peer nationalist groups	1	
Total		34	34

Koreans' are discovered and 'grievances' constructed. Consequently, what we need to explain is the acceptance of fictions such as 'special privileges for *Zainichi* Koreans' and the process that rouses activists to act (see Chapters 3 and 4).

To reiterate, most of the matters that become entry points into the nativist movement have an affinity with conservative political preferences. Let us investigate this point with reference to Table 2.5, which is a summary of the voting behavior of activists. If we look at Table 2.5, we see that most people have basically regarded turning out for elections as normal even though they have not been at all enthusiastic about politics. Similarly, the vast majority were voting for the LDP (*Jimintō*, a conservative party) well before they had any links with the nativist movement. Most of these people did not necessarily vote for the LDP because they supported it enthusiastically but largely because they had negative feelings about the Socialist Party and other opposition parties at the time. One of two supporters of the Democratic Party (*Minshutō*) became an

Table 2.5: Voting behavior of activists

Voting behavior			
Elections		**Party voted for**	
Vote	29	LDP	23
Occasional voter	1	Democratic	2
Abstain	2	Socialist/Communist	1
Minor	2	Democratic Socialist or LDP	1
Undecided	2		
Blank ballot	1		
Total	34		30

Note: Minor denotes activists who had only just turned 19 and 20 at the time of the survey, and who had never voted. When they are eligible to vote both will vote for ultra-right parties. They were asked who they would have voted for before participating in the movement, and it should be noted that at the time of the survey the number of parties increased with the appearance of 'Sunrise Party of Japan', 'Japan Restoration Party' and 'New Wind'.

activist as a result of having left a labor union (this was also the case for another person who supported the Democratic Socialist Party). One other person voted for the Democratic Party out of anti-war sentiments (this was also the case for one more person who was a socialist/communist). The person who cast a blank vote has been doing so for close to the past twenty years as an expression of his distrust of politics.

These results raise further doubts about mass society theory explanations. This is because if vague anxieties were to form the basis of the nativist movement, it would not have at its foundation a particular concentration of activists who had been conservative supporters. There are, in this sense, significant problems with Yasuda's opinion that *Zaitokukai* is made up of 'your neighbors'. There are certainly many activists in the nativist movement who are 'ordinary people' with jobs, but ideologically they are not 'neutral or apolitical'; they are conservative. It is only the two who had never voted in elections who could be described as 'neutral or apolitical'. The four who voted Democratic, Democratic Socialist and Communist underwent a political conversion at some point in time. There will be a detailed discussion of the process of political socialization in the next chapter, but these six turned concrete events into an opportunity and underwent a conversion. In contrast to this, larger numbers of people of a conservative persuasion became involved in the nativist movement without undergoing any major conversions.

In short, the investigations in this chapter suggest that it is political ideology rather than socioeconomic status that ought to be seen as making up the shared background of activists. In reviews of ultra-right movements in Europe and North America, the view that their supporters are 'the frustrated, downwardly mobile, and socially marginal' is also held to be mistaken (Blee and Creasap 2010: 271). Empirical studies of ultra-right organizations have been popular since the 1990s, and these have shed empirical light on the mistakes of mass society theory, which perceives ultra-right movements as belonging within the category of social pathology (Goodwin 2008b: 33).

The best approach for clarifying the realities concerning the nativist movement would be to analyze the process through which people with conservative ideologies are drawn into nativism. The primary causes for the appearance of the worst form of 'conservative movement' can best be elucidated by, first of all, taking statements of activists seriously, and not by seeing those in the conservative movement as 'excluded people who are venting their anger'. If we ignore the ideologies of activists, we end up overlooking the important issue of the links between transformations in existing conservative ideology and the nativist movement (see Chapter 6).

Resource mobilization base: the internet and movement culture
From the standpoint of social movement theory, mass society theory explanations dismiss yet another major point: the affective ties of informal networks which those who might look lonely actually possess (Goodwin, Jasper and Polletta 2000: 67). Whilst the view of mass society theory is that '*people who are atomized readily become mobilized*' (Kornhauser 1960: 33 [emphasis in original]), resource mobilization theory suggests the polar opposite. That is, it argues that because there are excessive costs in mobilizing atomized people, there need to be close links between social movement organizations and participants (Oberschall 1993: 24). It would be difficult to assemble large numbers of people unless the kind of mobilizing structure in which 'those collective vehicles, informal as well as formal, through which people mobilize and engage in collective action' (McAdam, McCarthy and Zald 1996: 3) preceded the movement. A mobilizing structure is also relevant to the nativist movement, and when we divide this structure into a hard aspect (the infrastructure for distributing resources) and a

soft aspect (the movement's cultural basis) we see that it possesses the following characteristics.

The hard side characteristic is the high degree of dependence on the internet. While ultra-right movements in Europe and North America also make active use of the internet (see Chapter 5), they engage in additional face-to-face canvassing at places such as schools (Blee 1996; Braunthal 2009, 2010). The degree of dependence on the internet in Japan's nativist movement, particularly in *Zaitokukai*, is by contrast extremely high. The movement renounced the paper medium for circulating information, from its outset, and this accounts for its trait of conspicuous reliance on the internet as its means of distributing information. Unspecified recipients are the subjects of the diffusion of information via the internet, and all that they have in common is the fact that they are all internet users.

Another of the soft characteristics is the active use of videos, in addition to the internet, to spread information. In fact, the spread of the internet and the increase in the transmission of videos have progressed in parallel. When a paper medium is used to transmit details of activities there is a time lag as well as a loss of any sense of presence and, on top of this, expenses are incurred for recording, printing, copying and mailing the details. A photographer is needed to make a video but the purchase of equipment and distribution comes at a cost that can easily be borne by an individual, and there is no need for any other follow-up work. Unlike the paper medium, which ends up being buried in amongst other documents, uploaded past videos can be retrieved by searching and this also introduces the opportunity for people to come across them by chance. Meanwhile, video is suitable for transmitting a large repertoire of actions such as political propaganda activity and demonstrations (see Chapter 5).

In terms of the soft dimension of mobilizing structures, ultra-right movements in Europe and North America have several distinct cultural bases. The first of these is their character as successors to the fascism of the past. The cult of relatives linked to the fascism and militarism of the past (Dechezelles 2013) and the use of symbols such as the swastika are examples of this. In Japan's nativist movement, a sense of past glory partially exists in talk about the personal war experiences of people close to oneself, but more than this it is to be found in the use of the naval ensign or the Japanese flag. However, as ultimately mere icons of the movement, these cannot be called the cultural foundation of the movement.

The second cultural base is to be found in the links between specific subcultures and the ultra-right movement. Hooligans and skinheads in Western Europe and the Protestant right wing in the United States form part of the organizational base of ultra-right movements (Fowler et al. 2010; Kaplan and Bjørgo 1998). Soccer games are often places where nationalism and racism are manifested, and hooligan and skinhead groups make up a certain proportion of nativist movements (Borusiak 2009; Jaschke 2013: 25; Kersten 2004: 178–9; Willems 1995: 168–71). In the United States, the Ku Klux Klan, which could be said to represent the white supremacist movement, has Christianity as its base and even incorporates Christian rituals extensively into its own rituals (Green and Rich 1998; McVeigh 2009). These days there are still numerous ultra-right movements with a strong religious hue, such as the Promise Keepers. These sorts of cultural bases have an 'attractiveness' that gives rise to pure longing, which makes persuasion possible (Miller-Idriss 2009: 119–20).[29] Other cultures that are also intimately connected with this include cultures that stress masculinity and those that link attacks on and violence against others with an ideal of masculinity (Kimmel 2007; Kimmel and Ferber 2000).

The visible subculture most likely to come to mind in Japan would be the right-wing students, encountered in the Introduction, who have been violent against Korean school children. The youth gang culture of Team Kansai, which has led to several criminal cases, is the one that is directly related to the nativist movement. Yasuda (2012a) reports on this saying that the yearning for 'an older brother figure on whom it is possible to rely' is one of the inducements to join the movement. However, this phenomenon is only visible in the Kansai region; there are no widespread subculture groups relying on hooligans, skinheads or the religious right. The internet subculture, as represented by Channel 2 of the massive Japanese-language electronic bulletin board could be thought of as their functional equivalent. To begin with, the very phrase 'special privileges for *Zainichi* Koreans' was coined on the internet. The lack of a sub-cultural group basis within the nativist movement may actually serve to heighten the influence of internet culture.

Towards a real understanding of the nativist movement

One of the gaps in mass society theory explanations is the propensity to overlook the diversity within ultra-right power (Kersten 2004: 182). Because mass society affects all of the people living in a particular society at a particular time, problems that arise from it must affect all of its members. The result of this is that all activists end up becoming victims of macro-social changes with the result that it is difficult to paint anything but a stereotypical image. The nativist movement, however, is not a homogeneous group. Historical forces influence society as a whole, but they are never felt equally by everyone in it (McAdam 1988b: 35). Yasuda (2012a) has portrayed the people in his writings in a way that allows us to glimpse their diversity. The fact that he ended up describing activists in generalized terms as 'stressed people' is what I, as a researcher who deals with these same subjects, find truly regrettable.

Mass society explanations fail to stand up to empirical analysis not only in Japan but also in Europe and North America (Mudde 2010). How then are we to explain the nativist movement? The present chapter has laid the groundwork for answering this question by confirming the following points. First of all, we cannot regard low levels of education or class as common denominators for Japan's nativist movement. Furthermore, more than half of the activists had had no contact with *Zainichi* Koreans, or indeed with any other foreigners, meaning that there are not even any shared direct experiences. What emerges in place of these various points as the common denominator is the fact that the activists are politically conservative. This is to be expected given that they are activists in the ultra-right movement, but there has been a baffling lack of attention to this point in statements regarding the nativist movement to date.

Next, the fictional nature of 'special privileges for *Zainichi* Koreans' was mentioned in the Introduction and this chapter has referred to the inability of objective 'competition' to explain the appearance of the nativist movement. Since the conditions for the occurrence of 'competition' have been disappearing increasingly in recent years, there is a need to explain the nativist movement in terms of other main causes. I have pointed out that it is first and foremost political conservatism that is at the foundation of the movement, and we can see this conservatism as the basis for the resonance of claims about 'special privileges for *Zainichi* Koreans' in the movement.

This is why Chapter 3 will use accounts of the life histories of activists to look at the ideologies that they have acquired in the process of political socialization. However, having a conservative ideology does not necessarily mean that one will immediately accept the idea of 'special privileges for *Zainichi* Koreans'. Chapter 4 will give detailed consideration to the question of why it is that the 'special privileges for *Zainichi* Koreans' frame, put forward by the nativist movement, has appeared so plausible. Chapter 5 will analyze resource mobilization processes using the internet – the device that has brought about a meeting between 'conservatives' and 'special privileges for *Zainichi* Koreans'. It is by following this sequence that we should be able to shed light on various aspects of the nativist movement that cannot be understood using simplistic arguments such as 'the eruption of grievance and anxiety in alienated individuals'.

3 Activists' Political Socialization and Ideology Formation

Diversity of activists and micromobilization processes

Micromobilization analysis attempts to elucidate the mechanisms which lead individuals to participate in movements. In reality, however, there are processes of ideological formation that occur before the mobilization stage, and these have been understood using the concept of political socialization. In order to clarify long-term processes towards movement participation, this chapter will examine the ideological background of activists by analyzing their life histories (for a methodological discussion of these life histories, see the Appendix).[1] Life histories are a particularly appropriate method for elucidating the motives behind radical movement participation, and they have also been used to shed light on the impact of socialization on political behavior (della Porta 1992).

Keniston's *Young Radicals* (1968) took the initiative in analyzing the life histories of activists. Just as Keniston had targeted the student movement, where the radicals were on the left wing, the 1990s saw an increase in analyses of the life histories of ultra-right activists (Blee 1996, 2002; Fangen 1999; Klandermans and Mayer 2006a; Linden and Klandermans 2007). Underpinning these sorts of studies is recognition of the fact that activists do not suddenly spring forth from nowhere and, therefore, of the importance of the process of the lives that they have lived to date; the sequence of events in their encounter with the movement; and the processes that led them to sympathize with the movement. Olson (1965) has devoted a whole book to clarifying the main causes that lead participants in movements to move beyond the temptation of just having a free ride. Olson's book and life history research share much in common despite differing theoretical premises regarding the start of movement participation: both emphasize the need to undergo multiple processes before movement participation occurs.

Individual participation in movements is not a simple matter; Figure 3.1 outlines this process and also the subject matter from Chapters 3 to 5. In this account, we will not see activists encountering the nativist movement itself until Chapter 4. Our focus in looking at the political socialization process will be on the formation of ideologies in general and attitudes to foreigners in particular and also on the source of influences. This is because these factors prescribe activists' reactions at the time of encountering the movement. This chapter also extends the period of analysis to just before contact with the nativist movement, unlike most studies which have limited themselves to the political socialization of minors (Okamura 1971). As we will see later, major incidents or chance opportunities can lead to significant changes in previously held ideologies, even after having become an adult.

Ideologies and political socialization: variables

In the previous chapter, we said that most activists in the nativist movement are politically conservative. Conservative is, however, a broad category, and the process by which an ideology is formed varies from person to person. Accordingly, this chapter will analyze activists' processes of ideology formation in a manner that takes account of the diversity of their life histories. Ideology, as it is used here, indicates the strength of one's anti-foreigner sentiments as well as one's location on a spectrum of political standpoints that stretches from progressive to conservative to right wing. The terms conservative and progressive will be used to indicate major differences in standpoint concerning the central issues of diplomacy and defense, which have been the focus of political confrontation in post-war Japan (Ōtake 1996). However, when analyzing the nativist movement, it is not sufficient to stop at the mainstream conservatives of the right; therefore, I have also dealt with forms of the 'right wing' which take a much harder line. In addition, whilst the group of politically disinterested people was small in number, it did exist and has, therefore, been placed just off the spectrum. The combined pattern, showing whether political disinterest and anti-foreigner sentiments were explicit or not, is set out in Figure 3.2 which also gives the relevant values for each.

The first point to note is that not a single person had held their current nativist movement ideology – right wing and explicitly oriented towards anti-foreigner sentiments – prior to their contact

Figure 3.1 Stages leading to movement participation

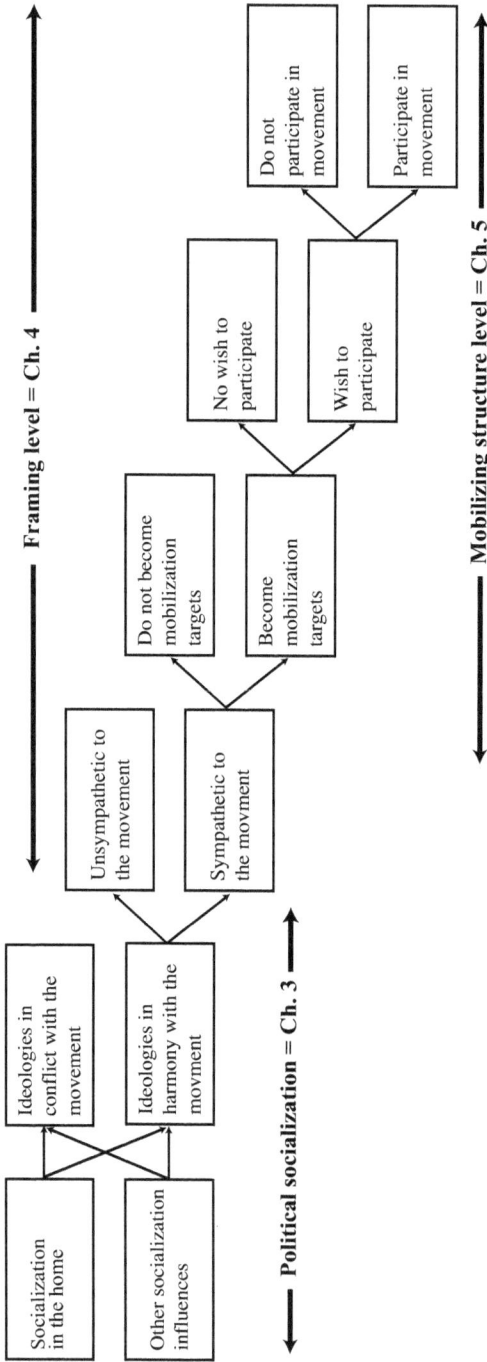

Source: Compiled by amalgamating Klandermans (1997: 23) and McAdam (1986: 69).

Figure 3.2: Ideologies predating connections with the nativist movement

Political standpoint

Progressive → Conservative/ultra-right

Anti-foreigner orientation	Disinterested	Conservative/ultra-right	Conservative	Ultra-right
Unambiguous	0	0	Nativist Articulation = 3	0
Vague	Non-political Awakenings = 3	Converts Alternation = 3	Grassroots conservatives Extension = 18	Right winger Amplification = 7

Source: For the names used for each type see Berger and Luckmann 1966; Blee 1996; Snow et al. 1986.

with the movement. However, most activists outside *Zaitokukai* had continuously had a right-wing ideology from a time prior to their connection with the nativist movement; seven out of thirty-four activists had belonged to the right wing. They had not had an interest in the 'foreigner problem' in the past, but the manner in which they became nativists served to 'amplify' their right-wing ideology. The vast majority, eighteen, were grass roots conservatives, who were conservative but did not necessarily hold explicit anti-foreigner sentiments. These men and women became right-wing nativists in a manner that 'extended' their own conservative orientation. Furthermore, in amongst those activists who belong to the conservative camp, there were three explicit nativists. They became activists by forcing an amalgamation of their anti-foreigner sentiments with the movement. However, only these three held explicit anti-foreigner sentiments; the true picture is that the vast majority of people were simply conservative or right wing. There were, in addition, three converts, who changed their creed from progressive to conservative and right wing, and for this reason this chapter will look at the process of 'alternation'. The disinterested three who were non-political had no ideological affinity with the nativist movement – it was the internet that 'awakened' them to become nativists.

In order to highlight the political socialization process, instead of using an explicit set of independent and dependent variables, I will posit 'loose' independent variables which clearly show the sources of influences on ideology formation. Accordingly, the concept of political socialization adopts the premise that political consciousness is established via the internalization of ideologies that are present in society. There are various vehicles for internalization but I will focus on 'political events' and 'social groups', treating them as loose independent variables. Political events are occurrences that exert a large influence on the formation of an individual's ideology; in the case of the nativist movement, the abduction issue would be the representative example.[2] In terms of groups, Naoi (1972a, 1972b) cites the influence of families, schools and workplaces, and reference will be made to each of these as relevant.

The process of political socialization

This section looks at how activists arrived at each of the five patterns – awakening, alternation, articulation, extension and amplification. In terms of independent variables, the biggest difference between this and previous studies concerns the influence of families. In the past, relations with parents have been held to be of decisive importance for political socialization (Demerath III, Marwell and Aiken 1971; Keniston 1968; McAdam 1988b). This is also pointed out in studies of ultra-right activists in Western Europe, which find that most were raised by ultra-right-wing parents (Klandermans and Mayer 2006a).[3]

Fewer nativist movement activists than previous studies would suggest referred to the influence of their parents; in fact, they referred more frequently to grandparents rather than parents. There were few examples of conservative and anti-foreigner attitudes having been handed down by parents. Oedipal-type rebellion such as opposing liberal parents (Keniston 1971) was present to a recognizable degree in one person only; in short, the family cannot be seen as the significant other in the political socialization of activists in this study. Although I asked about the influence of parents during interviews, the only type of reply that I got was almost always along the lines of 'there was none at all [parental influence] in my family. I can't discuss [politics] with my parents (Ms P. *Zaitokukai*, twenties)'. Let us look at how activists actually underwent the process of political socialization.

Awakening: from non-political to activist

Awakening indicates a situation in which non-political people, who have previously shown no interest in either 'politics' or 'foreigners', 'wake up' as a result of some impetus or other. As touched on in the previous chapter, since the majority of activists had taken a conservative stance from the start, only three correspond to this pattern. One of these, K, dropped out of a computer technical college and has assumed the important role of a *Zaitokukai* leader while currently working as a systems engineer. As he says in the following passage, before his contact with *Zaitokukai* he had never voted in an election.

I was what you would call non-political. Because I was not interested at all. Neither [left nor right] existed. I have never taken part [in an election]. I really was not interested at all. Since I had no interest in elections, I never thought that elections themselves were that

important, back then. I never [even talked about politics]. To begin
with, there was no one amongst my acquaintances and friends to
speak to about politics. (Mr K, *Zaitokukai*, forties)

K said, 'From the time that I was a child, I had heard about the bad
reputation of [*Zainichi*] Koreans when I was living in my hometown.
That talk was all that I had heard for a long time'. Prejudice against
Zainichi Koreans was not the source of K's 'awakening'.[4] That is
not to say, however, that he lacked the sort of foundation that would
make him receptive to the nativist movement; although he was not
knowledgeable about 'historical problems' he had picked up some
feelings of opposition to them. As seen below, it is his denial of the
cultural trauma of the 'comfort women' and of 'aggression towards
Asia' (Alexander et al. 2004) that brought him into contact with
Zaitokukai.

I had heard for a long time that Japan did terrible things in Asia, and
then when I became a working adult and also heard about the comfort
women issue, I felt that 'we shouldn't be fixating on every single issue
like this'. At that time, I wasn't in the slightest bit interested in the
problem of foreigners. (Mr K, *Zaitokukai*, forties)

In fact, it was starting to search the internet for information on
related matters that led to K ultimately joining *Zaitokukai*.

There was a massive [anti-Japanese] demonstration in Shanghai.[5]
During that demonstration I kept hearing that Japan had done terrible
things in China and Korea and that it was hated. At that time, all I
thought was that it had been wartime and that surely these were just
things that should be expected during war. But, given that such a
massive demonstration had broken out, I started doing some research
wondering just how terrible the things that Japan had done back then
were. However, after realizing that there were no facts, I ended up
where I am now. (Mr K, *Zaitokukai*, forties)

Although K's initial perception was that 'terrible things' were the
product of 'wartime' and they were 'things that should be expected',
he cannot be described as a historical revisionist as he did not glorify
these deeds. He subsequently became a historical revisionist on the
basis of information on the internet; after 'starting to search' and

finding 'no facts'. Now that he has been 'awakened' he says that he regrets having abstained from voting and that he now basically votes for the LDP. K's family had subscribed to a mainstream newspaper 'a long time ago' and then only to the sports paper that his father read, but after his father's death, they had not had any newspapers. Being raised in this sort of poor cultural environment could be seen as one sort of 'non-political' background.

Another person, G, describes himself saying, 'I did not go to a usual university or anything after finishing high school' and adds that he was disinterested in politics. However, just like K, he showed sporadic interest in historical issues, 'I got caught up in lots of things in my late twenties ... for example the person who assassinated Hirofumi Ito[6] ... When I looked it up on the net I thought, 'What! Some Korean guy assassinated him!' This is an example of how even non-political activists came into contact with the nativist movement. They took hold of the fine thread that led them to nativism in the same way as K and G made contact via historical issues.

Alternation: progressives' political conversion experiences

When people who had initially identified themselves as progressive convert, the degree of change that they display surpasses by far that of people who had been non-political. This is close to what Berger and Luckmann intend by 'alternation': 'pre-alternation biography is typically nihilated *in toto* by subsuming it under a negative category occupying a strategic position in the new legitimating apparatus' (Berger and Luckmann 1966: 179). As was the case with non-political activists, there were few converts – only three, but the changes that have accompanied their 180 degree shift away from their former selves surface in their conversation. A, out of all the activists, is what could be called a diehard fundamentalist, but until his thirties he had voted for left-wing political parties.

> It's embarrassing, but back then I voted for the Socialist Party at that time. When I think about it now, I really want to get in a time machine and go back and bash that me. I really do! I even voted for the Communist Party. [The ultra-right politician] Ishihara was the Governor of the city of Tokyo, and I voted for him although only from his second term of office. That was because I supported someone else for the first term. I started voting for the LDP after

the abduction issue. I was no good before that. I thought that being
a liberal was a good thing, and voted for leftist members of the Diet.
(Mr A, *Zaitokukai*, forties)

Why did A, who had thought that it was a good thing to be a liberal,
undergo such a degree of alternation that he 'want[ed] to ... bash
that me'? 'The decisive point ... was the year when the abductions
came to light. That year, I felt a clear and sudden change of direction
take place inside me'. There were four activists for whom the
abduction issue was the impetus, and there is no doubt that this
was a social factor that led to an increase in the number of nativists.
However, in order for the extreme sort of change that A underwent
to occur, an environment for alternation – that is, remaking one's
socialization – is necessary; the contemporary impact of an
incident is not sufficient. An exemplar of alternation is religious
conversion, and it is because 'the religious community "provides the
indispensable plausibility structure for the new reality"' (Berger and
Luckmann 1966: 178) that people are able to establish themselves
as converts. In the same manner, C (*Zaitokukai*, thirties male), who
experienced alternation, found himself identifying with γ, a veteran
activist: 'I almost always participated with γ ... he must have wanted
to say, "you disgust me"'.

A did not have this kind of 'significant other'. However, the flood
of information about the abduction issue and the subsequent changes
most likely made it viable to separate oneself from 'Japanese society
as one had existed in it previously'. Both South Korea and China
have more victims of abduction than Japan, but the focus of their
interest has been the North Korean nuclear program. On the other
hand, Japan's obsession with the abduction issue has been conspicuous
since Prime Minister Koizumi's September 2002 visit to North
Korea (Shirai 2013; Williams and Mobrand 2010).[7] While Berger and
Luckmann (1966: 182) regard religion as the exemplar of a system
that produces long-term change, they illustrate that military service
and short-term hospitalization are examples that lead to extreme
short-term changes. This is an example of what Goffman (1961) calls
total institution, and without this kind of environment, it would be
difficult for alternation to arise. In short, it could be said that it was
the shift to a condition akin to a total institution, such as a hospital or
the military, that supported A's alternation; we could perhaps say that
this condition applied in Japan after Koizumi's visit to North Korea.

Moreover, given that alternation is accompanied by a comprehensive rejection of past views, A goes as far as rejecting not only North Korea but relations with the 'victorious countries' of World War II; he comprehensively rejects Japan's 'post-war regime'.

I realized how preposterous countries that we have been toadying to are – countries like North Korea and Communist China. North Korea is the model of just how terrible socialist states are. Put simply, Japan has been besieged by the victorious countries and at the mercy of them. I also noticed how their logic was so irresponsible – they really were irresponsible – what incredible detachment from reality! I felt this like a clang inside me, there wasn't a real sound of course, but I certainly felt a sudden severing feeling. (Mr A, *Zaitokukai*, forties)

One of the activists who, unlike A, displayed a marked influence from her family was X, who was also one of the few females. As X points out below, her father was a municipal public servant and she grew up in a family who were members of a municipal workers union. In her early twenties she voted for the Socialist Party, in accordance with her parents' wishes. In her late twenties, she ended up working full time for the labor union at her place of employment, where she was engaged in promoting gender equality. At this time, she was helping a candidate, whom the union supported, in the election.

My parents – my family worked in local government – were public servants. 'The LDP is the rich people's party so don't vote for them'. I feel, 'Oh, that's right.' Is it right? I thought that the LDP was only for rich people who don't do any work. I don't know. I haven't looked into it. Since my parents were in *Jichirō* (All-Japan Prefectural and Municipal Workers' Union), I voted [in elections] for whoever *Jichirō* supported. (Ms X, *Zaitokukai*, forties)

X's union was affiliated with *Dōmei* (Japanese Confederation of Labor), a right-leaning confederation, but X says that when she was working full time for the union she felt that there was a 'whiff of the left wing' when they did things like call strikes. As a result, she continued in a state of accumulating stress; 'Inside myself I held tightly to the idea that I loved Japan, but I couldn't say it out aloud'. At the point in time that she is referring to here, the feelings that she was experiencing were not particularly strong. The opportunity that made her sense of not belonging explicit was provided by a self-development group that she joined called 'I Want to Change Myself'. X says that she felt that she 'was guided correctly' in this group and that she was able to gain a sense of 'feeling an exact fit'. What is meant here by 'feeling an exact fit' is that feelings that she had suppressed about her 'tremendous love of Japanese culture and language' were affirmed.

However, this was incompatible with the world to which she had belonged, her family and workplace. If all she had had to do in her workplace was to complete the work assigned to her, this might not have led to such a big problem. However, as X says below, as a union official she was the one who had to call for the thoroughgoing abolition of gender discrimination amongst other union members, but work became unsatisfying after her conversion.

> Things like gender equality and so on don't suit me. I can't explain it to union members. I say this and that. I can't say anything plausible. I can no longer muster the persuasiveness to explain things to others that I don't think are important. That's why it's become tough. (Ms X, *Zaitokukai*, forties)

As a result of this, she has not only resigned from her full-time work in the union but from the company itself and has even moved to an area far away and different from the environment that she had been in to date. This is one type of alternation; X herself has 'a feeling of having to be aware of social matters'. 'It would be good if people could see' that what has changed 'is that the aim has moved in this or that direction'. In addition to being a rejection of her way of life to date as a full-time union employee, this also signifies her independence from her parents. Unlike her act of leaving the union, she has not severed relations with her parents but maintains the kind of rapport with them in which she does not talk about her activities in *Zaitokukai*.

> My mother and father see and recognize it as an extreme step. I seldom talk with my father. Maybe my mother and I have a mutual understanding as women, and on the basis of that sort of intuition we are constantly talking about daily dramas and the like. But I become all formal in front of my father. (Ms X, *Zaitokukai*, forties)

Although her alternation has been in the opposite direction to her father's values, this has not become the cause of conflict. X continues to respect her father and to keep him at a distance just as she always has, and even though she has escaped his ideological influence they both avoid the topic. This type of father–daughter relationship may not be particularly unusual in Japan; it may well be one of the Oedipal types of rebellion that were mentioned above. Her experience of alternation allows X greater breadth and weakens her feelings of resistance towards extreme things.

Articulation: circumstances that breed nativists

Most activists in the nativist movement were not explicitly nativists from the outset. As Figure 3.2 above shows, only three had had 'negative concerns about foreigners'. One of these, H, was raised in a conservative family, in which his father was a Shinto priest and his family inculcated into him the sort of anti-foreigner sentiments that he mentions below.

> I was interested in the foreigner problem. Actually, there was a community of Koreans in X ward [near where I grew up] and my father brought me up not to mix with Koreans, and he taught me that it is dangerous to have anything to do with their sort. That's what our generation were taught. So, I was brought up with the extreme view that Koreans are the enemy. (Mr H, *Zaitokukai*, thirties)

H attends a prestigious national university, and says that because the president of his university makes statements advocating for *Zainichi* Koreans, he joined a 'sort of resistance movement' group that attacks *Zainichi* Koreans. He continues to take part in this group activity, and joining the nativist movement was an extension of this. H left *Zaitokukai* in 2013, but this was not a change of doctrine, he moved to another group that he thought would be a more effective movement. For H, it was not a matter of accepting a new set of facts, such as we see in alternation, but of finding an organization that meshed neatly with his own anti-foreigner sentiments. If we start counting from his student days, H has changed groups four times in search an organization that suited him.[8]

H was the only activist who spoke about an awareness of prejudice against *Zainichi* Koreans in this way and who put his words into practice. The other two were led to nativism as a consequence of beginning to have contact with foreigners in their regions and workplaces following an increase in the number of newcomers. η had close contact with *Zainichi* Koreans because he lived in the Kansai factory belt, but his anti-foreigner sentiments were directed towards newcomer foreigners.

> I was in middle school around the time of the bubble [economy], and there was talk about factories in the neighborhood employing Iranians, Chinese and the like ... Foreigners are extremely difficult to deal with; it's just not straightforward ... They listen to what the company president says, but they ignore other leaders and cause trouble with other employees; real problems of this sort have come up in conversations between adults. I have also heard these sorts of childlike conversations and felt that it's just not straightforward ... if numbers keep increasing steadily in this unchecked way – as we go on about internationalization this and internationalization that – we are probably going to end up in a bad way, and this is why I became interested. (Mr η, non-*Zaitokukai*, thirties)

This is the situation hypothesized by competition theory in which the influx of migrants leads to an increase in nativism, but η was not influenced by the adults around him. As we see below, the tendency was for the adults at his school and in the area to say, 'You must not discriminate against foreigners'. He also makes a point of saying that there was no internet at that time either. Back then, people with preferences such as those of η could not meet any other flesh-and-blood people who shared their consciousness, nor could they look up information on the internet or come across 'like-minded' people; there was nothing for them to do but hold onto their shameful feelings. This is a point of major divergence with H, who had a history of being educated in these issues by his father.

> Those days, there just wasn't anyone [with thoughts of exclusion]; the trend was instead to say you must not discriminate against foreigners. In places like factories things went as far as the hiring of people who were here illegally – there was absolutely no anxiety about whether we should be excluding foreigners or what we should do when there were problems, so I ended up thinking that this was quite bad. Teachers at school would not instruct us on this, adults

in the area would not instruct us, and there was as yet no internet at the time. (Mr η, non-*Zaitokukai*, thirties)

To the extent that η's feelings in middle school were not just a transient phenomenon that went away but continued after his graduation from high school and even after he had started work, he differed from the others. After having become a working adult, he took the opportunity to join the nativist movement (articulation) and began his life as an activist (this process will be discussed in detail in Chapter 5). 'I was neither interested in the LDP nor opposition parties at that time', says η, but 'longed for someone who would protect the country'. Consequently, 'anything to do with the Self-Defense Forces or Self-Defense Force vehicles passing by [would draw my] interest'. This turned into an ideology of support for the conservatives, which still continues, and can be regarded as the cause that lit the spark of his nativism.

Extension: diverse patterns of grassroots conservatives

Grassroots conservatives form the majority of those interviewed and are thus the most representative pattern of conservatives. These men and women did not necessarily hold explicitly anti-foreign sentiments nor had most of them ever had any contact with foreigners. Although they are already conservatives, since they are not extremists, in order for them to resonate with the nativist movement, there needs to be a considerable expansion of their 'conservative' ideologies. Let us now investigate how grassroots conservatives experience political socialization and what kind of common ground with the nativist movement this potentially produces.

Urban and rural grassroots conservatives

To begin with, I would like to introduce two prototype grassroots conservatives – one rural and one urban. B, an office worker in the accounting field, said, 'originally, I didn't read newspapers or anything else; I wasn't interested in anything that was going on in the world outside my hobbies'. He did not even see getting into university as having any merit so he randomly chose something to study, and since he had no hopes for the future either he did not make any decisions about finding employment. However, while continuing to lack any interest in politics, he continued with what was, as we will see below, typical conservative voting behavior.

> Voting was the only thing that I always did. I thought that it was something that I had to do – exercizing my right to vote ... I had always [voted] LDP. For the political party. My family home was in a rural area, the sort of place where there is a big conservative class, and since I'd grown up hearing this sort of talk, I just ended up voting that way. I hadn't ever thought in terms of the LDP as a conservative political party. (Mr B, *Zaitokukai*, thirties)

If this were all there was to it, it would be difficult to discern the foundation of his having become a nativist. The clue lies in his patriotism, which had its roots in childhood experiences, as is illustrated by his use below of the word 'inevitable' with regard to the fact that they also ate the meat form the beef cattle that they reared.

> My mother's side of the family were rice farmers and kept two beef cattle ... because they were beef cattle, they would disappear after two years ... But, I was in my sixth grade of primary school before I realized that we had eaten them ... It tells me that inevitability formed what I am now. ... the fact that I was originally born in this country; that I was born of my mum and dad – I think that everything is inevitable and that there is no such thing as chance. When I had this thought, I thought about how we sometimes think we love or hate this country, don't we? Do you love Japan? What a nonsensical question! Whether we love or hate it, we were born and raised in this country so I think that we have no option but to love it. (Mr B, *Zaitokukai*, thirties)

Basing himself on the contradiction of eating the cattle that he was fond of, and accepting this as inevitable, B discovered the foundation of his own life. Similarly, having decided that it was inevitable that he should have been born and raised in Japan, he arrives at the resulting affirmation of the status quo: that 'we have no option but to love it'. This was expanded into, 'I hate people who are wrecking Japan by saying I hate it, I hate it' and ultimately led him to nativism.[9]

Meanwhile, E, who was born and raised in the suburbs of Tokyo – stronghold areas for conservatism – has no interest in politics but was a typical member of the support base for the LDP, which is founded on a lifestyle conservatism that supports the status quo. She first acquired the right to vote at the time of the Nakasone cabinet and, even though she had no interest in Nakasone as a hawk, she voted for the LDP under the 1955 political system which had seen the LDP stay in power since 1955, thinking that they would probably 'do what was right for the country'.

> I had no interest at all in politics. The LDP had been in power for a very long time so there was a feeling that it didn't particularly matter if ordinary people didn't do anything because the people in charge would probably do what was right for the country. I turned out [for the elections] because it is a citizen's duty to do so. I went to all of them. [My vote] went to the LDP. Everyone said that Kiichi Miyazawa [former Prime Minister] was no good, but from my viewpoint he was okay and doing well enough although I wouldn't give him full marks. (Ms E, *Zaitokukai*, forties)

Nonetheless, when the 1955 political system collapsed she began voting for other conservative parties; it seems that she was not a steadfast member of the LDP support base. The nature of her political realignment could have led her to become a more independent swinging voter. E detested violent acts, such as those of Team Kansai, and was likewise opposed to anything radical. Despite this, her joining the nativist movement was, nonetheless, a result of her lifestyle conservatism.

> I think that I'd like to turn Japan back, probably to the 1990s. The '80s or the '90s. Back to the period when the old LDP held power; the period when you could get on with your life normally, without having to think about anything. I suppose that, as a woman, there is an aspect of wanting to safeguard my present lifestyle. (Ms E, *Zaitokukai*, forties)

Lifestyle conservatism has been identified as the background to the conservative revival that arose in the 1980s, but E felt nostalgic for the 1980s and 1990s, a period 'when you could get on with your life normally, without having to think about anything'.[10] There is a foundation that draws this sort of grassroots conservative to nativism, and in this case 'a vague anxiety regarding the collapse of Japan' could be seen as providing the backdrop. However, people experiencing anxiety based on E's variety of lifestyle conservatism are a background minority – sensible category – who form a 'moderate' faction within the nativist movement.

Family influence
As mentioned above, few activists spoke about the influence of
family, and the proportion was even lower amongst grassroots
conservatives. V is an exception and the person who, of all the
activists I interviewed, conveyed a strong sense of sincerity. At
least a part of his sincerity comes from having been raised in a large
conservative family, something that is seen comparatively often (it
is not exceptional) and, as we see below, from the influence of his
conservative grandfather.

> When we were children, my grandfather would hoist the Japanese flag
> on festival days. We'd stopped flying it by the time that I was in middle
> school, but we hoisted it without fail when I was in kindergarten and
> lower primary school. As to an interest in politics, he disciplined
> me to know the slightest [thing] as a working adult, so he told me to
> watch the news and to read the newspaper every day. When I asked
> him about things that I didn't understand, he would explain them to
> me. I am basically an LDP supporter. My grandfather liked the LDP
> and he used to think along the lines of 'if we just vote in the LDP.' It
> was a wish for political stability. (Mr V, *Zaitokukai*, forties)

V's grandfather displayed not only the conservative attitude of
flying the flag, which is usually a nationalist practice in Japan, but
was also in the habit of the social practice of reading the newspaper.
V's vote for the LDP was influenced by his grandfather; he was a
'system support' (Aiji Tanaka 1995, 1996) grassroots conservative,
that is, one who wishes to see political stability. This is one factor
that is common ground between nativism and a historical revisionist
viewpoint that is cultivated by listening to relatives talking about
the pre-war situation.[11]

> I had had doubts for a long time [about post-war education] when
> it came to the bits of conversation we had had about his previous
> [wartime] personal experiences. What we heard was considerably
> different from what I'd heard from my grandfather and others. When
> I used to listen to my mother telling me about her own grandfather
> who had been to the Korean Peninsula, when it was a colony, and had
> had a plantation there I felt a big disconnect between what she said
> and what I was hearing [at school]. My impression was that nothing

that terrible had happened, and yet ... What was different was my image of that country. (Mr V, *Zaitokukai*, forties)

Early childhood experiences of Japan's Self-Defense Forces could also be given as another of the characteristic factors that apply in V's case. A positive view of the Self-Defense Forces bred an interest in the military and the international news. As an adolescent, he subscribed to the right-wing magazine *SAPIO* and also bought books by the right-wing journalist Nobuhiko Ochiai; these works helped to shape his attitude to *Sōren*.

> There was an Air Self-Defense Force base near my home and that is why I liked planes. I was allowed to attend air shows from a young age and I used to watch the aircraft fighters fly ... I have been reading *SAPIO* for quite a long time. Nobuhiko Ochiai and others had been writing about problems like the abduction issue for a long time, therefore, I had known about it long before Megumi Yokota [a victim of abduction by North Korean agents] and others publicized it in their comments ... It was also books that came out around this time that wrote about Korean people's organizations and groups [referring to *Sōren*]. The fact that *Sōren* continued to exist even after the abductions had come to light left me with some vague feelings of uncertainty. Feelings like: why doesn't it just go away? (Mr V, *Zaitokukai*, forties)

People who have had contact with the Self-Defense Forces are undoubtedly a minority in Japanese society, but V's experience was a result of the special nature of the area in which he lived. Moreover, living in the area, V's family took the children to Self-Defense Force festivals as a fun day out. His historical revisionism also resulted from the influence of his relatives; he did not acquire it via the internet. In short, the factor that led to his acceptance of nativism was his primary socialization process mediated by his relatives and region; the polar opposite of the image of an internet right winger who is isolated from any social groups. There are not necessarily large numbers of people like V in the nativist movement. However, we can say that *Zaitokukai* has been able to establish branches in many cities and prefectures, including under-populated areas, because of the existence of people who were raised 'decently' in conservative environments in the provinces who flock to the movement because they have sincere 'doubts'.[12]

Historical revisionism

As seen above, family influence, particularly from grandparents, is
one of the routes by which people become historical revisionists.
An additional characteristic is the large proportion of people who
talk about a feeling of malaise towards their school education. This
is not the same as the hostile view of others that adults have as part
of their 'masochistic view of history'; it is a feeling of rebellion
that they had held as children. This does not depend on family
influence but is a refutation built on knowledge that one has gained
from reading history and other books on one's own. Following
the spread of the internet, it appears that there are large numbers
of hits on the historical revisionism home page in the process of
'comprehensive learning, the use of personal computers and the
like' (Mr U, *Zaitokukai*, twenties). In L's case, his interest in history
started as a child, and it was the inconsistencies between what he
learned at school and the contents of related works that he read on
his own that aroused his suspicions. As in L's case, however, it is not
unusual for these feelings to be based on mistaken understandings
encountered in the contents of education such as the idea that 'Japan
was the aggressor against its partner the United States'.

> I was sceptical about the masochistic view of history. For example, the
> idea in history education that Japan was the aggressor. I had also had
> a long-standing interest in that [period] so I knew that 'that was just
> not right'. I had a personal interest so I had books on the war. I knew
> that it was impossible that Japan would simply do something like plot
> aggression against the United States ... Because I was interested in the
> war and had done a certain amount of specialist study on the subject, I
> regarded the shallow content that middle school students were taught
> at school as nonsense. (Mr L, *Zaitokukai*, forties)

Another female leader, P, had also had doubts from the time of her
childhood about information and school education regarding the
past war. P's grades at school had not been good, but she had a
strong interest in history and still recalled even detailed descriptions
from her textbooks.

> I was quite interested from about the time that I was in kindergarten,
> in issues like the war. In August there are special war features
> on television, aren't there? It was because I had my doubts about

why they had to keep repeating that Japan was bad that I ended up moving to the right, no one else told me about it. As I got older, I did some research of my own, apart from what we were taught at school, and realized, 'Oh, this is different from reality'. (Ms P, *Zaitokukai*, twenties)

According to P, 'If all that people get is an education that is based on saying that Japan was bad, they end up, conversely, wanting to rebel a little against this'. The 'comfort women' issue became a symbol for this. There were several other activists, aside from P, for whom the 'comfort women' issue was the original cause that led them to nativism. This has become the most important target of attack for historical revisionism as a whole, and there is also a segment that has followed this issue exclusively. This is not all, however; the existence of the 'comfort women' issue at the points of overlap between the South Korean government, the Korean people and *Zainichi* Koreans within the political process produces a circuit of interest in 'comfort women' → nativism.

Throughout school, people like me had the absurd sort of education in which we were told that the Japanese military forced Korean women to become comfort women and raped them. It was as a result of the simple doubt, 'Could this, actually, really be true?' that my interest was sparked. People on the left keep squawking that we must pay compensation so I think that if this is not true, then we have to speak out and also rebut it. (Ms P, *Zaitokukai*, twenties)

P kept reading books about history even after graduating from high school and this was linked to her active participation in elections and her support for the conservatives, 'the LDP for the present'. In P's case, her interest was confined to history when she was a minor, but she displayed age-appropriate development by voting because she was thinking about her country's future once she became an adult. She then joined the conservative community on *Mixi*, an online Japanese social networking site, and even took to the streets as a *Zaitokukai* leader, something that can be seen as a natural result of her political socialization to that point in time.

You can vote once you are twenty, can't you. From there, I naturally started to turn my attention [to politics]. Before that, I was just fooling

around. I had no or practically no interest. I didn't even really read
the newspaper except for maybe some human interest stories or the
television columns. But being able to vote once I was twenty gave me
a feeling of responsibility as I realized that my one vote would have
some influence on Japan. For the moment, I vote LDP. (P, *Zaitokukai*,
twenties female)

P was working as a hostess but, just on the basis of her statements
thus far, it would be difficult to link the state of her occupational
class with her participation in *Zaitokukai*. Given that an internet
community like *Mixi* played the role of breeding her interest in
politics and her ideology, we should instead shift our attention to
the mobilizing structure.

Significant incidents

One typical pattern is to have started off as a conservative and then
developed an anti-foreign interest as a result of a specific incident.
The word 'incident' is wide-ranging in its coverage: from minor
matters that would only interest internet right wingers to major
news items such as the collision of Chinese fishing boats and
Japan Coast Guard vessels in the Senkaku Islands. Also, it is not
unusual for sport to provide the introduction to nativism, as can
be seen in the first volume of *Manga kenkanryū*, which began with
the 2002 Soccer World Cup and has had an impact on nativism,[13]
and in the case of the hooligans mentioned in Chapter 2. S, one
of the oldest members of the *Zaitokukai* leadership, exemplifies
this same sort of experience during the World Baseball Classic
(WBC). S had belonged to a baseball team since he was a child
and, inspired by his younger sister who had spent a short period
studying in London, he got a working holiday visa and went off to
Canada, where he was next to the United States which he admired
as the home of baseball.[14]

Don't you remember the incident, during the WBC, when Japan played
South Korea and lost, and then the South Korean team stuck their flag
into the mound? That incident happened. As I said earlier, for people
who play baseball, there is no more sacred place than the ground and
within this the baseball mound is even more revered. For that very
reason, how should I put it? In terms of feeling, it is as sacred as Christ
or Mary. The mound! Seeing them stick a flag into it made me think,

'What are they doing?' and the anger welled up inside me. That was the
start. I basically started [hating Koreans]. (Mr S, *Zaitokukai*, thirties)

It is, nonetheless, the major incidents which agitate the mass media
that most people cite. At the outset of the interviews, J, who had
many opportunities to interact with foreigners in the Language
Department of his university, said 'I am in no way – let me tell you
from the start – a nativist'. He joined the nativist movement primarily
out of political conservatism. As we see below, he explained his weak
support for the LDP using the old-fashioned term 'anti-communist'.

As you'd expect, [my vote] is LDP ... Democratic Party, which, at a
glance, includes not only conservative MPs, but also more from the
former Socialist Party. I guess I am anti-communist. In any case, I
hate the Communist Party, communism and socialism. No matter
what, I am opposed to voting for the Communist or the Socialist
Parties. I guess I choose the LDP for negative reasons after all. (Mr
J, *Zaitokukai*, forties)

J started hating China as a result of the Tiananmen Square Massacre,
and says that his feelings of not being able to trust China grew
stronger with 'incidents such as that of the poisoned *gyōza* and
the Nagano riots at the time of the Beijing Olympics'. Then, the
September 2010 collision between a Chinese fishing boat and a
Japanese patrol boat off the coast of the Senkaku Islands proved
a decisive incident. However, J saw this as a problem in terms of
the Japanese government's reaction, and from that time on felt an
increasing distrust of the mass media, which he felt had displayed
a weak attitude, and he began to rely increasingly on the internet.

The decisive event [that led to activism] was Senkaku. I knew that
China was a country that did that sort of thing, but it was the reaction
of the Japanese government rather than China's actions that angered
me. (Mr J, *Zaitokukai*, forties)

Seen in this way, J's case looks like an example of the typical pattern
for becoming an internet right winger, but the foundations had been
there for far longer. J continued feeling hatred for socialist countries,
as in his statement 'I hate the Soviet Union too'. J's case is best seen
as him already having what can be called a classic, anti-communist

consciousness and his hatred then becoming fixed as a result of various 'incidents' that occurred in China and served to augment this consciousness.

Amplification: self-formation as right wing

The seven people referred to here as right wing were to the 'right' of the LDP before joining the nativist movement. Most of them had achieved their self-formation in a right-wing direction from puberty. In order to come into contact with right-wing ideas while one is a minor requires the guidance of a 'significant other' and, consequently, organizations that mediate political socialization – families and schools – play a certain role. In D's case, he was brought up by a feudal father and, as we see below, underwent the sort of family education that is rarely seen in Japan these days. He says that, as a result, he acquired a consciousness of 'I think that it is natural to obey what the emperor says because it is what he says'.

> Anyhow, when I was in primary school, I was made to memorize things like the Imperial Rescript on Education. In the first year of middle school, I was also made to memorize the Imperial Decree ending the Pacific War, and to this day I can usually still recite it ... His Majesty, the late emperor said 'my sorrow gnaws at my very insides' which, in short, means that it was such a painful thing that it was like feeling that one's intestines would burst. As I speak I am gradually being overcome by the urge to cry. (Mr D, *Zaitokukai*, thirties)

γ was raised by his grandparents and this became, he says, the foundation for his acquisition not of historical revisionism but traditional conservatism. It is not a reaction of hostility towards 'anti-Japanese education' that characterizes the people who have been categorized as right wing, but the fact that they feel adoration for the Emperor and for the right-wing ideas connected with him.

> I naturally learned to respect the emperor from my grandfather who raised me and taught me to bow to a photograph of the emperor in his house everyday ... It probably can't even be taught at school. Maybe that's why I didn't understand [what the emperor meant]. Although I hadn't even thought about the existence of the emperor himself, after my grandfather started taking care of me, when I was in high school, he drilled into me daily that the emperor had to be

respected, and I think that this was the foundation for me. (Mr γ, non-*Zaitokukai*, forties)

When he was at university, γ found out about Shūsuke Nomura, a right-wing activist who appeared on a television talk show that he liked called *Asamade nama terebi*. A friend introduced γ to Nomura's writings and, admiring these, he contacted Nomura's office whereupon he was introduced to the small ultra-right party, *Shinpu*, and embarked on his life as an activist. Later, he left *Shinpu*, which was poorly managed and while he was being an independent activist he came across *Zaitokukai* and became involved in the nativist movement.

I was massively interested in politics and *Asamade nama terebi* on television was a tremendous hit with me. That was when I learnt about Shusuke Nomura and, although I didn't really know what a right winger was, I understood that there were people who were thinking seriously about Japan and its people and, moreover, that there were still people who were taking action now ... I gradually ended up talking a lot about politics with my friends and I probably talked about right wingers. Undoubtedly. Surely. Then, a friend bought me a book from a second-hand bookshop saying, 'I got a book that I thought you'd like'. That was a book by Mr Nomura, and it all started from that, I instantly got all worked up about things. (Mr γ, non-*Zaitokukai*, forties)

The activist δ, in his twenties, was from a family that subscribed to the Asahi Newspaper, which is known for its liberal tone, and since his parents told him that he could do as he wished he was not influenced by them on the political socialization front. It was a teacher at school who introduced him to the comics of Yoshinori Kobayashi, who was active in spreading historical revisionism, and this was when his contact with the ultra-right began.

There was my homeroom teacher and a supplementary teacher – the former was thoroughly left wing. But, one day, the homeroom teacher had to stay in bed because of a bad cold so he didn't come to school. That day we had a young female supplementary teacher, and in the homeroom in the afternoon, she said, 'Your homeroom teacher always tells you things in that [masochistic] way but you are all Japanese. Be proud that you are Japanese, and so that you can study what pride as a Japanese person means and what a Japanese person is, I recommend that you all look at the very readable works of Yoshinori Kobayashi, such as *On War*.' (Mr δ, non-*Zaitokukai*, twenties)

Two people said that they had come into contact with revisionist information during their comprehensive education but only δ spoke about having been influenced by a teacher. Also, as we can see from the passage quoted above, he was not directly influenced by the supplementary teacher; she merely suggested where they might look for more information. If, however, we look at blogs by people who are active in the nativist movement, large numbers of youths have been influenced by their school or cram school teachers. Murai (1997a, 1997b) discusses teachers who sympathize with revisionist viewpoints, and these sorts of teachers do produce youth who accept the ideas of revisionism and nativism.

> When I searched for *On War*, *Gōmanizumu manifesto* came up ... The entry said 'I dislike right wingers, but I also understand what Satoshi Akao and Shusuke Nomura are saying'. This sent me off to the library where I found a book this big called *The Encyclopaedia of Japanese Names*. I searched through this massive book for Satoshi Akao under A and Shusuke Nomura under N, and when I looked at their names and how they had been living their lives I thought, 'Wow, what amazing lives they are living'. (Mr δ, non-*Zaitokukai*, twenties)

In δ's case, he was full of enthusiasm and ended up reading Yoshinori Kobayashi's comic after hearing about it from the aforementioned teacher. This is where he came across Shusuke Nomura's name, and having immersed himself in his writings, decided to go on to Kokushikan University, which is well known for being right wing. In the case of people who become right wing in this way, if something causes an amplification of elements such as 'love of Japan' and 'protecting Japan', the distance between their ideologies and nativism is rapidly reduced. They are a good match with the nativists and also the group that is best able to participate in the nativist movement without any feelings of resistance.

Fertile ground for the acceptance of nativism

The discussion thus far has confirmed that activists are not particularly homogeneous and that the differences between them are even more pronounced before they begin taking part in activism. Young ultra-right activists in Europe tend to have had a history of belonging to deviant subcultures beforehand (Fangen 1999: 370), but this has not been the case in Japan. This can be seen as one of the main reasons for the diversity that precedes participation in activism in Japan. In addition, there is considerable variation amongst activists regarding whether the foundation for their acceptance of nativism was formed through a process of political socialization or not. A mere three activists had harbored explicit anti-foreigner sentiments from the outset and, what is more, two of them were xenophobic towards newcomers not *Zainichi* Koreans.

Most of the others were not drawn to nativism via the 'foreigner problem' but via other routes. One of the most prominent of these other routes is historical revisionism, which has been advocated since the 1950s and is not at all new (Gluck 2007). Similarly, there have no doubt always been people who feel particular hostility towards the descriptions of World War Two in textbooks. It was in the 1990s that the circulation of historical revisionist information in a form that could be easily accessed began. These sorts of changes in the 'supply' side produced a cluster of people who had previously not been able to put into words their sense of malaise regarding history, but who now began to use the words given to them by historical revisionists. Actually, those people who internalized historical revisionism before nativism are the generation who underwent a period of self-formation following the 1990s and achieved political socialization with the assistance of historical revisionist information.[15]

Next, the fact that Japan's nativist movement is a variant of historical revisionism increases the influence of significant others in the political socialization process. The proportion of people who are conscious of having been influenced by others around them in their process of political socialization is low, and if they were influenced it was largely not by their parents but by their grandparents. This is because the sort of historical revisionism that has its basis in personal wartime experiences is handed down not by one's parents but one's grandparents. Studies of the ultra-right in Western Europe cite the preponderance of people who were raised in an ultra-right milieu as a major background factor (Klandermans and Mayer 2006a), but it is difficult to argue that this is the case overall in Japan. In Figure 3.2 above, most of the people classified as right wing had been influenced by their surroundings (parents and school). This means that developing right-wing thinking was not something that happened for them once they were adults; they needed the guidance of 'significant others' as children.

People who replied that they did not particularly have any 'significant others' in their political socialization had some sort of 'incident' that acted as a functional equivalent. To give some examples mentioned during the interviews, 'the abduction issue', 'the WBC', 'the Senkaku issue' and 'anti-Japanese demonstrations in China' acted as the impetus for a progressive inclination towards nativism. This was the case for all the people who had been non-political, converts and grassroots conservatives; it is an influential route to becoming an activist. Moreover, almost everyone followed the steps of initially acquiring their information from the mass media and then moving away from print mass media and turning instead to the internet. It appears that had these men and women not moved on to the internet but simply stopped at becoming enraged after seeing what was in the mass media, they would not have become activists.

Finally, *Zaitokukai*'s base is to be found particularly in grassroots conservatism, which displayed the greatest degree of diversity within the conservative category. This is not just a matter of numbers, but probably results from the fact that this group is made up of 'rural conservatives' and 'urban conservatives', as discussed at the beginning of the previous section. It was also difficult to detect factors that linked the segment of non-political people and the segment of conservatives to the nativist movement via processes of political socialization. In short, there were considerable differences in the degree of agreement with the nativist movement prior to coming into contact with it, but this declines considerably once people become participants. The question of how this decline occurs will be addressed, from the viewpoint of accepting the frames of the movement, in Chapter 4, and from the viewpoint of the information infrastructure that brings them into contact with nativism, in Chapter 5.

4 Resonating with the Nativist Movement

Constructed grievance – the locus of the problem

In the previous chapter, we looked at the case of potential activists who had some ideological affinity with the nativist movement (or mobilization potential), but no particular interest in the 'foreigner problem'. How do these conservative citizens come to be attracted to the nativist movement? This chapter will deal with their cognitive processes from encounter with the movement to participation in it; we will attempt to trace their thought processes from their narratives. We will use the notion of frame in social movement research because it deals with the process by which movements persuade individuals.[1] The descriptive nature of a frame as a concept, which even its proponents acknowledge (Benford 1997), will not be problematic for this chapter. This is because the 'resonance of nativism' – that is, the processes by which potential constituents are attracted to the movement frame – and its causes will be explained in the following section.[2]

Firstly, let us identify the premises of the argument. The appearance of resource mobilization theory in social movement research in the 1970s began to raise doubts about the link between grievance and anxiety and movement participation. The gist of these doubts was that whilst grievance is a necessary condition for movement participation, it is of no more than secondary importance compared to other factors such as mobilizing structure and political opportunity. In contrast to this thinking, new studies in the 1980s once again began to focus on the link between grievance and movement participation. The formularized concepts of frame and the framing process developed by Snow et al. (Benford 1993a, 1993b; Gamson, Fireman and Rytina 1982; Snow et al. 1986; Snow and Benford 1988, 1992) are the most commonly used, but there have also been numerous other similar arguments (Gamson 1992;

Klandermans 1992). As the aim of this chapter is to analyze the cognitive processes of potential constituents, I will only use the concept of frame.

Framing theory has some points in common with classical social movement theory, in that they both focus on grievance as the central object of analysis, but there are three major differences between them. Firstly, classical social movement theory assumed an almost automatic linkage between grievance and movement participation (Snow et al. 1986: 465). In contrast to this, newer theories regard grievance as being something that is constructed through interpretation (Codena-Roa 2002: 202) and focus on processes that define specific realities as something unjust to be solved by collective action.

Secondly, framing theory differs from classical social movement theory in the sense that it sees isolated individuals as being less likely to be recruited to social movements. As with resource mobilization theory, potential constituents have some sort of link with the movement, and it is assumed that they go through a communication process. However, unlike resource mobilization theory's mechanical view of the relationship between existing important relationships and movement participation, framing theory stresses the diversity of interpretive processes that lead to participation (Snow et al. 1986: 467). The fact that activists in racist movements are actually quite heterogeneous (Blee 2002: 4) lends added importance to this point.

Thirdly, unlike the manner in which classical social movement theory treated movement participation as the eruption of irrational feelings, recent theories do not regard it as a negative factor. These theories, which emphasize the role of emotions in social movements, treat emotions as positives rather than negatives (Goodwin 2001; Goodwin, Jasper and Polletta 2001; Jasper 1997). I also think that it is best to avoid seeing people's motives for participating in the nativist movement as strictly negative. This view was the context for my criticism of the conventional perception of nativist movements as irrational responses to social disorganization.

Frame alignment between the movement and individuals

The notion of frame analysis, which originates from Goffman's work, is a 'schemata of interpretation' referring to 'the linkage of individual and SMO [social movement organizations] interpretive orientations' (Snow et al. 1986: 464). Social movements use ideology as a cultural resource for their frame alignment (Snow and Benford 2000: 58) and create their frame from existing ideologies. Moreover, when the ideology of potential constituents and the frame of the movement are well aligned, they resonate with the frame, which motivates constituents to participate in the movement. Undoubtedly the most well-known and representative frame is that of 'special privileges for *Zainichi* Koreans (*zainichi tokken*)'. Names of other organizations also embody the movement's frame: such names as 'restoration of sovereignty', 'deportation of criminal foreigners' and 'expulsion of harmful foreigners' also fall into this category. Of these, the problematization of 'crimes by foreigners' continued from the late 1990s on and was also taken up by all the national newspapers, but organization around this issue remained extremely small scale. In contrast to this, the phrase 'special privileges for *Zainichi* Koreans' was initially ignored by newspapers and television and not even acknowledged in the right-wing world of criticism; the only place where it was used was in a comic that first appeared on internet bulletin boards (see Chapter 6). Nevertheless, many have been attracted to *Zaitokukai*'s use of this frame. How did the frame alignment processes succeed in recruiting large numbers of people?

Snow et al. classify frame alignment into four types: frame bridging, frame amplification, frame extension and frame transformation. However, this division does not have a logical foundation; it remains mere empirical generalization. A minor modification of this typology is needed because of the particularly vague nature of the distinction between frame amplification from frame extension. Frames make use of existing ideologies, but they are neither determined by nor simple copies of ideology (Snow and Benford 2000: 58). As Swidler (1986) says, movements use ideology as a tool kit to establish a frame. Similarly, potential constituents, who are the targets of frame alignment, are attracted to a frame on the basis of their own ideologies.

This chapter analyzes how the ideologies of potential constituents resonate with the movement's frame; there is a certain variation in the frame alignment depending on the degree of consistency between the two. I will classify frame alignment into four types, as shown on Figure 4.1, depending on the affinity between the ideology of potential constituents and the movement's frame. Although there is an easy attraction to the 'special privileges for *Zainichi* Koreans' frame when there is a high level of affinity, the points of contact

Figure 4.1 Relationship between ideology and the frame alignment process

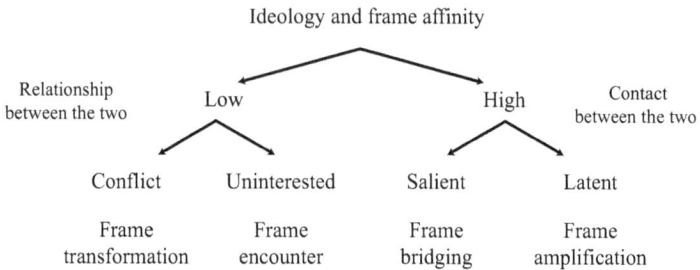

Ideology and frame affinity

Relationship between the two	Low	High	Contact between the two

Conflict	Uninterested	Salient	Latent
Frame transformation	Frame encounter	Frame bridging	Frame amplification

between the two could be salient or latent. The former refers to cases in which potential constituents already had the sort of ideological interest that is connected to 'special privileges for *Zainichi* Koreans' before coming into contact with the movement. We will regard this pattern of frame resonance as frame bridging: 'the linkage of two or more ideologically congruent but structurally unconnected frames regarding a particular issue or problem' (Snow et al. 1986: 467). As long as the two have the opportunity to meet, they become easily linked and drive movement participation.

However, even when potential constituents have an ideological affinity with the 'special privileges for *Zainichi* Koreans' frame this does not necessarily mean that they have a strong interest in the issue. In cases where the nexus of the two remains latent, potential constituents are likely to overlook the movement's frame. In these cases, frame amplification in which there is 'the clarification and invigoration of an interpretive frame that bears on a particular issue, problem or set of events' (Snow et al. 1986: 469) is needed.

Next, we will consider cases where the nativist movement recruits those with a low ideological affinity using the 'special privileges for *Zainichi* Koreans' frame. Where the two are incompatible, a frame transformation is needed in which there is 'changing old understanding and meanings and/or generating new ones' (Benford and Snow 2000: 625). In reality, major transformations only happen rarely, but it is possible to imagine that a transformation might be produced which 'departs from one's past self' in the case of a movement that makes extreme claims.

Finally, the patterns considered thus far have assumed that potential constituents have a clear-cut ideology concerning the frame put forward by movements, whether one of attraction or rejection. It is not the case, however, that everyone has a clear-cut ideology; the non-political stand seen in the previous chapter represents another possibility. In these cases, potential constituents become interested in the frame put forward by movements as a result of some opportunity or other and are then attracted to that frame. We will refer to this process that produces changes in which non-political people become activists – albeit without the same level of change as that which accompanies frame transformation – as frame encounter. Because frame encounters occur by chance, as it were, they are also largely prescribed by frame outreach: how many potential constituents connect with movement frames.

The frame alignment process in the narratives of activists

As stated in the previous chapter, most activists start off with a conservative political stance. This means that whilst a high proportion of activists have an ideological affinity to the 'special privileges for *Zainichi* Koreans' frame, there are also a certain number who do not. Even though people may show an ideological affinity, there remain certain disparities in the manner in which the frame is encountered and also in the manner in which the frame resonates. I would like to clarify the mechanism that leads to resonance with a frame by analyzing examples that correspond to each case.

Frame bridging

Most activists had not even been aware of the phrase 'special privileges for *Zainichi* Koreans' before coming into contact with *Zaitokukai*. There are also, however, some who already had a nativist ideology before contact, and these people had come across the term while actively searching for a nativist discourse. Those who resonated with the movement via frame bridging make up the largest group: fourteen out of thirty (excluding the four who were amongst the organizers of the nativist movement from the outset). This type is characterized by the fact that they came across to and then began participating in the nativist movement, seeing it as the embodiment of their own thinking. When the potential constituents' ideologies and the movement frame are compatible, participation will only ensue should the two happen to come into contact. H, the engineer encountered in the previous chapter, is a representative example of this; he had a negative view of *Zainichi* Koreans planted in him by his family and was active in a historical revisionist club during his student days. Even as a working adult who had moved out of home he continued his activism as outlined below.

> I set up a debating club with the others. It was between friends. There wasn't even the internet then so we just chatted on a really small bulletin board. I think that it was a local bulletin board. That was right at the time of the outbreak of the comfort women campaign issue, and we had a debating match against the people in the social movement who were claiming that the comfort women had existed. More than *zainichi*, it was the comfort women campaign issue that was the start of things for me. (Mr H, *Zaitokukai*, thirties)

H said that following the breakup of this group because of problems such as disputes over male–female relations he started searching, wondering whether there might be another similar group. This was around the time of the occurrence of the incident in which only the child of a Filipino irregular migrant family in Japan was granted special permission to reside, while both parents were forcibly repatriated. He came across *Zaitokukai* while searching the internet because his interest had been aroused by this issue, which took its name from that of the family – the 'Calderon Issue'.

> It was when I watched an uploaded video about the Calderon Issue that I first learnt about *Zaitokukai*. Those people who proclaim special privileges for *Zainichi* Koreans had already been so active in various movements. When I wondered why such movements were still continuing, I came to the conclusion that it was probably because no one had said, 'Stop it!' in a loud voice, that's how I saw it. *Zaitokukai* were the ones who were standing face-to-face with those guys and saying, 'Stop it'! I thought that this was fantastic, and that was why I joined *Zaitokukai*. (Mr H, *Zaitokukai*, thirties)

H says that 'it was *Zaitokukai*' that put his own 'way of thinking' into practice. For him, *Zaitokukai* embodied his own ideology and, consequently, he was immediately drawn to the 'special privileges for *Zainichi* Koreans' frame. M, encountered in the Introduction as the female who read the right-wing journal *Seiron*, also began her activism with *Zaitokukai* via this same incident. She had had a conservative ideology from the outset, but she had not necessarily had negative feelings toward *Zainichi* Koreans previously. Even after becoming a working adult, she had no contact with historical revisionism or nativism. But M felt uneasy when she came across reports of the 'Calderon Issue'.

I was interested in historical problems and also felt that they were problems, but I didn't really know much about the *zainichi* issue. It was because of the Filipino Calderon family that I joined *Zaitokukai*. It made me think 'What's going on? The media is really ridiculous!' [The family's story] was on [television]. There was a sense of 'something sad' [about it]. 'What's sad, you'? [I thought]. I thought that there was something ridiculous about the television coverage – that was before I found that video. I asked the people around me what they thought about it. As you'd expect, quite a few thought there was something a bit ridiculous about it. So I realized that I wasn't just a narrow-minded human being. (Ms M, *Zaitokukai*, thirties)

In M's case also, her own ideology and *Zaitokukai*'s frame were a match, but she did not go as far as actively searching and gathering information, as H had done. What had built the bridge in both cases was a chance viewing of an internet video.

By chance, on YouTube, Mr Sakurai was carrying out propaganda activities about the 'Calderon Issue' in front of the Immigration Bureau. I just happened to see it and thought 'so there are people who think like that' ... Seeing that overwhelming propaganda action, I thought it was amazing. (Ms M, *Zaitokukai*, thirties)

The impetus was the 'Calderon Issue' but M says the following. 'I hate South Koreans and North Koreans ... [because] they are liars. They are always demanding an apology and compensation!' In short, she was attracted to the 'special privileges for *Zainichi* Koreans' frame from a historical revisionism standpoint. A characteristic of revisionists for whom the 'special privileges for *Zainichi* Koreans' frame resonates is their lack of clarity regarding who is intended by the terms 'South Korean and North Korean'. 'An apology and compensation' have become major problems between Japan and

South Korea, but they have no connection with either North Korea or 'special privileges for *Zainichi* Koreans'. In M's eyes, however, South Korea, North Korea, *Zainichi* Koreans and 'Korean people' are all enemies thus bridging historical revisionism and the 'special privileges for *Zainichi* Koreans' frame (see Chapter 8).

H and M differ with regard to the fact that only one of them found *Zaitokukai* by doing some searching of their own. However, both of them approached the 'Calderon Issue' with an existing anti-foreigner attitude and ended up participating in *Zaitokukai* because it matched their ideologies. Cognitive change leading to adjustments between ideology and frame and then attraction to the frame were not essential to movement participation in these examples. Blee (2007: 27) says that many members of white supremacist groups become ardent racists as a result of having joined these movements. In the case of those for whom frame bridging led to resonance with the nativist movement, however, they were already nativists prior to their contact with the movement; they did not become nativists as a result of movement participation. What was important for them was learning of the existence of a movement that embodied their own ideologies, *Zaitokukai*. In such cases, the major cause prompting movement participation was none other than the internet, which served to connect them with the movement.

Frame amplification

Frame amplification was the process by which thirteen out of the thirty activists in this category found that their ideas resonated with the nativist movement, roughly the same number as with frame bridging. Whilst possessing a conservative ideology, most of them are not necessarily interested in '*zainichi*' or the 'foreigner problem'. Most of these activists discover the 'problem' of 'special privileges for *Zainichi* Koreans' as a result of chance encounters with *Zaitokukai* videos. This phenomenon is not just limited to Japan; most female activists in the Ku Klux Klan, for example, had their initial contact with the organization via a chance meeting (Blee 2003).

One of the activists who joined *Zaitokukai* through frame amplification, O, identified himself as a conservative although he had come into contact with Marxism as a student: 'I understand left thinking too, but it just doesn't come naturally to me'. He had not been particularly interested in the 'foreigner problem' but, coming across a *Zaitokukai* video on YouTube by chance, he was surprised to see 'special privileges for *Zainichi* Koreans' being criticized openly.

> I was just having a look around on YouTube and thought 'What's this? What is it saying?' So, there's a group carrying out this kind of movement, is there? … When I was growing up, people would get beaten up [by Koreans] just for making remarks about Koreans so it was a period when we had to refrain from talking about Koreans. It was taboo. Then, this was openly saying 'Koreans get out!' It was wondering 'What is this movement?' that became the impetus. Speaking out defiantly, attacking – it's alright to say '*chōsenjin* (Koreans)' isn't it? It must be. You can say French for French people so there's nothing wrong with calling Koreans Koreans. (Mr O, *Zaitokukai*, fifties)

O, himself, had always had a negative sense of *Zainichi* Koreans but, as his use of the term taboo shows, this had never been the focus of his thoughts. However, as a result of the 'special privileges for *Zainichi* Koreans' frame being defined for him by the language of ostracism that was being shouted out on the video, he had a pleasant feeling of the taboo lifting. It was as though he was feeling excited about the use in public of the term *chōsenjin*, which is laden with discriminatory nuances towards Koreans. O's repeated searches of the internet led him to the knowledge of the following sorts of 'facts'.

> When I looked into it, I found that they have lots of special privileges that Japanese people don't have. That's weird. They can use lots of different names; have as much as they like in their bank accounts; they can even use an alias on their licenses and they can have multiple names; and they are not honest when it comes to paying their taxes. They get staggering amounts of welfare. Five or six times what the rest of the Japanese population get – much, much more. One in four is on welfare. They are sponging off welfare. All this sort of suff kept coming up, one after another. (Mr O, *Zaitokukai*, fifties)

L, who says 'I was sceptical about the so-called masochistic view of history', also experienced the amplification of one part of his own ideology via the 'special privileges for *Zainichi* Koreans' frame.

> By chance I caught a video by [*Zaitokukai*] President Sakurai on
> YouTube and thought he was interesting. The President and about
> thirty other people were making a protest video in the midst of several
> thousand Koreans who were holding a demonstration demanding
> municipal voting rights. Mr Sakurai was yelling, 'Rubbish in the
> rubbish bin and Koreans on the Korean Peninsula!' I thought, he's
> someone who speaks in quite an interesting way in public. (Mr L,
> *Zaitokukai*, forties)

L set up a blog because he resented the fact that 'when Keizō Obuchi
was Prime Minister, he said that he would send rice, as aid, to North
Korea' and, in his blog, L commented on 'what should be done' from
a patriotic viewpoint when there is news of an incident. He did not,
however, participate in any specific movement nor was he aware of
'special privileges for *Zainichi* Koreans'. It was when he came into
contact with the *Zaitokukai* video that he discovered a specific enemy
towards which to direct his 'patriotic' consciousness. L had always
felt a sense of prejudice regarding minorities in general, and this is
likely to be linked to his lack of resistance to the idea of 'special
privileges for *Zainichi* Koreans'.

D says, with regard to South and North Koreans, 'I neither hate
nor like them, and nor am I interested in them'. D, who identifies
himself as a 'monarchist' and who had been able to satisfy his own
conservative orientation by reading historical novels, has been
influenced in this by the ultra-right's homepage.

> I think that maybe I am closest to being a 'monarchist'. Thinking
> about it now. To put it simply, I think that it is natural to obey what
> the emperor says because it is what he says ... On Channel Sakura's
> forerunner site they were always presenting conservative things on the
> internet. That had a tremendous influence. (Mr D, *Zaitokukai*, forties)

D had been handing out anti-Human Rights Law leaflets on the
street before having any contact with *Zaitokukai*, but this had
been purely a personal and intermittent activity. He was, however,
continually browsing ultra-right sites such as Channel Sakura. In
this sense, he was not ideologically far apart from the nativist
movement, but it was 'conservatism' that he was fixated on and
he had no interest in the 'foreigner problem'. It was when he
encountered a frame that was focussed on 'special privileges for

Zainichi Koreans' that he was drawn to the clarity of a frame 'with an extremely well-defined focus'.

> The first thing that made me want to join *Zaitokukai* was its great name. 'Against Special Privileges for *Zainichi*' – isn't that an extremely well-defined focus? I did think 'special privileges for *Zainichi* Koreans' – what's that? But, coincidentally, there was that fraud in Mie, fraud by a civil servant was uncovered. It also exposed the fact that Koreans had been paying only half of the municipal tax for fifty years, permanently paying only half. 'Oh, so it seems that special privileges for *Zainichi* Koreans do exist', I thought. That is why I joined *Zaitokukai*. (Mr D, *Zaitokukai*, thirties)

D got involved in *Zaitokukai* when he came across this news which was 'proof' of 'special privileges for *Zainichi* Koreans'. He found out about *Zaitokukai* via Channel Sakura, but it was when he actually felt 'Oh, there really are 'special privileges for *Zainichi* Koreans', that's no good,' that for the first time he was impelled to join. In short, the empirical credibility of the frame (Snow and Benford 1988: 209)[3] caused D to believe in 'special privileges for *Zainichi* Koreans'. D had also known of other ultra-right organizations, but had not joined any as he 'had felt that they were only ever right-wing groups, with no sense of citizens' groups or conservative citizens' groups about them'. For D, who says that while other groups 'were all full of serious people who were giving their lives to a cause', *Zaitokukai* – whose appeal was enhanced by the appearance of 'Citizen's Association' in its name – was easy to join. In short, in addition to 'special privileges for *Zainichi* Koreans', the name 'Citizen's Association' can also be thought of as having functioned as a secondary frame bringing down the barriers to entry.

Finally, I would like to confirm that the 'special privileges for *Zainichi* Koreans' frame was not created by the existing right-wing organizations; rather, one part of the right wing was drawn to it. η was involved with a movement agitating for the expulsion of foreign workers more than ten years before *Zaitokukai* was launched, and he joined the movement through frame bridging. He encountered the nativist movement when watching a television program about it.

> When I was on a night shift, I went into the break room – during my night break – and there was a program on television. At that time,

there was a news show called *Space J* on TBS, and there was a feature which talked about how there were ultra-right groups in Japan too that practiced discrimination and racism, like the Alliance of National Socialists. This was a time when I had been thinking aren't there any adults at all in Japan who express the problems with foreigners and assert their anger about this, and I realized that there were also people who think in this way in Japan. It made me feel really animated. (Mr η, non-*Zaitokukai*, thirties)

The childhood experience of seeing an increase in migrant workers in his neighborhood had led η to become interested in the exclusion of foreigners. This interest did not fade even when he became a working adult, and he searched amongst the local right-wing groups for somewhere to become active, but he says, 'many of the groups that I found were virtually inactive. Or, even if they were active, didn't touch on the foreigner problem'. In the midst of all this, he encountered the Alliance of National Socialists on television and, thinking 'I have to take part in this too', he quit his job and became an activist affiliated with this group that had its origins in the new right. What η experienced at this stage was precisely frame bridging, but at this point in time he was not even aware of the '*zainichi* problem' and, as he says below, he was drawn to the 'special privileges for *Zainichi* Koreans' frame later.

[My interest in 'special privileges for *Zainichi* Koreans'] began after I started writing a blog, around 2007. In the comments column, there were people who kept writing about *Zainichi* Koreans over again. At first, I thought, 'What is it with these people who keep writing about *Zainichi* Koreans'? But as I was thinking this, I became interested in *Zainichi* Koreans too. I talked about the problem of people staying here illegally, but received comments advising me to focus on *Zainichi* Koreans because the *zainichi* problem was the background issue. It was the people making these comments who had greater awareness, more discernment and knowledge. If anything, they were capable of teaching me. That's how it is, I thought. (Mr η, non-*Zaitokukai*, thirties)

Whilst η's ideology and the 'special privileges for *Zainichi* Koreans' frame were quite compatible, as his comments above make clear, he simply was not aware of '*zainichi*'. Receiving comments emphasising the importance of 'special privileges for *Zainichi* Koreans' from the readers of his blog amplified η's 'expulsion of foreigners' frame to extend to 'special privileges for *Zainichi* Koreans'. The influence of internet right wingers on nativism activists affiliated with old right-wing organizations is extensive when it comes to 'special privileges for *Zainichi* Koreans'; it is not limited to η's case. [4]

Frame encounter

It is not only 'special privileges for *Zainichi* Koreans' but also the 'foreigner problem' that has failed to attract wide attention. As a consequence, even when presented with the 'special privileges for *Zainichi* Koreans' frame most people ignore it as suspect information, shut down any discussion with an 'I don't know', or simply feign disinterest. However, some activists made a complete turnaround from this state of disinterest; they became attracted to the 'special privileges for *Zainichi* Koreans' frame and actually started participating. This was recruitment through frame encounter, and three out of thirty of the activists interviewed fall into this category. I, one of these three, had lacked any knowledge of foreigners living in Japan because he lived in an area with a low proportion of foreigners. The opportunity for his first encounter with the 'special privileges for *Zainichi* Koreans' frame came as a result of seeing a video, by chance, that had been uploaded onto the internet.

There was a first-rate video, in amongst the Japanese videos, it was called something like 'A body that will smash *Sōka Gakkai*', and I thought 'what's this'? I thought 'you'd probably get killed if you picked a fight with that lot' ... [I became interested] after the video speech that I listened to caught my interest. All along, I had also been someone who thought that the abductions by North Korea had nothing to do with me. Like the vast majority of people! (Mr I, *Zaitokukai*, thirties)

I's encounter came via a video 'criticizing *Sōka Gakkai*'. Criticism of *Sōka Gakkai*, Japan's largest new religion, had been a topic for a time in the nativist movement, and I had stumbled on a case of street oratory on this theme. Even though he came across a video about 'special privileges for *Zainichi* Koreans' at this time, he was not drawn to watching it. However, he did feel negatively towards *Sōka Gakkai* because of his experience of having had faith forced on him as a child.

My uncle's wife was a staunch member of *Sōka Gakkai*; it seemed like she had massive statues of Buddha all the way up to the ceiling of her house. When I spent time at that aunt's house, she would take me to the '*Tōei* Summer Movie Festival', and before going to the festival we would go to a large room that was like a packed gymnasium, where an enormous number of adults in suits were chanting different sutras from the ones we used at home, and I was forced to chant sutras that I didn't know along with them. This was because if I endured this agonizing ritual, I would then get to see *Pro-golfer Monkey Versus Meka Golfer* [a movie]. (Mr I, *Zaitokukai*, thirties)

The nativist movement sees both the *Kōmeitō* (Clean Government Party, founded by members of *Sōka Gakkai*) and *Sōka Gakkai*, which are positive about voting rights for foreign residents, as enemies, and has repeatedly criticized the latter. I accidentally saw and heard part of this in a video, and he was won over as he thought, 'It's really alright to say these sorts of amazing things?' And so it was that I 'watched movies for half a day on my days off work, once or twice a month' and as he came into contact with various bits of information the frame began to resonate with him.

G lived in Saitama Prefecture, which was the area where the 'Calderon Issue' occurred, and he had known about this before coming across *Zaitokukai*. His encounter with a *Zaitokukai* video had been a chance occurrence but he says that the fact that the video had dealt with an event that he knew about and that it had asserted an opinion diametrically opposed to that of the mass media 'raised this as a problem'.

> *Zaitokukai* first caught my attention when I was watching a video by our president [Sakurai]. Seeing him speaking out on the streets about the Calderon Issue, I thought, 'There are people doing these sorts of things'. It was the most popular video on the website called *Niko-niko Dōga*. Up until then, I had heard the name [Calderon] on the news and that there had been an incident, and then there was the President's way of thinking. I didn't just think that it was interesting; it had an intense impact on me. I felt like it had been problematized inside me. I started to search Google for terms like *zainichi* and permanent resident, and I found that these problems did exist. (Mr G, *Zaitokukai*, thirties)

What these two activists have in common is the extent of the impact on them of coming across a video. Because they started from a position of lack of interest, their encounters with the 'special privileges for *Zainichi* Koreans' frame were chance occurrences not the result of active searching by them. However, even after a chance encounter a nativist movement video will amount to no more than just another fragment of surfing the internet if the video does not attract one's interest. Snow and Benford (1988: 198) point out 'centrality' as the main factor prescribing the degree of resonance of a frame; they say that whether or not one sees the frame as important exerts an influence. In the cases of I and G, the fact that they had had real contact with '*Sōka Gakkai*' and 'local issues' respectively forms part of the background to their interest in the videos. In this sense, the question of whether or not one shows an interest in the matters raised by a frame is influenced by its consistency with real experiences.

Resonances with the 'special privileges' frame

Let us now address the main causes of the resonance of the 'special privileges for *Zainichi* Koreans' frame, with reference to the arguments thus far.[5] Among our informants, no one joined the nativist movement through frame transformation, and a mere three experienced frame encounter. Others were divided into people who actively sought contact with the nativist movement themselves and those who encountered the nativist movement by chance and, having low ideological resistance, accepted it. In this sense, the process of political socialization had already equipped most activists with the ideology that would make the 'special privileges for *Zainichi* Koreans' frame attractive to them. To put it another way, alternation away from the left wing had occurred before contact with the nativist movement: they came into contact with the movement after they had already undergone ideological change.

According to Blee, activists tend to mention ideological changes as having been specific and important in becoming racists. However, in reality, they only ever talk about abstract and trivial things when discussing their attraction to and participation in racist groups (Blee 1996: 692). This only applies partially to the Japanese nativist movement. On the one hand, activists already possessed the sort of ideology that drew them to the movement before they had joined it. In this sense, there were hardly any people who were conscious of having changed very much as a result of movement participation.

On the other hand, this ideological foundation was not necessarily directly linked to the resonance of the frame. The activists who had been immediately attracted to the 'special privileges for *Zainichi* Koreans' frame were limited to those who already had feelings of hostility towards *Zainichi* Koreans before joining *Zaitokukai* – one segment of those who come under frame bridging. In the case of the rest, the discovery of 'special privileges for *Zainichi* Koreans' was a new event, and a factor that would mediate between ideology and frame was needed.

The first factor is competition for 'empirical credibility' produced by the occurrence of an 'incident' that is of interest to an individual. This process was discernible in the case of the activist who felt a sense of unease about information in the media concerning the 'Calderon Issue', which then led to sympathy with a *Zaitokukai* video which they came across by chance. In addition, there is also the following case in which F felt animosity towards the Korean team in the 2002 FIFA World Cup.

> I wondered if they'd bribed the referee. You can generally tell. There were some extremely intolerable parts to the Koreans' rough play. It doesn't happen with other countries. It's because they play rough, usually. Referees made repeated suspicious calls even when [the South Korean team] 'had just committed a foul'. (Mr F, *Zaitokukai*, thirties)

These are examples of frame contradictions (Nepstad 1997) that arise notably between the mass media and nativism on the internet – contradictions in both sides' interpretations of a specific dispute. Potential constituents are only more readily attracted to nativism on the internet when they are not persuaded by the mass media frame. When, as far as they are concerned, the nativist frame on the internet has greater 'empirical credibility' they turn to the internet to find out 'what really happened'. This produces a sense of efficacy, in the sense that if one can be informed about the truth on the internet, then reality changes and this can promote movement participation (Nepstad 1997: 482–3). Since the 'special privileges for *Zainichi* Koreans' frame has no empirical basis, potential constituents will not see it as having 'empirical credibility' and will not be attracted to it if they sift through the frame from the starting point of their own experiences. However, the sorts of 'incidents' mentioned above, which have points of contact with the 'special privileges for *Zainichi* Koreans' frame, can produce 'empirical credibility' amongst potential constituents. In these cases, there is no shaking off of the frame as a fabrication and it, therefore, resonates effortlessly with the 'special privileges for *Zainichi* Koreans' frame.

Secondly, there were few cases in which 'special privileges for *Zainichi* Koreans' actually held immediate 'empirical credibility'. A far larger number of activists were influenced by the existence of the master frames (Snow and Benford 1992) of a 'masochistic view of history' and 'anti-Japanese' which govern right-wing social movements as a whole.[6] It is hard to find politicians who make statements about 'special privileges for *Zainichi* Koreans', but many go on in detail about historical revisionism and hostility to Japan's neighboring countries. The 'special privileges for *Zainichi* Koreans' frame can be thought of as one of the sub-frames under these sorts of 'masochistic view of history' and 'anti-Japanese' frames. In other words, 'special privileges for *Zainichi* Koreans', a frame with low 'empirical credibility', is reinforced by the 'masochistic view of history' and 'anti-Japanese' frames that treat their enemies –neighboring countries, *Zainichi* Koreans and the Japanese left wing – as one and the same body (see Chapter 8). As we saw in the previous chapter, historical revisionism and hostility towards neighboring countries exerted an important influence at the time when over half of the activists formed their ideologies. After the 'masochistic view of history' and 'anti-Japanese' frames had first resonated with them they were then also drawn to the 'special privileges for *Zainichi* Koreans' frame, which they saw as being very closely related to these other frames. And thus the fiction of '*zainichi* privilege' is accepted under the umbrella of comprehensive historical revisionism. We are now able to give an answer for the reason why 'special privileges for *Zainichi* Koreans' and not the 'foreigner problem' came to be constructed: no matter just how much the former lacks any basis in reality, it is able to draw in potential constituents by borrowing historical revisionism's power to attract.

Thirdly, there is the issue of 'centrality' (Snow and Benford 1988): the extent to which the issues put up by a movement attract the interest of potential constituents. People who experienced frame encounter came across nativist movement videos by chance, but they developed a strong interest in them because they were already the sort of people who had a sensationalist approach to events in which they were interested. The sudden rise in *Zaitokukai* members as a result of the 'fishing boat collision in the Senkaku Islands' is a case in point.

Chance encounters with the nativist movement

What becomes clear from the above is that we are dealing with a group of people who were already treading a path towards becoming nativists before their encounter with the movement. While these were chance encounters, the movement's frame was able to resonate rather easily with them. Viewers of videos become potential constituents at the point when they feel no sense of scorn and repugnance even after seeing street propaganda and demonstrations in which hatred is openly expressed. From the analysis in the previous and this chapter we can say that the major basis for becoming potential constituents is ideological proximity. Ideological distance is even more important than a lack of interest in the 'foreigner problem'. However, micromobilization is not as simple as ideological proximity being enough for potential constituents to become activists; some mechanism is needed to make them take the steps towards activism.

Firstly, we need a two-step model to explain the articulation between ideology and frame. Activists first form an ideology that has affinity with the nativist movement through a process of political socialization, which makes potential constituents of them. Encounter with the nativist movement frame, as the second step, results in resonance with the frame; they gain a motive for participation. At this point, if there is no discrepancy between ideology and frame – as in frame bridging – resonance is likely to occur easily. When this is not the case, attraction to the 'special privileges for *Zainichi* Koreans' frame occurs on the basis of support from three factors, which compensate for the frame's own fictitiousness: empirical credibility; dependence on the master frame; and centrality. This two-stage process to people becoming activists means that we cannot analyze the appeal of the nativist movement by just looking at the 'special privileges for *Zainichi* Koreans' frame. We need to interpret the various processes which lead to nativism, and these are more complicated than popular discourse on nativism would suggest.

Finally, it must be emphasized that it was communication via the medium of the internet that set the stage for these sorts of changes in cognition to emerge. Consequently, without an analysis of the particular role played by the internet, we cannot give an overview of the micromobilization process. The following chapter, which will be the last step in the analysis of the micromobilization process, will elucidate the stage-setting role played by the internet in the nativist movement.

5 The Internet and Resource Mobilization

The internet and the nativist movement

We have already glimpsed the extremely important role played by the internet in the political socialization and framing processes for activists. However, the internet is no more than a means for mediating ideology and action. I would like to set out the reasons why, despite this, we are discussing the role of the internet.

Firstly, alarm about new controls on and monitoring of the internet notwithstanding, it has been argued that internet-induced social change has benefitted the left wing most of all (e.g. Castells 2001): the anti-globalization movement being a representative example (Bennett 2005; della Porta et al. 2006). However, since the internet is used for an endless number of purposes, it is also a means for social movements on the 'right' to spread their message.[1] In fact, previous studies have pointed out the important role played by the internet in ultra-right movements. In the United States, for example, an internet forum called Stormfront specializes in racism and white supremacy (Bowman-Grieve 2009; Caren, Jowers and Gaby 2012; Weatherby and Scoggins 2005). Its web pages do not just post relevant opinions: its activities encompass a 'whites only dating' site; education and health; and hobbies (Back 2002; Bowman-Grieve 2009). There are also many home pages aside from those attacking others, including aesthetic contributions such as racists narcissistically posting their own photographs.

These elements of the ultra-right movements in the United States and Europe can also be found in magazines. The particular contributions of the spread of the internet have been to make activism much more visible and also to make it easier to understand movement and activist networks by looking at links on the web. This has led to a large volume of literature on the internet and ultra-right movements (Adams and Roscigno 2005; Back 2002; Burris, Smith and Strahm 2000; Caiani and Parenti 2009, 2013; Caiani, della Porta and Wagemann 2012; Daniels 2009; James 2001; Ray and Marsh 2001; Reid and Chen 2007; Tateo 2005; Waeber and Rodeheaver 2003, 2004). The fact that the spread of the internet and the rise of the internet nativist movement are closely related is another reason for the need to discuss the influence of the internet in Japan.

Secondly, the internet's trait of reducing communication costs has exerted a bigger influence on those who have few resources than on those with plentiful resources.[2] If we compare political parties that have large national organizations with social movement organizations that are in the course of being formed, it is easy to guess which one has benefitted more considerably from the internet (van de Donk et al. 2004: 5). For established organizations, the internet has 'enhanced' various activities, but not 'enabled' many.[3] It would, by contrast, be no exaggeration to say that Japan's nativist movement, which started from a base that was close to zero, first materialized as a result of the internet.

What has been enabled by the internet? The first thing that should be made clear with regard to the nativist movement is that it is characterized by a digitally-enabled mobilizing structure, which has recruited considerable numbers of people. However, the previous studies mentioned above tell us little about this point. These studies are limited to analyses of the contents of the web and bulletin boards or network analysis of web pages; they only use information that can be obtained from the internet.[4] The influence of the internet on mobilizing ultra-right activists still awaits clarification.

As we saw in Chapter 3, in an era when the internet did not exist, most people's participation in ultra-right movements occurred via personal networks such as the family. In Japan also, it seems that locally-based ultra-right movements continue to rely, even now, on existing organizational bases and personal networks. In Suzuki's (2013) study of the ultra-right movement in Ehime, almost all of her informants had belonged to existing conservative organizations. Yamaguchi, Saito and Ogiue (2012) also report on ultra-right activists with local roots.

However, recent studies have shown that most BNP activists became members by first contacting the party's home page. In this sense, the home page shoulders a central role in the process of recruiting activists (Goodwin 2011: 134–5). This is especially the case with *Zaitokukai,* in which an overwhelming majority of members had no previous experience of having belonged to an organization. It was the internet that became the de facto organizational basis of the movement; without it, the nativist movement would not have emerged. In this sense, the connection between the internet and the nativist movement is the key point in the clarification of our research question. This chapter will do what prior research has not done: it will analyze the use of the internet by individual activists, focusing on the role played by the technical base in the process of becoming a nativist. This amounts to an attempt to revise our perceptions of cognitive change, discussed in Chapters 3 and 4, from the perspective of technical infrastructure.

The internet and changes in the mobilizing structure

Micromobilization contexts and movement participation

As stated in Chapter 2, although isolated and socially deprived individuals may have grievances it is difficult for them to participate in movements (McCarthy and Zald 1987: 18, 28, 58). By contrast, people with existing links to organizations and to other people tend to become attracted to and to join movements more easily. Micromobilization processes are driven by this sort of 'small group setting in which processes of collective attribution are combined with rudimentary forms of organization to produce mobilization for collective action' (McAdam 1988a: 134–5). However, while six out of nine people in organizations other than *Zaitokukai* participated in the nativist movement through personal connections, in the case of *Zaitokukai* the number was confined to three out of twenty-five.

There are several reasons why small groups have been held to be important to date. Firstly, communication costs are reduced by disseminating information via small groups. Let us look at the example of γ, whom we met in Chapter 3 and who has been engaged in right-wing activism since the 1990s because of his admiration for a famous right winger, Shusuke Nomura. The decision to host the G8 Hokkaido Toyako Summit in 2008 was the impetus that led him to join the nativist movement, and at first he stood on the street alone making anti-Chinese speeches. He decided to join a new internet-based movement because the right-wing group that he had been in was quite slow paced.

After Toyako [Hokkaido] became the venue of the G8 Summit, I took to the streets ... I didn't say don't hold the summit, but if it's going ahead at all costs, then summon Hu Jintao as well. Let's question him about what on earth is happening on the issue of Tibet ... At that time, the Free Tibet Movement got going and they started recruiting on Channel 2 or some place on the internet, and I heard that the Free Tibet Movement had also started in Hokkaido. I thought it would be an opportunity to organize demonstrations and launch a conservative movement in Hokkaido, so I voluntarily joined the Free Tibet movement. (Mr γ, non-*Zaitokukai*, forties)

When γ slipped out of an existing right-wing group and joined the nativist movement, he acted on the basis of hearing about a new movement from existing acquaintances. He then got to know the President of *Zaitokukai* and began to help out with activities. It was also 'after encountering *Zaitokukai*' that he became interested in the 'foreigner problem'. γ was recruited to the nativist movement through his existing right-wing network.[5] As an activist with a wealth of experience, he subsequently took on the role of intermediary between the two groups; he managed young activists, hosting barbecues at his home and carrying out other activities.

Secondly, acquaintances from small groups create the social incentive that is essential for movement participation. X, who was introduced in Chapter 3 as an example of alternation from her full-time work for a labor union, became a volunteer on a matter relating to Taiwan as a result of her activities in a qigong group.[6] X went to Nagano with other members of this group to see the Beijing Olympic torch relay and she felt surprised thinking, 'It really should have been in Japan, the air is different'. Seeing large numbers of Chinese people there, she felt as if there had been a Chinese occupation. It was after this that she went on to become involved in nativism.

At the very beginning of my activism, I had found Free Tibet objectionable. This is why [my activism] started at the [Beijing] Olympic torch relay in Nagano where people were opposing China and saying things like stop the massacres and oppression in Tibet. [At that time] I was a volunteer. I was doing qigong, and there was a sort of group of us volunteering together ... As an extension of the activity, I thought that I'd just go and see what it was like. (Ms X, *Zaitokukai*, forties)

In X's case, she went to Nagano because her group was going. Small groups promote movement participation with personal relationships acting as the social incentive. From the point of view of movement organizers, organizations serve as the basis of bloc recruitment collecting together participants and bringing them along (see Oberschall 1972). However, when there is an environment of opposition to a particular movement, small groups can instead hinder movement participation. N was the only person interviewed who was recruited to *Zaitokukai* via a face-to-face relationship (by his girlfriend) but, at the outset, he was against activism because he was worried about her safety.

> She [his girlfriend] has been a work colleague for a long time ... I didn't know when we became friends that [my girlfriend] had been into this sort of activism. [At first she] asked me to drive her to propaganda venues on the street ... I was against it at first. When I thought about the risks, taking part in those sorts of activities with a woman's body, there were lots of risks. I had doubts about these activities being full of risk ... Slowly, slowly [I got involved], because I got interested too. I thought, so there are people like this around. (Mr N, *Zaitokukai*, thirties)

Opposition from 'significant others', as in the example above, often brings about the abandonment and reconsideration of activism (Klandermans and Oegema 1987; McAdam 1988b; Snow, Zurcher and Ekland-Olson 1980). Given the particularly widespread opposition to the nativist movement, it is difficult for social incentive to be effective in promoting participation in its case. One of the reasons why N, who was initially opposed, was drawn in by his girlfriend is the fact that she was the one who took the initiative in their relationship. Furthermore, his opposition had been based on concerns about the risks that accompany activism, and not on a hatred of nativism itself.[7] This sort of case belongs, however, to the rare category. One activist, B, broke off his relationship and threw himself into the movement; 'I ultimately broke up with my girlfriend, because she hated these kinds of activities'. In B's case, even his most significant other did not act as a break on his activism.

When, as in γ's case, a person joins the nativist movement from an existing right-wing network, small groups are the primary factor promoting movement participation. Most of the activists aside from those in *Zaitokukai* ended up joining the nativist movement as a result of these sorts of connections. However, the majority of groups in society feel negatively towards the nativist movement, and group affiliation may ultimately turn out to be an obstacle to participation in its case. In this sense, the finding that existing groups and networks are important is somewhat obsolete in the case of *Zaitokukai*. The rapid expansion of *Zaitokukai*, compared to all other nativist movement organizations, can be seen as a consequence of its extremely high degree of reliance on the internet. The overwhelming presence of single people in the ranks of *Zaitokukai* activists could be caused by the absence of the restraining effect of family opposition on them. 'Footloose' individuals who look at the internet and rush to the movement on the strength of their own volition are the biggest target of recruitment.[8]

The internet and the changing micromobilization process

Another implication of the previous section is that the internet has become the new micromobilization base, eclipsing small groups which had formerly acted as this base. In its widespread progress in encouraging people to join the movement, without using existing organizations as intermediaries, the internet has the potential to significantly change the concept of mobilization itself.[9] That is to say, the transition from 'the logic of collective action', with which social movement theory is well acquainted, to the 'logic of connective action', which is organized by digital media (Bennett and Segerberg 2012: 752), is now dominant in the nativist movement. Under the logic of collective action, rational individuals have a free ride on the contributions of others (Olson 1965). It is argued that small groups are necessary to minimize free riders who in large groups think 'even if I don't do anything, someone else will' (Oberschall 1972; McAdam and Fernandez 1990). Under the logic of connective action, the need for small groups to prevent free riding largely disappears because digital media reduces mobilization costs. This is seen, for example, in A's experience in the following gathering of strangers.

> Three of us, who had only just met for the first time, were at a site [for activism], and we had just said that we'd go and get some lunch when a policeman suddenly came along and questioned us. He asked us, 'When did you three start your activism together?' [The answer

was] 'fifteen minutes ago' ... 'We gathered here because there was an
appeal on the bulletin board. I didn't post the appeal and neither did
the others; someone else did, and that person isn't here. The people
who have turned up are us three, and because we have only seen each
other for the first time today, we have no idea about where we live or
each others' names. So, if asked when we started engaging in activism
together, we can only answer that it was fifteen minutes ago'. (Mr A,
Zaitokukai, forties)

This type of mobilizing structure differs greatly from citizen
movements that rely heavily on print media and interpersonal
networks.[10] Not only has *Zaitokukai* never published a paper medium
newsletter, but web videos have been its most important medium
for recruitment. With its history of having emerged from internet
activism, the nativist movement has largely mobilized through the
medium of the internet. We could also see its poorer mobilizing
structure as a latecomer movement having left it with no choice but
to rely on the internet. What has changed as a result of the use of
the internet? Some of the answers that have been given by previous
studies are: a reduction in mobilizing costs (Caiani and Parenti
2013: 154; Earl and Kimport 2011; Van Laer 2010; Salter 2003);
transnational diffusion (Bennett 2005; della Porta et al. 2006); the
simultaneity and bi-directionality of the transfer of information
(Eltantawy and Wiest 2011); the advent of online forms of protest
(Garrett 2006; Van Laer and Van Aelst 2010); and the availability of
information from alternative sources (Carty and Onyett 2006).[11] Of
these, a reduction in costs and information from alternative sources
are the two that are the most relevant to the nativist movement. I
will, therefore, focus on these two factors in my discussion of the
relationship between the internet and the nativist movement.

It is essential to distinguish aspects that have been enhanced
from those that have been enabled by the use of the internet (Earl
and Kimport 2011). When printed materials are replaced by email
magazines, publication costs are comprehensively reduced and
increases in the numbers of addressees do not become a burden. It
would, however, be difficult to call this an 'enabled' factor merely
as a result of the transposition of a paper to an electronic medium.
By way of contrast, during a time of information control in Egypt,
it would have been difficult, for example, for the heavy use of
SNS – which made it possible to evade repression and to mobilize

Figure 5.1: Contact with the movement: the role of the internet in framing

Framing process

		Enhanced by internet	Enabled by internet
Mobilization process	*Enabled by internet*	(3) Discoverers 9	(4) Brainwashed 2
	Enhanced by internet	(1) Searchers 10	(2) Net surfers 4

Source: Compilation inspired by ideas from Earl and Kimport 2011; Van Laer and Van Aelst 2010. In addition to activists included in the table, there were 7 who had been active since before the spread of the internet and 2 who had been invited to join by other people.

extensively – to have occurred without the internet (Eltantawy and Wiest 2011).

The matrix in Figure 5.1 sets out the framework of this chapter. The reduction of mobilizing costs influences micromobilization processes, while alternative information sources affect framing processes, which are enhanced or enabled by the internet. Firstly, as the marginal costs of transmitting information fall, a reduction in mobilization costs has the effect of expanding mobilization potential (Earl and Kimport 2011: 104). However, Carty and Onyett (2006) argue that the diffusion of information through digital media merely enhances recruitment processes since most of the people browsing the web are activists who would have been mobilized even without the internet.

Information from alternative sources has the potential to change framing processes in the sense that it exposes hidden issues and thereby heightens the motivation to participate. As we have seen thus far, most activists have been won over to the nativist movement as a result of coming into contact with information on the internet. This is why digitally-enabled framing processes also need to be taken into account.

It should be noted that the shift from the enhanced to the enabled is a gradual rather than a two-stage process. Whilst the classification of individuals is thus also necessarily a makeshift matter, the twenty-five people who participated in the nativist movement via the intermediary of the internet can be divided into the types seen in Figure 5.1. The next section will take a detailed look at the role played by the internet on each of the following types of micromobilization processes: searchers, net surfers, discoverers and the brainwashed.

Micromobilization processes for the nativist movement

Searchers: internet enhancement

The internet plays an important role in both how activists make contact with the movement and how they are attracted to the movement's frame, but its role in these processes is not indispensible. The first type – and largest single group – was made up of ten activists who were searchers; that is, people who came across the nativist movement when they looked for nativist information on the web. This may seem an obvious course of action that would readily come to mind these days, but before the spread of the internet even finding the nativist movement was not easy. Daisuke Arikado, who became an activist in the 1990s, learned of the existence of a neo-Nazi group in Tokyo from a television program while he was living in Osaka. It turned out to be a good match with his anti-foreigner orientation, but it took considerable effort for him to find that group.

> He quit work a few days after seeing the program and set off for Tokyo pretty much with just what he had on his back. Without knowing either the address or the telephone number of the Alliance of National Socialists, he walked around and tenaciously kept searching for where the Alliance's office might be. 'I walked around for hours, and finally I found an Alliance flyer on a telegraph pole near the West Exit of Shinjuku Station. I practically flew to their office, and have been with them ever since. (Yasuda, 2012a: 164)

The location of public organizations may have been readily available before the spread of the internet, but finding the nativist movement would not have been easy. Given that most people do not possess Arikado's passion, perhaps the fact that people can now find information easily just by searching has enhanced movement participation. P, encountered in Chapter 3, fits this type; one year after joining the virtual community *Mixi*, she joined its conservative community. Responding to calls on that site, she participated in handing out leaflets opposing voting rights for foreign residents. Since this was limited to a one-off action, she searched the net herself because she was seeking a place to be active.

> I searched the internet thinking surely there must be a group opposed to privileges for foreigners when the very first hit came up with this group [*Zaitokukai*], which sounded like the right sort of name for that kind of group, so I thought that I would join it. I didn't watch any videos, I still don't look at videos ... I joined immediately – joining is easy. Once I had done that, I started getting emails telling me when demonstrations would be held, and so I took part in them. (Ms P, *Zaitokukai*, twenties)

P had been interested in historical revisionism before she started using the internet. Nativism was simply an extension of historical revisionism, and her encounter with *Zaitokukai* is likewise not a matter of fate. It is simply a matter of her having joined *Zaitokukai* because it came up as a hit when she was searching the internet looking precisely for an organization like *Zaitokukai*. Similarly, when she took part in street demonstrations she was not in fact bewildered; rather, as we see below, she experienced such a degree of excitement that she repeats the word 'momentous' three times.

> [I tried participating] and it was momentous. I thought this is momentous. Up until this moment, there haven't been any ordinary people standing up to *Sōren* and saying, Hey you! We were practically saying 'Get out!' ... I thought that standing face to face with them and challenging them was momentous. (Ms P, *Zaitokukai*, twenties)

C, the enthusiastic activist from Chapter 3, who underwent alternation, usually listened to the radio while he was doing his delivery work. The first step for him came when he started listening periodically to a history-related program on the community FM station that he had on because it was 'lively'.

> As I kept listening [to the program], I found myself thinking that the views of the so-called right-wing side on the Pacific War were somewhat different from mine and, wondering what was going on, I

began looking up things ... [That program] was, if anything, on the conservative side ... Oh, is that right? Oh, so there are these sorts of views too? By trying to step away a little from what the people on the left were saying and from their views, it became apparent to me that there was a history made up of different truths ... I also listened to a lot of my grandmother's stories. About leaving for the front, about the American air raids ... she also showed me my grandfather's photograph from when he went to the army. He was on a horse, a white horse, wearing his sword like this; he looked so gallant! (Mr C, *Zaitokukai*, thirties)

C started collecting historical revisionist information on the internet, which he had just started using. As he was a blue-collar worker without a computer, he would go to an internet cafe on his days off work.

As I searched for various things on the internet, I began to understand that there was a difference between what is shown on television and what really happened ... Since I didn't have a computer at home I went to an internet cafe. I would spend hours there, watching videos. (Mr C, *Zaitokukai*, thirties)

C, who until that point had acted alone, 'watching by myself and tapping away on the keyboard', experienced a turning point in 2009. Feeling that he 'couldn't stay like this forever – tapping away at a keyboard', C set about transforming himself after having been stuck as an online right winger for several years.

Thinking that surely there would be something happening on the fifteenth of August [the anniversary of Japan's defeat], I started searching. That's when I got a hit [on a blog by a right-wing activist.] I thought 'I'd really like to go and have a look', so I went, and that was where I came across *Zaitokukai*. That was the beginning, when I really came in contact with it. (Mr C, *Zaitokukai*, thirties)

In C's case, his search led him to find a blog by a right-wing activist in his home area as a result of looking for an event that he could take part in on the anniversary of defeat. He saw an announcement and took part in an event at a shrine honoring the war dead, and after that he became active and stuck closely to a particular right-wing activist. It was because this right-wing activist was also connected with *Zaitokukai* that C learned of its existence. Originally, C had come into contact with historical revisionism through the old-style media of FM radio, and it had been the similarly traditional medium of word of mouth that led him to join *Zaitokukai*. C, who was not in the habit of reading books, made his way enthusiastically through the internet pages on historical revisionism. On the internet, there were 'facts' that supported his alternation, such as 'the Declaration of War that Prime Minister Tōjō had read out'. Although we cannot call the information on the internet independent, it held considerable meaning for C, who was not familiar with printed books. Even when he joined activities, he kept using the internet as a bulletin board as it was useful for searches. In short, in the case of searchers, the function of the internet can be said to have been largely limited to that of reducing the opportunity costs of obtaining information.

Net surfers: digitally-enabled framing processes

For the net surfers group, to which four of the activists belonged, it was the internet that both promoted contact with the movement and enabled frame resonance. People who fall into this category gain information about the movement in the course of searching on their own, but while browsing they move away from their initial interests and begin to incline towards nativism. During the 2002 FIFA World Cup, for example, there was a lot of talk about 'South Korea's rough play' on the internet. Even if we allow that this may have become a reason for 'hatred towards Korea', there is no link between it and a belief in 'special privileges for *Zainichi* Koreans'. However, the internet does link these sorts of unrelated matters via its links function. F, who played rugby during his student days, also had an interest in soccer, and when he watched the game with South Korea he experienced feelings such as, 'that was a foul just now, but the referees did not award it'.

> The reporting on Korea regarding the World Cup [was the impetus]. As you would expect, the most symbolic thing was the fact that, at the start, they held a meeting on their own in Japan. In Korea, they had talked about being one together, and I had thought that maybe they were preparing for this, but none of that preparation had been done ... We were joint sponsors so we should have been mutually supporting

one another, but nothing of the sort ... Clearly, soccer influenced me considerably, it was one of the major reasons for starting to get involved in this kind of movement. (Mr F, *Zaitokukai*, thirties)

F says that he had had 'no interest at all' in foreigners in Japan and that he had 'never noticed anything' about 'special privileges for *Zainichi* Koreans'. While thinking that something was 'strange' with the Korean team and researching it, he ended up putting aside his initial questions about soccer and was left instead with 'a critical eye towards Korea' and a sense of mistrust that 'the mass media was not telling us the truth, after all'. As his browsing continues, he begins to denounce 'special privileges for *Zainichi* Koreans', a topic which he had ostensibly not been interested in originally. F says, 'when I became aware of it, they had got away with so much', but his thinking resulted from the manner in which totally unconnected things had been connected via links, in the same manner as internet surfing.

> Searching on the internet, I noticed that some new information had been added. I saw this by chance, then I searched actively. I began to have a better understanding that something was strange, and then a convincing reply surfaced. That is how I came to think, Oh, it's the special privileges of *Zainichi* Koreans. (Mr F, *Zaitokukai*, thirties)

U, who is in his early twenties, 'had used computers during comprehensive education', and had also used the home computer for looking things up since he was in primary school. 'I was interested in history, particularly modern and recent history – I was really interested in these'. This intellectual curiosity also inclined him to read books and watch television programs on history. Up until this point, he had had some episodes on the internet but, as we see below, it is when he discovers a sequence of information on the internet 'that suited me perfectly' that he becomes attracted to the movement.

> I guess that the biggest factor was the net ... I grew up in the period when it spread into homes. Information related to politics started appearing on it. People on both the left and the right were making statements. And there happened to be items that really suited my own views. I guess that these caught my interest, that's how I felt. One thing that I looked up particularly early was the Annexation of Korea by

Japan. Issues that arose after this, things that bothered me in connection with this; I think that was the impetus. (Mr U, *Zaitokukai*, twenties)

Sunstein (2001) argues that browsing for personalized news on the internet facilitates group polarization. In general, browsing home pages with a specific viewpoint will take the reader to another home page with a similar viewpoint. Consequently, people who look at home pages out of interest in a particular viewpoint have few opportunities to see opposing opinions and they become fanatical about one particular viewpoint. This is a situation that has arisen in the nativist movement also but, as we see below, the internet has yet another trait.

I don't really remember [the details of how I came across *Zaitokukai*]. When you surf the net, before you realize it, you end up having found a completely different home page. It really felt like that. I got a friend to give me the name of a site, and after that, I think that searching, searching, searching I ended up finding *Zaitokukai*. That guy liked the net and he looked at a lot of stuff on it; that's why he casually came across it … It was by chance, really by chance. So, in that sense, that sort of thing often happens in a net society – that's how it seems. (Mr U, *Zaitokukai*, twenties)

Most internet users are likely to have had the experience of 'searching, searching, searching' and then realizing that they 'have ended up finding a completely different home page'. U started off on a home page that his friend had told him about, but he cannot remember what that was now. He then started searching to look into what he had found there and he ended up on yet another page where, in the course of conducting another search, he came across *Zaitokukai*. U had started off being interested in 'the annexation of Korea' and then, through the mediation of the internet, his interest had 'shifted to the social problems of relations between Japan and Korea, and relations between Japan and China' and from here he ended up at 'the foreigner problem'. In the course of repeatedly following the links that the home page deems to be relevant, one ends up looking at content that is far removed from what was being looked at initially. This differs from Sunstein's point; it suggests a kind of group polarization in which people's acquaintance with nativism is an unintended consequence.

Discoverers: chance meetings with nativism when surfing the net

There were nine activists of this type, whose discovery that nativist content on the internet resonated with them was incidental; that is, they made this discovery not as a result of conducting their own searches but just as a result of browsing. B, the rural conservative from Chapter 3, is a manager in a business that runs *pachinko* parlors, a well-known ethnic niche for *Zainichi* Koreans. Although he had had considerable contact with *Zainichi* Koreans, he says that he 'initially had no' nativist sentiments. The event that changed all this was hearing an internet radio program 'on a rainy September day' in which 'someone was talking to Lee Teng-hui'.

> I had basically gone through post-war education, and then there was a Taiwanese person talking on the net – I think that I heard him on RealPlayer or something like that. He talked about how Japan used to be like this in the past and that it had such and such a history, and present-day Japanese people were responding to this with nothing but criticism of how bad Japan had been in the past. (Mr B, *Zaitokukai*, thirties)

B had no interest in social matters nor was he accustomed to looking at internet pages on society and politics. B, himself, could not recall 'why I watched it or why I listened to it', but he says that 'strangely, I remember' the contents of this program. His understanding is that 'being told these things not by a Japanese person but by a foreigner had a big effect', and he then began collecting historical revisionist information.

> I don't normally access sites concerned with politics so ... I just happened to pick that one for some reason or other. Picking it and listening to it, something about it suddenly made something shift inside me. That was when I started doing bits of research – on the net, in books that I got from the library. The place where I used to live was very close to the library. It was about ten minutes by car, so I'd drop in. I'd research on the net, I'd do searches and if there was anything, I'd read it. (Mr B, *Zaitokukai*, thirties)

Via this process he came across Makoto Sakurai's home page, which could be called *Zaitokukai*'s predecessor, and started listening to his radio program. This was not limited to listening online; B was such an enthusiastic listener that he would download the program onto a portable player. Then, he also came across a notice about the founding of *Zaitokukai* and immediately decided to join.[12]

> The current president, Sakurai, used to have a radio program 'Korea, a Strange Country'. I used to download it from the net and listen to it while I was commuting to work, when I went on business trips and when I did work outdoors ... That net radio had been going for quite a long time ... *Zaitokukai* didn't exist back then. They used to broadcast a thirty-minute or an hour discussion format, which I listened to. Then *Zaitokukai* got going, and I thought why not join. (Mr B, *Zaitokukai*, thirties)

There were hardly any others who could recall in the way that B does what the impetus had been for browsing, but many had detailed recollections of the content that they saw on those occasions. This not only indicates the degree of the impact that browsing had on the people concerned but also that the browsing was incidental. The 'amount of material' containing nativist information circulating on the internet is a background factor to the likelihood of this sort of accidental browsing occurring. Another activist, E, worked in irregular employment as, despite being a university graduate, he had not been able to get a job as a government worker. He 'just work[s] to cover living expenses' and because he 'was not good at doing things I didn't like' he tried to earn a livelihood by trading shares, and this is how he came into contact with the internet.

> ADSL technology became available in 2000, and I also signed a contract with them on 12 September, 2002, and that enabled me to have uninterrupted all-day connection to the net. This changed my lifestyle dramatically ... That is, it's unlimited so if I'm at home all day, and I don't have any work to do, I can keep looking at the computer from morning to night. (Mr E, non-*Zaitokukai*, forties)

Since the advent of uninterrupted all-day connection there appears to have been a rapid increase in the number of people who surf the internet to kill time. E is no exception, but in his case the impetus was not simply surfing the net. He had been transacting shares when some information about 'hatred of Korea' appeared on a site related to his work, and this was the start of his interest.

I wasn't just [looking at] shares. I surf the net in my spare time and to kill time. Channel 2, Yahoo's bulletin board and things like that. At that time, there was the Japan–Korea World Cup, in which there were lots of problems such as with the Korean people's manner. As a result, what's called hatred of Korea copy-and-paste, stuff like ASCII art that abused Koreans, was on the net. So much material abusing Koreans and that sort of thing had been pasted up. It also ended up on unrelated boards on market conditions and the like that I was looking at; stuff that slanders Koreans ... so, even though I didn't like it, I ended up coming face to face with it. (Mr E, non-*Zaitokukai*, forties)

His contact with information full of hatred of Korea came about by chance, but it was his own long-standing interest in history that explains why he was actively looking at history-related bulletin boards. It was his historical revisionist posts on these bulletin boards that made him stand out as an internet right winger.

I follow historical discussions on net bulletin boards closely. The net right wing, the left and *Zainichi* Koreans have had lots of disputes in discussions of various history topics, in particular the colonial period, so when I come across something strange or something that I'm interested in I join in those discussions. (Mr E, non-*Zaitokukai*, forties)

As we see below, E began to advocate nativism explicitly at the time of the July 2005 selection of textbooks (municipalities select the text books that will be used in schools every four years). At this time, the movement to block historical revisionist textbooks was largely being conducted by a group related to the existing progressive political parties, but *Mindan* was also protesting against the selection that had been made. E perceived this as '*Zainichi* Koreans and the left conspiring to damage Japan', and felt that it was no longer enough to just be on the net but that it was essential to belong to a group and become active.

The municipality said that it would adopt *Tsukurukai*'s textbooks. The people protesting against this, surrounding the city hall by making a human chain, had an incredible presence for some time on the net ... This was it, the opportunity to build nativism towards Korea. Why is *Mindan* finding fault with Japanese history textbooks? I found it extremely disagreeable. (Mr E, non-*Zaitokukai*, forties)

This was the impetus for E, who had wandered between organizations ranging from a group related to the Yasukuni Shrine to a hate group targeting Chinese residents, before becoming an activist. However, the biggest climax in the selection of historical revisionist textbooks had come not in 2005 but 2001. The reason for E's lack of interest at that time is not explained by the fact that he was not yet browsing historical revisionist bulletin boards. As someone who did not read newspapers or watch television, E's first contact with real-time news came via his uninterrupted all-day connection to the internet. In this sense, without the internet, E would not even have been interested in the workings of society, let alone have been attracted to nativism. However, in this case, the function of the internet was merely as an alternative to newspapers and television; it would be difficult to argue that attracting people to nativism is a function peculiar to the internet.

The brainwashed: net-enabled processes

This type, which describes two activists, refers to people who happened to be browsing content on the internet that was not directly related to nativism and who ended up being attracted to nativism after following various links. One of the traits of the internet as indicated by the experiences of I, who we met briefly in Chapter 4, is that the degree to which nativism comes to the notice of the public increases in proportion to the frequency of browsing.

> There was a first-rate video, in amongst the Japanese videos, it was called something like 'A body that will smash *Sōka Gakkai*' and I thought, 'What's this?' I thought 'you'd probably get killed if you picked a fight with that lot' ... That was the impetus. (Mr I, *Zaitokukai*, thirties)

This video is of '[ultra-right wing activist] Hiroyuki Seto's street oratory when announcing his candidacy for the House of Councilors election'. This same link also included videos by the Association for the Restoration of Sovereignty and *Zaitokukai*. A video slandering *Sōka Gakkai* had provided the initial impetus, but I then became more interested in the nativism material on the link saying, 'To use a stereotypically mass media term, I was brainwashed'. After this, he 'watched videos once or twice a month, for half a day on my days off work', and several years later he took part in a demonstration as it was on a day when he was not working. The impact of 'hatred of Korea' information is not simply due to its volume of material resources. The self-reproductive processes of internet browsing lead to an increase in the number of people who sympathize with the nativist movement: there is a cycle in which an increase in the number of playbacks itself brings about another playback. This resembles a spiral of silence, but it happens even if anti-nativists watch a video. The act of browsing itself has the effect of spreading information and it plays the role of indirectly expanding the nativist movement.

Finally, Q also ended up reading about 'special privileges for *Zainichi* Koreans' when he looked at a video attacking *Sōka Gakkai*. As a systems engineer, he was familiar with computers and also frequently surfed the internet. While surfing, he came across a video by ultra-right activist, Hiroyuki Seto.

> The impetus was an encounter with a person who was spreading his message on a video ... As to the impetus for watching that video, it was just by chance, I can only say that I just happened to catch it. I had only watched a smattering of things on the internet ... Somehow, the link jumped ... and the video that came up was of Mr Hiroyuki Seto ... On that occasion, he was criticizing *Sōka Gakkai*. I wondered how long it would be before someone killed this person, so from then on I frequently checked to see when his home page would stop. I started reading with interest; my first impression was that he was saying interesting things. (Mr Q, *Zaitokukai*, thirties)

Q then made a practice of browsing Seto's home page, which served as the connection that led to his interest in the 'foreigner problem' and to him starting to research it on the internet. His initial interest was in a video of Seto abusing *Sōka Gakkai*; he says that his interest was piqued by the video's reference to something that he had thought was a kind of taboo. The path that Q pursued had started on a site completely unrelated to *Sōka Gakkai* → a video abusing *Sōka Gakkai* contained in the link → the home page of the speaker on the video → the discovery of the 'foreigner problem'.

> Then, there was immediately a discussion of politics and also of foreigners and Koreans. That's when I started researching: it

was because I got interested in the foreigner problem. A lot of substantiating material also emerged; I kept researching various things. Problems that made me think that these bad things had happened. (Mr Q, *Zaitokukai*, thirties)

As Q says, he 'kept researching', and 'facts' (as he saw them) that substantiated 'the foreigner problem' emerged in rapid succession during his searches. On the internet, there is complete harmony between the contents of historical revisionism, the slander of neighboring countries and nativism. Via the same process in which clicking on link after link while surfing the internet ultimately leads to a site that has no connection whatsoever with the initial browsing subject, 'special privileges for *Zainichi* Koreans' will ultimately leap up in front of someone who was initially surfing an unrelated topic. This person is, as it were, like a butterfly flying around in a virtual empty room and getting caught in a spider's web spun by a nativist; this may be a phenomenon that is particular to the internet.

Late development effects on resource mobilization

Hiroyuki Seto, one of the leaders of the nativist movement, has said that 'patriotism is showing a rapid rise as a result of the spread of the internet' (Seto 2007: 346) and that 'there is a complete discrepancy between the existing mass media and internet media' (Seto 2007: 4). This is a partially correct assessment of the real situation; the right wing is overwhelming the left wing in terms of providing ease of access to a large amount of information (leaving aside the issue of its poor quality) circulating on the internet and videos. This is a late development effect characteristic of an emergent nativist movement that arose from internet bulletin boards, which were its sole base. Finally, let us summarize the ways in which the internet alters the micromobilization process.

Firstly, recruitment via the internet hints at the effectiveness of social embeddedness (Granovetter 1985) and the strength of weak ties (Granovetter 1973) in mobilization. Resource mobilization theory predicted mobilization via the internet's special characteristics regarding the costs of disseminating information. It does not, however, offer any solution for resolving the problem of free riders beyond stating the importance of small groups, which form the base of the movement. Its viewpoint was basically that individuals embedded in social relations participate in the movement. Previous research has found that participation in small groups, which form the basis of the movement (embeddedness), is also meaningful in internet-mediated mobilization (Van Laer 2010).

However, the case of the Japanese nativist movement suggests another possibility: it is persuasion via the internet, without the mediation of small groups, which has been effective in mobilization. Subculture groups that might make up the base of the nativist movement (such as, hooligans and skinheads) do not exist in any substantial way in Japan. These groups not only function as small groups that are effective at recruiting participants; they also become a cultural base for removing antipathy towards the nativist movement. When this sort of base is lacking, group affiliation generally hinders participation in the nativist movement. In this respect, belonging to a net culture in which nativism has gained a certain status, is a factor that eliminates antipathy towards the movement. Belonging to a net culture indisputably generates no more than weak ties, which do not provide social incentives (Van Laer and Van Aelst 2010: 18). However, the strength of weak ties lies in the fact that they extend to a large number and variety of people, and this is a characteristic of virtual bases. In this sense, there is a divergence between narrow and deep 'real bases' and shallow and wide 'virtual bases', and the nativist movement can be seen as a new movement that specializes in the latter.

Secondly, the internet is able to exert a variety of influences on micromobilization, but this influence is limited in its extent. Twenty-five of the thirty-four people included in Figure 5.1, above, were mobilized via the internet. Among them, ten simply saw the search function as something that was convenient to use. Nine browsed nativism content accidentally, which can be regarded as a recruitment process enabled by the internet (see Carty and Onyett 2006). However, we only see internet-mediated framing in six cases. In short, the internet functions well as a place where new information can be gained, but it does not have the influence to change political standpoints; it is best to think of it as a mediator that expands existing standpoints.[13] The fact that, as we saw in Chapter 3, people who were already politically conservative become activists is in part due to this trait of the internet.

Thirdly, mobilization which relies on a virtual base cannot rely on selective incentive because of the inherent anonymity. Even if the organizational goal of abolishing 'special privileges for *Zainichi* Koreans' were to be achieved, activists would not reap any benefits. This means that activists in the nativist movement rush to join the movement purely as a moral protest (Jasper 1997). This would suggest that the motive is attraction to a great cause, but it is usually difficult to understand why they find a good reason to participate in the nativist movement instead of despising it. Consequently, one is likely to assume an alternative incentive such as the venting of anger at misfortune, but the starting point of this book is based on the rejection of this kind of explanation. How then should we understand this? We need to shift our attention to precisely those contexts where simple hate speech is displayed in the guise of a moral protest. Accordingly, the following chapter will move on to an analysis of the relationship between the nativist movement and politics, which should clarify the background factors to nativist discourse.

6 The Nativist Movement and Politics

From micromobilization to a political opportunity

Thus far we have been using interview data to analyze the processes by which individual activists flock to the movement. However, without an understanding of the structural background out of which the nativist movement emerges, there cannot be any understanding of the issue as a whole. The nativist movement is highly political in the sense that it has organized campaigns closely related to the enforcement of particular laws and to issues connected with the national budget. It has been argued that it is nonsense to link discussions of the movement with politics or political ideologies (Yasuda 2012a), but can we really ignore its links with politics? The Introduction and Chapter 2 raised doubts about explanations focusing on economic recession and social disorganization. The remainder of this book will re-examine these points and analyze the origins and development of the nativist movement from the perspective of its links with politics.

As we saw in Chapter 1, studies on the ultra-right in Western Europe have empirically examined the validity of dominant theories. This led to doubts about 'losers of modernization' theory and to revisions of the image of ultra-right supporters. Empirical research in this area has just started in Japan, and we also need an examination of which theories can be applied to the Japanese case.

In this regard, Koopmans' (1996) argument underscores the need for the present study: he says that the lack of an ideal amount of research notwithstanding, it is still possible to reveal certain insights by making utmost use of the available data. On the question of the comparability of different data sets in his analysis of ultra-right violence in eight countries, Koopmans argued that clear trends and differences can lend themselves to meaningful interpretation. He examined the relevance of grievance versus opportunity in explaining ultra-right violence, and found the latter yielded more insights. Given the even more limited amount of data available in Japan we have no real choice but to employ the sort of method suggested by Koopmans. In this chapter, I will use data on movement organizations and the right-wing world of criticism to clarify how the nativist movement and politics are related.

The relationship between social movements and politics has been analyzed using the concept of political opportunity structure. This concept, which has shed light on the fact that movements emerge when political opportunity opens up, is suited to explaining the timing of a movement. In Chapter 2, we showed that economic factors and competition with migrants could not explain the rise of the nativist movement in the second half of the 2000s. In Chapter 4, we also argued that the emergence of the movement is strongly linked with the spread of the internet (especially video sharing services). Other Japanese sociologists have also paid attention to the trend to the right amongst youth; however, their focus has been simply on the role of subcultures and they have ignored that of politics (Kitada 2005; Nakanishi 2006; Ōsawa 2011; Suzuki 2005). It is precisely the relationship between the nativist movement and politics that is paramount if we are to elucidate this phenomenon of a shift to the right. The aim of this chapter is, therefore, to show that, in addition to the internet, certain political conditions have also promoted the rise of the nativist movement. What follows is an examination of the hypothesis that the appearance of the nativist movement has been influenced by the changing interests of existing conservative power.

A theory of discursive opportunities

Political opportunity structure and the nativist movement

A large number of studies have been conducted using the concepts of political opportunities or political opportunity structures (Jenkins and Klandermans 1995; Koopmans 1995; Kriesi et al. 1995; McAdam 1982; Tarrow 1989, 1998; Tilly 1978). The premise of these approaches is that political opportunity structures influence the rise and fall of social movements. An example of this is Russia's ultra-right movement's steps to take advantage of the government's anti-Georgia policy to attract new members and to make propaganda claims (Varga 2008: 572). According to Tarrow (1998), these political opportunities have four dimensions: increasing access, unstable alignments, divided elites and influential allies.

Is it possible then to shed light on the relationship between Japan's nativist movement and these sorts of institutional or 'hard' aspects of politics? Compared to countries with anti-discrimination laws, there are few restrictions on the activities of Japan's nativist movement when it comes to increasing access. In countries where anti-discrimination laws are in place and access is closed off, it becomes difficult for the nativist movement to target specific groups. However, if we leave aside these sorts of cross-national comparisons, increasing access is not a meaningful factor and it does not serve as an explanation for the rise of the nativist movement in the 2000s.

The remaining three factors – unstable alignments, divided elites and influential allies – refer to more volatile aspects of political opportunity structures: political instability generates a space in which movements can flourish and political elites favorable to movements can influence their rise and fall. These factors also had little to do with Japan's nativist movement before the rise of the Japan Restoration Party.[1] Following the Koizumi administration, the LDP government was in a state of instability as seen, for example, in the frequent changes of Prime Minister. It was the emergence of political realignment and divided elites that led to the establishment of ultra-right parties such as the Sunrise Party of Japan. However, these unstable alignments did not go on to become an opportunity for the ultra-right movement.

It was instead the existence of powerful allies that exerted an influence on the rise of the ultra-right movement. The abduction issue, which emerged as a matter of high priority following Prime Minister Koizumi's 2002 visit to North Korea, provided a major opportunity for the 'National Association for the Rescue of Japanese Kidnapped by North Korea' (*Sukuukai*). The abduction issue enabled *Sukuukai* to gain influential allies as politicians, en masse, showed their concern about the abduction issue. However, because the distance between the nativist movement and institutional politics was too great it is difficult to argue that this political change influenced the movement.

How the ideological position of political parties influences left-libertarian movements, which regard leftist parties as part of their alliance system, was analyzed by della Porta and Rucht (1995). *Nippon Ishin no Kai* (Japan Restoration Party), which made tremendous advances in the December 2012 general election, represented an opportunity for an ultra-right party to conceivably become an ally of the nativist movement. Its members also included regional Diet members who were active in *Zaitokukai*, and some *Zaitokukai* leaders attended political classes run by Shingo Nishimura, who had been re-elected to the Lower House for the Japan Restoration Party. The rise of these leaders had the potential to influence the nativist movement; however, as a party with seats in the Diet, the Japan Restoration Party could not openly avow its links with a nativist movement which had had many of its members arrested. The institutional, hard political opportunity structures, thus, remained closed to the nativist movement.[2]

Discursive opportunities theory

However, political opportunities are not limited to the political system and political actors; some discussions of political opportunities focus on cultural, soft aspects (Gamson and Meyer 1996). These aspects are not so different from institutional political structures in the sense that they explain the trajectories of social movements within various polities. Certain political cultures, political trends in a particular period and issues regarding the legitimacy of political power can provide opportunities for movements. The political discourse of a movement tends to correspond to politico-cultural opportunities; if it did not, the movement would find it difficult to gain support (Diani 1996). Similarly, the influence of politico-cultural trends will be greater where political opportunities for a new movement are in flux and on the way to becoming institutionalized (Brand 1990: 27). This leads us to hypothesize that there was a connection between the appearance of the nativist movement and Japan's dominant political discourse in the 2000s.

These various arguments have produced a theory of discursive opportunities that aims to synthesize framing and political opportunity structures (Koopmans and Muis 2009: 648; Koopmans and Statham 1999: 228).[3] This theory can be characterized as 'institutionally anchored ways of thinking that provide a gradient of relative political acceptability to specific packages of ideas' (Ferre 2003: 309). Discursive opportunities shape which frames will stand out, how plausible constructed realities appear and what kind of demand looks legitimate in a given political system at a given time (Koopmans and Statham 1999: 228). When a movement is constructed in keeping with discursive opportunities it finds it easier to gain support, while movements that run counter to them are less likely to gain support.[4]

Just as with institutional opportunity structures, there are also a variety of discursive opportunities ranging in characteristics from the stable to the volatile. The abortion issue, which is dominated by individualistic discourse (privacy rights) in the United States and focused on protecting the family in Germany, is a good example of stable characteristics. As the courts make use of different principles to come to their decisions, pro-life movements also adapt to these changing principles (Ferre 2003). Another example of stable characteristics comes from the Netherlands, where ultra-right parties claim that Muslims threaten the Dutch culture of tolerance that embraces different religions, feminism and homosexuals. Japan's nativist movement tends to make use of 'freedom of expression' arguments because of their strong opposition to restrictions on hate speech which are the result of the influence of United States-style liberalism.[5] An ultra-right movement will switch to different principles if the political culture changes, thus producing the differences between movements in each country.

The volatile characteristic is exemplified by the intimate relationship, in the 1990s, between the revision of asylum rights and ultra-right violence in Germany (Koopmans and Olzak 2004). This issue was a matter of highest priority for politicians and the media for a year and a half, and ultra-right violence increased as movements took advantage of this controversy. Although there was criticism of this violence, many supported the view that refugees and asylum seekers had become an unendurable burden on Germany. Ultra-right violence did not break out because of grievances concerning the socioeconomic conditions into which Germany had been plunged following re-unification, but because the discursive opportunities in Germany had become anti-migrant.[6]

My interest lies in the influence that discursive opportunities exert on the nativist movement (see McAdam 1994). Stable discursive opportunities are typified in the view that Japan's deep-seated 'contempt towards Asia' prompted the appearance of the nativist movement. In reality, the repeated array of reckless remarks that politicians have been uttering have had an influence on discursive opportunities for some time (Takasaki 2002; Wakamiya

2006). A Japanese-style orientalism has put down deep social and political roots.

However, even if we regard entrenched orientalism in Japanese society as the cause, it does not provide answers to the questions raised in this book. Just as the argument that orientalism and racism form the background to the rise of the ultra-right in Western Europe is correct in itself, it does not provide an explanation for the phenomenon. If contempt towards various Asian countries is ever-present, then it cannot be the factor that explains why the nativist movement arose in the late 2000s and not at some other time. It may be that the spread of the internet enabled racist mobilization, in which case the change of mobilizing structure, rather than discursive opportunities, triggered the emergence of the movement.

Before we can suggest an explanation, however, we first need to examine whether discursive opportunities have or have not changed, and whether or not this change has had any influence on the nativist movement. In order to do this, we need to focus on the volatile aspect of discursive opportunities, especially at the beginning of the 2000s. In my view, the ultra-right movement's connections with politics caused it to change in the manner set out in Figure 6.1. This figure combines two opportunity structures and shows their influence on the degree of openness of the movement.

Of these structures, it is the Japan Society for History Textbook Reform (*Tsukurukai*) and the National Association for the Rescue of Japanese Kidnapped by North Korea (*Sukuukai*) that enjoyed both discursive resonance and institutional connections. The history textbook movement itself has been continually bogged down by inept organizational management, such as infighting. However, it has influential allies such as the Japanese Parliamentary Association for Reflecting on Future Prospects and History Education (*Nihon no zento to rekishi kyōiku o kangaeru giin no kai*), made up mainly of the LDP right wing, who have provided the group with considerable advantages such as backing at the time of textbook selection and parliamentary questions. Also in the case of *Sukuukai*, it has had strong links with the Alliance of Diet Members for the Rescue of Japanese Suspected of Having Been Kidnapped by North Korea (*Kita chōsen rakuchi giwaku nihonjin kyūsai giin renmei*).

Whilst institutional opportunities remained closed to the nativist movement, even though it was part of the ultra-right movement, discursive opportunities opened up in the 2000s. The nativist movement continued to be radicalized and its repertoire was mostly limited to direct action because it lacked a foothold in institutional politics. It was, however, able to mobilize continually because its discourses attracted a cluster of potential constituents. On the other hand, following the disappearance of hostilities with the (former) Soviet Union, the appeal of anti-communism and territorial disputes, issues to which the existing right wing had held tenaciously, decreased.[7] This closure of discursive opportunities resulted in the marginalization of the existing right wing.

Hierarchies inside discursive opportunities

The idea of discursive opportunities is based on the premise that the culture of social movements borrows part of the dominant culture, and for that reason operates under structural constraints (see Steinberg 1999). Most of the discourse of the nativist movement has also been appropriated from the discourse of the right-wing elite. It is not that the discourse of the two is directly linked, but the movement's discourse can increase its appeal by appropriating that of the right-wing elite. As was discussed briefly in the Introduction, there is an affinity between the discourse of the nativist movement and the statements of politicians and the media in Japan (Chong 2013: 9). In this chapter, we will examine the extent to which this view is correct.

In addition, because the nativist movement traces its origins partly to the internet right wing, it should also be seen as appropriating the discourse of the latter's subcultures, such as the internet and *manga*. A portion of subculture discourse is in turn constructed by appropriating the discourse of the dominant culture while displaying a degree of independence from it. Figure 6.2 sets out the relationship between these various elements in the form of a hierarchical structure: mass media – right-wing world of criticism – *manga* and *mooks* – anti-foreigner sites – the nativist movement. Hierarchy as used here refers to a relationship in which the actors in the top tiers appropriate the discourse of the bottom tiers. Under this structure, the legitimacy of the discourse declines as we move up the tiers away from the mass media in the bottom tier, and its content also becomes increasingly focused and radical. The relationship between these tiers is basically one of the actors at the top appropriating the discourse of the bottom tiers. However, given that this borrowing includes a process of

Figure 6.1: Political opportunity structures and the Japanese ultra-right movement in the 2000s

Institutional opportunities

		Open	*Closed*
Discursive opportunities	*Open*	Institutionalization Japan Society for History Textbook Reform National Association for the Rescue of Japanese Kidnapped by North Korea	Radicalization Nativist movement
	Closed	Populism	Marginalization Established right wing

Source: Compiled by author by modifying the table in Giugni et al. 2005: 149.

Figure 6.2 The nativist movement within discursive opportunities

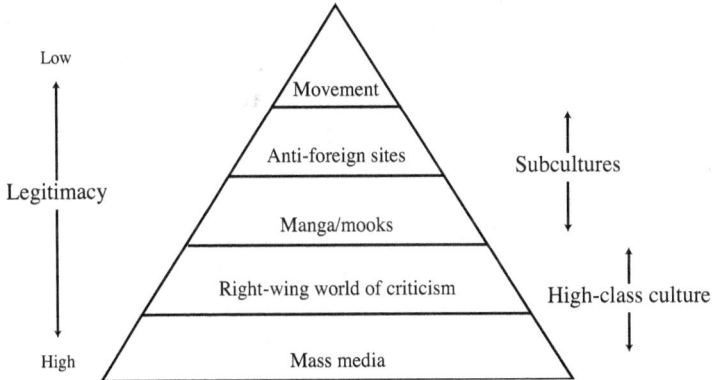

Source: Compiled by author based on Furuya (2012).

distinctive treatment of the discourse and not mere appropriation, it takes on a relatively independent character. I would like to pose and test the following hypotheses on the basis of this dual character.

Firstly, the change undergone by the right-wing world of criticism in the 2000s resulted in an opening up of discursive opportunities for the nativist movement. The right-wing world of criticism influences the discourse of the nativist movement, and the appropriations that the movement makes from the former's discourse have a significant impact on its own character. In other words, it was the impact of changes in the discourse of the right-wing world of criticism that led to the appearance of a nativist movement discourse: the emergence of the nativist movement and changes in the right-wing world of criticism are intimately related.

Secondly, the discourse of the nativist movement is not restricted to mere appropriations of the statements of the right-wing world of criticism. Steinberg (1999) emphasized the relationship between the dominant culture and a movement's discourse, but the nativist movement was also born of independent subcultures. In short, while the discourse in the subculture fields of *manga, mooks* and anti-foreigner websites continues to be influenced by the right-wing world of criticism, they also contain elements that have been produced independently within the subcultures. In addition to the right-wing world of criticism, the nativist movement also borrows its discourse from subcultures.

Koopmans et al. use data from newspaper articles to look at discursive opportunities, but the 'migrant problem' is a bigger problem in Western Europe than it is in Japan. For this reason, I decided to examine the discursive opportunities in magazines from the right-wing world of criticism, and built a database (see Appendix) out of headlines from the representative magazines *Seiron* and *Shokun!* (I replaced *Shokun!* with *WiLL* for 2009–12 because the former ceased publication). I also constructed databases covering the actions of the nativist movement and topics related to *Zaitokukai* events. These data are useful in clarifying whether the right-wing world of criticism did change in the first decade of the 2000s and whether these changes are exerting any influence on the actions of the nativist movement.

Discursive opportunities and the nativist movement

Two waves of change and interest in East Asia

Let us trace the changing interests of the right-wing world of criticism as represented in two graphs. Figure 6.3 plots the changes in the frequency with which the United States, the Soviet Union (Russia), China, South Korea and North Korea appear in articles.

Two broad changes emerge for the 1990s and the 2000s from this figure. Throughout the 1980s, the frequency for the Soviet Union, the imaginary enemy, remained at a high level. In the second half of the 1980s, the depiction of the United States as an economic rival also increased.[8] Conversely, the proportion for China, South Korea and North Korea remained disproportionately lower than these two countries. This was to change in the 1990s, and although the Soviet Union continued to be of interest until its dissolution, after that point its ratio dropped dramatically and failed to return to former levels.[9] As stated previously, this resulted in a striking closure of discursive opportunities for the existing ultra-right, and may be seen as one of the causes of its decline. In the 1990s, the interest of the right-wing world of criticism turned entirely inwards, and in the year 2000 the figure for all five countries combined fell to as low as ten per cent. The *Reader's Digest*, symbol of the conservative world of criticism in the United States, also showed a growing tendency towards introversion in the 1990s; this phenomenon was not limited to Japan alone, and could be seen as resulting from the demise of the Cold War (Sharp 2000).[10]

Signs of the changes that would flourish in the 2000s were already visible in the late 1990s, and Figure 6.4 shows the direction that they were taking. Until the mid-1980s – with the military budget increasing under the Nakasone Cabinet, interest in the Soviet Union also strong, and the state of Japan–United States defense cooperation under discussion – the number of articles related to military affairs and defense sometimes exceeded ten per cent. After that, military affairs and defense ceased to make up the central concerns of the right-wing world of criticism, and in their place history-related articles exceeded ten per cent for the first time in 1997.[11] One of the background factors to this was the fact that the *Sankei* Newspaper Company, which publishes *Seiron*, was backing its own revisionist history textbooks in 1997. In 2005, the year in which the proportion of history-related articles peaked at over twenty per cent, there was an overlapping of anti-Japanese demonstrations in China, Prime Minister Koizumi's visit to the Yasukuni Shrine and the selection of textbooks.

This increase in history-related articles was not, however, brought about by particular conditions or events of passing interest; from 1997 until the 2009 it constantly exceeded ten per cent as a result of the appearance of a new enemy – the Democratic Party government. [12] As the line graph in Figure 6.4 shows, from the second half of the 1980s when there was an increase in historical revisionist articles regarding the Nanjing Massacre, an increasingly pronounced connection emerges between historical issues and foreign countries. Prior to this, the majority of articles had been of a dilettantish nature on the subject of the history of the Shōwa period (1926–1989)[13] with some additional articles on the history of foreign issues. The next peak came with the outbreak of the 'comfort women' issue, but the actual proportion of articles dealing with historical issues was low at this point in time. It is not until the second half of the 1990s that the importance of historical issues increased and that they were linked to foreign countries, a situation which remains unchanged to the present day.

Figure 6.3 shows that articles about foreign countries began to increase following the simultaneous terrorist attacks on the United States, in 2001, and then again following Prime Minister Koizumi's visit to North Korea, in 2002. This increase did not indicate just a passing interest; articles about foreign countries maintained a constant level of over twenty per cent, the only exception coming at the time of the drubbing handed out by the Democratic Party when they took office in 2009. With the advent of this century, articles related to foreign countries increased and articles related to East Asia, which had made up less than five per cent in the first half of the 1980s, now made up around twenty per cent.[14] Furthermore, if we leave aside the new life breathed into the abduction issue by North Korea in 2003, China has attracted overwhelming attention. Following 2002, China considerably outstripped the United States.

Changes in discursive opportunities and the nativist movement

As pointed out in the previous section, historical issues began to appear in increasing numbers from the second half of the 1990s, and by the 2000s East Asian countries were being seen as the biggest enemies. The direct effect of these changes on the right-wing world of criticism was the institutionalization of *Sukuukai* and *Tsukurukai*. Although the nativist movement was not able to establish points of contact with institutional politics, it did link itself with the changing discursive opportunities surrounding 'history' and 'East Asia'. As we saw in Chapter 2, of the thirty-four activists asked about their impetus for having become involved in

Figure 6.3 Respective frequency of appearance of countries

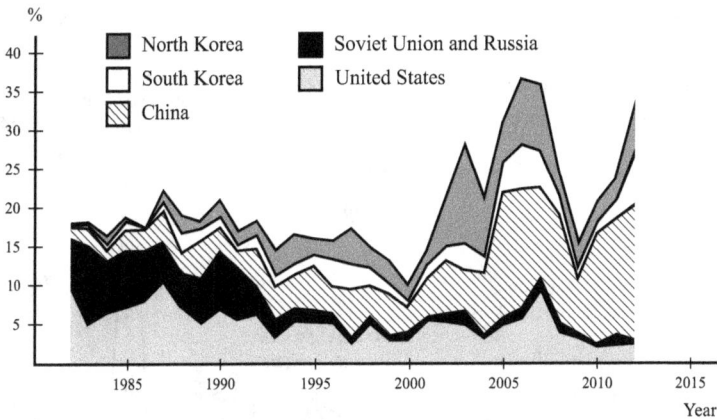

Figure 6.4 Ratio of appearance of military affairs, self-defense and
*   history*

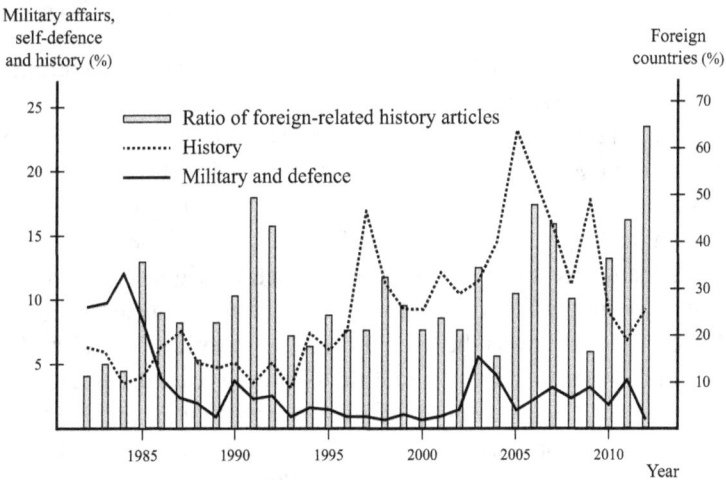

Note: The left y-axis denotes articles about military affairs, self-defense and history, whilst the right y-axis denotes the proportion of these articles that are about foreign countries.

the nativist movement, eleven gave events related to neighboring countries and eight mentioned historical problems, a total just short of sixty per cent. This result directly reflects the shift in focus of the right-wing world of criticism towards topics concerned with

Figure 6.5 Articles about foreigners in Japan

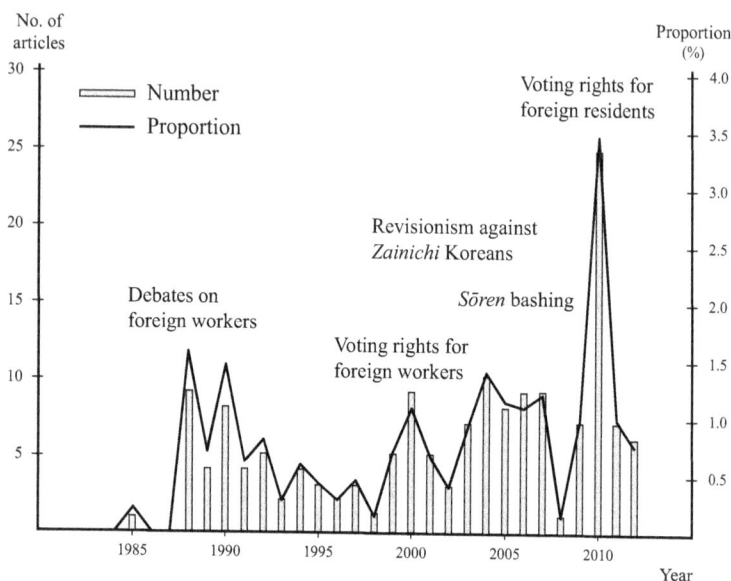

East Asia and history, and also shows that these were the entrance points into nativism.

The 'foreigner problem', by contrast, was cited by six activists, or fewer than twenty per cent. This number is consistent with Figure 6.5, which lists the total number of articles related to foreigners. However, even at its height, the proportion of interest in foreigners was never more than three and a half per cent; in fact, the right-wing world of criticism's interest in foreigners should be seen as quite low overall.[15] In other words, it was the altered right-wing world of criticism that began showing an interest in South and North Korea and China as well as in history, thus opening up discursive opportunities in these areas. The tendency for activists to show an interest in these neighboring countries and in history, rather than in the 'foreigner problem', was heightened by the opening up of these discursive opportunities.

Independently developed nativist discourse

However, changes in the right-wing world of criticism cannot explain why the nativist movement's core frame is 'special privileges for *Zainichi* Koreans'. To what extent does the nativist movement faithfully appropriate the discourse of the right-wing world of criticism and where are there divergences? Figure 6.6 indicates the right-wing world of criticism's level of interest in various topics following the establishment of *Zaitokukai*, in 2007. We can summarize the core interests of the right-wing world of criticism for the period concerned in the following manner.

Firstly, the proportion of interest in South Korea, North Korea and China, which had been 25 per cent in 2007, fell as low as 12 per cent in 2009, and then shot up to 31 per cent in 2012. This was the result of the redirection of attacks to the domestic sphere because of an increase in articles voicing their support for the 'Tamogami Incident' (discussed below) and criticizing the Democratic Party. The lack of any major incidents in connection with Japan's neighbors in 2009 also had an impact on this. The increase in 2012 was influenced by the reigniting of the Senkaku Islands issue and the death of the North Korean Supreme Leader Jong-il Kim.

Secondly, the proportion of interest in history, which had been 11 per cent in 2008, increased to as much as 18 per cent in 2009. This was the result of the large number of articles supporting Toshio Tamogami, Head of the Japanese Self Defense Forces, when a historical revisionist essay written by him caused problems. The rate fell once again to 9 per cent the following year, and has not reached ten per cent again.

Thirdly, while the proportion of articles criticizing the left wing (mainly the Democratic Party) was only 2 per cent in 2007, it rose to 16 per cent in 2010, and then fell again to 6 per cent in 2012.

These fluctuations show the annual changes in discursive opportunities. Figure 6.7 shows the proportion occupied by each topic in protest events connected with *Zaitokukai* (see the Appendix). Comparing Figures 6.6 and 6.7 allows us to confirm the existence of shared traits.[16] What is clear at a glance is that events that were directly anti-foreigner in nature made up less than forty per cent of all protest events. Rather, the areas where we can see similarities with the right-wing world of criticism are protest events about South Korea, North Korea and China and historical problems as well as 'the left'. How similar are the annual changes to the situation in the right-wing world of criticism? Let us confirm the extent to which the three traits identified above in connection with Figure 6.6 apply also to Figure 6.7.

Firstly, the proportion of *Zaitokukai* protest events targeting South Korea, North Korea and China was 64 per cent in 2007 and 46 per

Figure 6.6 Right-wing world of criticism areas of interest 2007–2012

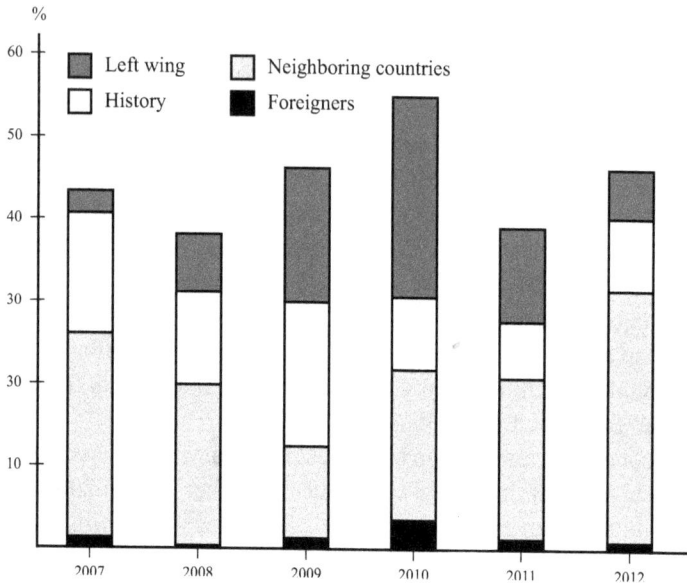

cent in 2008, then dropped rapidly to 26 per cent in 2009 and rose to 38 per cent in 2012. Quantitatively, this is similar to the changes in the right-wing world of criticism, and we can also see a similar qualitative trend up until 2009. However, the 2012 increase targeted South Korea rather than China, and it is precisely in this persistent focus on South Korea that we see a divergence from the right-wing world of criticism.

Secondly, in 2009, history-related protest events increased to 16, from 6 per cent the previous year, quantitatively consistent with the right-wing world of criticism. However, this increase in history-related events in this period is accounted for by harassment activities at local events, such as projects related to 'comfort women' and the obstruction of *Mindan*'s historical exhibitions. There was only one event in support of Tamogami; thus, the history-related trend cannot be said to have been influenced by discursive opportunities. Rather, history-related events began to be targeted as a result of change in organizational policies to attack local events.

Thirdly, offensives against the 'left wing' amounted to a slight increase to 9 per cent in 2009 from 7 per cent the previous year, figures that are at variance with the trend in the right-wing world of

Figure 6.7 Issues in Zaitokukai *protest events*

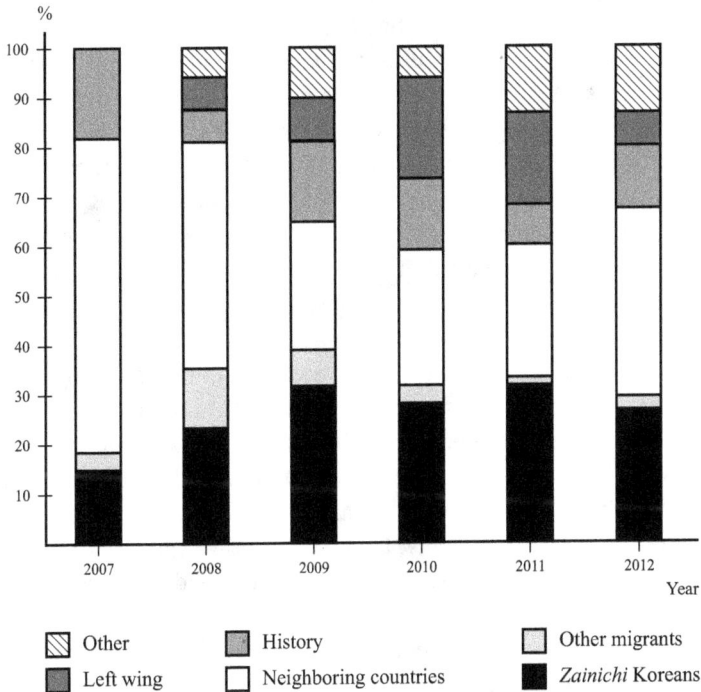

criticism. In 2010, however, there was an increase in anti-Democratic Party government events, making up as much as 20 per cent of the proportion of protest events. In 2011, this proportion maintained its high level with the addition of events harassing anti-nuclear protests, but in 2012, it fell as low as 7 per cent. With the exception of opposing anti-nuclear causes, this is consistent with the trend in the right-wing world of criticism.

Looked at it in this way, the quantitative changes are, on the whole, quite similar but if we delve into matters of substance, as we did with the history-related events, then we also find that there are areas where there is only the outward appearance of consistency. Nonetheless, offensives against South Korea, North Korea and China and 'the left' can be viewed as having shown a considerable degree of faithful response to discursive opportunities. The reason why *Zaitokukai* carries out numerous other protest events, aside from those centred on 'special privileges for *Zainichi* Koreans' is in part because the latter alone will not lead to an expansion of their power.

The nativist movement carried out a large number of events aside from those of an 'anti-foreigner' nature as a result of making use of the discursive opportunities that were opening up with regard to 'South Korea, North Korea and China', 'history' and 'anti-left wing' areas. Rather than seeing the nativist movement in terms of an illogical venting of anger without any clear purpose, it would, therefore, be more consistent with reality to see it as opportunistic protagonists reacting to discursive opportunities.

And yet two important points remain to be explained: the strength of the movement's hatred of South Korea and its persistent focus on 'migrant problems'. These stances are not directly influenced by discursive opportunities. Let us reconsider Figure 6.3. It was China that had an overwhelming presence in the right-wing world of criticism in the 2000s, with North Korea also assuming the role of villain some years because of the abduction issue. South Korea's frequency of appearance was no more than one third that of China and two thirds that of North Korea. However, *Zaitokukai* saw South Korea as its foremost enemy; the results of a web poll conducted by *Zaitokukai* were that of the 5,272 people who voted 78 per cent (4,123 people) said 'the country that I hate the most' is South Korea.[17] The scores for China, 12 per cent (652 people), and North Korea, 4 per cent (246 people), highlight this conspicuous 'hatred of South Korea'. If *Zaitokukai* were making use of the discursive opportunities of the right-wing world of criticism, then we should expect activities based on a hatred of China to be more likely to occur, but what has arisen in reality is a movement of hatred towards South Korea.

It is differences in the relative importance of historical problems specific to each country that provide a hint as to why this is so. Since the 1980s, there have always been historical problems concerning China, such as the Nanjing Massacre and history textbooks issues. In the case of South Korea, historical problems did not begin to influence bilateral relations until 1991, when former 'comfort women' came forward after the democratization of the country. The post-war reparations issue has not erupted anew between China and Japan, but the 'comfort women' issue continues to be one of the biggest unresolved diplomatic problems between South Korea and Japan. Similarly, in contrast to the broad uptake of stories about politics, economics and military affairs concerning China, after the 1990s the dominant trend regarding stories about South Korea was to

Figure 6.8 The relative importance of historical issues concerning South Korea and China

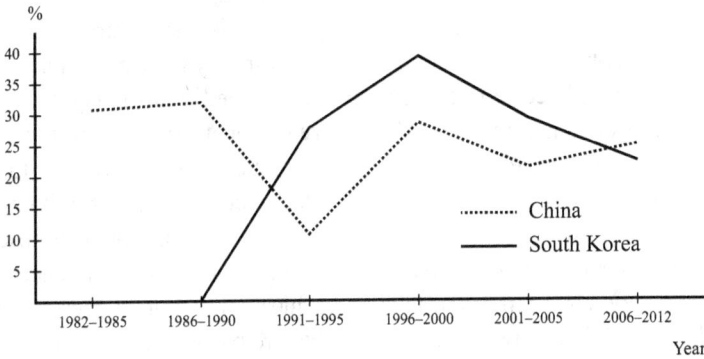

feature those with a historical bias. From 1991 until 2005 South Korea exceeded China by almost ten percentage points in terms of the proportion of historical issues discussed in relation to the country (see Figure 6.8).[18] This shows that whilst the biggest enemy for the right-wing world of criticism is China, with whom there is an all out confrontation including in military matters, South Korea is its enemy primarily with regard to the understanding of history. This is the common ground between the right-wing world of criticism and the nativist movement, and the origin of the nativist movement is to be found in historical revisionism's focus on Korea.

However, we are still not able to explain how the changing interests of the right-wing world of criticism are related to 'special privileges for *Zainichi* Koreans'. While Figure 6.7 shows the large proportion of *Zaitokukai* interest occupied by the 'foreigner problem', Figure 6.6 records the negligible interest of the right-wing world of criticism in this issue. Practically the only point of agreement between the right-wing world of criticism and the nativist movement is in the 2010 moves to oppose voting rights for foreign residents. In short, the movement's interest in foreigners cannot be explained by the changed concerns of the right-wing world of criticism. Might it be correct, then, to regard this part of the movement as consisting of the illogical elements that the existing right wing and journalism call 'venting one's anger' and 'bullying the weak'? In the interests of an integrated explanation, we now need to turn our attention to the area of subcultures.

Internet culture and the nativist movement

The tone of arguments on the internet could also be said to be a type of discursive opportunity in the sense that it is a structural element that individual social movements cannot directly control themselves. In the second section of this chapter, I argued that the right-wing world of criticism provides discursive opportunities that influence subcultures. At the same time, however, subcultures have a certain autonomous character. As we saw in the preceding chapter, it is easy for the nativist movement to be influenced by discursive opportunities on the internet because of the movement's high level of dependence on persuasion via the internet. This raises questions about the presence or absence of discursive opportunities that are particular to the internet and have little to do with the right-wing world of criticism; if we can answer these questions, we will be closer to an explanation of the exclusion of foreigners.

The differences between the internet and the right-wing world of criticism can be easily understood by looking at the terms 'hatred of Korea' and 'special privileges for *Zainichi* Koreans'. In the data for the right-wing world of criticism, the term 'hatred of Korea' is only used twice, in 1996 and 2005, and 'special privileges for *Zainichi* Koreans' does not make a single appearance. These terms do not exist in the lexicon of magazines from the right-wing world of criticism; the internet is where they have been constructed and where they circulate.[19] It was the comic, *Manga kenkanryū* (Hatred of Korea-style manga) (Yamano 2005, 2006a, 2007, 2009) that popularized these terms; the second volume contains a chapter with the title 'Special Privileges for *Zainichi* Koreans'. However, the right-wing world of criticism has basically ignored *Manga kenkanryū*, whose four volumes have sold close to one million copies, and also its author Sharin Yamano (Ōtsuki 2005). Although there is a marked difference in their levels of popularity, there is a certain contrast with the prominence accorded to *Gōmanizumu sengen*, a comic that popularized historical revisionism, and its author Yoshinori Kobayashi. The 'special privileges for *Zainichi* Koreans' discourse does not, of course, circulate in newspapers or indeed in magazines from the right-wing world of criticism; it has been propagated within the confines of the internet, *manga* and mooks.[20]

Sharin Yamano, the author of *Manga kenkanryū*, had been a browser of Channel 2 before he started his thread about South Korea,

North Korea and China. Yamano (2006b: 9) says that 'surveys are practically all on printed paper', but we can regard the internet – such as the Channel 2 bulletin board – as the source of his ideas and topics. Yamano recounts that he finished writing the *manga* in 2002, but because no publishers would take his work at the time he opened it up to the public on the internet. A short while later, September 2003, Makoto Sakurai, founder of *Zaitokukai*, also set up his own site.[21] We can think of the discourse of hatred of Korea, which was used with abandon in places like internet bulletin boards in this period, as having been systematized on individual sites. In fact, Sakurai (2006: 236) says that he built his site by 'collecting posted bulletin board comments'.

Behind the 2001–2002 cyber proliferation of a discourse of hatred of Korea lies easier access to information about South Korea on the internet. In this period, leading Korean newspapers opened online sites with Japanese editions and portal sites started to offer automatic translations between Japanese and Korean (Kimura 2007: 216). Sakurai (2006: 236) also says, 'my first opportunity to have a discussion with South Koreans was on the bulletin board for the translation of *Chūō nippō*' (A Korean newspaper).

Murakami's (2007) analysis of the song *Kankoku no Tsushima* (Korea's Tsushima Island) is highly instructive regarding the mechanisms for and traits of the spread of information on the internet in this period. This song first became known on the internet in October 2001; in August 2002, an article translating the song was circulated; and in November 2004, it had turned into a menacing argument about a Korean 'plan for the takeover of Tsushima'. The initial intention of this song was not to say that Tsushima is Korean territory, but to declare that Dokdo Island (Takeshima) is Korean territory. Because the information about this on the Japanese internet was spread with total disregard for context, it was turned into a menacing argument that 'Korea has its sights on Tsushima'. 'Special privileges for *Zainichi* Koreans' can also be thought of as having been born of an accumulation of similar distortions.

Manga kenkanryū was published by appropriating these internet discourses. Despite showing an unanticipated level of sales, this was a discourse that remained confined within the subculture. In this sense, the nativist movement, as epitomized by *Zaitokukai*, was confined to a subculture.[22] This shows that there are limits to the spread of a discourse on cyber space. Even so, *Manga kenkanryū* sold close to a million copies, attesting to the relative autonomy of subcultures.

A further trait of 'hatred of Korea' and 'special privileges for *Zainichi* Koreans' is that they are not confined to internet discourse but have come to have a sustained influence in the real world. Most researchers have pointed out that internet discourse has tended to appear in the real world as short-lived pranks. Maeda (2004) says that these incidents occur by rapid switching and alternation between facts and tales. However, 'special privileges for *Zainichi* Koreans' did not go on to disappear as an internet-based tale; it generated the solid 'fact' called *Zaitokukai* that we have been looking at in this book.

At this point, I would like to recall the activists' experiences discussed in the preceding chapter. In the course of following links on the internet, they ended up at 'special privileges for *Zainichi* Koreans', which had not been their initial search interest. On the internet, there is practically no distinction between 'history' and 'special privileges for *Zainichi* Koreans'. In this sense, the credibility of 'special privileges for *Zainichi* Koreans,' which was originally a mere tale, is secured by acceptance of the adjacent items of hostility towards South Korea, North Korea and China and also of historical revisionism. As a consequence, 'special privileges for *Zainichi* Koreans' has ended up being accepted not as fiction but as a real fact, leading to a real world movement. The difference between historical revisionism and 'special privileges for *Zainichi* Koreans' is not substantive; the latter is in circulation nowhere else but within a subculture, while the former has proliferated in every discursive field.

Unwanted child of the right-wing world of criticism

Arguments that see extreme left terrorism in Italy as having been born unexpectedly of the left are criticized by della Porta and Tarrow (1986) who say that this was, in fact, the logical consequence of the protest cycle. Japan's nativist movement is treated as an 'unwanted child' because it was transformed via the mediation of the internet. It was, however, the changes undergone by discursive opportunities in the 2000s that gave rise to the nativist movement.

In short, most of the factors leading to nativism were already in place when discursive opportunities opened up in the right-wing world of criticism. Merely adding another factor, technological change on the internet, was enough to produce nativist discourse.

Both of these factors, which were complete in the second half of the 2000s, can be used to explain the advent of the nativist movement. Similarly, as the protest events of the nativist movement suggest, they have responded to discursive opportunities to a considerable degree; it seems difficult to deny links between right-wing politics and the movement. In this sense, it is quite accurate for the nativist movement to acknowledge itself as 'conservative'. The eccentricity of the nativist movement needs to be analyzed in connection with changes in the appearance of 'conservatism'.

In this chapter, we have hypothesized relations of influence along the lines of right wing-world of criticism → (internet) → nativist movement. However, phenomena also emerge that are not confined to a causal relationship in which discourse 'deteriorates' as a result of this kind of one-way traffic. The arguments mentioned above of a 'Tsushima is at peril' kind were false rumors that originated on the internet, but they also ended up being discussed in major right-wing magazines. Even the visits to Tsushima by Korean tourists from Busan, across the Strait, are distorted into links in the chain of Korean designs for taking control of Tsushima (Yamamoto 2010). The argument that voting rights for foreign residents threaten Japan's isolated islands is also a false rumor that originated on the internet.

As we saw in the Prologue, these false rumors are being regurgitated by conservative politics in the form of questions in the Diet. If we take a long-term view, what we are seeing are discourse flows from the nativist movement into the right-wing world of criticism. Why do they believe these sorts of false rumors? In the following chapter, I will use the example of voting rights for foreign residents to make clear the main causes that are at work in the background to this state of affairs.

7 Will Votes for Foreign Residents Destroy Japan? Securitization of the Issue

Voting rights for foreign residents: a Japanese problem

Voting rights for foreign residents is a clear-cut term that arouses no academic debate. Politically, however, this is not the case; when I interviewed a certain Democratic Party Diet member, I was told that he would prefer that I did not use this term as it invites misunderstanding.[1] During another interview, a Democratic Party leader automatically corrected my use of 'voting rights for foreign residents' saying, 'Oh, the issue of *municipal* voting rights'.[2] He explained that this term was preferable because 'voting rights' might be understood to also include the right to vote at national elections, which would provoke opposition. The insistence on referring to municipal voting rights in no way changes the actual situation, but it does indicate that voting rights for foreign residents is a sensitive issue.

Voting rights for foreign residents is one of the most important issues for the nativist movement. Whilst I have argued that the nativist movement has taken advantage of changes in discursive opportunities, there are many issues, such as welfare payments for elderly *Zainichi* Koreans, which established right wingers ignore. When it comes to voting rights for foreign residents, however, there are marked similarities, both in terms of discourse and the actual movement, between established right wingers and the nativist movement. Voting rights for foreign residents has provoked strong opposition, based on spurious arguments, from the conservatives all the way through to the ultra-right.

We should recognize from the outset that this is actually a uniquely Japanese phenomenon. I am not arguing that political opposition to voting rights for foreign residents is not seen in other countries. In France, President François Mitterand publicly promised to grant voting rights to foreigners, but these never materialized because of opposition from the conservative and Communist parties (Moulier-Boutang 1985; Rath 1990). In Belgium, while voting rights for foreign residents had been on the political agenda since the 1970s, they only finally became a reality in 2004 after years of being thwarted (Earnest 2008: 113; Jacobs 1999; Jacobs and Swyngedouw 2002).[3] Japan stands out as the country with the strongest opposition to voting rights for foreign residents. In most countries, the government can easily enact laws to grant voting rights to foreign residents if legal barriers are resolved[4] (Hammar 1990). Japan is conspicuously unique in the sense that it is political opposition alone that is thwarting the realization of these rights.[5]

The difference between Japan and Western Europe stems in part from the fact that voting rights were not sought by the foreigners themselves but were initiatives advanced by European political elites as part of an integrated policy (Hammar 1990; Jacobs 1998). In short, they were pushed forward quietly in these countries, without either strong demands or strong opposition. In this sense, objective conditions are more favorable in Japan, where demands by *Zainichi* Koreans should make implementation rather easier.[6] However, the forces opposed to voting rights in Japan have become increasingly agitated over the years, and their arguments have also become more extreme. The theme of this and the subsequent chapter is to shed light on precisely what Japanese nativism is by focussing on its distinctive features. In this chapter, Campbell's (1998) method will provide the basis for attempting to achieve this goal. That is to say, my focus will be on outlining how the specific results that we see in Japan have been brought about by the particularly Japanese problematization of voting rights for foreign residents, rather than on the origins and causes of the issue. I will attempt to achieve this by analyzing the evolution of the issue using the concepts of denizenship and securitization.

Securitization of denizenship in the Japanese context

Japanese characteristics of voting rights arguments

Denizenship in Western Europe

Voting rights for foreign residents have become part of a new citizenship in which nationality and citizenship are separated.

Brubaker (1989) and Hammar (1990) provide the starting point in arguing for the political rights of foreigners. Behind these arguments lie increasing numbers of permanent settlers in Western Europe, who should be granted rights according to their periods of residence and living conditions.

Hammar, who added the term denizen to the existing dichotomy of foreigner and citizen in migration research, says the following about denizenship. '[Denizens] may have lived such a long period in the host country (15–20 years or more), their family ties may be so strong (parents or children are citizens) or they may hold such an honored position (as scientists, artists or sportsmen etc.) that they in fact constitute a new category of foreign citizens whose residence status is fully guaranteed or almost so' (Hammar 1990: 13).

Hammar uses the three-gate model in Figure 7.1 to explain where denizens are located: they sit between foreigners staying temporarily, who have passed through Gate 1, and citizens who hold citizenship in the country of residence, having passed through Gate 3. Each gate serves as a basis for dividing people into categories according to immigration controls and visa status.

As migrant workers in Western Europe began staying for longer periods and exhibiting low rates of naturalization, the previously very low number of denizens began to grow (Hammar 1990: 19). Hammar stresses that the increase in the number of denizens has led to rising numbers of residents who are unable to participate in democracy (with no right to vote), a situation which cannot be resolved merely by expanding naturalization (Hammar 1990: 24–5).[7] In countries with Nationality Acts founded upon *jus soli*, voting rights for foreign residents are not seen as important because the second generation will automatically become citizens. However, promoting both the acquisition of citizenship and the granting of voting rights is regarded as being conducive to political integration because there are increasing numbers of denizens as well as second generation migrants.[8] The political elites see the political integration of foreigners as more desirable than leaving them in a state of limbo because integration is linked to social stability.[9]

The main factors promoting voting rights for foreign residents in Japan
The notion of denizenship has been imported into the Japanese arguments about voting rights for foreign residents. In fact, without the introduction of voting rights for foreign residents in European

Figure 7.1 The three entrance gates

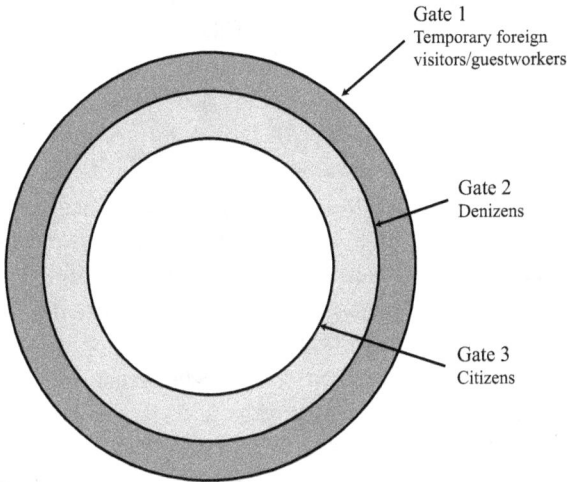

Gate 1
Temporary foreign
visitors/guestworkers

Gate 2
Denizens

Gate 3
Citizens

Source: Hammar (1990: 17).

countries, it would have been impossible for *Zainichi* Koreans to launch their movement for suffrage. Opponents stress that only a limited number of countries grant these rights to foreign residents. However, it should be noted that denizenship arguments deal with the political integration of migrants, which encompasses both voting rights and nationality laws. The political integration of migrants in Japan has been hindered by a *jus sanguinis*-based Japan Nationality Act combined with a lack of voting rights for foreign residents. The adoption of *jus soli* as the basis of the act would eliminate the present situation in which second generation *Zainichi* Koreans have no right to vote. Both the problem and the distinctiveness of the Japanese case are to be found in the fact that *Zainichi* Koreans have been excluded from democratic decision making for five generations.

On the other hand, there are many aspects of the politics surrounding voting rights for foreign residents in Japan that cannot be explained by denizenship arguments. Denizenship arguments have attempted to enhance the political integration of the migrants who came into Western Europe following the Second World War, but this is far from the main concern in the politics surrounding voting rights for foreign residents in Japan. Denizenship-based arguments began as an initiative of the Shimane Branch of the New Party Sakigake in

1994,[10] and were later also taken up by the DPJ. Thus far, the issue of migrants being unable to exercise political rights for long periods of time has been presented in terms of the principle of denizenship, but these arguments have not been able to exert any influence on the political process.

Up until the end of World War II, Japan's former colonial citizens had been able to vote at national elections, and it was the act of removing their voting rights that roused the political process to action.[11] *Zainichi* Koreans, the largest group of former colonial citizens, were the main focus of attempts to gain voting rights for foreign residents, and Japanese supporters also came to think of them as the main beneficiaries of this right. Inside the political process, securitization led to the exclusion of North Korean nationals becoming established procedure; there still remains a deep-seated view that *Zainichi* Koreans should be treated differently from other foreigners. It is the logic of the colonial settlement – that is, restoring rights that have been lost by 'past nationals' (Higuchi 2001a) – that bestirs politics.[12] We have ended up with an unproblematized status quo in which people who – whilst having been born in Japan – are not able to exercise the right to vote; in other words, an ongoing state of affairs in which some people are excluded from democracy.

Japan's 'migration and securitization' aspect

Securitization of migration

The words 'migration and security', like 'law and order' and 'peace and stability', have often been used together as a combination of kindred terms (Waters 2010: 217). This has led to migrants tending to be seen as a threat to security, particularly since the end of the Cold War. During the Cold War period, security was an issue concerned with threats, in the form of wars or their causes, emanating from outside the state, and the state existed to protect its people from hostile nations (Ibrahim 2005: 168). Security studies in the post-Cold War period have changed substantially in this regard (Krause and Williams 1997). Following the disappearance of the East–West conflict framework, the lack of agreement on how security is to be defined became a major topic in security studies (Terriff et al. 1999: 1).

On the one hand, there were moves to reconsider the very concept of security. Of particular relevance to this chapter are critical security studies that are based on the recognition that the security concept is unsophisticated and still developing (Buzan 1991: 3–12). In this approach, security is treated as 'a practice of making insecurities' (Huysmans 2011: 2).[13] In traditional security studies, insecurity was thought of as something objective that was determined by a balance of national power and military affairs and the degree of hostility. However, critical security studies do not regard insecurity as a set of objectively determined given conditions but rather as being produced deliberately through speech acts which state that something is insecure.[14]

In reality, it is not uncommon foreign policy practice to call something insecure and exclude it, even when the basis for saying this is weak (Campbell 1992; Hansen 2006). At the time of the Second Iraq War, declaring that Iraq's weapons of mass destruction – which ultimately did not exist – were dangerous, the United States plunged into war. Security action was decided not on the basis of the presence or absence of weapons of mass destruction but of whether or not the United States called Iraq dangerous. I will also take the critical security studies stance of not treating insecurity as a given, and will use the concept of securitization in its analysis. Securitization is 'a more extreme version of politicization' that is 'presented as an existential threat, requiring emergency measures and justifying actions outside the normal bounds of political procedure' (Buzan, Wæver and de Wilde 1998: 23–4). The task of this chapter is to adapt the concept of securitization to voting rights for foreign residents in order to examine 'how security problems emerge, evolve and dissolve' (Balzacq 2010: 56).[15]

Meanwhile, we are witnessing the expansion of the concept of security to include food, human, environmental and economic security. Military threats continue to exist, as in the past, but it is new threats to security that are important in the post-Cold War period; these are not produced on the state level but within society or one segment of society (Wæver et al. 1993: 2; McSweeney 1996: 85). One of the post-Cold War concerns is migrants, and discussion of the securitization of the migration issue is already underway (Bigo 2001, 2005; Ceyhan and Tsoukala, 2002; Huysman 1995, 2006; Quassoli 2001, 2004; Robinson 1998; Tsoukala 2005; Waters 2010).[16] The securitization of migration, which was accelerated by the events of 11 September, 2001 has developed as a result of (discourses about) increasing stresses following the demise of the Cold War, which have been caused by influxes of people from Eastern to Western Europe and from the south to the north.

It is individual migrants who are the targets of the securitization of migration; they are seen as creating insecurity domestically, rather than outside the country (Terriff et al. 1999: 160). Because migrants and refugees have a transnational character, which is beyond that of sovereign states, it becomes difficult for these states to exercise effective control, and migrants and refugees are thus seen as security threats. Since they are also regarded as being terrorists, spies and fifth columnists, consideration is even given to military responses in preparation for a state of emergency (Hettne and Abiri 1998: 190). The results produced by this are the tightening of border controls where migrants enter and the tendency to make resident migrants the objects of security measures.

Securitization, in the form of increasingly rigid border controls, is typified by the construction of 'walls around the West' (Andreas and Snyder 2000) while promoting regional integration. This includes building a physical wall on the United States–Mexico border (Andreas 2000; Andreas and Biersteker 2003) and tighter border controls in the European Union (Lavenex and Uçaper 2002; Léonard 2010; McMurray 2001). However, because this sort of securitization is often the result of the symbolic politics of being seen to be dealing with insecurity, it is not always effective; for example, as in the case of the tightening of border controls in the United States (Andreas 2000). A series of tightening of controls is also producing unintended consequences such as a lengthening of the period of stay by irregular migrants and an increase in deaths during border crossings (Massey, Durand and Malone 2002).

The advance of the form of securitization which makes resident migrants the objects of security measures occurs in areas where migrants live in large concentrations, as France's urban riots clearly show.[17] In neighborhoods with large concentrations of migrants, crime and terrorism are the chief contexts in which migrants are discussed, and this makes it easier to justify taking extraordinary political measures. Following urban riots, France even leapt to extreme arguments about revoking citizenship. The issue here is not whether migrant crime is really a threat or not. The problem is using the view that the crimes of migrants are a threat as the basis for promoting securitization and then taking extraordinary measures based on race and ethnicity; this is a subject that demands critical analysis.

Securitization of migration in Japan

The securitization of migration began in Japan in the 1990s. Although, *Zainichi* Koreans, chiefly *Sōren*, had constantly been under surveillance by the security police even before then, the criminal police had not regarded them as a problem. The rates of *Zainichi* Korean crime appear to have been low in absolute terms and, considering the severe employment discrimination that has underpinned their socioeconomic conditions they have been connected with surprisingly few cases of crime. This is what led to Kawai's assessment that 'it is not possible to talk about the causes of the low crime rates in Japan without mentioning that few crimes are committed by people referred to as *Zainichi* South and North Koreans' (Kawai 2004: 12).[18] As touched on in the Prologue, Muslims living in Japan eventually came under surveillance by the security police, but the securitization of migration in Japan has primarily been the jurisdiction of the criminal police.[19]

Securitization in this period applied not to crimes by *Zainichi* Koreans but to newcomer foreigners (*rainichi gaikokujin* in police parlance) (*Gaikokujin Sabetsu* Watch Network 2004, 2008).[20] In Japan at the end of the 1980s, serious arguments were unfolding concerning the acceptance of 'foreign workers', and foreigners were seen as 'workers'. By the latter half of the 1990s, the framing of the notion of 'foreigner crimes' had begun, and foreigners had come to be treated as 'criminals' (Takaya 2007). It could actually be argued that the securitization of crime by foreigners has been 'successful' in Japan where the results of polls show a conspicuously high rate of anxiety about foreigner crimes (Simon and Sikich 2007).

In contrast to Europe and North America, where dropping out and delinquency amongst migrant youth are recognized problems, in Japan, crimes committed by resident migrants are not even major social problems. This is because visa overstayers, rather than resident migrants, have been linked to crime in Japan, but we ought to qualify this by acknowledging that, to date, this has never become an issue. Given that the rate of advancement to secondary and tertiary education is quite low for newcomer youth, there is a high likelihood that they will become part of the poorest segment of the population. We cannot say that 'deviant behavior, crime and delinquency on the part of foreign youths living in Japan, who have failed to adapt to Japanese culture' will not be securitized in the future (Ayukawa 2001: 175). Furthermore, Japan has not seen the advent of the kind of securitization of border zones that has occurred in Europe and North America. There has been an increase in the number of immigration inspectors, but this is the result of increases in the numbers of people entering and leaving the country and also of resident foreigners; the increase cannot be said to be related to securitization. Government documents use the words 'illegal entry' and 'smuggling', but do not discuss them using the language of securitization.

Does this mean that it is meaningless to pose the problem of the 'securitization of border zones with reference to migration' in the case of Japan? It is true that the (irregular) influx of newcomer foreigners has not brought about the securitization of border zones in Japan; however, the issue of voting rights for foreign residents has promoted securitization. That is to say, securitization has again increased as *'Zainichi* Koreans' – who had not until that point been the target – have been merged with 'border zones' via baseless rumors. The acceptance of these rumors typifies what is characteristic about Japanese securitization.

Problematization of voting rights in Japan

Before the 1995 Supreme Court decision

Let us address the question of why it is only in Japan that voting rights for foreign residents have become a sensitive issue.[21] As Figure 7.2 shows, the three years 1995, 2000 and 2010 are the periods in which voting rights for foreign residents gained attention.[22] The 1995 peak was due to the handing down of the Supreme Court ruling on the trial cases seeking voting rights for foreign residents. The lawsuits were all rejected, but the Supreme Court judgement ruled that in the case of permanent residents, 'taking measures to grant voting rights should be interpreted as not violating the Constitution'.

Demands for voting rights started twenty years before the issue first peaked in 1975, when a Korean clergyman sent an open letter of enquiry to his local mayor and the prefectural governor. This was an individual act but, shortly after, voting rights also became a topic

Figure 7.2 Articles in leading national newspapers about voting rights for foreign residents

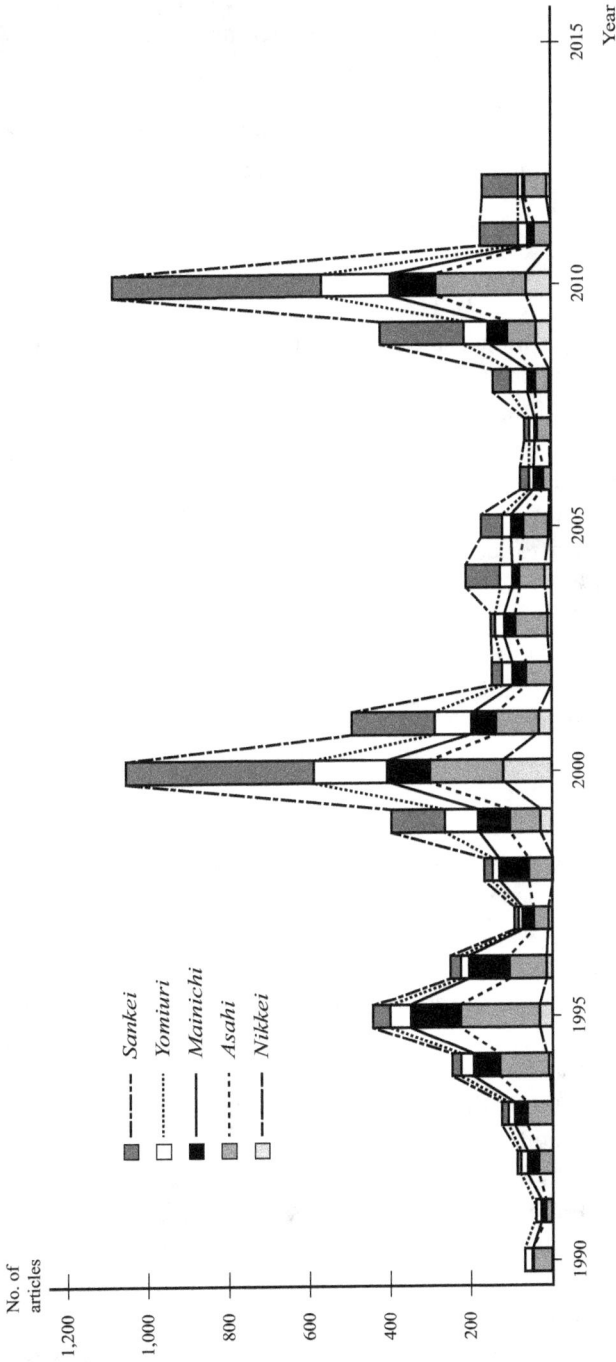

Note: This shows the number of cases that resulted in a hit using both foreigners and voting rights when retrieving articles on *Nikkei*'s teleconverter.

for discussion at a colloquium attended by *Mindan* and a caucus of Japanese and South Korean Diet members (*Zainihon Daikan Minkoku Kyoryū Mindan Chūō Honbu* 1982). The first organized moves to make concrete demands for voting rights for foreign residents first appeared in the second half of the 1980s. *Mintōren* (*Minzoku sabetsu to tatakau renraku kyōgikai* (Coordinated Action for Fighting against Racial Discrimination)), which was leading the citizens' movement by *Zainichi* Koreans, took up voting rights for foreign residents as one of its main topics in 1985 (*Minzoku sabetsu to tatakau renraku kyōgikai* 1985). In 1986, *Mindan* also publicly resolved to promote the movement for the acquisition of voting rights. These movements were partly triggered by the commencement, in 1985, of discussions about the problems of the legal status of third generation *Zainichi* Koreans. At that time, unresolved issues, including that of subjecting foreigners to fingerprinting, readily became topics of discussion. As the *Mintōren* plan for 'special permanent residents to possess local voting rights' (*Minzoku sabetsu to tatakau renkaku kyōgikai* 1989: 106) shows, at this time, voting rights were perceived as a *Zainichi* Korean issue.

Another issue, in addition to voting rights, that has greatly affected the status of *Zainichi* Koreans is Japan–Korea relations (Kang and Kim 1989; Kim 1995; Yi, Kimiya and Asano 2011). *Mindan* has managed to get topics listed for discussion as part of Japan–Korea diplomacy by conveying its requests to the South Korean government; that is, *Mindan* has managed to rouse the Japanese government to action via South Korea. Even in the case of matters that *Mindan* cannot influence by acting alone it has achieved some measure of success by using a boomerang effect whereby it has these matters reflected in South Korean government demands and then conveyed to the Japanese government in that form (Keck and Sikkink 1998). Voting rights for foreign residents is an issue that has been handled in this way; it was included as one of the demands in the nine items put forward by the South Korean government during negotiations concerning the legal status of *Zainichi* Koreans. Demands from South Korea follow a direct route to the Diet and the Ministry of Foreign Affairs by becoming topics for discussion in the Japan–Korea Diet caucus and also subjects for negotiation at summit meetings between the leaders of Japan and South Korea. Although the Japanese government rejected voting rights for foreign residents, a sentence was appended to the agreement exchanged between the two governments in 1991 stating that 'a request has been expressed by the government of South Korea regarding voting rights at local elections'. [23]

This negotiation process was also reported in the newspapers, but the focus of the media at the time was residence status and the abolition of fingerprinting. It was a legal struggle in the courts unconnected with diplomacy that made the existence of the voting rights for foreign residents issue widely known. Moreover, it was not a *Zainichi* Korean who took the initiative but a British person living in Osaka. In November 1989, he brought a lawsuit as a protest at not having been able to vote at the House of Councillors election. In the wake of this, *Zainichi* Koreans launched four legal battles, in rapid succession, in the courts from 1990 until 2000.[24] The most significant result was the February 1995 Supreme Court ruling.

The handing down of this decision also made it possible for Diet members to view the enacting of legislation as a realistic prospect.[25] The view that voting rights for foreign residents was not unconstitutional also became mainstream amongst scholars as they took advantage of the court's opinion (Hirota 2000; Nagao 2000). This period was characterized by the weakness of opposing arguments, as we see even in an editorial (March 2, 1995) of the conservative *Yomiuri* Newspaper, 'a groundbreaking decision that also opens the way for permanent resident foreigners to participate in local elections'. The ultra-right *Sankei* Newspaper also published a considerable number of opinions in favor of the court's decision in reader contributions and in its general reporting, even though its official editorial policy took a stand opposed to voting rights for foreign residents. The overall proportion occupied by *Yomiuri* and *Sankei* articles in this year was strikingly low, compared with the situation in the second and third peaks (see Figure 7.2 above).[26] They were not only not strongly opposed but not particularly interested either suggesting that, at the time of the Supreme Court decision, the right wing did not view voting rights for foreign residents as a threat.[27]

The first round of securitization: from the end of the 1990s until 2000

The peak in 2000 (Figure 7.2) began at the time of coalition government negotiations between the LDP, the Liberal Party (*Jiyūtō*) and the Clean Government Party (*Kōmeitō*). At these negotiations, it was a *Kōmeitō* idea to include legislating for voting rights for foreign residents as an item of agreement.[28] Following the earlier tentative decision on constitutional interpretation, the question shifted from one of the administration of justice to one of lawmaking[29], and in 1998 a Democratic Party/*Kōmeitō* bill and a Communist Party bill were submitted. There is a strong element of all this having been made possible by what has been called the high point in post-war Japan–Korea relations and the encouragement of President Dae-jung Kim (Chung 2010). According to *Mindan*, it cannot be said that Dae-jung Kim made particularly earnest efforts regarding voting rights for foreign residents, but when he visited Japan in November 1999, he unexpectedly used some of his time during the summit meeting with Prime Minister Keizō Obuchi and his speech to the Diet to refer to voting rights.[30] In preparation for this visit to Japan, the Democratic Party and *Kōmeitō* submitted a voting rights bill, and Obuchi also promised to proactively look into the matter when he visited South Korea.

The year 2000 was a peak year because the LDP was prevailed on to vote, on the pretext of the coalition agreement, and the focus of attention was on points of feasibility. At this time, the LDP argued 'from the standpoint of constitutionality, considering all other opinions to be abstractions', and released the opinion of the Election Systems Research Council that voting rights for foreign residents had a high likelihood of being unconstitutional.[31] Voices of opposition also began to grow within the LDP, making the prospect of a vote embarrassing. In the newspapers, the *Yomiuri* and *Sankei*, keeping pace with right-wing politicians, now became considerably more stridently opposed to voting rights for foreign residents in their reporting than the *Asahi* and *Mainichi*. At this time, however, there was not a conspicuous level of debate about this outside the parliament; the supporting faction had continued to express the same views since the 1990s, while the views of the opposing forces were now also being taken up to some extent by the right-wing world of criticism (Nakagawa 1996; Sakurai 2000; Takaichi and Momochi 2000; Takubo 2001; Yagi 1999).

Nevertheless, the appearance of a visibly influential force opposed to voting rights for foreign residents marked this time as different from the situation in the mid-1990s. Following the handing down of the 1998 bills, the Japan Conference (*Nippon Kaigi*) held a 'Meeting of Citizens Seeking to Rouse Diet Members to Protect Japan' with the aim of opposing voting rights in May 1999, but only several ultra-right Diet members attended.[32] It could be said that the sense of danger on the part of the opposing forces was relatively weak at this time. Sensing this, the Liberal Party and *Kōmeitō*, who were in the ruling coalition, submitted a bill for voting rights for foreign residents in January 2000, but the situation changed completely once the LDP began coordinating opinion internally. At this time, the establishment of voting rights for foreign residents was included as part of the articles of agreement for an LDP, Liberal Party and *Kōmeitō* alliance. The LDP voiced its disapproval but the Liberal Party aligned itself with the *Kōmeitō*, and an agreement was reached. Following the coalition agreement, the 'Group of Diet Members Demanding the Careful Handling of Voting Rights for Foreign Residents' was established in the LDP and this considerably bolstered the opposing faction.

This was a group of sympathetic Diet members but the substantive base for the opposing forces was Japan Conference. Japan Conference was established following the 1997 amalgamation of the 'National Conference for the Protection of Japan', whose principal aim was the legalizing of era names, and the 'Group for the Protection of Japan', a group of the religious right wing. If National Conference for the Protection of Japan had been the group that had broadly controlled the right wing, Japan Conference had enhanced its traditional character through the inclusion of the religious right – for example, the Association of Shinto Shrines. The fact that Japan Conference shouldered the task of being the initial voice of opposition meant that opposing arguments were predominantly based on conservatism (traditionalism). Actually, the following logic was how the 'Resolution Regarding the Bill to Grant Municipal Voting Rights to Foreigners' (13 October, 2000), which was adopted by the General Meeting of the Discussion Group of Japan Conference Diet Members, unfolded:[33]

- The Bill to Bestow Municipal Voting Rights on Foreigners is unconstitutional.
- There should first be efforts to relax the conditions for acquiring citizenship.
- Given the existence of opposing views in all parties, there should not be a hasty initiation of parliamentary debate.
- There ought first to be a unity of purpose between people from the Korean Peninsula.[34]

Because the basis of these arguments is simply conservatism, they alone do not enable us to say that there was a securitization of voting rights for foreign residents. It was precisely at this point, however, that securitization did begin, and it was initiated by those promoting voting rights. The bill submitted by the Liberal Party and *Kōmeitō* in 2000 overtook the 1998 Democratic Party/*Kōmeito* bill, but it diverged substantially from the proposals in the earlier version in that it called for North Korean nationals to be excluded. This was because Ichirō Ozawa, then leader of the Liberal Party, voiced his dissatisfaction with the bill saying that it would not pass if it included North Korean nationals.[35]

Ozawa, himself, may have sought the exclusion of North Koreans in order to soften the resistance of the opposing forces, but there can be no doubt that this was in blatant contravention of equality under the law. This is because while making special permanent resident or permanent resident visa status a prerequisite, a clause was added excluding only North Korean nationals who otherwise met all of the conditions. Fuyushiba, who submitted the bill, was forced to express himself in the following awkward manner, 'we have refrained from naming any particular country, the sorting was on the limited basis of people who have their nationality recorded in the nationality columns of their alien registration certificates' (in which North Korean nationals are specified just as 'Korean' instead of North Korean).[36] The primary direct cause of exclusion had been the 1998 missile launch by North Korea; using security as the reason, measures were taken that distorted the law.

Although there was opposition to this from citizens' groups, the mass media was effectively silent. At this time, the official editorials of the *Asahi* and *Mainichi*, which had earlier declared their support for voting rights, merely introduced the developments to readers; 'foreigners who have permanent residence and whose nationality is recorded as 'North Korean' are not covered'[37] and 'people with 'North Korean' nationality are actually excluded from consideration'.[38] There was absolutely no critique as to what this meant or how it ought to be evaluated. Since *Sōren* had declared its opposition to the bill on voting rights for foreign residents, it put up no resistance even though North Koreans were to be excluded from voting rights.[39] Under cover of *Sōren*'s stance, even the media that was in favor of voting rights also accepted the exclusion of those with North Korean nationality thus effectively leaving unquestioned the rights and wrongs of restricting the rights of foreign residents in the name of 'national defense'. The *Asahi* and

Mainichi opposed excluding permanent residents and only granting voting rights to special permanent residents as a means of getting the opposing faction to consider the bill because they felt that this would strengthen the post-war compensation nature of the bill. The exclusion of North Korean nationals, which should have carried the same level of importance, was, however, accepted without even being discussed.

At this time, no information about actual examples of Koreans with North Korean nationality 'abusing' voting rights was produced. And yet, this was the beginning of the securitization of the issue of voting rights for foreign residents, and it was also the precedent for excluding North Korean schools from their subsidized status in 2010. It would have been logically consistent to have limited voting rights for foreign residents to special permanent residents – not as denizenship, but with the aim of restoring the rights of 'past nationals'. Denizenship can always be added later via the process of broadening the range of those to whom voting rights are to be granted. If, however, we simply accept the logic of securitization, we will end up with no restraints on the arbitrary use of emergency measures in the case of someone who is regarded as a security threat.

Full-scale securitization under Democratic Party government

Following the September 2009 change of government to the Democratic Party, the third peak in the voting rights for foreign residents issue was ushered in as a result of the will shown to conclude the Voting Rights for Foreign Residents Bill by Yukio Hatoyama, then Prime Minister, and Ichirō Ozawa, then Chief Secretary of the Democratic Party. The faction opposed to implementing voting rights for foreign residents argued that their implementation would be a contravention of campaign pledges because it had not been included in the party's manifesto. However, the following description, which can be found in the policy INDEX, shows that the Democratic Party did not suddenly produce the voting rights bill from nowhere. 'At the time of the inception of the Democratic Party, we adopted, as part of our 'Basic Policies', 'the early implementation of matters such as voting rights for foreign residents who are permanent residents', and we will continue to maintain this policy from now on'.[40]

As the timing of the demonstrations in relation to voting rights for foreign residents in this period happened to occur when a group of Democratic Party Diet members led by Ozawa visited Korea and China, they had a strong semblance of being one link in the chain of Asian diplomacy. For the right wing, voting rights for foreign residents, along with the practice of separate names for married couples and laws for the protection of human rights, became the 'three bad laws', but the last two remained internal cabinet issues. Voting rights for foreign residents had, by contrast, also begun to be discussed in the context of 'hatred of Korea' and 'hatred of China', and had turned into a reflection of hostility towards these neighboring countries rather than a human rights issue. The LDP went so far as to produce flyers that read 'We are resolutely opposed to voting rights for foreign residents!' for use as materials to criticize the Democratic Party. The opposing forces took a firm stand, organizing gatherings and using right-wing newspapers and journals, while the supporting faction was instead on the defensive.[41]

Furthermore, arguments about the risks of granting voting rights to Chinese residents in Japan grew alongside China's burgeoning economic influence in the 2000s as trends suggested that in the future China's power would surpass even that of the United States. In Japan, which has long been in a process of decline, it is not simply the different political systems in the two countries that underpins this reaction but also a sense of dread when Japan is compared with a big neighboring country, which (one realizes) cannot be called friendly. However, Chinese residents are not the protagonists in demands for voting rights for foreign residents; their connection has not extended any further than that of a newcomer organization assenting to the proposal. This is why there had been few arguments directly linking the China threat and the voting rights issue. But then the Hatoyama Cabinet put forward its plan for an East Asian Community, and this ended up being linked to voting rights for foreign residents. This connection was constructed by the forces opposed to voting rights for foreign residents, who began to weave a narrative of arguments against the granting of voting rights on the basis of the existence of the China threat.[42] 'Participation in the East Asian Community initiative would mean coming under the domination of China ... The bill to give voting rights to foreigners will signal the cancellation of the United States–Japan Security Treaty and mark the first step towards the East Asian Community' (Nagao 2010: 62).

The Democratic Party had not imagined a situation in which voting rights for foreign residents and Japan–China relations would be linked. Nagao's argument, above, is nothing but arrant nonsense; however, the expression of opposition to voting rights in terms of East Asia is noteworthy. Securitization of Japan's border zone began its rapid progress after a collision between a Chinese fishing boat and a Japan Coast Guard patrol boat off the Senkaku Islands in September 2010. The 'defense of national borders' and voting rights for foreign residents are unrelated matters, but they are being linked together: 'The issue of voting rights for foreign residents is currently shifting its emphasis from a human rights issue for foreigners to a security issue for Japan' (Nagao 2011: 180). Every dispute in East Asia augments the plausibility of arguments promoting the securitization of the issue of voting rights for foreign residents. The resolution of a meeting of Japan Conference Diet members in 2000 that was discussed in the preceding section barely referred to East Asia, but by 2010 Japan Conference's arguments for opposing voting rights for foreign residents contained abundant references to foreign relations, as seen in the following excerpt from one of their leaflets.[43]

- The granting of voting rights to foreigners contains issues of unconstitutionality.
- They raise fears of growing intervention in our country's education.
- They will be a major obstacle to the resolution of territorial disputes.
- The granting of voting rights to foreigners is not a world trend
- They aim to influence Japanese politics.
- The Chinese government will mobilize permanent resident Chinese politically.
- Isolated islands in the border areas are being targeted.
- At this rate, we will end up allowing indirect aggression.

We now face the problem that the securitization process has been escalated without any actual remonstrance against the harm that these preposterous arguments are doing to the national interest.[44] Having reached this point, the politics concerning voting rights for foreign residents have moved away from a domestic issue concerning the rights of foreigners to a dependent variable of securitization concerning Japan, South Korea, North Korea and China.[45] This results in foreigners, who are Japan's denizens, not being seen as

minorities living in Japan; instead, they are forcibly cast as agents
for each of the nations in East Asia. What the opponents to voting
rights for foreign residents saw was not denizens living as minorities
in Japan but the phantoms behind them from neighboring countries.
It is these people who have been victimized by the securitization of
voting rights for foreign residents, and they continue to be excluded
from elections more than twenty years after the question of their
voting rights was first posed.[46]

Desecuritizing voting rights for foreign residents

Voting rights for foreign residents – whether as rights for 'past
nationals' or as denizenship – have broadened into a system that is
based on a reality that transcends the citizens/foreigners dichotomy.
Most Japanese citizens support voting rights for permanent resident
foreigners (Matsutani et al. 2005; Higuchi and Maruyama 2006),
and perhaps we ought to make this our starting point. By ignoring
this reality and by insisting on a simple dichotomy, securitization
ends up robbing society of the power to overcome dichotomous
thinking (Waters 2010: 219). Right-wing politicians chorus
that security must be prioritized in order to confront the harsh
environment of East Asian international relations, and this leads to
the suppression of the social support, based on sensible decisions,
that exists for voting rights for foreign residents.

The securitization concept is useful in revealing that: (1) this
kind of dichotomy deviates from reality and (2) this kind of
thinking never provides a solution to problems, but only gives
rise to various new problems. From a behavioral science point of
view, it is improbable that foreigners who have been given voting
rights would engage in 'unique' behavior that leads to security
threats. Arguments linking voting rights for foreign residents and
security threats are based on mistaken premises and conjecture,
and they end up producing a solution that in fact causes a worsening
of the situation. In Europe and North America, the targets of
securitization are irregular migrants who cross borders and thus
border zones have been closed. As mentioned already, border
control measures are basically ineffective; the only result of this
wasted expense has been the creation of victims.

The distinctiveness of Japan's approach to 'security and
migration' has been its targeting of permanent resident foreigners

who are thought of as likely to move to border zones to assist in the 'invasion' of these areas. In short, opponents make a forced association between 'South Korea, North Korea and China', which lie outside Japan, with the 'foreigners' who are inside Japan. The word 'border' is used as a geographical metaphor to create a space that connects these disparate entities; and herein lies the essence of the distinctiveness of Japanese-style nativism. However, given that securitization is carried out by speech acts, desecuritization, which would introduce evaluation criteria aside from threats to existence, should logically be possible (Huysmans 2006; Wæver 1995). The following chapter, in addition to analyzing the primary historical structural causes that give rise to this nativism, will also consider how to promote desecuritization.

8 East Asian Geopolitics and Japanese-style Nativism: Why are *Zainichi* Koreans Targeted?

East Asian geopolitics and *Zainichi* Koreans

In the previous chapter, we looked at how the speech acts that make up securitization have connected voting rights for foreign residents – as the rights of 'past nationals' and 'residents' – and territorial issues. However, border and territorial issues do not always provoke the securitization of 'foreigner problems'. Why do some people accept the credibility of the myth of 'foreigners moving en masse to border zones'? This problem is the same as the acceptance of the falsehood of 'special privileges for *Zainichi* Koreans'. In order to make clear what is happening we need to turn our thoughts again to East Asian geopolitics, which we touched on in the Prologue.

The following investigation will not deal with the entire East Asian geopolitical region; it will be limited to factors directly connected with *Zainichi* Koreans. The following lists, taken from other research works in this area, can be cited, firstly, as items that have brought about changes in Japan's relations with its nearest neighbors – South Korea, North Korea and China – and, secondly, as major domestic factors (Söderberg 2011b: 156–7). The events that have affected Japan's relations with its nearest neighbors are: the 'Japan–South Korea Normalization Treaty' of 1965; the Cold War and its ending; the death of Il-sung Kim; the economic development (or rather non-development) of North Korea; the abduction and nuclear-proliferation issues between Japan and North Korea; globalization and the inflow of new groups of migrants; changing power relations in Northeast Asia; and the rise of China. The major domestic factors have been: a more peaceful environment in Japanese politics since 1955; the increased flow of information; ratification of the 'International Covenant on Civil and Political Rights'; ratification of the 'Convention on the Elimination of All forms of Discrimination against Women'; the end of fingerprinting; and the introduction of special permanent resident status. How are these individual factors related to the nativist movement and also to distinctively Japanese nativism? The topic for this chapter is the elucidation of how the Japanese government organizes its policy towards *Zainichi* Koreans on the basis of its relationship with South Korea and North Korea, and the consequences of this.

Post-war Japan as a nationalizing state

Brubaker's Triad Model

Brubaker's studies of Eastern European nationalism provide a valuable guide when considering the situation in which *Zainichi* Koreans find themselves (Brubaker 1996, 1998, 2011). With the existence of multiple ethnic groups that could potentially constitute nation-states in the countries of Eastern Europe, including the former Soviet Union, the reconstruction of nations that accompanied the demise of the Cold War has led to a complex situation. Namely, the succession states to the previous multi-ethnic socialist states are redefining themselves as nation-states following the end of the Cold War. Examples such as the Soviet Union and Yugoslavia, where it was a case of nations splitting up, are easily understood, but other new problems erupted everywhere, such as that of the treatment of people of Belarusian descent within Poland. Brubaker sees the ethnic conflicts that arose as part of these processes of national reconstruction as resulting from the existence of a triad that includes a 'national minority', a 'nationalizing state' and a 'national homeland' (see Figure 8.1).

Nationalizing states are defined as 'ethnically heterogeneous yet conceived as nation-states, whose dominant elites promote (to varying degrees) the language, culture, demographic position, economic flourishing, or political hegemony of the nominally state-bearing nation' (Brubaker 1996: 57). For example, the socialist state of Czechoslovakia split into two independent states for the two main ethnic groups, the Czechs and the Slovaks, following the demise of the Cold War. In Brubaker's terminology, these are examples of the 'ethnically homogenous nation state' (Brubaker 1998), several of which were born in Eastern Europe. These are not, in reality, ethnically homogeneous nations; Slovakia is a multi-ethnic nation, which has

Figure 8.1 Triad model of the immigration issue

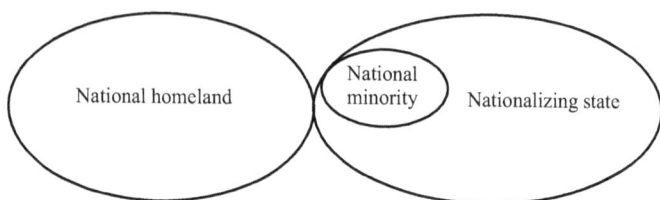

Hungarians in it from Hungary with which it shares a border, but it is an attempt to create a state made up predominantly of Slovakians.

National homeland refers to a situation when 'political or cultural elites define ethnonational kin in other states as members of one and the same nation, claim that they 'belong,' in some sense, to the state, and assert that their condition must be monitored and their interests protected and promoted by the state' (Brubaker 1996: 58). To return to the example in the previous paragraph, due to historical circumstances, in which Hungary had controlled Slovakia, the two countries cannot be described as having enjoyed amicable relations. However, in 1995, a treaty of friendship was concluded as a sign of historical rapprochement, and this led to the recognition of language and cultural rights for the Hungarians living in Slovakia (Vasilevich 2013). As the national homeland, Hungary exerted considerable influence on the rights of Hungarians in Slovakia.[1]

Finally, national minority is a 'political stance' which displays the following characteristics: '(1) the public claim to membership of an ethnocultural nation different from the numerically or politically dominant ethnocultural nation; (2) the demand for state recognition of this distinct ethnocultural nationality; and (3) the assertion, on the basis of this ethnocultural nationality, of certain collective cultural or political rights' (Brubaker 1996: 60). Instead of the dyad model, which regards relations between the national minority and the nationalizing state as being concluded domestically inside one nation, Brubaker explicitly established that they are affected by relations between the two nations. The destiny of national minorities is at the mercy of conflicts between the 'nationalizing state' and the 'national homeland' (Brubaker 1996: 5).

The triad model has been applied not only to Eastern Europe but also to Malaysia and Israel, and Brubaker says that it would be beneficial in analyzing overseas Chinese in South East Asia as well (Brubaker 1996: 6).[2] However, as with Eastern Europe following the end of the Cold War, this model manifests its effectiveness in cases where there is a fundamental redefinition of membership as a result of the collapse of the Eastern and Western blocs and the breaking up of nations. In Eastern Europe following the end of the Cold War there was not simply the breaking up of nations; there were also movements of people that we ought to call 'ethnic unmixing' (Brubaker 1998). Migrations such as the return of Germany's *Aussiedler* and the movement of East Europeans of Russian descent to Russia were generated to create 'ethnically homogeneous nation states' in Eastern Europe.

Whilst there was an aspect of labor migration to these movements, the main push factor was ethnic conflict and the main pull factor was ethnic affinity (Brubaker 1998: 1047). Ethnicity, which had retired into the background under socialist regimes, now became the basis for membership, and the state came to be depicted as belonging to the dominant ethnic group. The dominant ethnic group demanded a strengthening of its position, arguing that its condition was vulnerable and threatened by other groups (Brubaker 2011: 1786). It was this logic of ethnic homogeneity that promoted migrations, and the national minorities that stayed behind experienced the risk of deportations and strong pressures towards homogenization. The problem was further complicated by the triad relationship created by the participation of the national homeland.

Zainichi Koreans viewed from the triad model

SCAP and Japanese government policy towards *Zainichi* Koreans

How can we use the triad model to analyze the conditions of *Zainichi* Koreans after World War II? To begin with, there are several considerable differences between post-Cold War Eastern Europe and post-World War II East Asia.[3] Under the Cold War regime, the Korean Peninsula was divided into two successor states, South Korea and North Korea (China and Taiwan are a similar case). As touched on in the Prologue, the fact that Japan does not recognize North Korea as a state has resulted in *Zainichi* Koreans with North Korean citizenship suffering disadvantage. This division into two parts has even made its way into *Zainichi* Korean society; the major ethnic bodies are organized along north–south lines and there is no one untied body (Harajiri 1998: 131). Japan, as the nationalizing state and in pursuit of its own ends, has used this antagonism to divide and rule *Zainichi* Koreans.[4]

Ethnic issues that arose as an adjunct to the dismantling of the Japanese empire were strongly prescribed by United States policy, and had considerably more influence than that of the European Union on Eastern Europe after the Cold War.[5] To begin with, in keeping with Dower's (1999) use of the term Scapanese to describe Japan's post-war system, SCAP's (Supreme Commander for the Allied Powers) ideas of 'democratization' and 'anti-communism' are visible in plans developed for the organization of Japan's immigration control regime (Morris-Suzuki 2005). Following the San Francisco Peace Treaty, Japan–South Korea relations, which exerted a considerable influence on the legal status of *Zainichi* Koreans, also changed as a result of the Asia strategy of their common ally, the United States (Cha 1999). This also had an influence on the nativist movement, which we will analyze in the following section.[6]

The expansion and collapse of the Japanese empire brought about the ethnic mixing and unmixing of Japanese and Koreans, in a manner similar to events in Eastern Europe. That is, in the territories of the Japanese Empire, including the former 'Manchukuo' which was under the effective control of Japan, ethnic mixing proceeded as emigrants from Japan and migrants from the colonies mixed with each other. At that time, Japanese assimilation was seen as possible because the Japanese argued that they were ethnically diverse in order to win over and control different ethnic groups (Oguma 1995). After Japan's annexation of Korea, however, Koreans who crossed over to Japan from the Korean Peninsula were treated as Japanese under the law and Korean males had voting rights, including in national elections. The process of the dissolution of the Japanese Empire following defeat led to the liberation of the Korean Peninsula, and this saw the progressive evacuation of Japanese to Japan and the repatriation of Koreans to the Korean Peninsula (Araragi 2011; Wakatsuki 1991). This was a case of ethnic unmixing accompanying defeat and liberation (Brubaker 1998), but the problem is that the Japanese government now wished to see unmixing and promoted this in its policies (Tonomura 2013).

The Japanese government regarded *Zainichi* Koreans as politically dangerous, and thus the following policies were adopted: encouraging *Zainichi* Koreans to return to their own country;

limiting the rights of Koreans resident in Japan; and the granting of citizenship in exchange for the erasure of ethnicity. Putting this in the language of Figure 8.1, above, the creation of a 'nationalizing state' was to be promoted by forcing as many members as possible of the 'national minorities' to return to their 'national homeland' and by treating those who stayed behind inhospitably. In the immediate post-war period, encouraging repatriation was both GHQ and Japanese government policy. This is why 'transport ships heading for Japan carried Japanese evacuees, and transport ships bound for Korea and Taiwan sailed with Koreans and Taiwanese on board' (Ōnuma 1993: 36). In addition to this, in December 1945, the franchise was suspended for people from Japan's former colonies and they were thus divested of their voting rights.[7] This political decision was taken out of fear of the political influence of *Zainichi* Koreans (Mizuno 1996, 1997). This decision was, in fact, taken in the same period when SCAP ensured that Japanese women were given the vote; 'nationalization' resulted in the granting of rights to Japanese women and the removal of rights from *Zainichi* Koreans (Kim, Puja 2011: 59). In the closing years of the war, giving voting rights to Korea and Taiwan had been considered, but ultimately there was a sudden change of policy towards an 'ethnically homogeneous state'.

The occupation period was also the time when the immigration control regime that was established in 1952 was formulated.[8] To summarize, the Japanese government, with the acquiescence of SCAP, oriented itself towards ethnically homogeneous nation-state building, and this is the reason why they promoted the repatriation of *Zainichi* Koreans and the removal of their rights.[9] That is, from a certain point in time, the Japanese government stopped allowing *Zainichi* Koreans the right to choose their nationality (Ōnuma 1980a: 254–5) and attempted to make it easier to execute their forced repatriation through the application of the 'Immigration Control Ordinance'. Once the San Francisco Peace Treaty came into effect in 1952, people from Japan's former colonies, who had until then existed in an already ambiguous position, officially lost their Japanese citizenship (Mun 2007).[10]

Following this development, *Zainichi* Koreans, as foreign nationals, came under the control of the 'Immigration Control Act' and the 'Alien Registration Act'. These immigration laws had been developed by SCAP and the Japanese government on the advice of the United States Immigration and Naturalization Service (Kim 1997: 702; Morris-Suzuki 2010: Ch. 4). In short, until this point in time, raising the spectre of 'anti-communism' while being seen to give some consideration to 'democracy' made it possible to gain the approval of the United States even for a policy of 'unmixing'. As a result, the basic policy towards *Zainichi* Koreans was decided by the lopsided dyad of the Japanese government, which was aiming for the creation of an 'ethnically homogeneous nation-state', and *Zainichi* Koreans who had no one to back them.

The creation of special permanent residents

The sum of the changes that followed the Peace Treaty amounted to the discussion of the treatment of *Zainichi* Koreans at Japan–South Korea negotiations which had normalizing diplomatic relations between Japan and South Korea as their aim,[11] and where the triad prescribed policies. In addition, as the goal of the Japanese government at this time was unmixing, its initial proposals at the Japan–Korea negotiations were restrictive: fresh applications would have to be made to qualify for permanent residence and welfare recipients were to be forcibly repatriated (Choe 2011). In reality, the Japanese government regarded *Zainichi* Koreans as a burden, and gave substantial assistance to efforts to return people to North Korea (Morris-Suzuki 2007, 2010). After the start of Chung-hee Park's administration, however, *Mindan* came under its control and support (Roh 2011), and this enabled the joint negotiations to resist Japan's efforts at unmixing. As a result of the negotiations, treaty permanent resident status was created in 1965, and the status of *Zainichi* Koreans with South Korean nationality thus became relatively stable. Although they were now called treaty permanent residents, the South Korean side ended up compromising on the clause for forced returns (Kobayashi 2011), and the Japanese government held on to the possibility of 'unmixing' as collateral. Also, despite the establishment of this more stable residence status *Zainichi* Koreans continued to be excluded from many of the social rights that were part of welfare.

Meanwhile, Law Number 126, a provisional measure, limited the residence status of people with North Korean citizenship and produced a division in legal status between them and the treaty permanent residents who held South Korean citizenship.[12] Moreover, there were repeated submissions, in 1966 and 1969 respectively, of the 'Schools for Foreigners Bill' (*Gaikokujin gakkō hōan*), aiming to exclude North Korean schools from licensing, and the 'Immigration Control Act', which included restrictions on political activities (Tanaka 1990: 27–8; Yun 1992: 212). When the triad, in addition to a nationalizing state (Japan) and a national minority (Koreans with North Korean nationality), includes a national homeland (North Korea) that is also an 'enemy state', this, unsurprisingly, produces movements that attempt to bring about 'unmixing.'[13]

It was the ratification of the 'United Nations Convention on Human Rights' and the 'Convention Relating to the Status of Refugees' – elements beyond the level of the triad – that promoted partial change to these conditions. International laws were thus the fourth influential factor, fulfilling a similar function to that of the European Union in Eastern Europe (Smith 2002). This led to legal changes in the form of the 'Immigration Control and Refugee Recognition Act', which resulted in a more stable residence status for the majority of *Zainichi* Koreans who fell outside of the treaty permanent resident category and who now had general permanent residency applied to them (Ōnuma 1993: 267–9). In addition, they were now given access to the social security system in areas such as government pensions, childcare allowances and access to public housing (Koto 1991). All this notwithstanding, Japan's policy towards *Zainichi* Koreans has been discriminatory: there had been no repeal of the nationality clause for welfare, which had been applied administratively since 1950, and the stabilization of their residence status had come too late to be useful. Without external pressures, such as the ratification of international laws, Japan had been unable to develop domestic laws to improve the status of *Zainichi* Koreans, a state of affairs that illustrates its character as a nationalizing state.

The final change came about as a result of negotiations on the legal status of third generation *Zainichi* Koreans, designed to review the 'Treaty on Basic Relations between Japan and the Republic of Korea' twenty-five years after it first came into being. At this time, the South Korean government released nine demands, taken from the ideas of *Mindan* and, following discussions with the Japanese government, the 'Agreement between Japan and the Republic of Korea Concerning the Legal Status and Treatment of the People of the Republic of Korea Residing in Japan' was released. This was a case of the triad that had excluded North Korean nationals effecting a revision of legal status. However, the 'Special Act on Immigration

Control' (*Shutsunyūkoku kanri tokureihō*), enacted in 1991, saw the application of special permanent resident status to both South and North Korean nationals for the first time. A highly ranked official of the Immigration Bureau sang the bureau's own praises saying that this was 'special treatment', 'favorable treatment in terms of the legal status of foreigners the likes of which is not to be found anywhere else in the world' and 'an unsurpassed stable status' (Sakanaka 1999: 88).

Institutional pathology produced by adherence to the triad
Are we thus able to say that with the 'Special Act on Immigration Control', which united all *Zainichi* Koreans under the one status of special permanent resident, there was a policy change from triad to dyad? To put it another way, is the treatment of the national minority still determined on the basis of relations with the 'national homeland' (South Korea or North Korea)? Has the 'nationalizing state' changed its policy of marginalizing foreigners, so as to recognize the rights of the national minority based on their actual conditions?

Although it is impossible to answer these questions by looking only at legal status, let us consider the legal status of 'special treatment'. The difference between special permanent resident and treaty permanent resident was, effectively, that in the case of the former there were no forced deportations;[14] the guarantee of permanent residence was extended to descendants; and North Korean nationals were also included. A consideration of the history of North Korean nationals as a national minority resulted in their inclusion under an extension of the status of special permanent resident. In this sense, the 'legal status of foreigners' can be judged to have experienced a shift towards a dyad despite the fact that it is based on the Japan–South Korea relationship. However, it took three generations to arrive at a residence status that grouped together all people from Japan's former colonies – special permanent residence. South Korea had already demanded the sort of treatment that now applies to special permanent residents before 1965, during negations surrounding the 'Treaty on Basic Relations between Japan and the Republic of Korea' (Kim 1991a, 1991b). The issue of legal status ought to have been decided back then. A response time of twenty-five years since the treaty for a resolution to appear is too slow.

Similarly, South Korea had also demanded voting rights for foreign residents in the mid-1980s, but the Japanese side refused to list these amongst the matters for consideration; instead, they confined themselves to the following wording at the end of the memorandum that was produced in 1991, 'there was an expression of demands by the government of the Republic of Korea'. It was a series of court actions that led to this becoming a policy matter, not any initiative on the part of the Japanese side. Furthermore, whilst there has been a tentative resolution of legal status after twenty-five years, under present conditions there is no likelihood that voting rights for foreign residents will become law, even after the passage of twenty-five years from the time when it was first raised. As we also saw in the previous chapter, following 2000, a bill has been submitted excluding North Korean nationals. Voting rights for foreign residents can only be conceived of in terms of a Cold War-style triad, that of Japan–South Korea–*Zainichi* Koreans who are South Korean nationals (with the exclusion of North Korean nationals as the flip side of this), and yet this is not sufficient for legislation.

If it was not possible to make voting rights for foreign residents a reality, there were other solutions: introducing a *jus soli* component to the 'Nationality Law'; restoring to people from former colonies the right to choose their nationality; and introducing dual citizenship. These are policies that have already been adopted by other countries; they take account of the political rights of *Zainichi* Koreans using methods other than voting rights.[15] In reality, however, no nationality-based measure was adopted for resolving the problem. Following the *Kōmeitō* and Liberal Party submission of a bill for voting rights for foreign residents in 2000, the LDP established a 'project team on nationality and other matters'. Far from being motivated by serious considerations of easing naturalization criteria as an alternative policy, this was nothing more than political manoeuvring in order to obstruct the progress of the voting rights bill.[16] As a result of this, applying for naturalization under administrative discretion is still the sole method for acquiring nationality; the reality is that even the right to acquire Japanese nationality must develop in the form of a social movement (Zainichi Korian no Nihon Kokuseki Shutokuken Kakuritsu Kyōgikai 2006).[17]

Let us now review the factors that prescribe the treatment of *Zainichi* Koreans, and changes in these factors, with reference to Table 8.1. It is first and foremost *Zainichi* Koreans' past as people of the Japanese Empire that prescribes the triad, and it is the influence of the logic of the colonial settlement that is the biggest difference between them and other foreigners. Also, the fact that the Korean Peninsula was divided into north and south and became the front line of the Cold War, and the fact that there has not been any significant change to this situation even after the demise of the Cold War have cast a large shadow over the triad. Additionally, the Japanese government can also no longer ignore the fact that *Zainichi* Koreans have built a foundation for their lives in Japan with their history of residence spanning multiple generations. These dyads and triads have prescribed policies and their contents at every stage.

At the time of the enactment of the 1952 'Immigration Control Law' and the 'Alien Registration Act' neither the colonial settlement nor the fact of residence in Japan were taken into account. As can be appreciated from the fact that the Japanese government saw repatriation operations to North Korea as an opportunity, its orientation was towards unmixing, according to which national minorities were made to return to their countries. When Japan and South Korea ratified the 'Treaty on Basic Relations' Japan did acknowledge the status of the national minority as treaty permanent residents despite its rejection of South Korean demands regarding the forced repatriation condition. This acknowledgement was, however, limited to legal status; in terms of social rights, they remained excluded as ever. In this sense, the Japanese government has given little consideration to treating *Zainichi* South Koreans as denizens on the basis of the dyad. Furthermore, the fact that the legal status of North Korean nationals did not change until 1982 demonstrates that the Japanese government not only ignored the dyad but kept the policy of 'unmixing' (to facilitate repatriation).

The limited change that has occurred has been due to the enactment in 1991 of the 'Special Act on Immigration Control'. Special permanent resident status, which includes North Korean nationals, can be regarded as the advancement of a colonial settlement that does not adhere to the logic of the Cold War.[18] However, just as *Zainichi* South Koreans had continued to be excluded from social rights even under the 'Treaty on Basic Relations between Japan and the Republic of Korea', the enactment of the 'Special Act on Immigration Control' did not usher in any change in the conditions of exclusion from political rights for *Zainichi* Koreans. The logic behind demands for voting rights for foreign residents is twofold: it originated in the colonial settlement

Table 8.1: Chronology of treatment of Zainichi Koreans

	1952	1965	1982	1991	Post-1991
Basis for periodization	Immigration Control and Refugee Recognition Act/enactment of Alien Registration Act	Treaty on Basic Relations between Japan and the Republic of Korea	Ratification of Convention Relating to the Status of Refugees	Agreement Concerning Legal Status	
Triad					
Cold War		Neglect of North Korean legal status			Exclusion of North Koreans from the Voting Rights for Foreign Residents Bill; Suppression of North Korean schools
Colonial settlement	Denial of right to choose nationality; no permanent resident status	Treaty permanent residency for South Koreans		Special permanent residency	Submission of Voting Rights for Foreign Residents Bill
International norms			Adoption of social security		
Dyad					
Integration			Application of permanent resident status to North Korean nationals	Special permanent resident status for both South and North Korean nationals	Submission of Voting Rights for Foreign Residents Bill

(the restoration of the rights that had been 'suspended' in December 1945), and then it acquired a denizenship dimension. This triad-dyad hybrid applied to both the oldcomer and newcomer waves of population movements, and was reasonable in the sense that it resolved the problems that had been left behind after the war.[19] However, the dyad withdrew into the background as North Korean nationals were excluded from a stable residence status by the logic of the Cold War, and Japan–South Korea diplomacy was left to deal with the status of South Korean nationals.[20]

Ultimately, there has been no fundamental change in the framework established in the early period of the Cold War with regard to either the immigration control regime, which was established to control and manage *Zainichi* Koreans, or the *jus sanguinis* principle in the 'Nationality Law' (Morris-Suzuki 2010: 245).[21] Why has this set of circumstances arisen? I am compelled to say that the answer lies in the fact that, when it comes to the status of *Zainichi* Koreans, the Japanese government has failed to see this as its own issue to resolve. It has managed to bring about a stabilization of legal status through its relations with South Korea, which has led to some improvements for North Korean nationals. However, in its examinations of the issue of voting rights for foreign residents, as part of its relations with South Korea, the Japanese government excludes North Korean nationals because of its relations with North Korea. It did not grant social rights to *Zainichi* Koreans until Japan ratified the 'United Nations Human Rights Convention' and the 'Convention Relating to the Status of Refugees'. When Japan–North Korea relations worsened, the Japanese government suppressed organizations affiliated with *Sōren*.

These are all actions that were prescribed by external relations; they are not based on a dyad in which the Japanese government meets face-to-face with *Zainichi* Koreans. In truth, the government has not once to date proactively set up an advisory body on policy concerning *Zainichi* Koreans.[22] The 'Taskforce for the Advancement of Multicultural Coexistence' (*Tabunka kyōsei no suishin ni kansuru kenkyūkai*) – the first advisory body aimed at improving the treatment of foreigners living in Japan – was, effectively, only interested in looking at newcomers; *Zainichi* Koreans were excluded.[23] This is partly because the government is reluctant to deal with historical and political issues regarding *Zainichi* Koreans. Beyond this, however, it is path-dependent policy making by the triad that hinders any initiatives to tackle this issue on the basis of a dyad.[24]

This tendency to be sensitive to the triad while ignoring the dyad is also apparent, for example, in the neglect of the issue of foreigners with no pension. When the government decided to apply the pension system to foreigners, it did not put in place any measures to make the national pension available to elderly foreigners. Since the Japanese government's sole consideration was consistency between domestic and international laws, it did not concern itself with whether elderly foreigners could receive the national pension. This is why elderly foreigners are ineligible for the national pension. In the case of nationality also, although the naturalization requirements have been relaxed on the practical level, the framework for naturalization applications continues unchanged. Even so, the number of special permanent residents, which peaked in 1991, has been declining by 10,000 people annually. As a result of marriages with Japanese people and naturalizations, the national minority of *Zainichi* Koreans who hold foreign nationality will become 'extinct' in the near future; it is just a matter of waiting quietly for this to happen. Even without the introduction of the right to choose nationality or the principle of *jus soli*, there is no need to lift a finger; time will deliver a resolution. It is unclear whether the Japanese government has thought that far ahead, but we can evaluate their policy as being one of anticipating a resolution via demographic assimilation without them having to take the status of *Zainichi* Koreans seriously.[25]

Dyads and local citizenship

Changes in *Zainichi* Koreans

In the previous section, we looked at Japanese government policy towards *Zainichi* Koreans and at how it has been prescribed by a triad. There is yet another policy history in which *Zainichi* Koreans have been regarded as residents in a dyad. The changing times and the appearance of new generations form the background to a process whereby *Zainichi* Koreans are undergoing a change of appearance.[26] The post-war history of *Zainichi* Koreans has been largely prescribed by the two factors of the north–south division and the colonial settlement. This is because the *zainichi* community has been divided between *Mindan* and *Sōren*, the organizations within it that have represented south and north respectively, and also because *Zainichi* Koreans were left in an indeterminate legal status until 1991. Strangely, even second and third generation members of the community had endured a precarious legal status until 1991; people born and raised in Japan had to apply for a renewal of their visa permit every three years.[27]

There has been a divergence between the legal status brought about by the stagnation of the colonial settlement and the sociological reality, which has greatly changed with each generation.[28] The biggest changes have been brought about by an increase in the generations born in Japan and by the appearance of two diverging branches: inter- and intra-generational. The first generation have had a strong consciousness of themselves as 'expatriates' and, regardless of how feasible the idea might be in reality, they have, to a certain degree, held a common desire to return to their country one day. In the case of the second and later generations, given that obvious links to the 'homeland' no longer exist for them, they inevitably develop a different consciousness from that of the first generation (see, for example, Ryang 1997, 2000).[29] This lack of ties to the homeland has promoted intra-generational differences. These are embodied in the later generations' definition of themselves which is based neither on returning to their country nor assimilation by naturalization: a third way is to define themselves as *Zainichi* Koreans – literally, Koreans living in Japan (Chapman 2008; Hester 2008). The 'third way' is not, however, a simple matter; divergence keeps occurring due to a combination of many factors.[30]

Figure 8.2 illustrates the divergent identity patterns of generations following the third generation (Fukuoka 1993; Fukuoka and Tsujiyama 1991). This figure combines two axes: (1) identification with a history in which *Zainichi* Koreans have been the victims of oppression and (2) the degree of attachment to Japan as the place where one was brought up. The patterns of 'homeland oriented', 'symbiosis oriented', 'individualist', 'naturalization oriented' and 'coethnic solidarity oriented' have been abstracted from the interplay of these two factors. Subsequent research has produced two broader approaches to the treatment of the 'homeland' factor.

One trend is effectively a modification of the homeland oriented in Fukuoka's typology. Whilst the 'national homeland' may provide a certain point of reference for the younger generations, they do not see it as a place to go back to. Nevertheless, they are not able to assimilate in Japan either. This state tends to be expressed using

Figure 8.2 Zainichi *Korean patterns of assimilation/alienation*
          orientation

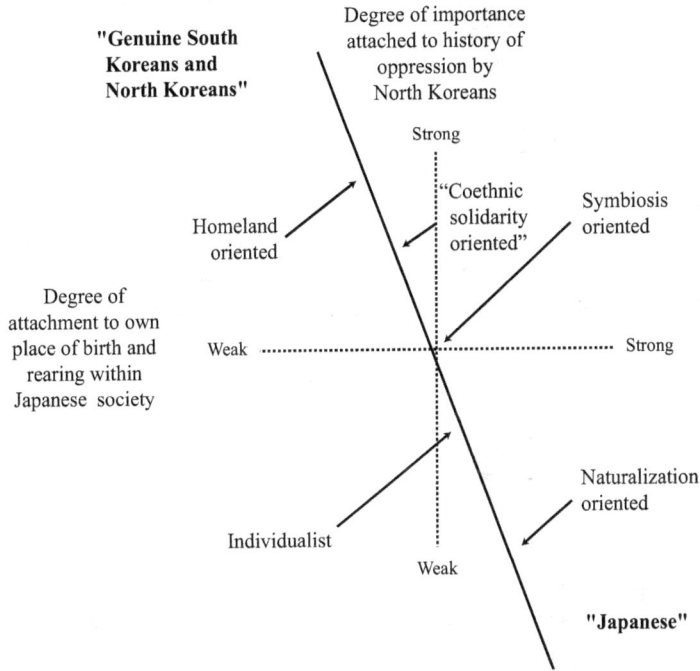

Source: Fukuoka (1993) page 103 and table on page 89. See also Fukuoka (2000) pages 49 and 59.

the terms 'diasporic nationalism', 'diaspora without homeland' and 'transnational diaspora' (Lie 2008; Oh 2012; Ryang and Lie 2009). While this can be perceived as an identity crisis, it could also be regarded as a desirable metaphysical state. Because they are examples of 'marginal man' *Zainichi* Koreans can view both the nationalizing state and the national homeland objectively, and this is potentially an orientation towards the deconstruction of the triad (Kang 1985b: 180).

A nother research approach is not to include the 'homeland' factor as part of the analysis, dealing instead with *Zainichi* Koreans as one of Japan's ethnic groups (Hashimoto 2010; Tani 2002).[31] These are not mutually contradictory approaches; the desirable base for *Zainichi* Koreans will converge not on nationality but on locality. The diasporic nature of *Zainichi* Koreans notwithstanding, they must reside in particular areas with attachments to their locality, regardless of the nation to which they belong. In short, the term 'citizens who are foreign nationals' is self-contradictory, but from the 1990s the term 'resident foreign nationals' was not only coined but has even been in official use.[32] Because it is hard for *Zainichi* Koreans to establish themselves as hyphenated Japanese, like Korean-Americans, naturalization effectively results in assimilation, in which their Korean ethnicity will die out. However, it is not unrealistic to maintain a sense of belonging to a national homeland in which one has never even resided. Consequently, the optimal unit of belonging might not be the national: attachment to the local enables *Zainichi* Koreans to avoid dilemmas of belonging. As residents, they can 'be committed to the 'local' while resisting it and resist while being committed' (Kang 1992: 46).[33]

The local as the foundation of the dyad

The dyad and local government policies regarding foreigners

Belonging to a local area leads to the development of policies for foreigners that are dyad-based (local government vis-à-vis foreign residents). Previous researchers have pointed out the contrast between the national government's lack of policy relating to foreigners and the leadership shown by some local governments (Ebashi 1993; Komai and Watado 1997; Miyajima 2000; Miyajima and Kajita 1996; Watado 1995). This is not limited to policy regarding newcomer foreigners; local governments have distanced themselves from the national government and its zeal for suppressing Korean schools, establishing instead a record of allowing them to exist as miscellaneous schools. Similarly, at the time of the movement against fingerprinting in the 1980s, while the Ministry of Justice rushed to control the situation, many local governments decided not to indict on the basis of decisions by mayors. Furthermore, in contrast to the inaction of the Japanese government, multiple local governments have been engaged in establishing consultative bodies and carrying out surveys concerning *Zainichi* Koreans since the 1980s.

Why is it that local governments, rather than the Japanese government, have been the ones to develop progressive policies? The following three observations can be made on the basis of what is generally known in migration studies (Ireland 1994; Pak 2000a, 2000b). Firstly, because migrants gather in particular areas they become a major issue for local governments with large concentrations of migrants, and this readily links them to the development of policies. Secondly, as the fact that leftist local governments handed down non-indictments for refusing to be fingerprinted shows, the protection of migrants' rights is a leftwing issue, and this trend is advancing in urban areas where the leftwing is strong. Thirdly, the internationalization policies of local governments, as suggested by the term 'internal internationalization' (Hatsuse 1988), have led to the development of forward looking and positive local policies for foreign residents.

These observations all form part of the truth but, as the discussion in this chapter shows, the cause is far simpler. The type of triadic thinking used by the Japanese government is unviable when local governments and foreign residents are face to face in a dyad. In this sense, local governments have just been carrying out their duty regarding policies towards foreign residents.[34] It is the Japanese government's response that is strange; we can see its persistent lack of policy as a consequence of having focussed solely on the triad and having ignored the dyad.

What kind of policy disparities do these differences produce? In the previous section I said that until the time of the ratification of the 'Convention Relating to the Status of Refugees' foreigners had been excluded from social security, but this is not entirely accurate. Before the ratification, some local governments had already guaranteed certain social security provisions such as access to public housing. Even when the Japanese government did nothing for *Zainichi* Koreans with no pension, some local governments provided welfare payments for them. As the national government was also shutting people out of assuming public office on the pretext of the 'natural legal principle', in the 1970s, the local governments of Osaka and Hyōgo abolished the nationality clause (Nakahara 1993: 63–4). These steps were the result of demands from various *Zainichi* Korean groups (Soh 1987). The high level of responsiveness on the part of local governments comes from the dyadic relation between authorities and foreign residents, in which the unreasonableness of the nationality clause is more easily understood.

Dyad-based voting rights for foreign residents

As argued in the previous chapter, the securitization of the voting rights issue is caused by a political process in which triadic relationships are highly influential. However, as the denizenship argument is at the very foundation of voting rights for foreign residents, it should be considered within the dyad of denizens and nation-state. In this sense, local governments' policies of voting rights for foreign residents, which are dyad based, offer an opening for desecuritization. In the case of voting rights for foreign residents, a major circuit for the movement – aside from going through the South Korean government – was also provided by lobbying local assemblies (Higuchi 2011). This has been quite successful as over half of the local assemblies are adopting resolutions calling for voting rights for foreign residents.[35]

There have also been dyad-based discussions about voting rights for foreign residents that referred to denizenship. In 2008, with the backing of Ichirō Ozawa, then leader of the Democratic Party of Japan (*Minshutō*), Katsuya Okada, a former Leader of the party, organized the 'Diet Members Group for Promoting an Improvement in the Legal Status of Permanent Resident Foreigners' (*Eijū gaikokujin hōteki chii kōjō suishin giin rennmei*).[36] The meeting of this group of Diet members was followed by a conference between Ozawa and the then South Korean Prime Minister Myung-bak Lee, but Okada ultimately came to a conclusion based on denizenship, which was unrelated to the Japan–Korea relationship. The final report released by this group reveals the following understanding of the status quo.[37]

> 'In the course of the sixty years since the end of the war, special permanent residents have grown old without seeing any end to the situation in which they are shut out of political participation'.
>
> 'It ought to be borne in mind that in the OECD (with thirty member countries), the only country that adopts *jus sanguinis*, fails to recognize dual citizenship and does not grant voting rights to foreign residents is Japan'.

It is a typical conclusion for a principled advocate such as Okada. However, after a change of government to the Democratic Party, it was the triad, not the dyad, that served as the primary factor influencing this issue. Following his inauguration in 2009, the then Prime Minister Yukio Hatoyama repeatedly spoke of his desire to see the legalization of voting rights for foreign residents, but said the following with regard to the political background to this issue.

Since China, as one country has an extremely large presence in the
East Asian Community – and even for this reason alone – how Japan
and South Korea cooperate with one another is exceedingly important
… Discussions about municipal voting rights are [important] also to
increasing understanding between Japan and Korea. Well, another
reason is because South Korea recognizes voting rights for permanent
residents, although these are not solely granted to its Japanese
residents. Historically, people were unable to go back to Korea, even
if they wanted to. And so, it would seem to me that granting municipal
voting rights to people who are determined to do their best in Japan
is the natural course of action. If we look back on history, within
the broad sweep of East Asian history, the bonds between Japan and
Korea must perforce be strong bonds. Given all of this, we ought to
make municipal voting rights a reality, especially because it is most
strongly desired by South Korea.[38]

Hatoyama thought voting rights for foreign residents necessary
because 'it is proper that administration and politics be conducted
by all of the people who live in a place'.[39] In reality, if attempts were
made at implementation and political costs taken into account, the
triad of Japan–South Korea–diplomacy would support the policy.
However, the triadic approach has triggered securitization which
argues, for example, that foreigners are massing in the border zones
of the nation to cast votes at municipal elections there.

Where then are the keys for promoting desecuritization? *Horumon
Bunka*, a journal emphasizing the everyday opinions of *Zainichi*
Koreans, called its special edition on voting rights 'The Day When
Zainichi Koreans will go to the Polls' (*Horumon Bunka* Editorial
Committee, 1992). At that time, a group of Koreans established The
Zainichi Party, a political group seeking voting rights, and appealed
for recognition of the fact that they were qualified by throwing their
hats into the ring for the upper house election in 1992 (Yi 1993). There
was also a sit-in protest because a *Zainichi* Korean singer was not
accepted as a candidate for the upper house election in 1995 (Asahi
Shinbun 7/7/1995). These examples show that voting rights are not
limited to an abstract right; they are a right to be exercised by every
individual *Zainichi* Korean. Just as with fingerprinting, if voting
rights had been understood as an issue of the dignity of human beings,
then they would hardly have been securitized in the way that we saw
in the previous chapter. What is needed is not only an improvement

Figure 8.3: Nativist movement targets

State

		Internal	External
Nation	*Internal*	'Anti-Japanese' left wing Democratic Party, Anti-nuclear movement	
	External	National minorities *Zainichi* Koreans	National homelands South Korea, China and North Korea

Source: Compiled by author on the basis of Mudde (2007).

of the triad (relations with neighboring countries), but a rethinking of matters concerning *Zainichi* Koreans as issues for the dyad.

Essentialism and justifications for the exclusion of foreigners

Finally, I will examine the worst outcome of a triad-based understanding: the mechanism by which the nativist movement attacks 'special privileges for *Zainichi* Koreans'. The ultra-right in Western Europe certainly sees the expulsion of migrants as the primary issue, but they do not only target migrants. They also have their staple enemies such as the domestic leftwing, established political parties and certain other countries. The same can be said of the Japanese nativist movement, and Figure 8.3 sets out its enemies. However, dyad-based arguments about the threat of *Zainichi* Koreans would be too implausible to mobilize potential members. Instead, *Zaitokukai* has relied on the triad to make their logic plausible: as we saw in Chapter 3, potential members initially felt hostile to the national homeland (neighboring countries), which then transformed into the rejection of the national minority.

The nativist movement, however, also has a dyad-based logic of exclusion that does not mediate its hostility towards South Korea, North Korea and China. For K, one of *Zaitokukai*'s leaders, anti-Japanese demonstrations in China provided the spark that led him to begin gathering related information on the internet. The starting point had been based on the triad, but the motivation for his activism today has changed in the way set out below.

I knew various things about the actual conditions. What angers me the most are the pension and the welfare issues. The problem is that, despite the fact that Japanese people don't get it, when it comes to foreigners, welfare is paid out quite readily. It's the same with the pension; Japanese people won't get it unless they have paid their instalments for twenty-five years, but foreigners – and without fail Koreans – get it despite never having contributed even a single yen, just because people feel sorry for them. (Mr K, *Zaitokukai*, forties)

This kind of nativism based on welfare chauvinism was referred to by several interviewees. Activists like K might leave the nativist movement if they were to be convinced that 'special privileges for *Zainichi* Koreans' is totally baseless. However, Japan's nativist movement differs from typical xenophobia; it also has at its base historical revisionism and relations with South Korea, North Korea and China. People like A below do not seem likely to revise their attitudes even though they are aware that 'special privileges for *Zainichi* Koreans' is a false rumor.

I insist on 'special privileges for *Zainichi* Koreans' because post-war problems are concentrated within the *zainichi* issue. Nishimoto, the *Asahi Newspaper* journalist, has come up with some splendid conclusions. He wrote that, judging by the expressions of the people at the meeting, most of them had different opinions regarding post-war issues, what made them gather for discussions was the issue of 'special privileges for *Zainichi* Koreans'. He pointed out that, in short, this is because the issue of 'special privileges for *Zainichi* Koreans' is symbolic of post-war problems ... GHQ drove the *zainichi* wedge into Japan, and then left ... Ultimately, I don't know whether or not there was a plan to hinder Japan by leaving us with a *zainichi* presence, but that is the reality. (Mr A, *Zaitokukai*, forties)

From A's point of view, Japan was 'encircled by victor nations, who were able to do just as they pleased', and the 'negative legacy' that they left for Japan is *Zainichi* Koreans. In this case, because the rejection of the post-war regime is rooted in enmity towards *Zainichi* Koreans, the actual nature of *Zainichi* Koreans, whatever it may be, becomes irrelevant. *Zainichi* Koreans become targets because they are seen as belonging to another government and a different regime, and not because of their nature as a group (Bigo

2005: 69). Yet no one else had displayed the same unshakeable belief as A in clearly connecting 'post-war issues' with the '*zainichi* issue'. With the exception of A and K, when asked how it was that they had arrived at the 'solution' of excluding *Zainichi* Koreans, most people reacted as if they had been caught off-guard by an enemy attack. U, whose middle school studies had been in an international school, developed an interest in his cultural traditions as his school experiences led him to reflect 'I am Japanese!' Why did this become linked to the nativist movement? U reacted in the following manner to my question.

> There are Japanese cultural traditions, and I felt that I wanted to protect them. Oh, I see … [How is this related to the 'foreigner problem?'] … Let me see. Now that I am being asked that for the first time I am thinking about it myself, but I wonder why it is. (Mr U, *Zaitokukai*, twenties)

U's participation in the nativist movement was part of his activities to 'protect Japan', but he had never considered why excluding foreigners would protect Japan. It seems that he saw South Korea, North Korea and China as raising objections about Japan's cultural traditions via historical issues. He could position the nativist movement in the role of counter attacking these efforts, but as to what the link between this and attacks against foreigners might be, he could not offer even vague reasoning. U's case is extreme, but there were a few members who talked as clearly as K about the expulsion of foreigners based on the dyad of 'the pension and welfare issues'. Most people mixed the 'national homeland' and the 'national minority' together within the triad, and they transformed their hostility towards the former into attacks against the latter. However, the grounds for this argument were vague even amongst its proponents, and they barely managed to join the two together with an essentialist view of ethnicity. In short, this is an understanding somewhat like F's: that South Korea, North Korea and China and those from these neighboring countries (*Zainichi* Koreans and Chinese) are the same indistinguishable people.

> It is because they are part of the same ethnic group. I don't even really know what ethnicity means. But, surely things like the way people live, their culture and customs can't be changed easily. If you think about

that, I think that *zainichi* too aren't that – they're not that different from Koreans. (Mr. F, *Zaitokukai*, thirties)

It has already been pointed out that the comic book *Manga kenkanryū* is based on an essentialist understanding of ethnic groups (Itagaki 2007). However, the essentialism of the nativist movement does not apply to ethnic groups in general; it is only adopted with regard to the main issue of 'anti-Japaneseness'. In brief, South Koreans, North Koreans and *Zainichi* Koreans are all understood in terms of a causal relationship in which they target Japan because they are an 'anti-Japanese ethnic group'. Nativists do not realize that the incomplete colonial settlement is the fundamental problem: it is the source of disputes such as Japan–South Korea historical issues and the movement for voting rights for foreign residents. If the causes of existing conditions in the 'nationalizing state' (the colonial settlement) are transposed onto essentialism ('anti-Japaneseness'), then Koreans can be held responsible for them. Viewing Koreans as essentially being 'anti-Japanese', nativists identify 'national minority' (*Zainichi* Koreans) with the 'national homeland' (South and North Korea). This is how vague arguments end up enabling the justification of the exclusion of *Zainichi* Koreans.

Epilogue

Yonaguni Island at the western extremity of Japan, which was mentioned briefly in the Prologue, has been troubled continuously since 2008 by the issue of the building of a military base there. This island which had a population of over 20,000 people active in 'smuggling' with Taiwan in the immediate post-war period is nowadays a 'lone island on the distant seas' with a population of only just over 1,500.[1] Few tourists visit, leaving the islanders to live a quiet life, and it was on this territory that all of a sudden 'myth' and 'reality' sprang into being. I would like to end this book with a reconsideration of nativism viewed in terms of the myths and realities of voting rights for foreign residents and the deployment of Japan's Self Defense Forces.

In March 2010, when the Hatoyama government stated its strong support for voting rights for foreign residents, the town council of Yonaguni adopted a resolution opposing these rights. Thereafter, this resolution was treated as the symbolic case in the campaign opposing voting rights for foreign residents. As we saw in the Prologue, the reasoning behind this is that if voting rights for foreign residents were to become a reality, then foreigners would move en masse to border areas, acquire the casting vote in their local elections and ultimately take over the islands on Japan's borders. Aside from public works, Yonaguni's industries amount to stock farming, fishing and tourism, and since they rely on small aeroplane and twice weekly cargo ship services for the delivery of goods, the cost of living is also high. The considerable difficulty of making a living on Yonaguni has led to an ongoing trend of population decline. Thus, it is argued that if China were to feel so inclined, it could easily take over this little island.

These arguments opposing voting rights for foreign residents could be called a kind of local nativism, but they cannot be explained away as simply a local issue. This is because the wild stories about 'Yonaguni being captured' were not fomented and inflated on the island but inspired externally. Japan Conference, Japan's largest ultra-right group, mounted a campaign opposing voting rights for foreign residents, in 2010, and asked the town council to also pass a resolution opposing them. The LDP members of Yonaguni's town council simply went along with this,[2] but once the resolution had been taken it would go on being used as proof that 'the border areas are experiencing a sense of danger' (Mihagi 2012). Red herrings used to link 'national borders' with 'national defense' turned voting rights for foreign residents, which are properly the rights of residents, into 'tools of aggression'.

At the same time as calls for voting rights for foreign residents were being treated as 'aggression by foreigners', what was actually taking shape in Yonaguni was a response to 'aggression by foreign countries'. The '2011–15 Construction Plan for Japan's Medium-term Defense Capability' includes 'the new deployment of coastal surveillance forces in the island areas of Japan's southwest region',[3] and plans are progressing for what is seen as the necessary deployment of Ground Self-Defense Forces to Yonaguni in 2014. There is no need to deploy the army, which has little to do with the 'defense of the Senkaku Islands' – the current military focus, to Yonaguni (Sado 2012).[4] However, policies and their implementation are constantly constructing 'insufficiently defended' national borders (Haddad 2007: 134). The 'China threat' is a ready resource when defending the vested interests of the Ground Self-Defense Forces.

This Self-Defense Plan itself has the air of having been invited by the island's own Self-Defense Association rather than of having been forcibly imposed from the outside. Taiwan, which is 111 kilometres to the west, is closer to Yonaguni Island than is Ishigaki Island, the regional centre, which is 124 kilometres to its east. Since Yonaguni had been part of Taiwan's economic sphere in the pre-war period – with inhabitants going to Taiwan for work – and given also that there continue to be exchanges of people and trade in the post-war period, the idea was conceived of a special exchange zone with Taiwan as a policy for regional revitalization. As this was rejected by the national government, the idea of attracting the Self-Defense Forces emerged as the next policy for regional revitalization.[5] This plan gave rise to an opposition movement amongst the islanders which, at two mayoral elections, backed a mayoral candidate opposed to the plan (the movement was ultimately defeated), and two of the six people who made up the legislative assembly, which had previously not had an opposition party, now became the opposition via town council elections. Because they had not won a majority in the legislative assembly, the faction opposing the plan to attract the Self-Defense Forces went as far as to make a direct appeal to local government under a public referendum ordinance, but this was rejected due to the opposition of ruling party members of the assembly.

In August 2013, the mayor – who was from the faction supporting the plan to attract the Self-Defense Forces – was re-elected and then, in February 2015, a local referendum showed a majority of residents were in favor of the plan. Consequently, more than one hundred Self-Defense Force officials and their families moved to Yonaguni as new residents in March 2016. In short, one hundred new voters, on an island with a population of 1,500, will have a hand in the administration of the town. We are not talking here about the migration of foreigners as part of some wild idea. What we are talking about is voters in the form of Self-Defense officials, who display a high level of homogeneity and who are ignorant about the administration of the town. I am not questioning here the political ideologies of Self-Defense Force officials. Whatever their political standpoint, for these Self-Defense Force officials who have been newly appointed to Yonaguni by chance, the island's politics can only ever remain a mystery. These sorts of voters would in all likelihood abstain from voting in local elections, but this is not what will happen in Yonaguni. This is because the vice president of the local Self-Defense Association, a body which supports the Self-Defense Forces, is the member of the town council who introduced the discussion of inviting the Self-Defense Forces to the area. This is likely to produce a solid organizational vote as the Self-Defense Association guides the Self-Defense officials, who are ignorant of the town's administration, on how to vote correctly.

There are doubts about the economic effect that the presence of the Self-Defense Forces will have given that they will consume provisions that they have brought with them and, therefore, there cannot be any expectations that they will buy anything on the island, and nor will they make any subsidiary aid payments. However, the political effect of an organizational vote that corresponds to just short of ten per cent of total votes in mayoral elections will be immense, and the administration of the town will soon faithfully reflect the 'logic of Self-Defense (the Self-Defense Association)'.[6] If Japan's nearest neighbors are provoked and the area is plunged into a state of tension, then a cycle will emerge in which there are further expansions of the Self-Defense Force presence. This represents the birth of the cycle of China threat → deployment of the Self-Defense Forces → diplomatic friction → further strengthening of defense capability → an island subordinate to national defense. Yonaguni will undergo transformation along the lines of: the entry point to Taiwan → a solitary island on the distant seas → the frontline of national defense.

A look back at history shows that this is not the first time that Yonaguni has been put at the mercy of the logic of self-defense. Yonaguni went through the bitter experience of having its smuggling activities with Taiwan, which had provided the island's post-war economic base, 'forcibly terminated' because of the Chinese Civil War and the Korean War. This termination came about because the United States military imposed a thorough crackdown on smuggling in order to address the problem of the flow of ammunition and brass from Yonaguni to China (Yakahi 2005: 51–2). Cut off from Taiwan, Yonaguni has subsequently followed a course of decline. If we call this the 'first tragedy' suffered by Yonaguni, then the 'second farce' is being played out in the form of the deployment of Self-Defense Forces. This farce has even spilt over to the textbook issue with the selection of a civics textbook published by Ikuhōsha, which gives favorable descriptions of 'territorial disputes' and 'the Self-Defense Forces' in the Yaeyama Islands sector, which includes Yonaguni.[7] What this series of events shows is that, under cover of shouts that 'distant islands would be taken over by foreigners', what we have before us is a set of circumstances that resemble a bad example of black humor in which 'distant islands will be taken over by national defense'.

The lesson of this book is that securitization must be resisted from the dual standpoints of local determination and national minorities. Taken to its extreme, the logic that justifies the exclusion of foreigners is national security, which historically has brought about many tragedies in the treatment of 'hostile peoples'. Seen from this viewpoint, the resolution opposing voting rights for foreign residents by the town council of Yonaguni is not a trivial exception. Once the logic of securitization, which takes advantage of 'threats', is adopted the concept of 'borders' comes to be applied everywhere and develops into a principle for controlling the whole of society. When the focus falls on strained relations with North Korea, Japanese society already has a 'track record' of suppressing people with North Korean nationality as a matter of course.

In response to this, methods for reducing 'threats' without relying on 'national defense' thinking in a desecuritization manner will be indispensible when it comes to stopping vicious cycles such as the one witnessed on Yonaguni. This sort of thinking highlights the necessity of returning to historical issues as the primary causes of 'threats' – that is, asking what makes enemies of all of Japan's nearest neighbors. The Cold War structure has permitted the vague treatment of war responsibility and the colonial settlement. It was being under the umbrella of the United States that allowed Japan to escape from its responsibility. However, economic development in East Asia and the politicization of 'cultural trauma' (Alexander et al. 2004) mean that Japan can no longer get away with the manner in which it has attempted to conduct its interactions as an extension of this past, even after the end of the Cold War. This notwithstanding, Japan's demonstrated lack of an ability to learn, seen in the outpouring of reckless remarks for domestic consumption immediately following the international apology to the victims of its wartime aggressions, has aggravated relations with our nearest neighbors. Japanese-style nativism is an extension of this behavior.

We have now reached the point where I can finally talk about the most important finding of this book, Japanese-style Nativism. As mentioned in the Prologue, Japanese-style nativism indicates a xenophobic movement that reflects relations with Japan's nearest neighbors, and is based on the colonial settlement and the Cold War.[8] *Zainichi* Koreans are the direct targets, but it is historical relations with Japan's nearest neighbors, rather than negative stereotypes of foreigners, that form the basis of xenophobic sentiments. In this sense, factors such as the increase in the numbers of foreigners and cultural competition, which are the main causes of nativism in other countries, are of little significance when it comes to explaining Japanese-style nativism.

The origins of Japanese-style nativism are to be found in the fact that, under the Cold War system, Japan has basked in the 'benefit' of leaving unattended the matter of settling its past accounts.[9] In Japan, 15 August, 1945 is designated as the date for marking the anniversary of the end of the war, but the Chinese Civil War was still raging and within a few years the Korean Peninsula was plunged into a state of full-scale war (Komagome 1996). The result was the division of both China and the Korean Peninsula, but it was actually this very situation that proved useful in ensuring that the issues of Japan's colonial rule and its war responsibility would remain vague. The United States also preferred securing supply bases to investigating Japan's war responsibility, and it was acquiescent in the construction of relations with Japan's nearest neighbors which left the issue of responsibility in an ambiguous state. The manner in which South Korea was treated at the time of the normalization of diplomatic relations with Japan can be summed up as one of taking advantage of another party which needs resources for its development. In short, the method of resolution that was adopted was logically contradictory; it was as if, while denying any case for reparations, the colonial settlement was resolved via the payment of development funds. We have already discussed the similar measures adopted with regard to *Zainichi* Koreans.

Meanwhile, another path – albeit one as delicate as a fine thread – has opened up aside from those of putting off a colonial settlement and of abandoning proactive interaction. This is dyad-based local-level experiences; local governments have worked hard to develop local citizenship that served as a type of asylum for foreign residents. However, these past few years, the abolition of subsidies to Korean schools has been carried out in a way that throws away the accomplishments of the dyad. These local integration policies were too fragile, however, to secure local citizenship for foreign residents. The triad penetrates even into local government policies, and this is the hard fact of the ongoing destruction of asylum.

However, initiatives on the local level persistently amount to no more than a side story. Without a reconstruction of the triad, which has clearly had a historical path marked out for it, Japanese-style nativism will keep erupting repeatedly. In this sense, the demise of the Cold War between East and West was a good opportunity for arriving at a rapprochement by altering what has been the historical path to date and, considering the existing state of affairs, the 'benefits' of having done so would have been enormous. Germany was actually able to rebuild its relations with Poland, at the time of the reunification of its western and eastern parts, by declaring publicly that it renounced territories to the east (Sakaki 2013; Sato, Shigeki 2008). Attempts of this kind were made under the Hosokawa and the Murayama governments, but ended in halfway measures without going as far as changing the path that Japan was on.[10] With regard to *Zainichi* Koreans, radical measures, including voting rights and choice of citizenship, ought to have been taken at the time of the creation of the requirements for Special Permanent Residence in 1991. Had we been able to rebuild relations with Japan's nearest neighbors at this point in time, a nativism which equates South Koreans, North Koreans and *Zainichi* Koreans would most likely not have gained credibility and the movement would also probably not have expanded rapidly.

I have been relentlessly critical of 'explanations that see anxiety as the cause' and 'explanations that see misfortune as the cause' because these fail to deal with structural problems which have produced deadlocks in Japanese diplomacy. On the other hand, it is not sufficient to understand Japanese-style nativism as a form of 'the continuous expressions of contempt for Asia', because this also fails to grasp particular historical causes such as post-war East Asian geopolitics. The nativist movement is not about the exclusion of *Zainichi* Koreans on the basis of simple racism. At its foundations lies the desire to erase *Zainichi* Koreans, whose existence is a manifestation of 'stories that strike a discordant note in mainstream history' (Gluck 2007: 310) and also of a disgraceful history.

Changing a path that has been close to seventy years in the making will be no easy matter, but the elucidation of this path and an exploration, based on this elucidation, of possibilities for changing it are urgently needed. Taking current political circumstances into account, it is difficult to imagine that even after having elucidated the path, any movements that would go as far as changing it would arise. Even so, the eruption of Japanese-style nativism seems to have aroused anti-racist movements in civil society and in politics. An embodiment of these is the movement against hate speech, a term that has gained such prominence that it was listed in the top ten buzzwords for 2013. However, Japanese-style nativism cannot itself be constrained by restrictions on hate speech. This is not just a matter of opposing hate speech; efforts must be made to come to grips with the issues in discursive opportunities which allow hate speech, and also with the issues between Japan and her nearest neighbors which post-war Japan has left unattended.

Appendix

Most of the data used in this book has been collected via fieldwork. For the sake of simplicity, I will outline the details of the data collection methods used for each chapter and when it was collected. There are numerous critiques of the ultra-right and nativists, but few empirical studies.[1] Japan is not alone in this. In the 2000s, there has been a rapid increase in knowledge about the ultra-right in Europe and the United States as a result of the vast accumulation of research on ultra-right parties. However, interviews with individual ultra-right activists are rare (Blee 2007; Goodwin 2008b).[2] This is, in part, because ultra-right activists are generally hostile to researchers and journalists (Andersson 2013; Blee 2007), which is why it is difficult to accumulate knowledge about extreme political violence (della Porta 2008). As I have also experienced difficulties because of the paucity of research in this area, I will make my information as publicly available as possible. The following is an outline of the data used in this book.

Interview data regarding activists

The data used in this study comes from my own records of interviews with thirty-four activists in the nativist movement. As stated above, there have been few fieldwork studies of ultra-right activists and, even when these exist obtaining accurate information is extremely difficult (Blee 1996: 687). Surveys are not reliable because there will be some false answers and structured interviews merely lead people to repeat their own convictions. Bearing all of this in mind, I gathered data from interviews about activists' life histories, an approach that resolves many of the methodological problems raised above. Unlike structured interviews, in which interviewees tend to repeat the ideologies and policies of their groups, life history interviews generate talk about personal experiences rather than the presentation of organizational goals as one's own (Blee and Taylor 2002).[3]

Given that life histories are post-hoc narratives by activists about their experiences, they cannot completely reconstruct the processes of political socialization or frame alignment. Even so, analyses of life histories are widely used in frame analysis (Johnston 1995). By listening as the person concerned relates their experiences and consciousness chronologically, contradictions in their narration readily become apparent. Repeated questioning also makes it possible to judge whether this is a post-hoc construction or not. This approach is also suited to collecting data regarding movement participation because it does not simply ask direct questions about motives but manages to take a detailed look at the semantic context (Blee and Taylor 2002). Also, because the interview transcripts are available on the web, and therefore potentially subject to falsification, I use my own data to analyze the processes leading to movement participation.[4]

Another reason for having adopted the life histories approach is because I did not want to use methods such as participant observation. In the case of *Zaitokukai*, formal requests were a condition of conducting surveys, but some local branches allowed participant observation. Given the existence of groups open to researchers, such as the Association for the Restoration of Sovereignty (*Shuken kaifuku o mezasu kai*), it would have been possible to carry out participant observation. The reason for not having done so was because I did not want to participate in the nativist movement, even as a researcher.[5]

Previous research on this issue stresses the fact that ultra-right activists are 'ordinary people' (Blee 1996, 2002; Ezekiel 2002; Goodwin 2008b; Jansson 2010; Klandermans and Mayer 2006b: 269). Research experience to date enabled me to predict that this would also hold true for Japanese activists. However, I postponed fieldwork for almost a year because I did not want to 'build a rapport' with people who were engaging in activities that I felt emotionally unable to condone (Higuchi 2013). Throughout my fieldwork, I first made clear my own political position and only then asked activists to tell me their life histories leading up to their participation in the movement. It would have been easy enough for them to discover my political orientation on the internet, and it may be that explicitly disclosing it from the start led some people to avoid answering interview questions from an 'enemy'.[6] Conversely, there were also people who were decidedly curious about speaking to an 'enemy', and there were several times when discussions continued even after the end of the interview.

Zaitokukai was the main site of activism for twenty-five of the people interviewed (including those who were still active), while the remaining nine were active in other groups.[7] When organizing the interviews, I sent a copy of the interview prospectus, either by letter or email, to groups in the nativist movement, along with my request for an interview. In many instances addresses were unclear, and in most cases emails remained unanswered. In the case of *Zaitokukai*, a mandatory formal procedure has been in place since the end of 2010 for those requesting interviews, and a condition of acceptance is the payment of a 'fee for cooperation in data collection' at the time of the interview. From the standpoint of interview ethics, informal interviews were not a possibility; there was no choice but to abide by *Zaitokukai* conditions in order to conduct the interviews.

The author was asked to pay approximately 10,000 yen for two hours with one participant, but a decision by the *Zaitokukai* secretariat led to occasional reductions. It was under these conditions that I carried out the interviews from February 2011 until October 2012, using recordings to produce transcripts of the interviews.[8] The attributes of participants were: gender – 4 females and 30 males; age – 4 people in their twenties, 13 in their thirties, 11 in their forties, 4 in their fifties, and 2 in their sixties.

Since random sampling was not possible, I will give a simple account of the sampling biases that exist. Given that they were in the midst of a financial crisis, *Zaitokukai* asked for a fee for cooperation in data collection and felt the need to introduce as many members as possible to the study. This did not lead to the 'selection' of members who were likely to improve the external image of the group; interviewees were recruited on the basis that they were the activists who were willing to be interviewed. As a consequence, twenty-one were officials at branch manager level and above, and four others. Most of the people whose main place of activism was groups other than *Zaitokukai* had had previous experience in right-wing movements and had only joined the nativist movement in recent years. All of these people, including the four from *Zaitokukai* who did not hold official positions, can be seen as sharing the characteristics of an 'activist class' – they participate proactively in the groups to which they belong. A point that arose several times in informal conversation was that when people heard that there were to be formal interviews with a university professor whom they did not know, most became hesitant about taking part in the interview.[9] Thus, those who became interview participants can be seen as people who tend to be positive communicators and types who cannot refuse a request. Interviews were often conducted in small groups of several people rather than one-on-one, and this may, in part, have been a way of keeping an eye on me.

Having established the characteristics of the people being interviewed, a contrast emerged with Kōichi Yasuda's famous reportage on *Zaitokukai*. As mentioned in the Introduction, Yasuda stated that many members of *Zaitokukai* had low levels of education and were in irregular employment, but later held that they were diverse in terms of class. One of the initial discrepancies between his work and mine can be seen as arising from differences in the subjects used for data collection. Perhaps because Yasuda was unable to gain practically any cooperation from *Zaitokukai*, he says that his approach included talking to 'rank-and-file members' at demonstrations and going to their homes to listen to what they had to say.[10] He also came into contact with people who came to public talks following the publication of *The Internet and Patriotism*. The differences between Yasuda's data collection, in which 'marginal members' were predominant, and my interviews, which targeted the activist class, are thus also – not surprisingly perhaps – reflected in class terms.

Another difference between the interview subjects in Yasuda's study and mine is to be found in the motives that led to their participation in nativism. Yasuda says that 'the majority of the people I interviewed replied that their "hatred of Korea was sparked by the Japan–South Korea World Cup"' (Kimura, Sei and Yasuda 2013: 43). In the case of my interviews, the majority gave historical revisionism or conflict with Japan's neighboring countries as the starting point for their activism and only one person cited the World Cup as the motivating factor (see Chapter 3). Yasuda's assertion that the World Cup was the motive is somewhat lacking in credibility as an explanation of the motivations of 'rank-and-file members'. A considerable amount of time had passed since the 2002 World Cup, and it is not as if 'rough play by the Korean team' had become a major social issue. Is it likely that, despite this, those 'rank-and-file members', having keenly sensed 'unfairness' when watching the Korean team's game, felt a sense of animosity which they then kept alive for close to ten years? It would seem reasonable to conclude that the 'World Cup issue' was an ex post facto construction.

Interviews about voting rights for foreign residents

Between May 2010 and April 2013, I carried out twenty-one interviews with nineteen people about enfranchisement for foreign residents. In addition to Yukio Hatoyama, former Prime Minister, and Tetsuzō Fuyushiba (deceased), former Minister of Land and Transportation, many others agreed to take part in an interview, on the condition of anonymity. The breakdown of participants is as follows: Diet members (Democratic Party 9; New *Kōmeitō* 2; LDP 1; Social Democratic Party 1; Sunrise Party of Japan 1); Secretaries to Diet members (Democratic Party 1); and 6 people from a variety of other organizations.

The Okinawa and Yaeyama Interviews

These interviews were carried out in collaboration with Mitsuru Matsutani. In November 2012, March 2013, February 2014 and February to March 2015 we carried out 29 interviews in Ishigaki City and the towns of Yonaguni and Taketomi concerning the selection of textbooks and the construction of Self-Defense Forces bases. The participants were: mayors 3; Diet members 1; city and town councillors 8; city and town personnel 3; and related organizations 14.

Data about right-wing world of criticism journals

This data providing a view of the discourse of established conservatives serves the purpose of elucidating the interests of the right-wing world of criticism and the changes in its designation of enemies.[11] I made the more right leaning *Shokun!* and *Seiron* the focus of data collection rather than the major journals of the right-wing world of criticism, *Bungei Shunjū* and *Chūō Kōron*. This was because it was necessary to deal with discourse that was further to the right than that of mainstream conservatives. However, as *Shokun!* ceased publication in 2009, I replaced it with *WiLL* from that point onwards. Kura (2006, 2008 and 2009) has carried out analyses of *SAPIO* articles, but these have not been used in this book because it is newly published and the articles are short.[12] *Voice* was another possible contender but I decided that it was possible to grasp the trends by looking at *Shokun!* and *Seiron*, which are representative right-wing world of criticism journals. *WiLL* was chosen partly because its editor-in-chief had previously worked for Bungei Shunjū (the publisher of *Shokun!*) and also because its layout resembles that of *Shokun!*

The reasons for citing articles from the years 1982–2012 are that *Nichigai* Associates began listing *Seiron* articles in their database in 1982 and also in order to look at the changes that occurred in the 1980s and the end of the 1990s. It has already been pointed out that there tend to be yearly changes in the right-wing world of criticism. Yoshimi (2003: 267) says that in the 1980s *Shokun!* shifted to a tendency to 'display open aggression' and that this grew substantially in the 1990s. While Jomaru cites arguments about the threat of the Soviet Union to point out the same shift as Yoshimi, he states that from the second half of the 1990s 'there has been a striking deterioration' (2011: 398) in writing styles, which frequently include terms such as 'anti-Japanese'.

Considering the constraints on the time and labor required to put together data, I abandoned the notion of compiling the data by scanning the contents of these articles (however, I exhaustively copied and scanned relevant articles, and cite these, as required, in the text). Instead, I have listed titles from 1982 to 2012, and have noted 'month and year of issue', 'geographic region dealt with', 'issue', 'whether the author is a politician (present/former Diet member) or not' and 'whether the term anti-Japanese is used or not'. All entries where it was not possible to make these determinations from the title alone have been recorded as unknown. Also, where one title referred to multiple nations or issues (for example, South Korea, China and history), it was regarded as relating to all of them. There are significant differences in the topics and nations dealt with by the three journals but this reflects discrepancies in the issues dealt with from year to year rather than in their nature. For example, *WiLL* had a large proportion of articles that dealt with the 'left wing' but this was because there was a Democratic Party government from 2009 until 2012. Conversely, the reason why there was a large proportion of articles about the Soviet Union and Russia in *Shokun!* was because they were covering the Cold War era.

Another point to note is that I am fundamentally describing proportions and not absolute numbers. There is a tendency for a year on year increase in the numbers of articles; this is likely to occur because the number of topics circulating in society increases as a whole due to the expansion in the fields of interest that accompanies increasing levels of education (McCombs and Zhu 1995). However, issues compete with one another as the scope for taking up topics popularly circulating in society at a given point in time is not limitless (Hilgartner and Bosk 1988). In short, rather than an overall increase in the interests of the right-wing world of criticism, it would be more accurate to view the total amount of interest at a particular point in time as fixed and then look at the proportion of this that is taken up by particular interests.

Data on *Zaitokukai* protest events

Social movement research after the 1970s has used event analysis which counts protest events by a movement. Event analysis indicates a method of analysis which gathers protest event data – using newspapers, public documents and the like – on a consistent basis; prepares a database by coding these; and then uses this data to carry out a quantitative analysis of the social movement. Protest events designate gatherings held by social movements for the purpose of achieving their aims, and the number, type and scale of protest events can be used as an index showing the dynamism of a social movement. This method came to be used in the 1960s for making international comparisons of collective violence and for analyzing the origins of race riots (Olzak 1992: 49). Subsequently, alongside international comparisons of social movements and the success of macro-analysis, there was an increase in studies using event analysis. Event analysis emerged as the most widely used methodology in articles on social movements appearing in the major sociology journals in the United States between 1987 and 1993 (Crist and McCarthy 1996: 95–6). Although event analysis has been used less frequently following the 2000s, it is an established methodology (Rucht and Ohlemacher 1992; Rucht, Koopmans and Neidhardt 1998). I have created a database in order to conduct an event analysis because I consider it to be effective for comprehending the characteristics of the nativist movement.

Newspapers are the most commonly used data sources for event analysis, but the nativist movement rarely appears in Japanese newspapers.[13] Official records, such as police records, are sometimes used regarding strikes and radical movements because of their comprehensiveness, but these are not a beneficial data source for the nativist movement. Ultimately, the only realistic method is to make use of the movement's own information, and I decided to use the blog of *Zaitokukai* founder Makoto Sakurai because of the consistency and comprehensiveness of the data contained in it.[14] Because Sakurai's blog covers events from the beginning of the formation of the movement and posts links to information about related events, information that is essential to coding can be gathered from it. Using this method, I have collected 1,006 protest events occurring between 2007 and 2012. I have entered the data for each of these respectively, coding them with the 'month and year', 'place of gathering', 'issue', 'target (the object at which the protest was directly aimed)' and 'repertoires of action'.

Notes

Prologue

1 However, this figure accounts for members who have registered by email; there is no obligation to disclose information concerning individuals or the payment of fees. Consequently, it would be more accurate to say that there are over 15,000 registered people rather than members.

2 *Zainichi* (literally, resident in Japan) is used largely to refer to ethnic Koreans living in Japan. As former colonial citizens they are granted special permanent resident status. The term covers several generations, but members of the most recent generations may share only the nationality of their elders as they have been educated and socialized in Japan.

3 Compared with 'anxiety', there are few other items that have been written about in the discourse that can be mentioned, but 'discrimination' is also a word that could (potentially) be used to explain the rise of the nativist movement. I do not mean to assert that anxiety and prejudice are unrelated to the rise of Japanese-style nativism, but nor do I think that it can be explained by them.

4 This is not to say that we can ignore the fact that following 9/11 the Japanese police have been keeping resident Muslims under constant surveillance. The realities of this are clear in the 2010 case of the leaking of public security files on the internet. For a more detailed discussion on this see Aoki, Azusawa and Kawasaki 2011.

5 When thinking about this problem, there are many aspects of Oguma's (1998: 661–7) concept of 'colored empire' and Kang's (1996) arguments about Japanese orientalism that can be used, with some reworking.

6 The concept of geopolitics was originally mainly used in connection with military affairs, and there is a strong tendency to take the respective strength of political parties as a given. However, this work grasps geopolitics as symbols and systems with socially-constructed meanings attached (Tuathail 1996: 52). If this were not the case, then the dyad/triad model in Chapter 8 would not stand.

Introduction

1 The features of the established right wing are: (1) absolute loyalty to the emperor and the nation; (2) opposition to and vigilance against communism,

socialism and any forces sympathetic to these; (3) an emphasis on action rather than theory; (4) maintenance of ethnic traditions and culture and vigilance against foreign ideas and cultures; (5) stressing duty, order and authority; (6) a national sense of duty; (7) an authoritarian command structure; (8) familist totalitarianism; (9) a conservative inclination; (10) patriarchal human relationships; (11) vigilance against the intellectual class; (12) a tendency towards lone wolves; and (13) elitism (*Shakai Mondai Kenkyūkai* 1976: 49). Of these, (4) could be called nativism, but it is (1) and (2) that have been the common denominator for the established right wing.

2 This does not mean that right-wing thinking does not include nativism, but simply that nativism has not become a focal point because of historical circumstances and the political environment.

3 The fact that voting rights for foreign residents is still an issue today is partly the consequence of the adoption of xenophobic policies which cannot imagine political integration for *Zainichi* Koreans (see Chapter 7 on this point).

4 The 'welfare problem' taken up by *Zaitokukai* was also problematized in the 1950s. There was *Zainichi* Korean-bashing with claims that a large proportion of this group were welfare recipients, which led to welfare cuts in the name of 'adjustment' (Yuichi Higuchi 2002: 183–6). The Japanese government deprived *Zainichi* Koreans of their voting rights out of fear of the political influence that they might wield in the immediate post-war period (Mizuno 1996, 1997). A system of re-entry permits was similarly applied for reasons to do with bilateral relations with North Korea (Chong 2012). These issues were all treated as if they were legal problems, but it would be more accurate to think of the law as actually being used for political reasons to restrict rights and then to justify these actions.

5 The massacre of Koreans at the time of the Great Kantō Earthquake in 1923 was a case of hate violence, but it was not an organized action. Although the state policies of social control were also profoundly connected to this massacre (Kang 2003), it is better to regard it as having been a spontaneous movement that was temporary and not well organized. The current nativist movement – despite its unstable base – is more continuous and more organized, and it requires an analytical framework that differs from that of classical studies of crowd behavior.

6 This group was based on a collection of contractors: they called themselves a right-wing organization as a front for illegal bid rigging. They started racist harassment when they saw large numbers of Iranians gathering in Tokyo's Ueno Park.

7 For a more detailed discussion see Higuchi (2013a). Hiroyuki Seto, a leader of this group, published a book regarding this matter (Seto 2000).

8 For more details see Higuchi (2012s, 2012x).

9 For *Tsukurukai* see Koo (2010), Murai (1997a, 1997b), Oguma and Ueno (2003) and Saaler (2005). *Tsukurukai* has experienced a certain degree of grassroots expansion, but the large-scale support that it receives from the established right wing, for example from Shinto and the Junior Chamber of Commerce, makes it different from the nativist movement (Tawara 2001).

10 There is, however, a discrepancy between parties with particularly strong support from youth under twenty-five and parties whose core support is made up of people aged in their late twenties to their forties. The latter

correspond to the British National Party and the Reform Party of Canada (Goodwin et al. 2010: 197; Nevitt et al. 1998: 188–9).

11 It was the group known as Team Kansai that orchestrated these events and also organized discriminatory agitation in front of a museum about *buraku* people. This group appears prominently in connection with criminal and civil cases.

12 Antiracism counter mobilization has the effect of curtailing support for the nativst movement and right-wing parties (Lloyd 1998; Willems 1995; Witte 1996). This curtailment effect by opposition movements can also be seen in Japan, but Japan seems to be relatively 'tolerant' towards ultra-right activists. In the Netherlands, for example, membership of an ultra-right organization carries with it political and social marginalization (Klandermans 2013; Linden and Klandermans 2006a, 2006b).In Germany, the strength of the social stigma surrounding skinheads makes it difficult for them to ever stop being skinheads (Backes and Mudde 2000).

13 It is also possible, however, that because this would lead to the radicalization of a minority within the movement (della Porta 1995; della Porta and Reiter 1998), even more serious hate crimes might occur.

14 I am also acquainted with some of the people from whom Yasuda collected data and, while he does not talk about them in his book, they cannot be called exclusively 'stressed people'. And even if they had been 'stressed people', it seems implausible in many cases to connect their respective difficulties with their commitment to the nativist movement.

15 The reference here to 'stressed people' indicates those suffering from either economic difficulties or emotional anxiety, or both.

16 According to some of the people concerned, after a bar owner assumed a leadership position more 'gang group' members started to gather while others tended to drift away, leading to a change in the organizational culture. Yasuda says, 'although I looked at the personal histories of members who had been arrested in incidents in Kyoto and Tokushima, [the fact that most *Zaitokukai* members bear no relevance to the 'elite'] is clear' (Yasuda 2011: 35). However, because the character of Team Kansai is exceptional rather than normal among *Zaitokukai* activists, it would be best to see using it to draw analogies about the whole as a mistake.

17 But then, this view was not limited to Yasuda; it was in common use in arguments that saw the movement as pathology (e.g. Hoffer 1951).

18 From the viewpoint of what Olson (1965) calls the problem of free riders, the initial act of participating in the movement is the one fraught with the most obstacles. It would be considerably easier for people to continue with the movement once they have overcome these obstacles and participated for the first time.

19 Mudde (2000:170) examines the degree to which nationalism, nativism, statism (law and order, militarism), welfare chauvinism, traditional ethics and revisionism apply in the case of the right-wing parties in each country. Just looking at this list one appreciates the considerable diversity contained within the single term ultra-right.

20 There are some areas on which the existing right wing and the nativist movement agree, such as opposition to voting rights for foreign residents.

It should instead be the case that they agree in most areas, but this point is left abstract while only discrepancies are picked up. In my opinion, the differences between the existing right wing and the nativist movement are largely in matters of style and not ideological.

21 This very phenomenon has also been observed in *Tsukurukai* and has not at all been unusual in right-wing citizens' movements in recent years (Oguma and Ueno 2003). It is not the case, however, that the emperor system has completely lost any meaning; there are new possibilities for linking it to nationalism (see Karube 2006 on this).

22 Any reading of the interview narratives of this Deputy President frankly and readily show that he did not participate in the movement out of any vague grievance or anxiety in his life. As might be expected, he participated because he agreed ideologically with the movement, but this aspect fell outside the consideration of Yasuda's work.

23 There are also groups, such as *Haigaisha*, within the nativist movement that focus on the expulsion of Chinese, but it is overwhelmingly *Zainichi* Koreans who are the target.

24 At a stretch, hate against Koreans has something in common with anti-Semitism, but it would be difficult to understand the exclusion of *Zainichi* Koreans using the anti-Semitism analogy.

25 To be precise, this residential status is applied to former colonial citizens and their descendants who have been living in Japan since before the defeat in World War Two.

26 Extracted from a leaflet on the *Zaitokukai* homepage: (http://www.zaitokukai.info/uploads/images/bira/z_bira_a01.jpg).

27 On the truth or otherwise of the 'hatred of Korea' discourse, which includes in part 'special privileges for *Zainichi* Koreans', see Noma (2013), Ōta et al. (2006), Tanaka Itagaki (2007) and Yasuda (2012a).

28 The spread of stereotypical views is not just limited to Japan; researchers who have carried out surveys of ultra-right activists in Europe also stress that supporters are 'ordinary people' (Blee 1996, 2002; Goodwin 2008b; Klandermans and Mayer 2006b: 269).

29 There has also been an increase in research using approaches that appreciate rationality regarding similar phenomena (Breton et al. 2002; Brustein 1996; Wintrobe 2006).

Chapter 1

1 I have consulted the following articles, which review the arguments in this field: (Ignazi 2002, 2003; Rydgren 2007; Eatwell 2003; Schain et al. 2002).

2 Moreover, the investigation in this book is mainly limited to Western Europe following the 1980s, but the forerunner to this was the research into fascism and McCarthyism in the United States (Husbands 2002).

3 However, the fact that trends in the ultra-right cannot be explained solely via a demand-side analysis has been pointed out repeatedly in Western European studies (Mudde 2010: 1168). In fact, variables on the 'supply' side can give a far better explanation of degrees of support for ultra-right parties (Van der Berg and Fennema 2007: 482). According to Carter, party

ideology, organization, leadership and inter-party competition significantly influence the number of votes for ultra-right parties (Carter 2005).

4 Kriesi argues that at the same time as the ultra-right was experiencing conflict, even more conflict was emerging in the new (left-wing) social movement inside the new middle class of specialists and technocrats, but we will not deal this. There are also other arguments about social changes having given rise to two disparate political parties, green parties and ultra-right parties (for example Ignazi 1992; Kitschelt 1995; Taggart 1996).

5 Looked at operationally, people who do not belong to any religion, labor union or stable lifeworld as a result of intergenerational social mobility tend to support the ultra-right (Lubbers, Scheepers and Billet 2000: 368–9).

6 This is based on a series of studies called ethnic competition theory, but it uses a simplified version of the original competition theory (Balazs et al. 2007).

7 On this point, see Van der Brug and Fennema (2003: 56).

8 There is also the view that the ultra-right needs to use political leadership to integrate different milieux because its support is not concentrated within one specific social milieu (Immerfall 1998: 258).

9 This disparity could be the result of social change in post-industrial societies, in which women rather than men tend to be left-wing (Inglehart and Norris 2003).

10 There is, however, a discrepancy between parties with particularly strong support from youth under twenty-five and parties whose core support is made up of people aged in their late twenties to their forties. The latter correspond to the British National Party and the Reform Party of Canada (Goodwin et al. 2010: 197; Nevitt et al. 1998: 188–9).

11 Another age effect is dealignment in support for political parties; that is, an irreversible increase of independent voters (Dalton and Wattenberg 2000; Knutsen 2006). This can be said to be weakening existing political parties' power to unify voters while also opening up opportunities for new political influences to emerge, including the ultra-right.

12 In this section we have been looking at the effect of each variable, but analyses by Arzheimer (2009) using the largest data set also confirm the same effects; these are robust results.

13 With regard to this, there is also the view that traditional class classifications are inadequate, and that we ought to also consider the fact that the logic of support for the ultra-right varies according to class (Lubbers and Güveli 2007).

14 Even in studies which categorize supporters of the British National Party as 'angry white men', the pseudo r square was no more than 0.065 when demographic variables and locality were included in the analysis (Ford and Goodwin 2010: 14).

15 Most advocates do not deny the fact that there is a link between some types of structural change and the rise of the ultra-right (Catellani and Milesi 2007; Mileti and Plomb 2007: 33). It is, however, the simple linking of this to deprivation that is being criticized.

16 This is close to the image of voters presented by participatory democracy theory, in recent years, as voting independently of organizations (Dalton 2004; Dalton and Wattenberg 2000).

17 However, Norris says that there was no significant connection between the proportion of migrant population in each country and the percentage of the vote for the ultra-right. This can be smoothed over as an ecological fallacy, but there needs to be precise clarification in future.

18 The connection between competition over jobs and the ultra-right vote is rejected, but there is also the argument that competition over housing is linked to support for the ultra-right (Bowyer 2008).

19 These are aggregate results from macro-data, but support for ultra-right parties in England has risen in local government areas with large racial minorities, particularly from Pakistan and Bangladesh (Bowyer 2008: 618).

20 It should be added that whilst the degree of political dissatisfaction amongst people who vote for the National Front in France is high, the extent of people who abstain from voting is higher than those who vote for the ultra-right (Lubbers and Scheepers 2002: 139).

21 However, results supporting protest vote theory do emerge in Belgium, where voting is compulsory. In an analysis of exit polls conducted by Swyngedouw (2001: 234), it was only ultra-right parties that garnered a significantly large number of protest votes. As voters do not have the choice of abstaining from voting they can end up choosing the ultra-right instead.

Chapter 2

1 There is also the argument that 'suddenly imposed grievances', such as the Three Mile Island nuclear accident, act as direct causes for the appearance of social movements (Walsh 1981). However, 'special privileges for *Zainichi* Koreans' clearly does not fall within this group, and even the increase in social movement mobilization that followed the Fukushima Number 1 Nuclear Reactor accident began more than a year after the accident (Hirabayashi 2013).

2 This is not just the case in Japan; identical stereotypes are rampant in all countries, even though they have been refuted empirically (Atkinson 1993; Mudde 2014).

3 However, it was also argued, in relation to the development of social movements, that Smelser's theory of collective action was the model for the subsequent resource mobilization theory, political process approach and frame analysis. Davies (1962, 1969) and Gurr (2011) were exponents of middle-range theory, which focussed on the relationship between the occurrence of grievance and social movements.

4 One reason that can be given for this is that mass society theory has treated social movements as undesirable pathological phenomena and regarded them as hostile (Bevington and Dixon 2005: 201). Criticism of the ultra-right was consistent with mass society theory's negative assessment of social movements, but this stance makes it difficult to have an accurate understanding of or to respond appropriately to the problem.

5 For an introduction that neatly summarizes this sort of simple theory of nationalism, see Honda (2007).

6 There was one person who dropped out of vocational school and another dropped out of university, but since they have been able to find work in their areas of specialization they have been treated as if they had graduated.

7 We can also see something of Murai (1997a, 1997b) in Oguma's description of the class nature of *Tsukurukai*.

8 Regarding attributes, we can reliably say that there are large numbers of single people – as touched on in the Introduction, males and residents of large cities, and that the average age is low (according to *Zaitokukai*'s home page, the male to female ratio of members is roughly 6:1, and, looked at by prefecture, membership numbers are higher than for the rest of the population in the Tokyo and Kansai areas). I do not think, however, that we can say that there are any other clear trends in terms of economic status. Male dominance is not just found in ultra-right parties, it is common throughout ultra-right movement research; there are numerous cases of females being invited by their spouses or partners, and participating in a subordinate manner (Blee and Linden 2012).

9 Adler (1996) and Van Dyke and Soule (2002) have analyzed ultra-right movements from this perspective. However, it is not possible to exclude the possibility of ecological fallacy in these works given that they do not use data about individual activists. Overall, there are inconsistencies in the knowledge that comes both from studies that have used micro-data and those that have used macro-data, and it is best to rely on the former from a procedural point of view.

10 Explanations based on competition theory are basically nonsense when it comes to Chinese migrants, who are expulsion targets although not to the same extent as *Zainichi* Koreans. Since 2007, the number of registered Chinese has become the largest group, surpassing the number of holders of South or North Korean citizenship. Despite this, the visible Chinatowns are effectively those built by the oldcomer Chinese in Yokohama, Kobe and Nagasaki, which are geared towards tourists; overall, Chinese visibility is low. As a whole, Chinese also have higher academic backgrounds than *Zainichi* Koreans (Omagari et al. 2011).

11 Fukuoka and Kim (1997) give an analytical clarification of the ethnicity of *Zainichi* Korean youth.

12 On *Zainichi* Korean marriage, see Hashimoto (2010). Hidenori Sakanaka (1999), a former Director of the Tokyo Immigration Bureau, has said that marriage will lead to a rapid decline in the number of *Zainichi* Koreans. Even though this preserves *jus sanguinis*, it relies on the prospect that assimilation through marriage is possible. Sakanaka is a nationalist, but from this realistic assimilationist standpoint, the view that *Zainichi* Koreans are dangerous looks nonsensical.

13 There are broadly two reasons for this. Firstly, there has been an increase in the numbers acquiring Japanese nationality, with an average of just under 10,000 people a year doing so since 1990. Secondly, since the children who are born of the increasing numbers of marriages with Japanese largely acquire Japanese citizenship there has also been a sharp drop in the number of people holding South or North Korean citizenship who were born overseas.

14 It is not that I do not regard the Korean schools that use Korean to educate students as rejecting assimilation, but the reasons why these schools have

been exclusion targets are, if anything, the result of Japan–Korea relations not cultural differences.

15 The dependency ratio is calculated for Japan as a whole, but because in the case of foreigners it is the number of households and not the number of individuals that is publicly released, the numbers used in Table 2.2 have been calculated individually and are closer to the real situation. Firstly, I have calculated the number of residents – such as, special permanent residents, permanent residents, permanent resident spouses and Japanese spouses – as the denominator in the foreign resident statistics. For the number of people actually receiving welfare, I have multiplied the number of households by the number of people in the households. In this case, where the head is a foreign national and all the other members of a household are Japanese citizens these household members have been recorded under the nationality of the head. Conversely, in cases where the head of a household holds Japanese nationality and other members of the household are foreign nationals they have not been included in the figures. These sorts of issues do arise, but I have made these figures available because they reflect the real situation more accurately.

16 The right to live forms the basis of welfare. The argument that guaranteeing the right to live is the responsibility of the country of nationality and not the country of residence is used to argue that foreigners in Japan have no right to receive welfare. Current practice in Japan is to apply welfare provisions, using administrative discretion, with changes as needed (Koto 1991).

17 The welfare payments put in place by a portion of local governments compensate for this, and these welfare payments have a strong compensatory nature as they address the policy defect of the failure to adopt transitional measures.

18 The Solidarity Network with Migrants' Poverty Project is shouldering the burden regarding welfare. See *Ijūren Hinkon Purōjekuto* (2011) for poverty amongst foreigners in general.

19 This data was obtained from a user-defined aggregation of the national census. For more detail see Inaba et al. (2014), Omagari et al. (2011), and Takaya et al. (2013, 2014 and 2015).

20 The possibility that the largely white-collar newcomer youth are bringing about a generation gap cannot entirely be denied. However, this trend is also clear in Kim and Inazuki (2000), and the gap may safely be seen as reducing.

21 In Japan also, the analytical conclusion has been that the segmented labor market is giving rise to anti-migrant sentiments (Nagayoshi 2012).

22 There is dispute on this point between ethnic competition and the cultural division of labor, but I will not go into this any further as it is not connected to the aim of this book. See Olzak (1992) and Hechter (1999) on both.

23 On the economic conditions of *Zainichi* Koreans, see Han (2010) and Park (2005).

24 This also overlaps with Yasuda's view, but it does not hold true as an explanation of reality.

25 *Pachinko* parlours (Japanese pinball gambling venues) are one of the most important economic niches for *Zainichi* Koreans. Hostility towards them is based on the political reasoning that profits from the *pachinko* industry flow out to North Korea. These sorts of arguments started being made in the

1980s, as in Takako Doi, former Japan Socialist Party leader's, 'misgivings about *pachinko*' which can be seen as a case of bashing.

26 The welfare payments made to elderly *Zainichi* Koreans by local governments that were mentioned earlier were the fruit of local movements demanding rights.

27 In addition to the discussions of *Zainichi* Korean social movements in this book see (Kim 2011; Park 1999; Tanaka 2005).

28 There is a considerable body of research that uses these two hypotheses. In connection with ultra-right movements, one study which uses the British National Party's register of party members has shown that party membership is low in areas where despite the presence of large numbers of people from South Asia they live mixed throughout rather than apart from the rest the community (Biggs and Knauss 2012).

29 In Germany, for example, efforts are underway to find a solution to the problem of high school students becoming interested in the ultra-right as a result of attraction to this sort of culture (Miller-Idriss 2009).

Chapter 3

1 The symbols assigned to activists in this book (Roman alphabet for *Zaitokukai* and Greek alphabet for others) correspond to my summary of interview records. In the text, I only refer to activists' ages and gender, but I provide more detailed information in Higuchi (2012a–x, 2013a–j).

2 Looked at from the perspective of generations and cohorts, the age at which specific political events are experienced is important (Braungart and Braungart 1986), but I was unable to gather any meaningful data on this.

3 Parental influences fall under authoritarianism in general (Adorno et al. 1950: Ch. 3).

4 He also says, 'I think that the problem that I feel most keenly would have to be that of *Zainichi* Koreans ... The immediate threat comes from *Zainichi* Koreans and from Chinese'. Therefore, we see that his adolescent prejudices led him to regard foreigners as immediate threats.

5 This refers to the anti-Japanese demonstrations that broke out in China's major cities in April, 2005.

6 The first Prime Minister of the Meiji government and the first Resident-General of Korea, assassinated by Korean nationalist Jung-geun An.

7 Leaving aside the value of Koizumi's visit to North Korea, one major change that it has brought about is a common understanding both of the right wing (Nakanishi 2007) and the left wing (Wada 2004).

8 Klandermans and others refer to these sorts of activists as 'wanderers' (Klandermans and Linden 2007), but there were only two amongst the activists surveyed for this book. This is no doubt partly due to the short history of the nativist movement.

9 The 'inevitability' of having been born and raised in Japan is also the case for the vast majority of *Zainichi* Koreans, but activists do not realize this. There is a detailed explanation of this in Chapter 8.

10 The Japan of the 1990s that she refers to here may be thought of as indicating, politically, the period preceding the collapse of the 1955 regime and, in

terms of the reality of people's lives, the period that preceded long-term economic recession.

11 The denial of past fascism and war responsibility is a fairly frequent point of reference in the speech of close relatives (Dechezelles 2013).

12 In Okinawa, where there is powerful hatred of military installations, not only has *Zaitokukai* been unable to establish a branch, but its membership figures are strikingly low. If it were the case that participation in the nativist movement is determined solely by socioeconomic factors, then membership figures should be high in Okinawa, which has a particularly high youth unemployment rate. The case of Okinawa thus suggests the necessity of introducing politico-cultural factors into the argument.

13 On this point, see Hwang (2003) and Kuroda (2003).

14 Since Japan does not have a working holiday agreement with the United States, it appears that he chose to have a working holiday in Canada, which was close enough to be able to go and see a match. In order to do this, he left his former job and saved enough to get himself to Canada by driving a taxi, a job in which it is possible to make money in a short time by working long hours.

15 Two of the three converts were converted with the assistance of a historical revisionist radio program and Yoshinori Kobayashi's *On War*.

Chapter 4

1 For a comprehensive introduction to frame analysis, see (Benford and Snow 2000; Noakes and Johnston 2005). A work which applies frame analysis to the ultra-right is McVeigh, Myers and Sikkink (2004). Frame analysis is characterized by the breadth of its usefulness: its extensive collection of research includes the 'master frame' used by the entire social movement of a particular period; frame construction by individual social movement organizations; and frame disputes between organizations and with antagonistic organizations. I limit myself to using the frame alignment process concerning 'movement participation by individuals', but there is surprisingly little empirical research on this as most studies look at the organizational level. The works directly consulted in writing this book were Benford (1993a, 1993b) and Johnston (1991, 1995).

2 As used in this book, the 'special privileges for *Zainichi* Koreans' frame indicates a cognitive framework in which, in addition to the four 'privileges' mentioned in the Introduction, *Zainichi* Koreans are seen as a threat to Japan.

3 This indicates the compatibility of the frame alignment process and world events.

4 This arises from the fact that the 'special privileges for *Zainichi* Koreans' frame itself was not a product of the right-wing movement or of the right-wing world of criticism but of the internet. See Chapter 6 for a more detailed discussion.

5 The discussion that follows will be 'tentative' because this is the first book to carry out an analysis of Japan's nativist movement on the level of the individual and because the body of research that ought to be available for

comparison does not exist. I also think that the validity of answers given in this book will be tested as we accumulate more interview data.

6   This is discussed in detail in Chapter 6 but, according to Jomaru, the use of the term 'anti-Japanese' increased in the magazines *Shokun!* and *Seiron*, from around 1996. He says that it was 'used both with reference to Chinese and Koreans, as well as Japanese' (Jomaru 2011: 390).

Chapter 5

1   On the situation emerging in Japan, see Gottlieb and McLelland (2001). The contents are highly descriptive, but there is a chapter on *Tsukurukai*.

2   The tide of research about the influence on social movements of changes in information technology tends to lean towards a focus on reductions in communication costs and repeatedly questioning the premises of resource mobilization theory. In short, it ends up questioning the free-rider issue and the pros and cons of the mobilization by organizations model (Bimber, Flanagan and Stohl 2005).

3   As will be discussed later, this distinction is based on Earl et al. (2010) and Earl and Kimport (2011).

4   An exception to this is a survey of thirty-eight users of a far-right chat room (Glaser, Dixit and Green 2002). I have also made use of email questionnaire answers from users of nativist homepages and blogs. However, as in most cases there was no clear email address, even when I sent emails I was not able to get an answer.

5   It is said that *Zaitokukai* provokes animosity within the existing right wing (Yasuda 2012a), but there are also many cases of joint action between the two in localities where activists are sparse.

6   The Taiwan connection mentioned here refers to activities that have an anti-China connotation.

7   He talks about the risk of injury as a result of her participation but, more generally, it is the social control risks that are more significant. The risk, in particular, of repeated convictions for *Zaitokukai*-related activities can be seen as effective in curtailing movement participation. For theoretical and empirical research on this, see (McAdam 1986; Opp and Roehl 1990; Opp, Voss and Gern 1995; Wiltfang and McAdam 1991).

8   This is a rule that applies to extreme groups in general, and it is possible that the spread of the internet has facilitated mobilization for them. It is also true that, as in the case of 'festivals' on the internet, although transient mobilization has become possible it is difficult to achieve stable mobilization.

9   In addition to the previously mentioned development of a global movement, we can also see movements which are solely online (electronic movements) as characteristic of the internet (Earl and Kimport 2011: 5–8). This is a valuable viewpoint in studies of the internet right wing, but in this book it will only be dealt with in connection with online mobilization.

10   Then again, the internet has become a new mobilizing structure in the movement for the abandonment of nuclear power following the Fukushima

Nuclear Reactor accident, which shows that technological innovation could also be possible in left-wing citizen movements. For empirical research on this point: see Hirabayashi (2013) regarding Japan, and Stalker and Wood (2013) for a comparative perspective looking at anti-G20 movements.

11 There are still questions of theoretical and empirical validity about the traits of mobilization via the internet. In research on the women's movement in the Netherlands, it is argued that the internet has been uniquely effective in the provision of information, recruiting, soliciting comments and networking with other organizations (Edwards 2004: 192).

12 B says, 'There was nowhere else that would accept you on the net apart from *Zaitokukai*. To begin with, there was no choice in those days. That's how it felt. So, if someone asks why I joined, that's the reason'. This is what Fischer (1975) calls the logic of homophiles. As I said at the outset, citizen movements used to be a left-wing phenomenon, but these days the nativist movement is being chosen by some as one of the citizen movements of the right. These sorts of potential constituents have not just emerged in the second half of the 2000s but have always existed to some extent; all that they lacked in the past was a mobilizing structure to organize them. Put another way, this stratum has not been organized by either the existing right wing or Japan Conference.

13 This recalls McLuhan's argument that the media is an extension of our bodies. The seven, out of twenty-five, people whose initial contact with the nativist movement had been via videos were fewer than I would have predicted. This does not, however, imply the limited effectiveness of videos; as we see below, in the case of a considerable number of those who came into contact with the nativist movement through written texts, watching videos can be seen as having provided the added incentive to participate. 'Anyway, the influence of videos is amazing, you know. Oh, so this is how you carry out street propaganda, it's amazing. Watching videos and starting to feel that there might just be something that I can do too, that was the impetus' (Mr W, *Zaitokukai*, forties).

Chapter 6

1 If the influence of the nativist movement continues to increase and it builds a constituency that cannot be ignored in urban areas, where there are significant numbers of independent voters, it is possible that a segment of the conservative class will ally themselves with the movement. If there had been a larger-scale nativist movement during the instability in Japanese politics under Democratic Party government, a portion of the Japan Restoration Party and the LDP could well have become its partners.

2 With regard to this point, Kimura (2013) makes interesting observations about the influence on far-right movements of links with the political elite. It had been comparatively easier for the government to control the ultra-right organzation 'National Conference to Protect Japan', which has very close ties with existing conservative power, when the latter was leading the compilation of historical revisionist textbooks in the 1980s. Kimura does not say so explicitly, but it could be argued that because the composition

of *Tsukurukai* in the 1990s differed from that of previous far-right groups it was difficult for the movement to be controlled by the government. The distance between the movement and existing conservative power is an added factor that makes the nativist movement difficult for the political elite to control.

3 There have been arguments concerning the connection between political opportunity structures and framing since the 1990s (Diani 1996; Snow and Benford 1992; Zdravomyslova 1996). My use of the concept of discursive opportunities aims for an unambiguous synthesis of the two.

4 A very interesting piece of research analyzing the influence of these sorts of variations on far-right political parties is Art (2006). My analysis is limited to the influence of opportunities on mobilzation, but they may also have an impact on the achievement of goals (McCammon et al. 2007: 731). The reason given for excluding Korean schools from subsidies was consideration for public opinion, and this calls for an analysis of the influence that the movement has on policy as it is being heeded as one part of this 'public opinion'.

5 In relation to this, the first ruling in a civil trial appeal by a Korean school in Kyoto on the matter of harassment was handed down in the Kyoto Civil Court on 7/10/2013. The ruling's affirmation of the illegality of the actions of the defendant (*Zaitokukai*) under the 'Convention on the Elimination of all Forms of Racial Discrimination' made it more difficult to carry out hate speech that targets specific institutions.

6 In his studies of Pim Fortuyn in the Netherlands, Koopmans also argues that it was discursive opportunities rather than socioeconomic conditions that led to the rise of the far right (Koopmans and Muis 2009).

7 This point has been discussed in terms of the relationship between the openness of political opportunity structures and the repertoire of actions. For more detail on this, see Kriesi et al. (1995); Koopmans (1995); Tarrow (1989); and Traugott (1995).

8 Following the 1990s, Japanese nationalism 'sought its main competitive rivals and threats in Asia, probably for the first time since the Sino-Japanese War' (Kimura 2007: 217).

9 On this point, although the United States may temporarily slump, it continues to display a stable, steady presence. In this sense, the United States is indisputably Japan's most significant other (Ōsawa 2008). Ōsawa has coined the term *daisansha shinkyū*: 'third party instance' to describe this.

10 A consequence of this increasing introspection was the bashing of feminism and national minorities in the United States (Sharp 2000), but this was not the case in Japan. Articles about gender had not been numerous to begin with, but reached two per cent for the first time in 2002 and then 2.2 per cent at their peak in 2005. Since there was an increase in articles bashing East Asian countries at this time, it would be difficult to argue that gender bashing occurred as a result of a failure to pay attention to foreign countries. In Japan's case, it was the historical problems set out in Figure 6.3 that filled the pages. Separate studies are needed regarding the background that gave rise to this result.

11 Oguma and Ueno (2003) have identified the anxiety that accompanies globalization as providing the background to the rise of *Tsukurukai*, but its

rise should, in fact, be linked to the opening up of discursive opportunities related to history.

12 The politicization of historical problems in this period and the very close links between this and nationalism was a phenomenon that occurred in numerous countries, not just in Japan (Gluck 2007; Kurosawa and Nishi 2011).

13 This interest in contemporary history is doubtlessly what Yoshino (1992) referred to as cultural nationalism. The problem is that historical revisionism, which is quite different from this substratum, grew rapidly and moreover became the mainstream historical description of the right wing; but, Yoshino's framework cannot account for this.

14 It is not possible to discuss North Korea within the context of historical problems in part because it does not have diplomatic relations with Japan. The abduction issue and the nuclear issue are the main topics that arise regarding North Korea, and the complexity of the relationship between these two East Asian countries is evident here also.

15 This can also be said of Prime Minister Shinzō Abe's views; he only makes two positive references to foreigners in his book (Abe 2006).

16 As right-wing world of criticism magazines also contain unrelated essays and reminiscences which are not political in nature, I give numbers that are the sum of the frequency of appearance of related articles. Given that basically all of *Zaitokukai*'s protest events are relevant, I have shown them as a proportion of all articles.

17 The results of the vote can be found at http://www.zaitokukai.info/modules/xoopspoll/pollresults.php?poll_id=78, retrieved 6/6/2013).

18 The 2006–12 decline in the proportion held by history was due to the increased proportion taken up by territorial disputes with South Korea.

19 This is in contrast to the term 'anti-Japanese', which has been used frequently by the right-wing world of criticism from the latter half of the 1990s (Jomaru 2011), and which the nativist movement also used freely.

20 *Manga kenkanryū* was initially sold as a mook, and books about it also appeared as mooks (*Bessatsu Takarajima Henshubu* 2005, 2006a, 2006b).

21 Despite repeated requests for an interview with Sakurai, he never agreed. He may have consented had it simply been a matter of having his opinions heard, but he probably did not want to take part in a survey aimed at getting him to tell his life history. Consequently, I have only been able to write about him using information obtained indirectly.

22 This is at variance with the historical revisionist movement, and it could be said that *Zaitokukai* was characterized by the fact that '[compared with *Tsukurukai*] it has operated much more in a manner that bypasses both the mass media and public education' (Itagaki 2007: 34).

Chapter 7

1 This is based on an interview with a Diet member who supports voting rights for foreign residents, on 21February, 2013.

2 This is based on interviews with a former Chief Cabinet Secretary on 22 April, 2013.

3　The linguistic wars between Flanders and Wallonia form the backdrop to the strong opposition in Belgium. As a result of the opposition of Flanders, which thought that the granting of voting rights would lead to electoral disadvantage, their legalization took more than thirty years (Earnest 2008: 120–3). In this sense, opposition in Belgium had its origins in the country's political system of consociational democracy, and its roots are to be found in a different context from that of the arguments against voting rights in Japan.

4　In Germany, voting rights for foreign residents did not come into law because they were deemed to be unconstitutional (Rubio-Marin 2000). Political participation for the second generation has instead become a reality via the introduction of *jus soli* into the nationality law.

5　Discussions of voting rights for foreign residents in Japan end up retreating into assertions about the pros and cons of voting rights and lack any analytical perspective on the heated background to these arguments. There are also several works in English that discuss voting rights for foreign residents in Japan, but I have not come across any that deal with the political aspects of these voting rights (Chapman 2008; Kalicki 2008).

6　There has, however, been no expansion of the movement seeking voting rights for foreign residents. A public opinion poll of *Zainichi* Koreans showed that approximately eighty per cent called for voting rights for foreign residents (Kinpara et al. 1986; *Kawasaki Gaikokuseki Shimin Ishiki Jittai Chōsa Kenkyū Iinkai* 1993), but this has not managed to translate into a mass movement of actual people voicing these demands.

7　Layton-Henry (1990) sheds light on different aspects from those in Hammar's arguments concerning the nature of rights. He stresses that political rights are the last civil rights to be acquired by foreigners. This means that political rights present the biggest hurdle in terms of sovereignty, but political participation for foreigners has nonetheless become an actual policy issue. This shows the maturity of democratic arguments, and there are ongoing efforts to address this issue (Pedroza forthcoming).

8　The holding of multiple citizenships is also being proposed as a means of reconciling identity considerations and the promotion of political integration (Jones-Correa 1998; Sejersen 2008).

9　Even though not quite so blunt, there is an aspect of the political integration of foreigners – who are 'dangerous others' – in denizenship arguments. Whilst I do not endorse this view, I do think that it contains a greater sense of reality than is seen in Japan, which has continued to exclude *Zainichi* Koreans politically, without coming up with even this sort of idea.

10　For the details concerning this, see the interview with former member of the Lower House, Jun Nishikiori, who was a Sakigake Shimane representative ('Hōkaisei genan o dashita 'Sakigake Shimane' daihyō Nishikiori Jun shi ni kiku' (Questioning Jun Nishikiori, representative of 'Sakigake Shimane which put forward the law reform motion)), *Kikan Sai* (Sai Quarterly), 14: 1994.

11　In reality, there are numerous cases of voting rights having been granted to people from former colonies, as in the examples of Spain and its former colonies, Britain and Ireland, and the various countries of the British Commonwealth. Even when Ireland withdrew from the British Commonwealth in 1949, it was not divested of its voting rights (Rath 1990:

139). In the case of Britain, the legal basis of voting rights is the fact that the Irish and the peoples of the various countries of the British Commonwealth are not strictly seen as foreigners, and there is also the consideration of the 'close ties' with Ireland (Rikihisa 2006).

12 If we use Hammar's 'naturalization model' and the 'voting rights model', then this argument leads to a revisionism that is dependent on the former. That is, voting rights for foreign residents will widen the gap between nationality and identity and between citizenship and ethnicity (Takigawa 2002; Tei 2010a, 2010b, 2010c). At first glance, this may appear logical, but the following two points render it inadequate as a solution. Firstly, this argument is, in reality, bankrupt because it ignores the fact that the gap is clearly a product of the colonial settlement. Special permanent residents exist as a result of the Japanese government's treatment of former colonial citizens. Revisionists denounce *Zainichi* Koreans for their insistence on Korean nationality, overlooking the responsibility of the Japanese government for the failure of the colonial settlement. Secondly, it ignores the fact that the appearance of the 'voting rights model' is a reflection of the fact that the 'naturalization model' does not work. If it were possible to resolve the gap simply via naturalization, there should be no need for the 'voting rights model'. This sort of argument merely approves of and justifies a status quo in which there are people who, never having been naturalized, reach the ends of their lives without ever having exercised their political rights. This is in keeping with the logic of the opposition faction which says, 'You should be naturalized if you want voting rights', but this unilateral insistence on naturalization is an unbalanced approach. If we are to see some logical consistency in the resolution of these gaps, it must be via the dual approach of a colonial settlement and the introduction of *jus soli* into the Nationality Act.

13 There are two schools in critical security studies: the Copenhagen School with its strong philosophical nature based on the notion of linguistic turn, and the Paris School, which has taken a sociological approach (Balzacq 2010, 2011). In this book, I mainly use the arguments from the Paris School, because of their affinity with empirical research, but I also quote from works of the Copenhagen School.

14 The position that stresses speech acts has been criticized for focussing on the elites – the group that speaks – but this is not strictly true as it also looks at the ultra-right movement as a speech subject (Wæver 1995).

15 To cite Krause (1998: 306), the aim of securitization studies is to clarify 'how threats are defined and constructed'.

16 Today's nation states must confront protagonists who do not share the rules that exist between nations; this also includes terrorists, who challenge nations' monopolization of the devices of violence. The logic of war as the extension of politics does not work in the case of terrorists. The nation state sees having a dialogue with or controlling 'illegal migrants' as impossible. Because of their transnational nature, migrants are seen far more as a security threat that opposes the nation-state than as a nation of hypothetical enemies.

17 There are a number of studies regarding migrants and crime, but they have mainly been positivist works focussed on the relation between the socioeconomic characteristics of groups and the crime rate (Martinez Jr. and

Valenzuela Jr. 2006; Peterson, Krivo and Hagan 2006; Tonry 1997; Waters 1999). The knowledge that can be gained from these studies is useful, but we need to be careful about turning this knowledge itself into an ingredient of securitization.

18 *Zainichi* Koreans have, however, been framed for crimes from the end of the war until the period of rapid economic growth (Takahashi 1969). Even now, activists in the nativist movement refer to links with 'the black market' and 'gangster organizations'; the undercurrent of securitization has not disappeared.

19 The events of 11 September, 2001 were also an impetus for the securitization of the migration issue in Japan (Furuya 2003). We cannot say, however, that they brought about any change in the meaning of migration (Bigo 2005: 66–7).

20 It should also be remembered that Tokyo Governor Shintarō Ishihara made a pronouncement to the Japan Self-Defense Forces in 2000: 'Large numbers of *sangokujin* who have entered Japan illegally are repeatedly committing atrocious crimes ... At these times, we send you (Self-Defense Forces) out ... we look to you to carry out one of your major duties, the maintenance of order' (*Mainichi Shinbun* 4/11/2000). In this, Ishihara is not only referring to 'illegal residents' but also summoning up recollections regarding *Zainichi* Koreans (Furuya 2005). Nativists have turned *Zainichi* Korean history into a ready access pool for revisionism. What is important in the context of the present book is the idea of sending out the Self-Defense Forces under 'exceptional circumstances', and we also ought to pay particular attention to the fact that the mental images conjured up by 'illegal' and atrocious' function to justify securitization.

21 For a summary of arguments about voting rights for foreign residents in Japan, see Higuchi (2001) and Rei Sato (2008).

22 Before this, there had been several letters to the editor and articles picking up on calls from *Mindan* branches for 'suffrage' not 'voting rights'.

23 'Agreement between Japan and the Republic of Korea Concerning the Legal Status and Treatment of the People of the Republic of Korea Residing in Japan', January 10, 1991.

24 So (1992, 1995) discusses these decisions in detail and includes the arguments by the parties concerned.

25 Tetsuzō Fuyushiba, former Chief Secretary of the *Kōmeitō* and one of the most enthusiastic promoters of the 'Voting Rights for Foreign Residents Bill' amongst parliamentarians, says that without this decision there would not have been any thought of legislation (Interview 22/10/2010).

26 However, changes in the method of counting articles recorded in the database has a certain impact on this. Because *Sankei* started recording articles published in Osaka and Tokyo separately, major articles appearing in the count for both head offices ended up being counted twice. Even taking this change into account, however, there has been a clearly discernible increasing trend following 2000.

27 Japan Conference, Japan's biggest ultra-right group, also showed no awareness of the appearance of a problem at this time. It says that it had not imagined that the promoters had become so powerful (Japan Conference Interview 19/2/2011). Books and articles about voting rights for foreign residents published in this period were principally by *Zainichi* Koreans, the

people making the demands, and they were practically unanimously in favor (*Horumon Bunka Henshu Iinkai* 1992; Kim 1994; Kondo 1996a, 1996b; Yi 1993; Niwa 1995; So 1992, 1995; *Teiju Gaikokujin no Chihō Sanseiken o Mezasu Shimin no Kai* 1998).

28 The LDP voiced its disapproval at this time but, as the Liberal Party and the *Kōmeitō* were in agreement, the LDP also ultimately agreed. When the Liberal Party withdrew from the coalition in 2000, the bill was resubmitted twice – by the *Kōmeitō* and the Conservative Party, and by the Democratic Party. See Kondo (2000) for the arguments against in this period and also for the counter arguments.

29 This means that following the Supreme Court decision, arguments maintaining that there were constitutional doubts regarding voting rights for foreign residents were, effectively, to be understood as political statements rather than as legal arguments.

30 Interview 19/7/2002.

31 The Liberal Democratic Party (Election Systems Research Council), *Draft Opinion Regarding the Issue of Local Voting Rights for Foreign Residents (Draft)*, May 2000. 'The examination is being carried out from the standpoint that if there is a need to explore the arguments for (the issue of local voting rights for foreign residents), then this ought to be done exclusively from the point of view of the constitution'.

32 *Nihon no ibuki* (Breath of Japan), 140 (July 1999), p 17.

33 'Both conservative theory and a recommendation of the General Meeting of the Discussion Group of Japan Conference Diet Members contain objections to voting rights for foreign residents and opposition to any broadening of voting rights'. *Nihon no ibuki*, 156 (November 2000).

34 Because external dispatches were effectively impossible following the abduction issue, *Sōren* continued to keep tight control over the matter, but the organization itself, under instruction from the home country, opposed voting rights for foreign residents. Voices of concern about this sort of internal division amongst *Zainichi* Koreans also existed amongst *Zainichi* Korean intellectuals (Kang 1994), and this came to be one of the arguments that was used against them.

35 Interview with Fuyushiba 22/10/2010. Whilst I have not conducted an interview with Ozawa, given that the exclusion of North Korean nationals became part of the bill via a joint Liberal Party and *Kōmeitō* proposal the facts seem clear.

36 Diet Member Fuyushiba's reply in the minutes of the Lower House 23/5/2000.

37 *Mainichi Shinbun*, Editorial, 24/1/2000.

38 *Asahi Shinbun*, Editorial, 12/2/2000.

39 For an opposing argument see Ryu (1996).

40 *Democratic Party Policy Proposals INDEX 2009*.

41 In this period there was persistent focus on constructing opposing arguments (Bessatsu Takarajima 2010; Hayase 2009a, 2009b, 2010, 2011; Inoue 2010; Iwata 2009; Mishina 2010; Momochi 2010; Nagao 2010; Nishimura 2010; Nishio 2010; Sakurai 2010; Takaichi 2010; Tei 2010a–d; Yamano 2010). The views of the supporting faction lagged behind, and even their continued existence seemed uncertain (Hosaka 2011; Koseki

2010; Niwa 2011; Park 2011; So 2010; Soh 2010, 2011a, 2011b; Tanaka 2010; Turunen 2011).

42 The following two arguments are just a sample of the multitude of such arguments. 'In the event of voting rights for foreign residents being applied to Chinese residents, the massive number of these residents would transfer their certificates of residence to Yonaguni, and it is even possible that we could see the emergence of a mayor who is pro-China (anti-Self-Defense Forces base)' (Hamaguchi 2010: 61). 'From the viewpoint of Chinese strategy, the participation of Chinese permanent residents in regional elections is an exceedingly welcome proposition because it would make it legally possible both to promote Japanese and United States estrangement and to prevent the deployment of the Self-Defense Forces by voting' (Hiramatsu 2010: 47).

43 I have referred directly to a Japan Conference leaflet but, as the following link shows, the opposing faction adopts practically the same format in making its arguments opposing voting rights: (http://www.nipponkaigi. org/opinion/archives/961#more-961).

44 We can find a vast change from 2000 to 2010 in the arguments of LDP member Sanae Takaichi (Takaichi 2010; Takaichi and Momochi 2010) against voting rights for foreign residents.

45 The alternative policy considered by the LDP to the 2000 'Voting Rights for Foreign Residents Bill' was the promotion of a simplification of the naturalization process. This amounted to nothing more than a means of blocking voting rights; the voting rights bill was left unchanged and has fizzled out. However, under conditions of progressive securitization, there is a strong likelihood that the acquisition of Japanese nationality will itself be seen as dangerous, and not even this measure will be adopted.

46 It is the rights of people like this that are at issue when we discuss voting rights for foreign residents and when we look at them in an international context. (In addition to the political research already covered, see Benhabib 2004; Munro 2008; Song 2009; and Soysal 1994 for a political theory approach.)

Chapter 8

1 However, as Slovakia and Hungary were signatories to the 'EU Convention for the Protection of National Minorities', the treatment of Hungary's nationals was not decided merely on the basis of diplomatic considerations.

2 Brubaker's arguments are particularly influential with Eastern European researchers, and the analysis of Malaysia and Israel has been carried out in books examining the possible broader applicability of this model (Iglesias, Stojanović and Weinblum 2013).

3 The prescription of the treatment of *Zainichi* Koreans as one link in the colonial settlement is one point of difference with the situation in Eastern Europe. There are, however, also some areas of similarity with the relationships between Russia, as the centre of the Soviet Union, and surrounding countries.

4 See So Kyon-Shik (1997) for more on this. On the one hand, ethnic schools would have been free from governmental pressure if they had been linked to *Mindan*, but because of their affiliation to *Sōren* their protests against 'emergency measures' were ignored. On the other hand, the LDP changed its tune and respected *Sōren's* opinion of opposition to voting rights for foreign residents. These are examples of how the Japanese government puts north-south divisions to convenient use in order to divide and rule.

5 United States actions to conclude a peace treaty and to position Japan as its strategic base for containing Asia, under the Cold War structure, were at odds with the nationalisms of Japan's neighbors (Yi 1996). It was the US policy of putting Japan back on the world stage while the issue of war responsibility was still ambiguous that resulted in postponing the resolution of numerous issues concerning war responsibility (these fall, to a certain extent, under territorial disputes – see Toyoshita 2012 for more on this). This past settlement has created difficulties in East Asian geopolitics that are comparable to the continuation of the Cold War.

6 Söderberg suggests a framework which also takes China's influence into account, in addition to that of Japan, South Korea and the United States (2011a: 11), and which is also useful for analyzing Japanese-style nativism. As describing this model in its entirety is, however, beyond my expertise, I will limit the discussion fundamentally to Brubaker's triad.

7 Demands for voting rights for foreign residents as 'past nationals' is based on the fact that they had formerly possessed these rights, and this is the point of issue that is most strongly emphasized by *Zainichi* Koreans at voting rights trials.

8 The sources used regarding SCAP and Japanese government trends in this period are Kim (1997) and Ōnuma (1993).

9 It is claimed that the reason for SCAP's low level of intervention in the legal treatment of people from the former colonies was the result of their low level of policy priority (Kim 1997; Morris-Suzuki 2010). Taking advantage of this, the Japanese government disadvantaged people from its former colonies by selectively regarding them as foreigners or Japanese, at its own convenience.

10 Some assert that this loss of citizenship was, by its very nature, illegal. (Chong 2003: Chapter 5).

11 For the differences in points of issue and initial drafts at these meetings, see Choe (2011).

12 Their children and grandchildren were subject to the residence qualifications of the Immigration Control Ordinance (4–1–16–2 aliens and 4–1–16–3 aliens) and found themselves in the insecure situation of having to apply for renewal every three years. For more on these points, see Ha (1976), Kim (1995), Ōnuma (1993) and Sakanaka (1999).

13 Despite oppression and employment discrimination, *Zainichi* Koreans have come to occupy a certain economic status (Higuchi 2016) and have even been able to develop a powerful movement that exerts influence on local governments. A substructure of ethnic businesses has served as the basis for economic and political activities. Although there have been restrictions such as the difficulty of obtaining finance other than from ethnic financial institutions, there have not been large numbers of legal restrictions on foreigners' businesses in Japan. In short, restrictions on national minorities

are not necessarily sweeping; in the case of Estonia and Latvia, for example, the economic activities of inhabitants of Russian descent were not restricted. Commercio (2008) calls this partial control, and argues that a national minority seeks to evade any worsening of problems by constructing an economic niche. If we conduct a historical analysis focussed on links between politics and economics, we can see that *Zainichi* Koreans also discover new realities for themselves.

14 Since the Japanese government has secured a forced deportation clause, there remains the possibility that this could happen. For North Korean *Zainichi* Koreans, in particular, there are situations in which they cannot avoid being anxious about this possibility. Given, however, that forced deportations are in reality extremely risky politically, it is difficult to imagine the Japanese government going to these barbaric lengths even though it may be full of ill will.

15 For more on this point see the detailed research done by Ōnuma more than thirty years ago (1979a–c; 1980 a–c).

16 This project team put together the 'Bill Concerning Special Cases of Acquisition of Nationality such as Special Permanent Resident', but having shelved the voting rights bill, their mission was over and it was never submitted to the Diet.

17 Several revisionists on the issue of *Zainichi* Koreans appear in this publication, and it even contains chapters which appear to be threats, citing 'the disadvantages of not becoming naturalized' (Sakanaka 2006). Works which extol Japanese nationality as a right tend, on the contrary, to show the difficulties inherent in the issue of the acquisition of citizenship.

18 This occurred not only with the demise of the Cold War but also around the time of the death of the ruler of the Japanese Empire, the Shōwa Emperor. In this sense, this period presented the ideal timing for 'a settlement of the perceptions and the historical views of Asia, foremost among these a view of North Korea that was synthesized from "a catalogue of prejudices"' (Kang 1989: 28. The present diplomatic stalemate and the nativist movement are the clear costs of the half-baked response of this period.

19 The lack of any conception of settling unresolved issues is not simply due to Japan being a nationalizing state but also to the absence of a department responsible for the issue. If there were the political will, then there might possibly be a response which formulated comprehensive guiding principles, as is the case with the Ainu (an indigenous people). The lack of political will simply resulted in fragmented policies based on departmental sectionalism.

20 Under Democratic Party government, the Hatoyama Cabinet's 2010 Diet session was the best opportunity for the submission of the 'Voting Rights for Foreign Residents Bill'. After missing this opportunity, voting rights for foreign residents were shelved, but there were moves, by a segment of Democratic Party Diet members under the Noda government, to submit a bill limited to special South Korean permanent residents. There was less opposition to this plan, but it could actually be argued that it exposed the issue of voting rights for foreign residents in Japan as being nothing more than a dependent variable of Japan–South Korea relations.

21 The biggest change to the 'Nationality Law' was the 1985 move from a patrilineal system to one that was both matrilineal and patrilineal (for more

detail, see Kashiwazaki 2002). The post facto recognition of illegitimate children could also be cited as a more recent significant change (Tanno 2013). This has had the consequence of children with foreign fathers becoming Japanese nationals, leading in turn to a considerable reduction in special permanent residents, but this does not change the fact that it is a *jus sanguinis* principle.

22 It is not to be expected that there will be any explicit changes to policy under these conditions. In light of government actions in the case of *buraku* and Ainu people such as formulating legislation and administrative guidelines, there is no option but to rate its stance on *Zainichi* Koreans as one of inaction.

23 'The Report of the Taskforce for the Advancement of Multicultural Coexistence – Towards Regional Multicultural Coexistence' (*Tabunka kyōsei no suishin ni kansuru kenkyūkai hōkokusho – chiiki ni okeru tabunka kyōsei no suishin ni muket*e), March 2006, Ministry of Internal Affairs and Communications. The policy ideal of multicultural coexistence has been created by eschewing history and politics, as the oppressively persistent indifference to organizations affiliated with *Sōren* shows (Fujioka 2007). If analyses of newcomer foreigners are not in sync with history and politics, we are likely to lose sight of many things (Buckley 2000: 324).

24 This is a path dependency problem that Favell (1998) has called 'institutional pathology'. Favell analyzed institutional pathology in Britain and France, but similar analyses of post-war *Zainichi* Koreans should also be possible.

25 For more on this point see Ōnuma (1980c: 476).

26 With regard to these sorts of changes, I would cite the case of John Lie, who was born in South Korea, spent his childhood in Japan, and was educated in North America. Lie (2008) attempts a comprehensive consolidation, with a particular focus on the area of discourse.

27 The ignoring of the dyad is plainly evident in the fact that this sort of legal status remained unchanged until the ratification of the 'Convention Relating to the Status of Refugees' (Ōnuma 1979a: 280).

28 For an explanation of this point, see Park (1999).

29 Ryang is the most explicit advocate of generations as an explanatory factor, and she also indicates major differences between the second and third generations (Ryang 1997), but in this book I am only concerned with the segmentation into first and second generations.

30 The third way policy was basically accepted by a majority of *Zainichi* Koreans. Disputes engaged in by Sang-jung Kang and others, during their youth in the 1980s, were tied up with the significance of the 'national homeland' factor for the third way (Isogai 1986; Kang 1985a, 1985b; Yang 1985, 1986).

31 In this approach, whilst the impact of pre-war colonization and the post-war division of the Korean Peninsula are pointed out, they are 'effectively' not included in the actual analysis.

32 The concept of local citizenship, on the basis of a separation of legal attribution and daily life, has also been cited as a right for the purposes of participating in community planning (Beauregard and Bounds 2000).

33 There is both an experiential and conceptual affinity between being a *Zainichi* Korean and having a local area as a point of reference. When

living in Japan as a South or North Korean, a local area can act as a point of reference while escaping the dilemmas of belonging and assimilation. On this point, I would refer the reader to research on *zainichi* literature by Wender (2005).

34 Because I have also surveyed local government policies for foreigners, I understand that there are differing degrees of commitment depending on the local government and that policy measures are not taken 'spontaneously' (Higuchi 2000a; 2000b; 2001a). The aim of my comments here is to draw a comparison with the central government's obstinate stance.

35 This is according to http://www.gaikokujinsanseiken.com. In 2010, Japan Conference promoted a campaign opposed to voting rights for foreign residents, but less than ten per cent of local assemblies actually adopted their resolution.

36 From an interview with the secretary of the then Secretary General of the Democratic Party, Katsuya Okada's, 2/11/2011.

37 They concluded that exclusion from political participation would have been undesirable as democratic society and a diversity of values ought to be appreciated, regardless of requests by South Korea (interview with Okada's secretary, 2/11/2011). However, the exclusion of North Koreans has carried over into the Democratic Party bill and it still has not been possible to remove the political cost arguments.

38 From an interview with Mr Hatoyama, 21/11/2011.

39 Quoted from the 'Waga riberaru yūai kakumei' homepage (http://www.hatoyama.gr.jp/speech/ot02_2.html).

Epilogue

1 For more on smuggiing in Yonaguni, see Ishihara (1982; 2002). Shukichi Hokama, present (2012) Mayor of Yonaguni, also points out that increasing the population is the biggest concern of the local administration and that luring the Self-Defense Forces to the area was part of a population strategy.

2 The 'Opinion Opposing Municipal Voting Rights for Permanent Resident Foreigners', adopted by the town council of Yonaguni on 23/3/2010, was closely modelled on Japan Conference wording.

3 'Plan for Improving Medium-Term Defense Capability' (2011–2015), 17/12/2010 Decision of the Security Council of Japan and a Cabinet Decision.

4 For more on the territorial issues concerning islands, including the Spratly Islands, see Emmers (2010).

5 The statement, 'the Self-Defense Forces are a superb business' (that's why we're luring them here) is being used confidently on the island. As a consequence, the conservative faction that is in favor of luring them to the island attaches no importance to whether they will actually be useful to the defense of the outlying islands or not.

6 The biggest concern for the faction opposed to the Self-Defense Force bases is that this will lead to the collapse of the conservative-reformist balance on the island and usher in a period of continuous rule by the conservatives. (From an interview on 13/3/2013)

7 The Self-Defense Forces are carrying out manoeuvres assuming a state of affairs such as the 2003 incident in which a trawler intruded into the territorial waters of 'the seas around the S (Senkaku) Islands' and 'rammed a patrol boat' (Maeda 2007: 136). The 2010 Senkaku Boat Collision Incident has even come to have an influence on politics, and Yaeyama's rising conservative powers are also making full use of this 'Chinese threat in Japan's border regions' (Nakashinshiro 2013; Nakayama 2013).
8 The exclusion of Jews, based on historical revisionism (Holocaust denial) is, of course, also to be found in the West, just as racism based on dyads also exists in Japan. The Japanese-style nativism referred to here is an ideal type of the characteristic elements in Japan.
9 For more on this and its relationship with historical issues, see Hyun (2008).
10 Forces oriented towards both historical revisionism and the strengthening of defense capability were mainstream in the 2000s (Samuels 2007), and this was what produced the current strained relations (Kwong 2005). In the face of this, insisting on establishing defense capability can only have the long-term result of demonstrating the unreality of realism.

Appendix

1 Exceptions include Murai (1997a, 1997b), Oguma and Ueno (2003), Suzuki (2013) and Yamaguchi, Saito and Ogiue (2011), but their number is far too limited to yield even an understanding of the general situation.
2 To the best of my knowledge, the following are the sole examples of empirical research in which individual activists have actually been approached: in comparative European research – Klandermans and Mayer (2006c); Northern Europe – Bjørgo (1998); the United States – Blazak (2001), Blee (1996, 2002), Ezekiel (2002), Simi and Futrell (2010); Britain – Art (2011), Goodwin (2010, 2011); Germany – Virchow (2007); France – Berezin (2007); the Netherlands – Linden and Klandermans (2007); Sweden – Kimmel (2007); Norway – Fangen (1998, 1999); and India – Schgal (2007).
3 For methodological points see Schiebel (2000).
4 In the case of researchers who use semi-structured interviews, accepted practice is to fully disclose the records of interviews so as to enable readers to judge the strengths and weaknesses of their interpretations (Blee and Taylor 2002). However, those sections that may make it possible to identify the person concerned are not made public unless consent for this has been given.
5 The following works make very interesting arguments regarding the methodological problems that accompany surveys of 'unpleasant' movements: Blee 2003; Esseveld and Eyerman 1992.
6 I had this same experience during my research on voting rights for foreign residents when requesting interviews with Diet members who are opposed to these rights.
7 I have made the interview records public for all but one of this group (Higuchi 2012a-x, 2013a-j), and these can all be searched for and downloaded.

8 In the interests of comprehensibility, I have made reordered versions, interview records and supplemented statements public. However, where it was necessary to conceal the birthplace of survey participants, I have changed participants' dialects to standard Japanese.

9 This tendency was particularly pronounced in the case of *Zaitokukai* because most of its members operate using an alias. The life history interviews, which were used to ensure the reliability of the interviews, also produce their own sampling bias. Since all interview methods have their biases, there is a critical necessity to accumulate research findings on nativist movements using a variety of methodologies.

10 This is based on direct exchanges with Kōichi Yasuda. The roots of this discrepancy are to be found in journalists collecting data by touting their right to know and in researchers conducting surveys based on survey ethics.

11 Jomaru (2011) is a case of existing research which has a direct methodological connection while Kato (2012) and Suzuki (2011) overlap with my work in terms of objectives and media.

12 During the interviews, *Shokun!*, *Seiron*, and *SAPIO* were each cited by precisely one person as their source of information.

13 Event analysis using newspapers is also actually being undertaken in Europe because there are constantly articles on the far right in newspapers (Caiani and Parenti 2013; Caiani, della Porta and Wagemann 2012; Koopmans and Olzak 2004).

14 Sakurai's blog can be found at http://ameblo.jp/doronpa01/page-1. html#main.h

Bibliography

Abe, Shinzō, 2006, *Utsukushii kuni e* (To a beautiful country), Tokyo: Bungei Shunjūsha.

Adams, Josh and Vincent J. Roscigno, 2005, 'White supremacists, oppositional culture and the world wide web,' *Social Forces*, 84 (2): pp. 759–78.

Adler, Marina A., 1996, 'Xenophobia and ethnoviolence in contemporary Germany,' *Critical Sociology*, 22 (1): pp. 29–51.

Adorno, Theodor et al., 1950, *Authoritarian Personality*, New York: Harper & Brothers.

Alexander, Jeffrey C. et al., 2004, *Cultural Trauma and Collective Identity*, Berkeley: University of California Press.

Allport, Gordon W., 1958, *The Nature of Prejudice*, New York: Doubleday.

Andersson, Christoph, 2013, 'Dealing with the extreme right,' in Ruth Wodak, Majid KhosraviNik and Brigitte Mral (eds.), *Right-Wing Populism in Europe: Politics and Discourse*, London: Bloomsbury.

Andreas, Peter, 2000, *Border Games: Policing the U.S.–Mexico Divide*, Itahaca: Cornell University Press.

————— and Timothy Snyder, 2000, *The Wall around the West: State Borders and Immigration Controls in North America and Europe*, Lanham: Rowman and Littlefield.

————— and Thomas J. Biersteker (eds.), 2003, *The Rebordering of North America: Integration and Exclusion in a New Security Context*, New York: Routledge.

Aoki, Osamu, Kazuyuki Azusawa and Kenichirō Kawasaki (eds.), 2011, *Kokka to jōhō – keishichō kōanbu 'isuramu sōsa' ryūshutsu shiryō o yomu* (The state and information: reading leaked documents from the Department of Public Security, Tokyo Metropolitan Police Department 'Islam Investigation'), Tokyo: Gendai Shokan.

Araragi, Shinzō, (ed.), 2011, *Teikoku hōkai to hito no saiidō: hikiage, sōkan, soshite zanryū* (The collapse of empire and the remigration of people: repatriation, evacuation and staying behind), Tokyo: Bensei Shuppan.

Arendt, Hannah, 1996, *The Origins of Totalitarianism*, (new edition), Orlando: Harcourt.

Arita, Yoshifu, 2013, *Heito supīchi to tatakau! Nihonban haigaishugi hihan* (Fighting hate speech! A critique of Japanese nativism), Tokyo: Iwanami Shoten.

Art, David, 2006, *The Politics of the Nazi Past in Germany and Austria*, Cambridge: Cambridge University Press.

—————, 2011, *Inside the Radical Right: The Development of Anti-Immigrant Parties in Western Europe*, Cambridge: Cambridge University Press.

Arzheimer, Kai, 2009, 'Contextual factors and the extreme right vote in Western Europe, 1980–2002,' *American Journal of Political Science*, 53 (2): pp. 259–75.

————, 2012, 'Working class parties 2.0? Competition between centre-left and extreme right parties,' in Jens Rydgren (ed.), *Class Politics and the Radical Right*, London: Routledge.

———— and Elizabeth Carter, 2006, 'Political opportunity structures and right-wing extremist party success,' *European Journal of Political Research*, 45: pp. 419–43.

Atkinson, Graeme, 1993, 'Germany: nationalism, Nazism and violence,' in Tore Bjørgo and Rob Witte (eds.), *Racist Violence in Europe*, New York: St Martin's Press.

Ayukawa, Jun, 2001, *Shōnen hanzai: hontōni tahatsuka kyōakuka shite iru no ka* (Juvenile crime: Is it really increasing in frequency and brutality?), Tokyo: Heibonsha.

Back, Les, 2002, 'Aryans reading Adorno: cyber-culture and twenty-first century racism,' *Ethnic and Racial Studies*, 25 (4): pp. 628–51.

Backes, Uwe and Cas Mudde, 2000, 'Germany: extremism without successful parties,' *Parliamentary Affairs*, 53: pp. 457–68.

Balazs, Gabrielle, Jean-Pierre Faguer and Pierre Rimbert, 2007, 'Widespread competition and political conversions,' in Jörg Flecker (ed.), *Changing Working Life and the Appeal of the Extreme Right*, Aldershot: Ashgate.

Balzacq, Thierry, 2010, 'Constructivism and securitization studies,' in Myriam Dunn Cavelty and Victor Mauer (eds.), *The Routledge Handbook of Security Studies*, London: Routledge.

————, 2011, 'A theory of securitization: origins, core assumptions and variants,' in Balzacq (ed.), *Securitization Theory: How Securitization Problems Emerge and Dissolve*, London: Routledge.

Beauregard, Robert A., and Anna Bounds, 2000, 'Urban citizenship,' in Engin F. Isin (ed.), *Democracy, Citizenship and the Global City*, London: Routledge.

Beck, Ulrich, 2000, 'Risk society revisited: theory, politics and research programmes,' in Barbara Adam, Ulrich Beck and Joost Van Loon (eds.), *The Risk Society and Beyond: Critical Issues for Social Theory*, London: Sage.

————, 2005, *Power in the Global Age: A New Global Political Economy*, Cambridge: Polity Press.

Benford, Robert, D., 1993a, 'Frame disputes within the nuclear disarmament movement,' *Social Forces*, 71: pp. 677–701.

————, 1993b, '"You could be the hundredth monkey": collective action frames and vocabularies of motive within the nuclear disarmament movement,' *Sociological Quarterly*, 34 (2): pp. 195–216.

————, 1997, 'An insider's critique of the social movement framing perspective,' *Sociological Inquiry*, 67 (4): pp. 409–30.

———— and David A. Snow, 2000, 'Framing processes and social movements: an overview and assessment,' *Annual Review of Sociology*, 26: pp. 611–39.

Benhabib, Seyla, 2004, *The Rights of Others: Aliens, Residents and Citizens*, Cambridge: Cambridge University Press

Bennett, W. Lance, 2005, 'Social movements beyond borders: understanding two eras of transnational activism,' in Donatella della Porta and Sidney Tarrow (eds.), *Transnational Protest and Global Activism*, Lanham: Rowman & Littelfield.

———— and Alexandra Segerberg, 2012, 'The logic of connective action: digital media and the personalization of contentious politics,' *Information, Communication and Society*, 15 (5): pp. 739–68.

Berezin, Mabel, 2007, 'Revisiting the French National Front: the ontology of a political mood,' *Journal of Contemporary Ethnography*, 36 (2): pp. 129–46.

————, 2009, *Illiberal Politics in Neoliberal Times: Culture, Security and Populism in the New Europe*, Cambridge: Cambridge University Press.

Berger, Peter and Thomas Luckmann, 1996, *The Social Construction of Reality: A Treatise in the Sociology of Knowledge*, New York: Doubleday.

Bessatsu Takarajima Henshūbu, (ed.), 2005, *Manga kenkanryū no shinjitsu! 'Kankoku/hantō tabū' chōnyūmon* (The reality of the wave of Korea hatred in manga! The introduction to 'Korean/peninsula taboos'), Tokyo: Takarajimasha.

————, 2006a, *Kenkanryū no shinjitsu! Za zainichi tokken* (The reality of the wave of Korea hatred! Special privileges for *Zainichi* Koreans), Tokyo: Takarajimasha.

————, 2006b, *Kenkanryū no shinjitsu! Jōgai rantōhen* (The reality of the wave of Korea hatred! Brawls outside stadiums volume), Tokyo: Takarajimasha.

————, 2010, *'Gaikokujin sanseiken' de nihon ga nakunaru hi* (The day when Japan will disappear as a result of voting rights for foreign residents), Tokyo: Takarajimasha.

Betz, Hans-Georg, 1990, 'Politics of resentment: right-wing radicalism in West Germany,' *Comparative Politics*, 23: pp. 45–60.

————, 1994, *Radical Right-Wing Populism in Western Europe*, New York: St Martin's Press.

———— and Stefan Immerfall, 1998, 'Introduction,' in Hans-Georg Betz and Stefan Immerfall (eds.), *The New Politics of the Right: Neo-Populist Parties and Movements in Established Democracies*, New York: St Martin's Press.

Bevington, Douglas and Chris Dixon, 2005, 'Movement-relevant theory: rethinking social movement scholarship and activism,' *Social Movement Studies*, 4 (3): pp. 185–208.

Biggs, Michael and Steven Knauss, 2012, 'Explaining membership of the British National Party: a multilevel analysis of contact and threat,' *European Sociological Review*, 28 (5): pp. 633–46.

Bigo, Didier, 2001, 'Migration and security,' in Christian Joppke and Virginia Guiraudon (eds.), *Controlling a New Migration World*, London: Routledge.

————, 2005, 'From foreigners to abnormal aliens: how the faces of the enemy have changed following September the 11th,' in Elspeth Guild and Joanne van Selm (eds.), *International Migration and Security: Opportunities and Challenges*, London: Routledge.

Billiet, Jaak B., 1995, 'Church involvement, ethnocentrism, and voting for a radical right-wing party: diverging behavioral outcomes of equal attitudinal dispositions,' *Sociology of Religion*, 56: pp. 303–26.

———— and Hans de Witte, 1995, 'Attitudinal dispositions to vote for a 'new' extreme right-wing party: the case of 'Vlaams Blok,' *European Journal of Political Research*, 27: pp. 181–202.

Bimber, Bruce, Andrew J, Flanagan and Cynthia Stohl, 2005, 'Reconceptualizing collective action in the contemporary media environment,' *Communication Theory*, 54: pp. 365–88.

Bjørgo, Tore, 1998, 'Entry, bridge-burning and exit options: what happens to young people who join racist groups – and want to leave?' in Jeffrey Kaplan and Tore Bjørgo (eds.), *Nation and Race: The Developing Euro-American Racist Subculture*, Boston: Northeastern University Press.

———— and Rob Witte (eds.), 1993, *Racist Violence in Europe*, New York: St. Martin's Press.

Blazak, Randy, 2001, 'White boys to terrorist men: target recruitment of Nazi skinheads,' *American Behavioral Scientist*, 44: pp. 982–1,000.

Blee, Kathleen M., 1996, 'Becoming a racist: women in contemporary Ku Klux Klan and Neo-Nazi groups,' *Gender and Society*, 10 (6): pp. 680–702.

————, 2002, *Inside Organized Racism: Women in the Hate Movement*, Berkeley: University of California Press.

————, 2003, 'Studying the enemy,' in Barry Glassner and Rosanna Hertz (eds.), *Our Studies, Ourselves: Sociologists' Lives and Work*, New York: Oxford University Press.

————, 2007, 'Ethnographies of the far right,' *Journal of Contemporary Ethnography*, 36 (2): pp. 119–28.

———— and Verta Taylor, 2002, 'Semi-structured interviewing in social movement research,' in Bert Klandermans and Suzanne Staggenborg (eds.), *Methods of Social Movement Research*, Minneapolis: University of Minnesota Press.

———— and Kimberley A. Creasap, 2010, 'Conservative and radical-right movements,' *Annual Review of Sociology*, 36: pp. 269–86.

———— and Annette Linden, 2012, 'Women in extreme right parties and movements: a comparison of the Netherlands and the United States,' in Kathleen M. Blee and Sandra McGee Deutsch (eds.), *Women of the Right: Comparisons and Interplay across Borders*, University Park: Pennsylvania State University Press.

Bonacich, Edna, 1972, 'A theory of ethnic antagonism: split labor market,' *American Sociological Review*, 37: pp. 547–59.

————, 1973, 'A theory of middleman minorities,' *American Sociological Review*, 38: pp. 583–94.

———— and John Modell, 1980, *Economic Basis of Ethnic Solidarity: Small Business in the Japanese American Community*, Berkeley: University of California Press.

Bornschier, Simon and Hanspeter Kriesi, 2012, 'The populist right, the working class, and the changing face of class politics,' in Jens Rydgren (ed.), *Class Politics and the Radical Right*, London: Routledge.

Borusiak, Liubov, 2009, 'Soccer as a catalyst of patriotism,' *Sociological Research*, 48 (4): pp. 57–81.

Bowman-Grieve, Lorraine, 2009, 'Exploring 'Stormfront': a virtual community of the radical right,' *Studies in Conflict & Terrorism*, 32: pp. 989–1,007.

Bowyer, Benjamin, 2008, 'Local context and extreme right support in England:

the British National Party in the 2002 and 2003 local elections,' *Electoral Studies*, 27: pp. 611–20.

Brand, Karl-Werner, 1990, 'Cyclical aspects of new social movements: waves of cultural criticism and mobilization cycles of new middle-class radicalism,' in Russel Dalton and Manfred Kuechler (eds.), *Challenging the Political Order: New Social and Political Movements in Western Democracies*, London: Polity Press.

Braungart, Richart G. and Margaret M. Braungart, 1986, 'Life-course and generational politics,' *Annual Review of Sociology*, 12: pp. 205–31.

Braunthal, Gerard, 2009, *Right-Wing Extremism in Contemporary Germany*, London: Palgrave Macmillan.

————, 2010, 'Right-extremism in Germany: recruitment of new members,' *German Politics and Society*, 28 (4): pp. 41–68.

Breton, Albert, Gianluigi Galeotti, Pierre Salmon and Ronald Wintrobe (eds.), 2002, *Political Extremism and Rationality*, Cambridge: Cambridge University Press.

Brubaker, Rogers, 1996, *Nationalism Reframed: Nationhood and the National Question in the New Europe*, New York, Cambridge University Press.

————, 1998, 'Migrations of ethnic unmixing in the "New Europe",' *International Migration Review*, 32: pp. 1,047–65.

————, 2011, 'Nationalizing states revisited: projects and processes of nationalization in Post-Soviet States,' *Ethnic and Racial Studies*, 34 (11): pp. 1,785–1,814.

———— (ed.), 1989, *Immigration and the Politics of Citizenship in Europe and North America*, Lanham: University Press of America.

Brustein, William, 1996, *The Logic of Evil: The Social Origins of the Nazi Party, 1925–1933*, New Haven: Yale University Press.

Buckley, Sandra, 2000, 'Japan and East Asia,' in Henry Schwarz and Sangeeta Ray (eds.), *A Companion to Postcolonial Studies*, Oxford: Blackwell.

Buechler, Steven M., 2004, 'The strange career of strain and breakdown theories,' in David A. Snow, Sarah A. Soule and Hanspeter Kriesi (eds.), *The Blackwell Companion to Social Movements*, Oxford: Blackwell.

Burris, Val, Emery Smith and Ann Strahm, 2000, 'White supremacist network on the internet,' *Sociological Focus*, 33 (2): pp. 215–34.

Buzan, Barry, 1991, *People, States, and Fear: An Agenda for International Security Studies in the Post-Cold War Era*, (second edition), Boulder: Lynne Rienner.

————, Ole Wæver and Jaap de Wilde, 1998, *Security: A New Framework for Analysis*, Boulder: Lynne Rienner.

Caiani, Manuela and Linda Parenti, 2009, 'The dark side of the web: Italian right-wing extremist groups and the internet,' *South European Society and Politics*, 14 (30): p. 273–94.

————, 2013, *European and American Extreme Right Groups and the Internet*, Aldershot: Ashgate.

Caiani, Manuela, Donatella della Porta and Claudius Wagemann, 2012, *Mobilizing on the Extreme Right: Germany, Italy, and the United States*, Oxford: Oxford University Press.

Campbell, David, 1992, *Writing Security: United States Foreign Policy and the Politics of Identity*, (revised edition), Minneapolis: University of Minnesota Press.

————, 1998, *National Deconstruction: Violence, Identity, and Justice in Bosnia*, Minneapolis: University of Minnesota Press.

Caren, Neal, Kay Jowers and Sarah Gaby, 2012, 'A social movement online community: Stormfront and the white nationalist movement,' *Research in Social Movements, Conflicts and Change*, 33: pp. 163–93.

Carter, Elisabeth L., 2005, *The Extreme Right in Western Europe: Success or Failure?* Manchester: Manchester University Press.

Carty, Victoria and Jake Onyett, 2006, 'Protest, cyberactivism and new social movements: the reemergence of the peace movement post 9/11,' *Social Movement Studies*, 5 (3): pp. 229–49.

Castells, Manuel, 2001, *The Internet Galaxy: Reflections on the Internet, Business and Society*, Oxford: Oxford University Press.

Catellani, Patrizia and Patrizia Milesi, 2007, 'The psychological routes to right-wing extremism: how Italian workers cope with change,' in Jörg Flecker (ed.), *Changing Working Life and the Appeal of the Extreme Right*, Aldershot: Ashgate.

Ceyhan, Ayse and Anastassia Tsoukala, 2002, 'The securitization of migration in Western societies: ambivalent discourses and policies,' *Alternatives: Global, Local, Political*, 25 (1): pp. 21–39.

Cha, Victor, D., 1999, *Alignment Despite Antagonism: The United States–Korea–Japan Security Triangle*, Palo Alto, CA: Stanford University Press.

Chapman, David, 2008, *Zainichi Korean Identity and Ethnicity*, London: Routledge.

Choe, Yongho, 2011, '*Shūsenchokugo no zainichi chōsenjin/kankokujin shakai ni okeru "hongoku" shikōsei to daiichiji nikkan kaidan* (Homeland orientation of *Zainichi* North and South Korean communities in postwar Japan and the inaugural Japan–Korea Conference),' in Jongwon Yi, Masafumi Kimiya and Toyomi Asano (eds.), *Rekishi toshite no nikkan kōkkoseijōka II: Datsushokuminchika hen* (The normalization of Japan–South Korea diplomatic relations as history II: Decolonization volume), Tokyo: Hōsei Daigaku Shuppankyoku.

Chong, Yonghae, 2003, '*Tami ga yo' seishō: aidentiti/kokumin kokka/jendā* (Singing 'the people's anthem' in unison: identity, nationality and gender), Tokyo: Iwanami Shoten.

Chong, Yonghwan, 2012, 'Nyūkanhō kaisei to sainyūkoku kyoka seido no saihen: 'Minashi sainyūkoku kyoka' seido to zainichi Chōsenjin (Revision of the Immigration Control and Refugee Recognition Act and reorganization of the approval system for re-entering Japan: 'Deemed approval system for re-entering Japan' and *Zainichi* Koreans),' *Hōritsu Jihō* (Legal bulletin), 84 (12), Tokyo: Nihon Hyōronsha.

————, 2013, '"Seisai" no seiji to zainichi Chōsenjin no kenri (The politics of "sanctions" and the rights of *Zainichi* Koreans),' *Migrants Network*, 156.

Chung, Erin Aeran, 2010, *Immigration and Citizenship in Japan*, Cambridge: Cambridge University Press.

Codena-Roa, Jorge, 2002, 'Strategic framing, emotions, and superbarrio: Mexico City's masked crusader,' *Mobilization*, 7 (2): pp. 201–16.

Coffé, Hilde, 2012, 'Gender, class, and radical right voting,' in Jens Rydgren (ed.), *Class Politics and the Radical Right*, London: Routledge.

————, Bruno Heyndels and Jan Vermeir, 2007, 'Fertile grounds for extreme right-wing parties: explaining the Vlaams Blok's electoral success,' *Electoral Studies*, 26: pp. 142–55.

Commercio, Michele E., 2008, 'Systems of partial control: ethnic dynamics in Post-Soviet Estonia and Latvia,' *Comparative International Development*, 43: pp. 81–100.

Costain, Ann, 1992, *Inviting Women's Rebellion: A Political Process Interpretation of the Women's Movement*, Baltimore: Johns Hopkins University Press.

Crist, John T. and John D. McCarthy, 1996, '"If I had a hammer": the changing methodological repertoire of collective behavior and social movement research,' *Mobilization*, 1 (1): pp. 87–102.

Cutts, David, Robert Ford and Matthew J. Goodwin, 2011, 'Anti-immigrant, politically disaffected or still racist after all? Examining the attitudinal drivers of extreme right support in Britain in the 2009 European elections,' *European Journal of Political Research*, 50: pp. 418–40.

Dalton, Russel J., 2004, *Democratic Challenges, Democratic Choices: The Erosion of Political Support in Advanced Industrial Democracies*, Oxford: Oxford University Press.

———— and Martin P. Wattenberg (eds.), 2000, *Parties without Partisans: Political Change in Advanced Industrial Democracies*, Oxford: Oxford University Press.

Daniels, Jessie, 2009, *Cyber Racism: White Supremacy Online and the New Attack on Civil Rights*, Lanham: Rowman & Littlefield.

Davis, James C., 1962, 'Toward a theory of revolution,' *American Sociological Review*, 27 (1): pp. 5–19.

————, 1969, 'The J-curve of rising and declining satisfactions as a cause of some great revolutions and a contained rebellion,' in Hugh Davis Graham and Ted Robert Gurr (eds.), *Violence in America: Historical and Comparative Perspectives*, Vol. II, Washington DC: U.S Government Printing Office.

de Bruijn, Simon and Mark Veenbrink, 2012, 'The gender gap in radical right voting: explaining differences in the Netherlands,' *Social Cosmos*, 10 (1): pp. 215–31.

Dechezelles, Stéphanie, 2013, 'Neo-fascists and Padans: the cultural and sociological basis of youth involvement in Italian extreme-right organizations,' in Andrea Mammone, Emmanuel Godin and Brian Jenkins (eds.), *Varieties of Right-Wing Extremism in Europe*, London: Routledge.

della Porta, Donatella, 1992, 'Life histories in the analysis of social movement activists,' Mario Diani and Ron Eyerman (eds.), *Studying Collective Action*, London: Sage.

————, 1995, *Social Movements, Political Violence, and the State: A Comparative Analysis of Italy and Germany*, Cambridge: Cambridge University Press.

————, 2008, 'Research on social sovements and political violence,' *Qualitative Sociology*, 31: pp. 221–30.

———— and Sidney Tarrow, 1986, 'Unwanted children: political violence and cycles of protest in Italy, 1966–1973,' *European Journal of Political Research*, 14: pp. 607–32.

————— and Dieter Rucht, 1995, 'Left-liberation movements in context: a comparison of Italy and West Germany, 1965–1990,' in J. Craig Jenkins and Bert Klandermans (eds.), *The Politics of Social Protest: Comparative Perspectives on States and Social Movements*, London: UCL Press.

————— and Herbert Reiter, (eds.), 1998, *Policing Protest: The Control of Mass Demonstrations in Western Democracies*, Minneapolis: University of Minnesota Press.

—————, Massimiliano Andretta, Lorenzo Mosca and Herbert Reiter, 2006, *Globalization from Below: Transnational Activists and Protest Networks*, Minneapolis: University of Minnesota Press.

Demerath III, N.J., Gerald Marwell and Michael T. Aiken, 1971, *Dynamics of Idealism*, San Francisco: Jossey-Bass.

De Weert, Yves, Patrizia Catellani, Hans De Witte and Patrizia Milesi, 2007, 'Perceived socio-economic change and right-wing extremism: results of the SIREN – Survey among European workers,' in Jörg Flecker (ed.), *Changing Working Life and the Appeal of the Extreme Right*, Aldershot: Ashgate.

De Weerdt, Yves and Hans De Witte, 2007, 'Public safety – private right: the public-private divide and receptiveness of employees to right-wing extremism in Flanders (Belgium),' in Jörg Flecker (ed.), *Changing Working Life and the Appeal of the Extreme Right*, Aldershot: Ashgate.

Diani, Mario, 1996, 'Linking mobilization frames and political opportunities: insights from regional populism in Italy,' *American Sociological Review*, 61: pp. 1,053–69.

Dower, John W., 1999, *Embracing Defeat: Japan in the Wake of World War Two*, New York: W. W. Norton.

Earl, Jennifer et al., 2010, 'Changing the world one web page at a time: conceptualizing and explaining internet activism,' *Mobilization*, (15) 4: pp. 425–46.

Earl, Jennifer and Katrina Kimport, 2011, *Digitally Enabled Social Change: Activism in the Internet Age*, Cambridge, MA: MIT Press.

Earnest, David C., 2008, *Old Nations, New Voters: Nationalism, Trans-nationalism, and Democracy in the Era of Global Migration*, Albany: State University of New York Press.

Eatwell, Roger, 2003, 'Ten theories of the extreme right,' in Peter H. Merkl and L. Weinberg (eds.), *Right-Wing Extremism in the Twenty-First Century*, London: Frank Cass.

————— and Matthew J. Goodwin (eds.), 2010, *The New Extremism in 21st Century Britain*, London: Routledge.

Ebashi, Takashi, (ed.), 1993, *Gaikokujin wa jūmin desu* (Foreigners are residents), Tokyo: Gakuyō Shobō.

Ebata, Michi, 1997, 'Right-wing extremism: in search of a definition,' in Aurel Braun and Stephen Scheinberg (eds.), *The Extreme Right: Freedom and Security at Risk*, Boulder: Westview Press.

Edward, Arthur, 2004, 'The Dutch women's movement online: internet and the organizational infrastructure of a social movement,' in Wim van de Donk, Brian D. Loader, Paul G. Nixon and Dieter Rucht (eds.), *Cyberprotest: New Media, New Citizens and Social Movements*, London: Routledge.

Eltantawy, Nahed and Julie B. Wiest, 2011, 'Social media in the Egyptian Revolution: reconsidering resource mobilization theory,' *International Journal of Communication*, 5: pp. 1,207–24.

Emmers, Ralf, 2010, *Geopolitics and Maritime Territorial Disputes in East Asia*, London: Routledge.

Esseveld, Johanna and Ron Eyerman, 1992, 'Which side are you on? Reflections on methodological issues in the study of 'distasteful' social movements,' in Mario Diani and Ron Eyerman (eds.), *Studying Collective Action*, London: Sage.

Ezekiel, Raphael S., 2002, 'An ethnographer looks at Neo-Nazi and Klan groups: the racist mind revisited,' *American Behavioral Scientist*, 46: pp. 51–71.

Fangen, Katrine, 1998, 'Living out our ethnic instincts: ideological beliefs among right-wing activists in Norway,' in Jeffrey Kaplan and Tore Bjørgo (eds.), *Nation and Race: The Developing Euro-American Racist Subculture*, Boston: Northeastern University Press.

Fangen, Katrine, 1999, 'On the margins of life: life stories of radical nationalists,' *Acta Sociologica*, 42: pp.357–73.

Favell, Adrian, 1998, *Philosophies of Integration: Immigration and the Idea of Citizenship in France and Britain*, London: Macmillan.

Fennema, Meindert, 1997, 'Some conceptual issues and problems in the comparison of anti-immigrant parties in Western Europe,' *Party Politics*, 3 (4): pp. 473–92.

Ferre, Myra Marx, 2003, 'Resonance and radicalism: feminist framing in the abortion debates of the United States and Germany,' *American Journal of Sociology*, 109: pp. 304–44.

Fischer, Claude S., 1975, 'Toward a subcultural theory of urbanism,' *American Journal of Sociology*, 95: pp. 1,319–41.

———— , 1982, *To Dwell Among Friends: Personal Networks in Town and City*, Berkeley: University of California Press.

———— , 1984, *The Urban Experience*, (second edition), San Diego: Harcourt Brace Jovanovich.

———— , 1995, 'The subcultural theory of urbanism: a twentieth year assessment,' *American Journal of Sociology*, 101: pp. 543–77.

Flanagan, Constance A. and Lonnie R. Sherrod, 1998, 'Youth political development: an introduction,' *Journal of Social Issues*, 54 (3): pp. 447–56.

Flecker, Jörg, Gudrun Hentges and Gabrielle Balazs, 2007, 'Potentials of political subjectivity and the various approaches to the extreme right: findings of the qualitative research,' in Jörg Flecker (ed.), *Changing Working Life and the Appeal of the Extreme Right*, Aldershot: Ashgate.

Fontana, Marie-Christine, Andreas Sidler and Sibylle Hardmeier, 2006, 'The "new right" vote: an analysis of the gender gap in the vote choice for the SVP,' *Swiss Political Science Review*, 12(4): pp. 234–71.

Ford, Robert and Matthew J. Goodwin, 2010, 'Angry white men: individual and contextual predictors of support for the British National Party,' *Political Studies*, 58: pp. 1–25.

Fowler, Robert Booth et al., 2010, *Religion and Politics in America: Faith, Culture, and Strategic Choices*, (fourth edition), Boulder: Westview Press.

Franklin, Mark et al., 2009, *Electoral Change: Responses to Evolving Social and Attitudinal Structures in Western Countries*, Colchester: ECPR Press.

Fromm, Erich, 1941, *Escape from Freedom*, New York: Holt, Rinehart and Winston.

Fujioka, Mieko, 2007, 'Shokuminchishugi no kokufuku to "tabunka kyōsei" ron' (Overcoming colonialism and "multicultural symbiosis" theory),' in Kenji Nakano (ed.), *Seisairon o koete – Chōsen hantō to Nihon no 'heiwa' o tsumugu (*Beyond sanctions – spinning peace between the Korean Peninsula and Japan), Tokyo: Shinhyōron.

Fujita, Tomohiro, 2011, 'Intānetto to haigaisei no kanren ni okeru bunkasa: Nihon–Amerika hikaku chōsa no bunseki kara (Cultural disparities in the connection between the internet and nativism: viewed from an analysis of a comparative Japanese–American survey),' *Nenpō Ningen Kagaku* (Human Sciences Annual Report), 32.

Fukuoka, Yasunori, 1993, *Zainichi Kankoku, Chōsenjin: wakai sedai no aidentiti* (*Zainichi* South and North Koreans: identities of the younger generations), Tokyo: Chuō Kōronsha.

————— and Yukiko Tsujiyama, 1991, *Dōka to ika no hazama de: zainichi wakamono sedai no aidentiti kattō* (Between assimilation and differentiation: identity conflicts of the younger generations of *zainichi*), Tokyo: Shinkansha.

————— and Myongsoo Kim, 1997, *Zainichi Kankokujin seinen no seikatsu to ishiki* (Lives and consciousness of *Zainichi* Korean youth), Tokyo: Tokyo Daigaku Shuppankai.

Furuya, Satoru, 2003, 'Migrants, national security and September 11: the case of Japan,' *Race and Class*, 44 (4): pp. 52–62.

————— , 2005, 'Mirareru mono to miru mono: kanshi shakai to gaikokujin (The seen and the seers: surveillance society and foreigners),' in Toshimaru Ogura (ed.), *Gurōbaruka to kanshi keisatsu kokka e no teikō: senji denshi seifu no kenshō to hihan* (Standing up to globalization and a surveillance police state: examination and criticism of the wartime electronic administration), Tokyo: Kinohanasha.

————— , 2012, 'Nihon ni okeru heito supīchi: Osaka shūkai komento memo (Hate speech in Japan: Osaka Conference Comment Memo).

Gamson, William A., 1992, 'The psychology of collective action,' in Aldon D. Morris and Carol M. Mueller (eds.), *Frontiers in Social Movement Theory*, New Haven: Yale University Press.

————— , Bruce Fireman and Steven Rytina, 1982, *Encounters with Unjust Authority*, Homewood: The Dorsey Press.

————— and David S. Meyer, 1996, 'Framing political opportunity,' in Doug McAdam, John D. McCarthy and Mayer N. Zald (eds.), *Comparative Perspective on Social Movements: Political Opportunities, Mobilizing Structures, and Cultural Framing*, Cambridge: Cambridge University Press.

Gans, Herbert, 1979, 'Symbolic ethnicity: the future of ethnic groups and cultures in America,' *Ethnic and Racial Studies*, 2 (1): pp. 1–20.

————— , 1994, 'Symbolic ethnicity and symbolic religiosity: towards a comparison of ethnic and religious acculturation,' *Ethnic and Racial Studies*, 17 (4): pp. 577–92.

Gaikokujin sabetsu Watch Network, (ed.), 2004, *Gaikokujin hōimō: 'chian akka' no sukēpugōto* (Foreigner encirclement: scapegoats for 'worsening public order'), Tokyo: Gendai Jinbunsha.

————, (ed.), 2008, *Gaikokujin hōimō Part 2: Kyōka sareru kanri shisutemu* (Foreigner encirclement, Part 2: Enhanced systems of control), Tokyo: Gendai Jinbunsha.

Garrett, Kelly, 2006, 'Protest in an informational society: a review of literature on social movments and new ICTs,' *Information, Communication, and Society*, 9 (2): pp. 202–24.

Gidengil, Elisabeth et al., 2005, 'Explaining the gender gap in support for the radical right: the case of Canada,' *Comparative Political Studies*, 38 (10): pp. 1,171–95.

Giugni, Marco, Ruud Koopmans, Florence Passey and Paul Statham, 2005, 'Institutional and discursive opportunities for extreme-right mobilization in five countries,' *Mobilization*, 10 (1): pp. 145–62.

Givens, Terrie, 2004, 'The radical right gender gap,' *Comparative Political Studies*, 37 (1): pp. 30–54.

————, 2005, *Voting Radical Right in Western Europe*, Cambridge: Cambridge University Press.

Glaser, Jack, Jay Dixit and Donald P. Green, 2002, 'Studying hate crimes with the internet: What makes racists advocate racial violence?' *Journal of Social Issues*, 58 (1): pp. 177–93.

Gluck, Carol, 2007, *Rekishi de kangaeru* (Thinking with the past), Tokyo: Iwanami Shoten.

Goffman, Erving, 1961, *Asylum: Essays on the Social Situation of Mental Patients and Other Inmates*, New York: Anchor.

Goodwin, Jeff, James M. Jasper and Francesca Polletta, 2000, 'The return of the repressed: the fall and rise of emotions in social movement theory,' *Mobilization*, 5 (1): pp. 65–83.

————, 2001, 'Introduction: why emotions matter,' in Jeff Goodwin, James M. Jasper and Francesca Polletta (eds.), *Passionate Politics: Emotions and Social Movements*, Chicago: University of Chicago Press.

Goodwin Matthew J., 2008a, 'Backlash in the 'hood: determinants of support for the British National Party (BNP) at the Local Level,' *Journal of Contemporary European Studies*, 16 (3): pp. 347–61.

————, 2008b, 'Research, revisionists and the radical right,' *Politics*, 28 (1): pp. 33–40.

————, 2010, 'Activism in contemporary extreme right parties: the case of the British National Party (BNP),' *Journal of Elections, Public Opinion and Parties*, 20 (1): pp. 31–54.

————, 2011, *New British Fascism: Rise of the British National Party*, London: Routledge.

————, et al., 2010, 'Who votes extreme right in twenty-first century Britain? The social bases of support for the National Front and the British National Party,' in Roger Eatwell and Matthew J. Goodwin (eds.), *The New Extremism in 21ˢᵗ Century Britain*, London: Routledge.

Gordon, Milton M., 1964, *Assimilation in American Life*, New York: Oxford University Press.

Gottlieb, Nanette and Mark McLelland (eds.), 2001, *Japanese Cybercultures*, London: Routledge.

Granovetter, Mark, 1973, 'The strength of weak ties,' *American Journal of Sociology*, 78: pp. 1,360–80.

————— , 1985, 'Economic action and social structure: the problem of embeddedness,' *American Journal of Sociology*, 91: pp. 481–510.

Green, Donald P. and Andrew Rich, 1998, 'White supremacist activity and crossburnings in North Carolina,' *Journal of Quantitative Criminology*, 14 (3): pp. 263–82.

Gurr, Ted Robert, 2011, *Why Men Rebel*, (Fortieth Anniversary Edition), Boulder: Paradigm.

Gusfield, Joseph R., 1994, 'The reflexivity of social movements: collective behavior and mass society theory revisited,' in Enrique Laraña, Hank Johnston and Joseph R. Gusfield (eds.), *New Social Movements: From Ideology to Identity*, Philadelphia: Temple University Press.

Ha, Changok, 1976, '*Zainichi* Chōsenjin no jinken mondai (Human rights issues for *Zainichi* Koreans), in Seikichi Ueda and Udai Fujishima (eds.), *Chōsen no tōitsu to jinken* (Korean unification and human rights), Tokyo: Gōdō Shuppan.

Haddad, Emma, 2007, 'Danger happens at the border,' in Prem Kumar Rajaram and Carl Grundy-Warr (eds.), *Borderscapes: Hidden Geographies and Politics at Territory's Edge*, Minneapolis: University of Minnesota Press.

Hamaguchi, Kazuhisa, 2010, 'Hatoyama seiken to ryōdo mondai no kiki (The Hatoyama government and the crisis of territorial disputes),' *Sokoku to Seinen* (Homeland and youth), 377.

Hammar, Tomas, 1990, *Democracy and the Nation State*, Aldershot: Avebury.

Han, Jaehyang, 2010, '*Zainichi kigyō*' no sangyō keizai shi (Industrial economic history of *Zainichi* Korean firms), Nagoya: Nagoya Daigaku Shuppankai.

Han, Tong-hyun, 2006, *Chima chogori seifuku no minzokushi: sono tanjō to Chōsen gakkō no joseitachi* (Ethnography of traditional Korean dress uniforms: their origins and female students in Korean schools), Tokyo: Sofusha.

Hansen, Lene, 2006, *Security as Practice: Discourse Analysis and the Bosnian War*, London: Routledge.

Harajiri, Hideki, 1998, '*Zainichi*' toshite no Korian (Koreans as '*Zainichi*'), Tokyo: Kodansha.

Hashimoto, Miyuki, 2010, *Zainichi Kankoku/Chōsenjin no shinmitsuken: haigūsha sentaku no sutōrī kara yomu 'minzoku' no genzai* (Intimate spheres of Zainichi Koreans: reading 'ethnicity' today from stories about choice of partners), Tokyo: Shakai Hyōronsha.

Hatsuse, Ryuhei (ed.), 1998, *Uchinaru kokusaika, kaitei zōho han* (Internal internationalization, revised and enlarged edition), Tokyo: Sanrei Shobō.

Hayase, Yoshihiko, 2009a, 'Zainichi Daikan Minkoku Mindan to gaikokujin sanseiken fuyo seisaku (Association of Koreans in Japan and the policy of granting voting rights to foreign residents),' *Reihyō*, 6 (3).

————— , 2009b, 'Shogaikoku ni okeru gaikokujin sanseiken dōnyū no keii to sono jittai (The particulars and realities of the introduction of voting rights for foreign residents in several countries),' *Reihyō*, 6, (4).

————— , 2010, 'Nihon ni okeru gaikokujin sanseiken mondai: dōnyūron

shutsugen no haikei to genjō (The voting rights for foreign residents
problem in Japan: the emergence of arguments for their introduction),'
Reihyō, 7 (1).

————, 2011, 'Zainichi gaikokujin no chii to sanseiken mondai: kokuseki,
hōseido no shiten kara (The status of foreigners in Japan and the
problem of their voting rights: from the viewpoint of nationality and
the legal system)' *Reihyō*, 8 (1).

Hechter, Michael, 1999, *Internal Colonialism: The Celtic Fringe in British
National Development*, Second edition, New Brunswick: Transaction.

Hester, Jeffry, 2008, 'Datsu zainichi-ron: an emerging discourse on belonging
among ethnic Koreans in Japan,' in Nelson H.H. Graburn, John Ertl
and Kenji Tierney (eds.), *Multiculturalism in the New Japan: Crossing
the Boundaries Within*, New York: Berghahn Books.

Hettne, Björn and Elisabeth Abiri, 1998, 'The securitization of cross-border
migration: Sweden in the era of globalization,' in Nana Poku and
David T. Graham (eds.), *Redefining Security: Population Movements
and National Security*, New York: Praeger.

Higuchi, Naoto, 2000a, 'Taikō to kyōryoku: shisei kettei mekanizumu no
naka de (Opposition and cooperation: inside municipal government
decision-making mechanisms)', in Takashi Miyajima (ed.), *Gaikoujin
shimin to seiji sanka* (Foreign residents and political participation),
Tokyo: Yūshindō.

————, 2000b, 'Jichitai no kokusaika seisaku to shimon kikan (Internationalization policies of municipalities and consultative bodies),' in
Takashi Miyajima (ed.), in *Gaikokuseki jūmin to shakaiteki, bunkateki
ukeire shisaku* (Foreign residents and measures for social and cultural
incorporation), Tokyo: Final report for Grant-in-Aid for Scientific
Research.

————, 2001a, 'Gaikokujin sanseikenron no nihonteki kōzu: shimin ken
ron kara no apurōchi (The Japanese construction of voting rights for
foreigners arguments: a citizenship approach),' in NIRA Citizenship
Kenkyūkai (ed.), *Tabunka shakai no sentaku: 'shitizenshippu' no
shiten kara* (Choosing a multicultural society: from a 'citizenship'
viewpoint), Tokyo: Nihon Keizai Hyōronsha.

————, 2001b, 'Gaikokujin no gyōsei sanka shisutemu: gaikokujin shimon
kikan no kentō o tsūjite (Systems for administrative participation by
foreigners: examining the role of foreigner consultative bodies),' *Toshi
mondai* (Municipal problems), 57 (4).

————, 2011, 'Higashi Ajia chiseigaku to gaikokujin sanseiken: Nihonban
denizenshippu o meguru aporia (East Asian geopolitics and voting
rights for foreigners: Japanese aporia surrounding denizenship),'
Shakai Shirin, 57 (4).

————, 2012a, 'Zaitokukai no ronri (1): Rachi mondai de 'kaji ga kirikawatta'
A shi no baai (The logic of *Zaitokukai* activists (1): the case of A, who
experienced alternation as a result of the abduction issue),' *Tokushima
Daigaku Shakai Kagaku Kenkyū* (Social Science Research University
of Tokushima), 25.

————, 2012b, 'Zaitokukai no ronri (2): "kokorofurueru rekishi" o keiken
shita B shi no baai (The logic of *Zaitokukai* activists (2): the case of

B who experienced "stirring history"),' *Tokushima Daigaku Shakai Kagaku Kenkyū*, 25.

————, 2012c, 'Zaitokukai no ronri (3): "uppunbarashi ja tsuzukanai" C shi no baai (The logic of *Zaitokukai* activists (3): the case of C for whom "venting his anger" was not the motive for participation),' *Tokushima Daigaku Shakai Kagaku Kenkyū*, 25.

————, 2012d, 'Zaitokukai no ronri (4): Kyōiku chokugo o anki shite iru D shi no baai (The logic of *Zaitokukai* activists (4): the case of D who has memorized the Imperial Rescript on Education),' *Tokushima Daigaku Shakai Kagaku Kenkyū*, 25.

————, 2012e, 'Zaitokukai no ronri (5): "Futsū ni seikatsu dekiru jidai" o torimodoshitai E shi no baai (The logic of *Zaitokukai* activists (5): the case of E who wants to go back to "the time when it was possible to live normally"),' *Tokushima Daigaku Shakai Kagaku Kenkyū*, 25.

————, 2012f, 'Zaitokukai no ronri (6): Wārudo kappu ga kikkake to natta F shi no baai (The logic of *Zaitokukai* activists (6): the case of F for whom the World Cup was the turning point),' *Tokushima Daigaku Shakai Kagaku Kenkyū*, 25.

————, 2012g, 'Zaitokukai no ronri (7): 'Jibun no naka de mondai teiki sareta G shi no baai (The logic of *Zaitokukai* activists (7): the case of G who found himself questioning things),' *Tokushima Daigaku Shakai Kagaku Kenkyū*, 25.

————, 2012h, 'Zaitokukai no ronri (8): "Kenkanryū' o ji de iku H shi no baai" (The logic of *Zaitokukai* activists (8): the case of H who put his "Korea hatred" into actual practice),' *Tokushima Daigaku Chiiki Kagaku Kenkyū* (Tokushima University Regional Studies), 1.

————, 2012i, 'Zaitokukai no ronri (9): "Sōka Gakkai o tsubusu" dōga ni hikikomareta I shi no baai (The logic of *Zaitokukai* activists (9): the case of I who was won over by a "Smash *Sōka Gakkai*" video),' *Tokushima Daigaku Chiiki Kagaku Kenkyū*, 1.

————, 2012j, 'Zaitokukai no ronri (10): Aikokushin to haigaishugi no aida, J shi no baai (The logic of *Zaitokukai* activists (10): the case of J, between patriotism and nativism),' *Osaka Keizai Hōka Daigaku Ajia Taiheiyō Kenkyū Sentā Nenpō* (Annual Report of the Asia Pacific Research Centre, Osaka University of Economics and Law), 8.

————, 2012k, 'Zaitokukai no ronri (11): Nonpori tenjite katsudōka ni natta K shi no baai (The logic of *Zaitokukai* activists (11): the case of K who became an activist whilst being non-political),' *Tokushima Daigaku Chiiki Kagaku Kenkyū*, 2.

————, 2012l, 'Zaitokukai no ronri (12): Zaitokukai ga ōku no hito ni yūki o ataeta to iu L shi no baai (The logic of *Zaitokukai* activists (12): the case of L who claimed that *Zaitokukai* had supplied many people with courage),' *Tokushima Daigaku Chiiki Kagaku Kenkyū*, 2.

————, 2012m, 'Zaitokukai no ronri (13): Daigaku jidai kara "Seiron" o yonde ita M shi no baai (The logic of *Zaitokukai* activists (13): the case of M who had been reading *Seiron* since her university days),' *Tokushima Daigaku Chiiki Kagaku Kenkyū*, 2.

————, 2012n, 'Zaitokukai no ronri (14): Kōsai aite ni kanyū sareta N shi no baai (The logic of *Zaitokukai* activists (14): the case of N who was recruited by his girlfriend),' *Tokushima Daigaku Chiiki Kagaku Kenkyū*, 2.

———, 2012o, 'Zaitokukai no ronri (15): "Motomoto migi datta" O shi no baai (The logic of *Zaitokukai* activists (15): the case of O who "had been on the right from the start"),' *Tokushima Daigaku Shakai Kagaku Kenkyū*, 26.

———, 2012p, 'Zaitokukai no ronri (16): Rekishi mondai ga ki ni kakatte ita P shi no baai (The logic of *Zaitokukai* activists (16): the case of P who was concerned about historical issues),' *Tokushima Daigaku Shakai Kagaku Kenkyū*, 26.

———, 2012q, 'Zaitokukai no ronri (17): Hitori de gaisen shite ita dōga ni hikikomareta Q shi no baai (The logic of *Zaitokukai* activists (17): the case of Q who was fascinated by a video of a lone figure carrying out street demonstrations),' *Tokushima Daigaku Shakai Kagaku Kenkyū*, 26.

———, 2012r, 'Zaitokukai no ronri (18): Shokuba ni atta Sankei Shinbun o ki ni itta R shi no baai (The logic of *Zaitokukai* activists (18): the case of R who liked the *Sankei Shinbun* at his workplace),' *Tokushima Daigaku Shakai Kagaku Kenkyū*, 26.

———, 2012s, 'Kōdō suru hoshu' no ronri (1): Chūgoku ga jūyō to iu α shi no baai (The logic of "active conservatives" (1): the case of α who says that China is important),' *Tokushima Daigaku Chiiki Kagaku Kenkyū*, 1.

———, 2012t, '"Kōdō suru hoshu" no ronri (2): gaikokujin sanseiken ni hantai suru β shi no baai (The logic of "active conservatives" (2): the case of β who opposes voting rights for foreign residents),' *Tokushima Daigaku Chiiki Kagaku Kenkyū*, 1.

———, 2012u, '"Kōdō suru hoshu" no ronri (3): Zaitokukai kara mananda γ shi no baai (The logic of "active conservatives" (3): the case of γ who learnt from *Zaitokukai*),' *Tokushima Daigaku Chiiki Kagaku Kenkyū*, 1.

———, 2012v, 'Kōdō suru hoshu' no ronri (4): 'saranaru migi' toshite no haigaishugi o jissen suru δ shi no baai (The logic of "active conservatives" (4): the case of δ who practised a form of nativism even more to the right),' *Ibaraki Daigaku Chiiki Sōgō Kenkyūjo Nenpō* (Annual Report of Institute of Regional Studies, Ibaraki University), 45.

———, 2012w, '"Kōdō suru hoshu" no ronri (5): *tondemo* hon kara rekishi mondai o meguru kenokan e - ε shi no baai (The logic of "active conservatives" (3): the case of ε whose hatred of historical problems began with an antisemitic book),' *Tokushima Daigaku Chiiki Kagaku Kenkyū*, 1.

———, 2012x, '"Kōdō suru hoshu" no ronri (6): Chūgoku ga jūyō to iu α shi no baai, sai (The logic of "active conservatives" (6): the case of α who says that China is important, second interview),' *Tokushima Daigaku Chiiki Kagaku Kenkyū*, 2.

———, 2012y, 'Nihon no esunikku bijinesu o meguru mitorizu (Overview of ethnic businesses in Japan),' in Naoto Higuchi (ed.), *Nihon no esunikku bijinesu* (Ethnic businesses in Japan), Kyoto: Sekai Shisōsha.

———, 2013a, '"Kōdō suru hoshu" no ronri (7): uyoku ni deshiiri shita η shi no baai (The logic of "active conservatives" (7): the case of η who enrolled in the far right),' *Ajia Taiheiyō Kenkyū Sentā Nenpō*, 9.

————, 2013b, ' "Kōdō suru hoshu" no ronri (8): "netto uyoku no karisuma" Z shi no baai (The logic of "active conservatives" (8): the case of Z, "the charisma of internet right wingers"),' *Ibaraki Daigaku Chiiki Sōgō Kenkyūjo Nenpō*, 46.

————, 2013c, 'Zaitokukai no ronri (19): Kanada de kawatta S shi no baai (The logic of *Zaitokukai* activists (19): the case of S who underwent change in Canada),' *Tokushima Daigaku Shakai Kagaku Kenkyū*, 27.

————, 2013d, 'Zaitokukai no ronri (20): Totsuka Yotto Sukūru ni kyōmei shita T shi no baai (The logic of *Zaitokukai* activists (20): the case of T who empathized with the Totsuka Yacht School),' *Tokushima Daigaku Shakai Kagaku Kenkyū*, 27.

————, 2013e, 'Zaitokukai no ronri (21): intānashonaru sukūru de manande ita U shi no baai (The logic of *Zaitokukai* activists (21): the case of U who was a student at an international school),' *Tokushima Daigaku Shakai Kagaku Kenkyū*, 27.

————, 2013f, 'Zaitokukai no ronri (22): "hi no maru o jīchan ga kakageta" V shi no baai (The logic of *Zaitokukai* activists (22): the case of V whose grandfather flew the Japanese flag),' *Tokushima Daigaku Chiiki Kagaku Kenkyū*, 3.

————, 2013g, 'Zaitokukai no ronri (23): intānetto de sekai ga kawatta W shi no baai' (The logic of *Zaitokukai* activists (23): the case of W for whom the world changed on the internet),' *Tokushima Daigaku Chiiki Kagaku Kenkyū*, 3.

————, 2013h, 'Zaitokukai no ronri (24): Rōso senjū kara migisenkai shita X shi no baai (The logic of *Zaitokukai* activists (24): the case of X who moved to the right after being a union activist),' *Tokushima Daigaku Chiiki Kagaku Kenkyū*, 3.

————, 2013i, 'Zaitokukai no ronri (25): benkyō sākuru toshite no Zaitokukai ni sanka shita Y shi no baai (The logic of *Zaitokukai* activists (25): the case of Y who participated in *Zaitokukai* as a study circle),' *Tokushima Daigaku Chiiki Kagaku Kenkyū*, 3.

————, 2013j, ' "Kōdō suru hoshu" no ronri (9): kokka kakushin no ichibu toshite haigaishugi undō ni sanka suru θ shi no baai (The logic of "active conservatives" (9): the case of θ who participates in nativism as a part of national reform),' *Tokushima Daigaku Chiiki Kagaku Kenkyū*, 3.

————, 2013l, 'Haigaishugi undō no kakushin o tsukamu: Zaitokukai chōsa kara miete kita mono (Comprehending the heart of the nativist movement: findings of research on *Zaitokuai*),' *Journalism*, 282.

————, 2014, 'Japan's far right in East Asian geopolitics: the anatomy of new xenophobic movements,' *University of Tokushima Social Science Research*, 28: pp. 163–83.

————, 2016, 'Dynamics of occupational status among Koreans in Japan: analyzing census data between 1980 to 2010,' *Seoul Journal of Japanese Studies*, 2 (in press).

———— and Masao Murayama, 2006, 'Gaikokujin sanseiken to yoron' (Voting rights for foreigners and public opinion),' in Hiroshi Tanaka and Kim Kyondok (eds.), *Nikkan 'kyōsei shakai' no tenbō: kankoku de jitsugen shita gaikokujin chihō sanseiken* (Prospects for a Japan–Korea symbiosis: the implementation of voting rights for foreign residents in South Korea), Tokyo: Shinkansha.

————— and Mitsuru Matsutani, 2016, 'Support for the radical right in Japan: converging to the European politics?' *Social Theory and Dynamics*, 1: 61–70.

Higuchi, Yūichi, 2002, *Nihon no Chōsen, Kankokujin* (Japan's North and South Koreans), Tokyo: Dōseisha.

Hilgartner, Stephen and Charles L. Bosk, 1988, 'The rise and fall of social problems: a public arenas model,' *American Journal of Sociology*, 94: pp. 53–78.

Hirabayashi, Yūko, 2013, 'Nani ga "demo no aru shakai" o tsukuru no ka: posuto 3.11 no akutibizumu to media' (What creates a "demonstrataion society"?: post-3.11 activism and the media),' in Shigeyoshi Tanaka, Harutoshi Funabashi, Toshiyuki Masamura (eds.), *Higashi Nihon daishinsai to shakaigaku: daisaigai o umidashita shakai* (The great earthquake of Eastern Japan and sociology: the society that produced a great disaster), Kyoto: Minerva Shobō.

Hiramatsu, Shigeo, 2010, 'Kuni o ayauku suru "gaikokujin chihō sanseiken" (Municipal voting rights for foreign residents which put the nation in imminent danger),' *Chian fōramu* (Public order forum), 16 (4).

Hirota, Masao, 2000, 'Gaikokujin shisei sanka no hōteki kentō (A legal analysis of foreigner participation in municipal government),' in Takashi Miyajima (ed.), *Gaikokujin shimin to seiji sanka* (Foreign residents and political participation), Tokyo: Yūshindō.

Hoffer, Eric, 1951, *The True Believer: Thoughts on the Nature of Mass Movements*, New York: Harper & Brothers.

Hokama, Shukichi, 2012, 'Yonagunichō no shōrai tenbō: jinkō zōka to iu kadai' (Yonaguni's future outlook: the subject of population increases),' *Bessatsu kan*, 19.

Honda, Yuki, 2007, 'Focusing in on contemporary Japan's "youth" nationalism,' *Social Science Japan Journal*, 10 (2): 281–6.

Hori, Yukio, 1993, *Zōho sengo no uyoku seiryoku* (The post-war far right), (enlarged edition), Tokyo: Keisō Shobō.

'Horumon Bunka' Henshū Iinkai (ed.), 1992, *Zainichi Chōsenjin ga senkyo ni iku hi* (The day that *Zainichi Koreans vote*), Tokyo: Shinkansha.

Hosaka, Nobuto, 2011, 'Seijiteki ni "inai" sonzai o nakusu tame ni (Correcting a politically "bereft" existence),' *Buraku Kaihō*, 644.

Husbands, Christopher, T., 2002, 'How to tame the dragon, or what goes around comes around: a critical review of some major contemporary attempts to account for extreme-right racist politics in Western Europe,' in Martin Schain, Aristide Zolberg and Patrick Hossay (eds.), *Shadows Over Europe: The Development and Impact of the Extreme Right in Western Europe*, London: Palgrave.

Huysmans, Jef, 1995, 'Migrants as a security problem: dangers of securitizing societal issues,' in Robert Miles and Dietrich Thränhardt (eds.), *Migration and European Integration: The Dynamics of Inclusion and Exclusion*, London: Pinter.

————— , 2006, *The Politics of Insecurity: Fear, Migration and Asylum in the EU*, London: Routledge.

————, 2011, 'What's in an act? On security speech acts and little security nothings,' *Security Dialogue*, 42 (4–5): pp. 371–83.

Hwang, Seongbin, 2003, 'W-hai to Nihon no jigazō, soshite Kankoku to iu tasha (The Soccer World Cup and Japan's self-portrait, and South Korea as other),' *Masu Komyunikēshon Kenkyū* (Mass Communication Studies), 62.

Hyun, Mooam, 2008, 'Gurōbaruka suru jinken: "hannichi" no Nikkan dōjidai shi (The globalization of human rights: contemporary Japanese–South Korean history of "anti-Japanese sentiment"),' in Minoru Iwasaki et al. (eds.), *Sengo Nihon Sutadīzu, 3: 1980–1990 nendai* (Post-war Japanese studies, 3: the 1980s and 1990s), Tokyo: Kinokuniya Shoten.

Ibrahim, Maggie, 2005, 'The securitization of migration: a racial discourse,' *International Migration*, 43 (5): pp.163–87.

Iglesias, Julien Danero, Nenad Stojanović and Sharon Weinblum (eds.), 2013, *New Nation-States and National Minorities*, Colchester: ECPR Press.

Ignazi, Piero, 1992, 'The silent counter-revolution: hypotheses on the emergence of extreme right parties in Europe,' *European Journal of Political Research*, 22: pp. 3–34.

————, 2002, 'The extreme right: defining the object and assessing the causes,' in Martin Schain, Aristide Zolberg and Patrick Hossay (eds.), *Shadows Over Europe: The Development and Impact of the Extreme Right in Western Europe*, London: Palgrave.

————, 2003, *Extreme Right Parties in Western Europe*, Oxford: Oxford University Press.

Ijūren Hinkon Project (ed.), 2011, *Nihon de kurasu Ijūsha no hinkon* (Poverty amongst migrants living in Japan), Tokyo: Gendai Jinbunsha.

Immerfall, Stefan, 1998, 'The neo-populist agenda,' in Hans-Georg Betz and Stefan Immerfall (eds.), *The New Politics of the Right: Neo-Populist Parties and Movements in Established Democracies*, New York: St Martin's Press.

Inaba, Nanako, Yukiko Omagiri, Sachi Takaya, Naoto Higuchi and Itaru Kaji, 2014, '1985 nen kokusei chōsa ni miru zainichi gaikokujin no shigoto (Jobs held by Japan's foreign residents: views from the 1985 national census data),' *Ibaraki Daigaku Jinbun Komyunikēshon gakka ronshū* (Collected Essays of the Human Communications Department of Ibaraki University), 17.

Ingelhart, Ronald and Pippa Norris, 2003, *Rising Tide: Gender Equality and Cultural Change around the World*, New York: Cambridge University Press.

Inoue, Kaoru, 2010, *Koko ga okashii, gaikokujin sanseiken* (This is strange, voting rights for foreign residents), Tokyo: Bungei Shunjūsha.

Ireland, Patrick, 1994, *The Policy Challenge of Ethnic Diversity: Immigrant Politics in France and Switzerland*, Cambridge, MA: Harvard University Press.

Ishihara, Masaie, 1982, *Dai mitsu bōeki no jidai: senryō shoki Okinawa no minshū seikatsu* (The era of smuggling: people's lives in early post-war Okinawa), Tokyo: Bansansha.

————, 2000, *Kūhaku no Okinawa shakai shi: senka to mitsu bōeki no jidai* (The social history of Okinawa as a vacuum: the ravages of war and smuggling), Tokyo: Bansansha.

Isogai, Haruyoshi, 1986, '"Zainichi" no shisō, ikikata o yomu (Reading the thoughts and way of life of "zainichi"),' *Kikan Sanzenri*, 46.

Itagaki, Ryūta, 2007, '"Manga kenkanryū" to jinshushugi, kokuminshugi no kōzō ("Wave of Korea hatred" comics and the structure of racism and nationalism),' *Zenya* (Eve), 11.

Ivarsflaten, Elisabeth, 2005, 'The vulnerable populist right parties: no economic realignment fuelling their electoral success,' *European Journal of Political Research*, 44: pp. 465–92.

———, 2008, 'What unites right-wing populists in Western Europe? Re-examing grievance mobilization models in seven successful cases,' *Comparative Political Studies*, 41 (1): 3–23.

——— and Rune Stubager, 2012, 'Voting for the populist radical right in Western Europe: the role of education,' in Jens Rydgren, (ed.), *Class Politics and the Radical Right*, London: Routledge.

Iwata, Atsushi, 2009, 'Kokumin kokka no keisei: gaikokujin sanseiken mondai kenkyū josetsu (The formation of a nation state: An introduction to the study of voting rights for foreign residents issue),' *Reihyō*, 6 (4).

Jacobs, Dirk, 1998, 'Discourses, politics and policy: the Dutch parliamentary debate about voting rights for foreign residents,' *International Migration Review*, 32: pp. 350–73.

———, 1999, 'The debate over enfranchisement of foreign residents in Belgium,' *Journal of Ethnic and Migration Studies*, 25 (4): pp. 649–63.

———, and Marc Swyngedouw, 2002, 'The extreme right and enfranchisement of immigrants: issues in the public "debate" on integration in Belgium,' *Journal of International Migration and Integration*, 3 (34): pp. 329–44.

James, Nigel, 2001, 'Militias, the patriot movement and the internet: the ideology of conspiracism,' in Jane Parish and Martin Parker (eds.), *The Age of Anxiety: Conspiracy Theories and the Human Sciences*, Oxford: Wiley-Blackwell.

Jansson, David, 2010, 'The head vs. the gut: emotions, positionality, and the challenge of fieldwork with a southern nationalist movement,' *Geoforum*, 41: 19–22.

Jaschke, Hans-Gerd, 2013, 'Right-wing extremism and populism in contemporary Germany and Western Europe,' in Sabine von Mering and Timothy Wyman McCarty (eds.), *Right-wing Radicalism Today: Perspectives from Europe and the US*, London: Routledge.

Jasper, James, M., 1997, *The Art of Moral Protest: Culture, Biography, and Creativity in Social Movements*, Chicago: University of Chicago Press.

Jenkins, J. Craig, 1985, *The Politics of Insurgency: The Farm Worker Movement in the 1960s*, New York: Columbia University Press.

——— and Bert Klandermans (eds.), 1995, *The Politics of Social Protest: Comparative Perspectives on States and Social Movements*, London: UCL Press.

Jiyū Minshūtō Seimu Chōsakai Yonagunichō Chōsadan (Parliamentary Committee of the LDP, Yonaguni Town Commission), 2010, 'Gaikokujin chihō sanseiken mondai "shiryōshū" (Municipal voting rights for foreign residents issue "Documents"),' *Seisaku Tokuhō* (Policy News), 1,355.

Johnston, Hank, 1991, *Tales of Nationalism: Catalonia, 1939–1979*, New Brunswick: Rutgers University Press.

————, 1995, 'A methodology for frame analysis: from discourse to cognitive schemata,' in Hank Johnston and Bert Klandermans (eds.), *Social Movements and Culture*, London: UCL Press.

Jōmaru, Yōichi, 2011, *'Shokun!', 'Seiron' no kenkyū: hoshu genron wa dō henyō shite kita ka* (Studies of 'Shokun!' and 'Seiron': how has conservative discourse changed?), Tokyo: Iwanami Shoten.

Jones-Correa, Michael, 1998, *Between Two Nations: The Political Predicament of Latinos in New York City*, Ithaca: Cornell University Press.

Kalicki, Konrad, 2008, 'Voting rights of the "marginal": the contested logic of political membership in Japan,' *Ethnopolitics*, 7: pp. 265–86.

Kallis, Aristotle, 2013, 'Breaking taboos and "mainstreaming the extreme": the debates on restricting Islamic symbols in contemporary Europe,' in Ruth Wodak, Majid KhosraviNik and Brigitte Mral (eds.), *Right-wing Populism in Europe: Politics and Discourse*, London: Bloomsbury.

Kang, Chae-on and Donfun Kim, 1989, *Zainichi Kankoku, Chōsenjin: rekishi to tenbō* (*Zainichi* South and North Koreans: history and outlook), Tokyo: Rōdō Keizaisha.

Kang, Sang Jung, 1985a, '"Zainichi" no genzai to mirai no aida (Between the present and future for "*zainichi*"),' *Kikan sanzenri*, 42.

————, 1985b, 'Hōhō toshite no "zainichi" ("*Zainichi*" as a means),' *Kikan sanzenri*, 44.

————, 1989, 'Shōwa no shūen to gendai Nihon no "shinshō chiri=rekishi": kyōkasho no naka no Chōsen o chūshin toshite' (The end of Shōwa and "imagined geography=history" in present-day Japan: a focus on Korea in textbooks),' *Shisō*, 786.

————, 1992, '"Zainichi" no aratana kijiku o motomete: teikō to sanka no hazama de (Seeking a new "*zainichi*" plan: between resistance and participation),' *Seikyu*, 13.

————, 1994, 'Tenkeiki no "zainichi" to sanseiken ("Zainichi" in a transformative period and voting rights),' *Seikyu*, 20.

————, 1996, *Orientarizumu no kanata e: kindai bunka hihan* (Beyond orientalism: a critique of modern culture), Tokyo: Iwanami Shoten.

Kang, Tok-sang, 2003, *'Shinpan' Kantō daishinsai, gyakusatsu no kioku* (The great Kantō earthquake and massacre), (new edition), Tokyo: Seikyū Bunkasha.

Kawasakishi Gaikokuseki Shimin Ishiki Jittai Chōsa Kenkyū Iinkai, 1993, *Kawasakishi gaikokuseki shimin ishiki jittai chōsa hōkokusho* (Report of the survey on the foreign residents of Kawasaki City).

Kaplan, Jeffrey and Tore Bjørgo (eds.), 1998, *Nation and Race: The Developing Euro-American Racist Subculture*, Boston: Northeastern University Press.

Karube, Tadashi, 2006, 'Fuyū suru rekishi: 1990 nendai no tennōron (Drifting history: 1990s debates about the emperor),' *Shakai kagaku kenkyū* (Social Science Research), 58 (1).

Karvonen, Lauri, 2004, 'The new extreme right-wingers in Western Europe: attitudes, world views and social characteristics,' in Peter Merkl and

Leonard Weingberg (eds.), *The Revival of Right-Wing Extremism in the Nineties*, London: Frank Cass.

Kashiwazaki, Chikako, 2002, 'Kokuseki no arikata: bunkateki tayōsei no shōnin ni mukete (The state of nationality: towards a recognition of cultural diversity),' in Atsushi Kondo (ed.), *Gaikokujin no hōteki chii to jinken yōgo* (The legal status of foreigners and human rights protection), Tokyo: Akashi Shoten.

Kashiwazaki, Masanori, 2011, 'Gendai Nihon ni okeru haigai nashonarizumu to shokuminchishugi no hinin: hihan no tameni (Anti-foreign nationalism in present-day Japan and the denial of colonialism: its critics),' in Minoru Iwasaki, Kuan-Hsing Chen and Shunya Yoshimi (eds.), *Karuchararu sutadīzu de yomitoku Ajia* (Deciphering Asia through cultural studies), Tokyo: Serika Shobō.

Kato, Haruno, 2012, 'Hoshu undō kanten kara no jendā basshingu gensetsu: furēmu bunseki o shiyō shite (Gender bashing discourses from the perspective of the conservative movement: using frame analysis),' *Kakusa senshitibuna ningen hattatsu kagaku no sōsei kōbo kenkyū seika ronbunshū* (Anthology of the results of creative research from developmental science on sensitivity to differences), 20.

Kawai, Mikio, 2004, *Anzen shinwa hōkai no paradokkusu: chian no hōshakaigaku* (The paradox of crumbling safety myths: the sociology of public order law), Tokyo: Iwanami Shoten.

Keck, Margalet E. and Kathryn Sikkink, 1998, *Activists beyond Borders: Advocacy Networks in International Politics*, Ithaca: Cornell University Press.

Keniston, Kenneth, 1968, *Young Radicals: Notes on Committed Youth*, New York: Harcourt, Brace & World.

———— , 1971, *Youth and Dissent: The Rise of a New Opposition*, New York: Harcourt Brace Jovanovich.

Kersten, Joachim, 2004, 'The right-wing network and the role of extremist youth groupings in unified Germany,' in Angelica Fenner and Eric D. Weitz (eds.), *Fascism and Neo-Fascism: Critical Writings on the Radical Right in Europe*, London: Palgrave Macmillan.

Kessler, Alan E. and Gary P. Freeman, 2005, 'Support for extreme right-wing parties in Western Europe: individual attributes, political attitudes, and national context,' *Comparative European Politics*, 3: pp. 261–88.

Kim, Dongfun, 1994, *Gaikokujin jūmin no sanseiken* (Voting rights for foreign residents), Tokyo: Akashi Shoten.

Kim, Kyongdoku, 1995, *Zainichi Korian no aidentiti to hōteki chii* (*Zainichi* Korean identity and legal status), Tokyo: Akashi Shoten.

Kim, Kyongmook, 2011, 'Nihon no naka no "zainichi" to shakai undō: shimin undō to kokusai rentai ni yoru saikentō ("Zainichi" in Japan and social movements: a review via international solidarity of citizen movements),' in Jongwon Yi, Masafumi Kimiya and Toyomi Asano (eds.), *Rekishi toshite no Nikkan kokkō seijōka I: higashi Ajia reisen hen* (The normalization of Japan–South Korea diplomatic relations as history I: East Asia Cold War volume), Tokyo: Hōsei Daigaku Shuppankyoku.

Kim, Myongsoo and Tadashi Inazuki, 2000, 'Zainichi Kankokujin no shakai idō (Social mobility of *Zainichi* South Koreans),' in Kenji Kosaka (ed.), *Kaisō shakai kara atarashii shimin shakai e* (From a stratified society to a new citizen society), Tokyo: Tokyo Daigaku Shuppankai.

Kim, Puja, 2011, *Keizoku suru shokuminchishugi to jendā: 'kokumin' gainen; josei no shintai; kioku to sekinin* (Enduring colonialism and gender: the concept of 'nation'; women's bodies; and memory and responsibility), Tokyo: Seori Shobō.

Kim, Taeki, 1991a, 'Zainichi Kankokujin sansei no hōteki chii to "1965 nen Kannichi Kyōtei" (1) (The legal status of third generation *zainichi* Koreans and "the 1965 South Korea–Japan Agreement"),' *Ikkyo ronsō* (Hitotsubashi Essay Collection), 105 (1).

————, 1991b, 'Zainichi Kankokujin sansei no hōteki chii to "1965 nen Kannichi Kyōtei" (2),' *Ikkyo Ronsō*, 106 (1).

————, 1997, *Sengo Nihon seiji to zainichi Chōsenjin mondai: SCAP no taizainichi Chōsenjin seisaku 1945–1952 nen* (Post-war Japanese politics and the *Zainichi* Korean issue: SCAP policy towards *Zainichi* Koreans 1945–1952), Tokyo: Keisō Shobō.

Kim, Yong, 2008, 'Zainichi Chōsenjin danatsu kara miru Nihon no shokumunchishugi to gunjika (Japan's colonialism and militarization seen from the oppression of *Zainichi* Koreans),' in Puja Kim and Toshio Nakano (eds.), *Rekishi to sekinin: 'ianfu' mondai to 1990 nendai* (History and responsibility: the 'comfort women' issue and the 1990s), Tokyo: Seikyūsha.

Kimmel, Michael, 2007, 'Racism as adolescent male rite of passage: ex-Nazis in Scandinavia,' *Journal of Contemporary Ethnography*, 36 (2): pp. 202–18.

———— and Abby L. Ferber, 2000, '"White men are this nation": right-wing militias and the restoration of rural American masculinity,' *Rural Sociology*, 65 (4): pp. 582–604.

Kimura, Kan, 2007, 'Būmu wa nani o nokoshita ka: nashonarizumu no naka no kanryū (What has the boom left behind?: The South Korean popular culture boom in the midst of nationalism),' in Saeko Ishida, Kan Kimura and Chie Yamanaka (eds.), *Posuto kanryū no media shakaigaku* (Sociology of the media following the South Korean popular culture boom), Kyoto: Minerva Shobō.

————, 2013, 'Nikkan rekishi mondai ni dō mukiau ka (31): henka suru Nihon shakai (How to confront Japanese-Korean historical issues (31): Changing Japanese society),' *Kyū*, 31.

Kimura, Motohiko, Yoshiaki Sei and Kōichi Yasuda, 2013, 'Sakkā to aikoku no kimyōna kankei (The strange relationship between soccer and patriotism),' *Shūkan Asahi*, 118 (45).

Kimura, Motohiko, Shion Sono and Kōichi Yasuda, 2013, *Nashonarizumu no yūwaku* (The lure of nationalism), Tokyo: Korokara.

Kinoshita, Chigaya, 2010, 'Nihon no haigaishugi undō no yukue (The future of Japan's nativist movement), *Migrants Network*, 127.

Kinpara, Samon et al., 1986, *Nihon no naka no Kankoku, Chōsenjin, Chūgokujin* (North and South Koreans and Chinese in Japan), Tokyo: Akashi Shoten.

Kitada, Akihiro, 2005, *Warau Nihon no 'nashonarizumu'* (Japan's laughing 'nationalism'), Tokyo: Nihon Hōsō Shuppan Kyōkai.

Kitschelt, Herbert, 1995, *The Radical Right in Western Europe: A Comparative Analysis*, Ann Arbor: University of Michigan Press.

Klandermans, Bert, 1992, 'Social construction of protest and the multi-organizational field,' in Aldon D. Morris and Carol M. Muller (eds.), *Frontiers in Social Movement Theory*, New Haven: Yale University Press.

————, *Social Psychology of Collective Action*, Oxford: Blackwell.

————, 'Extreme right activists: recruitment and experience,' in Sabine von Mering and Timothy Wyman McCarthy (eds.), *Right-Wing Radicalism Today: Perspectives from Europe and the US*, London: Routledge.

———— and Dirk Oegema, 1987, 'Potentials, networks, motivations and barriers: steps towards participation in social movements,' *American Sociological Review*, 52 (4): pp. 519–31.

————, Marlene Roefs and Johan Olivier, 2001, 'Grievance formation in a country in transition: South Africa, 1994–1998,' *Social Psychology Quarterly*, 64 (1): pp. 41–54.

———— and Nonna Mayer, 2006a, 'Right-wing extremism as a social movement,' in Bert Klandermans and Nonna Mayer (eds.), *Extreme Right Activists in Europe: Through the Magnifying Glass*, London: Routledge.

———— and Nonna Mayer, 2006b, 'Through the magnifying glass: the world of extreme right activists,' in Bert Klandermans and Nonna Mayer (eds.), *Extreme Right Activists in Europe: Through the Magnifying Glass*, London: Routledge.

————, Jojanneke van der Toorn and Jacquelien van Stekelenburg, 2008, 'Embeddedness and identity: how immigrants turn grievances into action,' *American Sociological Review*, 73: pp. 992–1,012.

Knigge, Pia, 1998, 'The ecological correlates of right-wing extremism in Western Europe,' *European Journal of Political Research*, 34: pp. 249–79.

Knutsen, Oddbjørn, 2006, *Class Voting in Western Europe: A Comparative Longitudinal Study*, Lanham: Lexington Books.

Kobayashi, Reiko, 2011, 'Nikkan kaidan to "zainichi" no hōteki chii mondai: taikyo kyōsei o chūshin ni (Japan–South Korea Conference and the issue of the legal status of "zainichi": a focus on forced deportations),' in Jongwon Yi, Masafumi Kimiya and Toyomi Asano (eds.), *Rekishi toshite no Nikkan kokkō seijōka II: datsu shokuminchika hen* (The normalization of diplomatic relations between Japan and South Korea as history II: Decolonization volume), Tokyo: Hōsei Daigaku Shuppankyoku.

Komagome, Takeshi, 1996, *Shokuminchi teikoku Nihon no bunka tōgō* (Cultural integration in the Japanese colonial empire), Tokyo: Iwanami Shoten.

Komai, Hiroshi and Ichirō Watado (eds.), 1997, *Jichitai no gaikokujin seisaku* (Local government foreigner policies), Tokyo: Akashi Shoten.

Kondo, Atsushi, 1996a, *'Gaikokujin' no sanseiken* (Voting rights of 'foreigners'), Tokyo: Akashi Shoten.

————, 1996b, *Gaikokujin sanseiken to kokuseki* (Voting rights for foreigners and nationality), Tokyo: Akashi Shoten.

————, 2000, 'Eijū gaikokujin no chihō sanseiken o meguru saikin no ronten (Recent issues regarding municipal voting rights for permanent resident foreigners),' *Hōgaku seminā* (Law Seminar), 552.

Kondo, Ruman and Akira Tanizaki (eds.), 2007, *Netto uyoku to sabukaru minshushugi: mai demokurashī shōkōgun* (Net right wing and subculture democracy: my democracy syndrome), Tokyo: Sanichi Shobō.

Koo, Yoojin, 2009, ' "Atarashii rekishi kyōkasho o tsukuru kai" no Exit, Voice, Loyalty: higashi Ajia kokusai kankei e no gani o chūshin ni (Exit, Voice, Loyalty of the "Society for History Textbook Reform": a focus on the implications for East Asian international relations),' *Sōkan shakaigaku*, 19.

Koopmans, Ruud, 1995, *Democracy from Below: New Social Movements and the Political System in West Germany*, Boulder: Westview Press.

———, 1996, 'Explaining the rise of racist and extreme right violence in Western Europe: grievances or opportunities,' *European Journal of Political Research*, 30: pp. 185–216.

——— and Paul Statham, 1999, 'Ethnic and civic competitions of nationhood and the differentiated success of the extreme right in Germany and Italy,' in Marco Giugni, Doug McAdam and Charles Tilly (eds.), *How Social Movements Matter*, Minneapolis: University of Minnesota Press.

——— and Susan Olzak, 2004, 'Discursive opportunities and the evolution of right-wing violence in Germany,' *American Journal of Sociology*, 119 (1): pp. 198–230.

———, Paul Statham, Marco Giugni and Florence Passy, 2005, *Contested Citizenship: Immigration and Cultural Diversity in Europe*, Minneapolis: University of Minnesota Press.

——— and Jasper Muis, 2009, 'The rise of right-wing populist Pim Fortuyn in the Netherlands: a discursive opportunity approach,' *European Journal of Political Research*, 48: pp. 642–64.

Kornhauser, William, 1960, *The Politics of Mass Society*, London: Routledge and Kegan Paul.

Koseki, Shōichi, 2010, 'Teikoku shinmin kara gaikokujin e: ataerare, ubawarete kita Chōsenjin, Taiwanjin no sanseiken (From imperial subjects to foreigners: the voting rights granted and snatched away from Koreans and Taiwanese),' *Sekai*, 809.

Koto, Akira, 1991, 'Gaikokujin rōdōsha to wagakuni no shakai hoshō hōsei (Foreign workers and Japan's social security laws), Shakai Hoshō Kenkyūjo (ed.), *Gaikokujin rōdōsha to shakai hoshō* (Foreign workers and social security), Tokyo: Tokyo Daigaku Shuppankai.

Krause, Keith, 1998, 'Critical theories and security studies: the research programme of "Critical Security Studies" ' *Cooperation and Conflict*, 33 (3): pp. 298–333.

——— and Michael C. Williams (eds.), 1997, *Critical Security Studies: Concepts and Cases*, Minneapolis: University of Minnesota Press.

Kriesi, Hanspeter, 1999, 'Movements of the left, movements of the right: putting the mobilization of two new types of social movements into political context,' in Herbert Kitschelt et al. (eds.), *Continuity and Change in Contemporary Capitalism*, Cambridge: Cambridge University Press.

Kura, Shinichi, 2006, 'Hoshukei opinion shi ni okeru gaikokujin gensetsu (1): 1990 nendai made no zasshi "SAPIO" o chūshin ni (Discourse on foreigners in conservative opinion magazines (1): a focus on the magazine "SAPIO" up until the 1990s),' *Miyazaki Kōritsu Daigaku Jinbungakubu Kiyō* (Bulletin of the Faculty of Humanities, Miyazaki Prefectural University), 14 (1).

————, 2008, 'Hoshukei opinionshi ni okeru gaikokujin gensetsu (2): 1990 nendai kōhan ni okeru zasshi "SAPIO" o chūshin ni (Discourse on foreigners in conservative opinion magazines (2): a focus on the magazine "SAPIO" in the late 1990s),' *Miyazaki Kōritsu Daigaku Jinbungakubu Kiyō*, 15 (1).

————, 2009, 'Hoshukei opinionshi ni okeru gaikokujin gensetsu (3): 2000 nendai ni okeru zasshi "SAPIO" o chūshin ni (Discourse on foreigners in conservative opinion magazines (3): a focus on the magazine "SAPIO" in the 2000s),' *Miyazaki Kōritsu Daigaku Jinbungakubu Kiyō*, 16 (1).

Kuroda, Isamu, 2003, 'Nikkan wārudo kappu to media (The South Korea–Japan World Cup and the media),' *Supōtsu shakaigaku kenkyū* (Studies in the sociology of sport), 11.

Kurosawa, Fumitaka and Ian Nishi (eds.), 2011, *Rekishi to wakai* (History and reconciliation), Tokyo: Tokyo Daigaku Shuppankai.

Kwong, Kwak-Tae, 2005, 'Nikkan kankei to "rentai" no mondai (Japan–South Korea relations and the "solidarity" issue),' *Gendai shisō* (Modern thought), 33 (6).

Lavenex, Sandra and Emek M. Uçaper, 2002, *Migration and the Externalities of European Integration,* Lanham: Lexington Books.

Layton-Henry, Zig, 1990, 'The challenge of political rights,' in Zig Layton-Henry (ed.), *The Political Rights of Migrant Workers in Western Europe*, London: Sage.

Le Bon, Gustave, 1895, *Psychologie des Foules*, Paris: Alcan.

Léonard, Sarah, 2010, 'EU border security and migration into the European Union: FRONTEX and securitisation through practices,' *European Security*, 19: pp. 231–54.

Lie, John, 2008, *Zainichi (Koreans in Japan): Diasporic Nationalism and Postcolonial Identity,* Berkeley: University of California Press.

Linden, Annette and Bert Klandermans, 2006a, 'The Netherlands: stigmatized outsiders,' in Bert Klandermans and Nonna Mayer (eds.), *Extreme Right Activists in Europe: Through the Magnifying Glass*, London: Routledge.

————, 2006b, 'Stigmatization and repression of extreme-right activism in the Netherlands,' *Mobilization*, 11 (2): pp. 213–28.

————, 2007, 'Revolutionaries, wanderers, converts, and compliants: life histories of extreme right activists,' *Journal of Contemporary Ethnography*, 36 (2): pp. 184–200.

Lloyd, Cathie, 1998, 'Antiracist mobilization in France and Britain in the 1970s and 1980s,' in Danièle Joly (ed.), *Scapegoats and Social Actors: The Exclusion and Integration of Minorities in Western and Eastern Europe*, Basingstoke: Macmillan.

Lubbers, Marcel, Merove Gijsberts and Peer Scheepers, 2002, 'Extreme right-wing voting in Western Europe,' in *European Journal of Political Research,* 41: pp. 345–78.

Lubbers, Marcel and Ayse Güveli, 2007, 'Voting LPF: stratification and the varying importance of attitudes,' *Journal of Elections, Public Opinion & Parties*, 17 (1): pp. 21–47.

Lubbers, Marcel and Peer Scheepers, 2000, 'Individual and contextual characteristics of the German extreme right-wing vote in the 1990s: a test of complementary theories,' *European Journal of Political Research*, 38: pp. 63–94.

————, 2001, 'Explaining the trends in extreme right-wing voting: Germany 1989–1998,' *European Sociological Review*, 17: pp. 431–49.

————, 2002, 'French Front national voting: a micro and macro perspective,' *Ethnic and Racial Studies*, 25(1): pp. 120–49.

————, 2005, 'Political versus instrumental Euro-scepticism: mapping scepticism in European countries and regions,' *European Union Politics*, 6 (2): pp. 223–42.

———— and Jaak Billet, 2000, 'Multilevel modeling of Vlaams Blok voting: individual and contextual characteristics of the Vlaams Blok vote,' *Acta Politica*, 35 (4): pp. 363–98.

Maeda, Noritaka, 2004, 'Genjitsu kara monogatari e/monogatari kara genjitsu e (From fact to fiction/from fiction to fact),' in Kiyoshi Abe and Kōji Nanba (eds.), *Media bunka o yomitoku gihō: karuchuraru sutadīzu Japan* (The art of reading and understanding media culture: cultural studies Japan), Kyoto: Sekai Shisōsha.

Maeda, Tetsuo, 2007, *Jieitai: henyō no yukue* (Japan Self-Defense Forces: direction of change), Tokyo: Iwanami Shoten.

Martinez Jr., Ramiro and Abel Valenzuela Jr. (eds.), 2006, *Immigration and Crime: Race, Ethnicity and Violence*, New York: New York University Press.

Massey, Douglas S., Jorge Durand and Nolan J. Malone, 2002, *Beyond Smoke and Mirrors: Mexican Immigration in an Era of Economic Integration*, New York: Russell Sage Foundation.

Matsutani, Mitsuru, 2011, 'Popyurizumu no taitō to sono gensen (The rise of populism and its sources), *Sekai*, 815.

Mayer, Nonna and Pascal Perrineau, 1992, 'Why do they vote for Le Pen?' *European Journal of Political Research*, 22: pp. 123–41.

McAdam, Doug, 1982, *Political Process and the Development of Black Insurgency, 1930–1970*, Chicago: University of Chicago Press.

————, 1986, 'Recruitment to high-risk activism: the case of Freedom Summer,' *American Journal of Sociology*, 92 (1): pp. 64–90.

————, 1988a, 'Micromobilization contexts and recruitment to activism,' *International Social Movement Research*, 1: pp. 125–54.

————, 1988b, *Freedom Summer*, New York: Oxford University Press.

————, 1994, 'Culture and social movements,' in Enrique Laraña, Hank Johnston and Joseph R. Gusfield (eds.), *New Social Movements: From Ideology to Identity*, Philadelphia: Temple University Press.

————, 1996, 'Conceptual origins, problems, future directions,' in Doug McAdam, John D. McCarthy and Mayer N. Zald (eds.), *Comparative Perspectives on Social Movements: Political Opportunities, Mobilizing Structures, and Cultural Framings*, Cambridge: Cambridge University Press.

———— and Roberto M. Fernandez, 1990, 'Microstructural bases of recruitment to social movements,' *Research in Social Movements, Conflict and Change*, 12: pp.1–33.

———— and Ronnelle Paulsen, 1993, 'Specifying the relationship between social ties and activism,' *American Journal of Sociology*, 99 (3): pp. 640–67.

———— John D. McCarthy and Mayer N. Zald, 1996, 'Introduction: opportunities, mobilizing structures, and framing processes,' in Doug McAdam, John D. McCarthy and Mayer N. Zald (eds.), *Comparative Perspectives on Social Movements: Political Opportunities, Mobilizing Structures, and Cultural Framings*, Cambridge: Cambridge University Press.

McCammon, Holly J., Courtney Sanders Muse, Harmony D. Newman and Teresa M. Terell, 2007, 'Movement framing and discursive opportunity structures: the political success of the U.S. women's jury movements,' *American Sociological Review*, 72: pp. 725–49.

McCarthy, John D. and Mayer N. Zald, 1987, *Social Movements in an Organizational Society*, Piscataway: Transaction.

McCombos, Maxwell and Jian-Hua Zhu, 1995, 'Capacity, diversity, and volatility of the public agenda: trends from 1954 to 1994,' *Public Opinion Quarterly*, 59: pp. 495–525.

McDonald, Maryon, 2006, ''New nationalisms in the EU: occupying the available space,' in Andre Gingrich and Marcus Banks (eds.), *Neo-Nationalism in Europe and Beyond: Perspectives from Social Anthropology*, New York: Berghahn Books.

McMurray, David A., 2001, *In & out of Morocco: Smuggling and Migration in a Frontier Boomtown*, Minneapolis: University of Minnesota Press.

McSweeney, Bill, 1996, 'Identity and security: Buzan and the Copenhagen School,' *Review of International Studies*, 22(1): pp. 81–93.

McVeigh, Rory, 2009, *The Rise of the Ku Klux Klan: Right-Wing Movements and National Politics*, Minneapolis: University of Minnesota Press.

———— , Daniel J. Myers, and David Sikkink, 2004, 'Corn, klansmen, and Coolidge: structure and framing in social movements,' *Social Forces*, 83: pp. 653–90.

Merkl, Peter, 2004, 'Why are they so strong now? Comparative reflections on the revival of the radical right in Europe,' in Peter Merkl and Leonard Weingberg (eds.), *The Revival of Right-Wing Extremism in the Nineties*, London: Frank Cass.

Michael, George, 2003, *Confronting Right-Wing Extremism and Terrorism in the USA*, London: Routledge.

Mileti, Francesca Poglia and Fabrice Plomb, 2007, 'Addressing the link between socio-economic change and right-wing populism and extremism: a critical review of the literature,' in Jörg Flecker (ed.), *Changing Working Life and the Appeal of the Extreme Right*, Aldershot: Ashgate.

Miller-Idriss, Cynthia, 2009, *Blood and Culture: Youth, Right-Wing Extremism, and National Belonging in Contemporary Germany*, Durham: Duke University Press.

Minzoku Sabetsu to Tatakau Renraku Kyōgikai, 1985, *Dai11kai mintōren zenkoku kōryū shūkai shiryōshū* (Document collection of the 11th meeting of the national *Mintōren* network).

———— (ed.), 1989, *Zainichi Kankoku, Chōsenjin no hoshō, jinkenhō* (Reparations and human rights legislation for *zainichi* South and North Koreans), Tokyo: Shinkansha.

Mihagi, Sho, 2012, *Obiyakasareru kokkyō no shima, Yonaguni: Senkakau dake ga kiki dewa nai!* (Yonaguni, threatened island: Senkaku is not the only island in crisis), Tokyo: Meiseisha.

Mishina, Jun, 2010, 'Gaikokujin sanseiken ni hisomu Nihon shihai no shinario: seiji ni eikyōryoku o motsu zainichi Kankokujin to sayoku no bukimina ugoki (The domination of Japan scenario concealed within voting rights for foreign residents: ominous movements of politically influential *zainichi* Koreans and left wingers),' *Seiron*, 455.

Miyajima, Takashi (ed.), 2000, *Gaikokujin shimin to seiji sanka* (Foreign residents and political participation), Tokyo: Yushindo.

———— and Takamichi Kajita (eds.), 1996, *Gaikokujin rōdōsha kara shimin e* (From foreign workers to citizens), Tokyo: Yūhikaku.

Mizuno, Naoki, 1996, 'Zainichi Chōsenjin Taiwanjin sanseiken 'teishi' jōkō no seiritsu: zainichi Chōsenjin sanseiken mondai no rekishiteki kentō (1)' (The bringing into effect of the stipulations "suspending" the voting rights of *zainichi* Koreans and Taiwanese: a historical examination of the *zainichi* Korean voting rights issue (1)), *Sekai jinken mondai kenkyū sentā kenkyū kiyō* (Research Bulletin of the World Human Rights Issues Research Centre), 1.

————, 1997, 'Zainichi Chōsenjin Taiwanjin sanseiken 'teishi' jōkō no seiritsu: zainichi Chōsenjin sanseiken mondai no rekishiteki kentō (2)' *Sekai jinken mondai kenkyū sentā kenkyū kiyō*, 2.

Momochi, Akira, 2010, *Kaiteiban gaikokujin no sanseiken mondai Q&A: chihō senkyoken fuyo mo kenpō ihan* (Voting rights for foreigners issue Q&A: even granting municipal voting rights is unconstitutional), (revised edition), Tokyo: Meiseisha.

Morris-Suzuki, Tessa, 2005, 'Senryō gun e no yūgaina kōdō: haisengo Nihon ni okeru imin kanri to zainichi Chōsenjin (Behavior harmful to the occupation army: immigrant control in Japan after defeat and *Zainichi* Koreans),' in Minoru Iwasaki et al., (eds.), *Keizoku suru shokuminchishugi: jendā/minzoku/jinshu/kaikyū* (Enduring colonialism: gender/ethnicity/race/class), Tokyo: Seikyūsha.

Morris-Suzuki, Tessa, 2007, *Exodus to North Korea: Shadows from Japan's Cold War*, Lanham, MD: Rowman & Littlefield.

————, 2010, *Borderline Japan: Foreigners and Frontier Controls in the Postwar Era*, Cambridge: Cambridge University Press.

Moulier-Boutang, Yann, 1985, 'Resistance to the political representation of alien populations: the European paradox,' *International Migration Review*, 19: pp. 485–92.

Mudde, Cas, 2000, *The Ideology of the Extreme Right*, Manchester: Manchester University Press.

————, 2007, *Populist Radical Right Parties in Europe*, Cambridge: Cambridge University Press.

————, 2010, 'The populist radical right: a pathological normalcy,' *West European Politics*, 33(6): pp. 1,167–86.

————, 2013, 'Three decades of populist radical right parties in Western Europe: so what?' *European Journal of Political Research*, 52: pp. 1–19.

————— (ed.), 2014, *Youth and the Extreme Right*, New York: IDEBATE Press.

Mughan, Anthony and Pamela Paxton, 2006, 'Anti-immigrant sentiment, policy preferences and populist party voting in Australia,' *British Journal of Political Science*, 36: pp. 341–58.

Mun, Kyongsu, 2007, *Zainichi Chōsenjin mondai no kigen* (The origins of the *Zainichi* Korean issue), Tokyo: Kurein.

Munro, Daniel, 2008, 'Integration through participation: non-citizen resident voting rights in an era of globalization,' *Journal of International Migration and Integration*, 9: 63–80.

Murai, Atsushi, 1997a, *Rekishi ninshiki to jugyō kaikaku* (Historical recognition and teaching reform), Tokyo: Kyōiku Shiryō Shuppankai.

————— , 1997b, 'Jiyūshugi shikan kenkyūkai no kyōshitachi: genba kyōshi e no kikitori chōsa kara (Interviews with teaching members of the Teachers with a Liberal Historical View Colloquium),' *Sekai*, 633.

Murakami, Kazuhiro, 2007, 'Intānetto no naka no Tsushima: aru "kenkan" genshō o megutte (Tsushima on the internet: certain "hatred of Korea" phenomena),' in Saeko Ishida, Kan Kimura and Chie Yamanaka (eds.), *Posuto kanryū no media shakaishugi* (Sociology of the media following the Korean popular culture boom), Kyoto: Minerva Shobō.

Nagao, Kazuhiro, 2000, *Gaikokujin no sanseiken* (Voting rights for foreigners), Kyoto: Sekai Shisōsha.

————— , 2010, 'Gaikokujin sanseiken wa "akirakani iken" (Voting rights for foreign residents are "clearly unconstitutional"),' *Seiron*, 458.

————— , 2011, *Nihonkoku kenpō zentei dai 4 han* (Japanese Constitution 4th revised edition), Kyoto: Sekai Shisōsha.

Nagayoshi, Kikuko, 2012, 'Nihonjin no haigai ishiki ni taisuru bundan rōdō shijō no eikyō (The influence of a segmented labor market on Japanese people's anti-foreigner consciousness),' *Shakaigaku hyōron* (Japanese sociological review), 63 (1).

Nakagawa, Hachiyo, 1996, ' "Kokuseki jōkō" teppai toiu "hannichi" undō: "hikokumin tachi" no kōmuinken, sanseiken wa "muketsu shinryaku" ("Anti-Japanese" movements to repeal the "nationality clause": the right to work in government jobs and voting rights for people who are "non-citizens" constitutes a "bloodless invasion"),' *Seiron*, 292.

Nakahara, Ryōji, 1993, *Zainichi Kankoku, Chōsenjin no shūshoku sabetsu to kokuseki jōkō* (Employment discrimination against *Zainichi* Koreans and the nationality clause), Tokyo: Akashi Shoten.

Nakamura, Ilsung, 2014, *Rupo Kyōto Chōsen gakkō shūgeki jiken: 'heito-kuraimu' ni kō shite* (Reportage – Attack on Korean school in Kyoto: resisting 'hate crime'), Tokyo: Iwanami Shoten.

Nakanishi, Shintarō, 2006, 'Poppu karuchā to seiji, kaika suru "J nasho-narizumu": "kenkanryū" o tekusuto ni (Pop culture and politics – blossoming "Japanese nationalism": critique of "the wave of Korea hatred")),' *Sekai*, 749.

Nakanishi, Terumasa, 2007, ' "9.17 no chikai" to Nihon no kakusei' ("The pledge of 9.17" and Japan's awakening)', *Shokun!*, 39 (10).

Nakashinshiro, Makoto, 2013, *Kokkyō no shima no "hannichi" kyōkasho kyanpēn: Okinawa to Yaeyama no muhō ideorogī* (The "anti-Japanese" textbook campaign of Japan's border islands: The unreasonable Okinawa and Yaeyama ideology), Tokyo: Sankei Shinbun Shuppan.

Nakayama, Yoshitaka, 2013, *Chūgoku ga mimi o fusagu Senkaku shotō no futsugōna shinjitsu: Ishigaki shichō ga kataru Nihon gaikō no arubeki sugata* (The inconvenient reality about the Senkaku Islands which China disregards: the ideal shape of Japanese diplomacy as narrated by the Mayor of Ishigaki), Tokyo: Wani Books.

Naoi, Michiko, 1972a, 'Seijiteki shakaika katei ni okeru shūdan no yakuwari (The role of groups in the political socialization process),' *Shakaigaku hyōron*, 22 (3).

————, 1972b, 'Seijiteki shakaika katei ni okeru shūdan no yakuwari (2),' *Shakaigaku hyōron*, 23, (1).

Nepstad, Sharon Erickson, 1997, 'The process of cognitive liberation: cultural synapses, links, and frame contradictions in the U.S.–Central America peace movement,' *Sociological Inquiry*, 67 (4): pp. 470–87.

Nevitt, Neil et al., 1998, 'The populist right in Canada: the rise of the Reform Party of Canada,' in Hans-Georg Betz and Stefan Immerfall (eds.), *The New Politics of the Right: Neo-Populist Parties and Movements in Established Democracies*, New York: St. Martin's Press.

Nishimura, Koyu (ed.), 2010, *Gekiron mukku gaikokujin sanseiken no shinjitsu* (Gekiron mook – the reality of voting rights for foreigners), Tokyo: Okura Shuppan.

———— and Kōichi Yasuda, 2013, '"Nettouyo bōkokuron" ni igi ari! (There are objections to the "devastated country theory of the net right"!),' *WiLL*, 98.

Nishio, Kanji, 2010, 'Gaikokujin sanseiken: Oranda, Doitsu no sanjō (Voting rights for foreign residents: the disastrous spectacle of the Netherlands and Germany),' *WiLL*, 64.

Niwa, Masao, 1995, 'Zainichi Kankoku, Chōsenjin no chihō sanseiken' (Municipal voting rights for *Zainichi* North and South Koreans),' *Seikyu*, 22.

Noakes, John A. and Hank Johnston, 2005, 'Frames of protest: a road map to a perspective,' in Hank Johnston and John A. Noakes (eds.), *Frames of Protest: Social Movements and the Framing Perspective*, Lanham: Rowman & Littlefield.

Noma, Yasumichi, 2013, *'Zainichi tokken' no kyokō: netto kūkan ga umidashita heito supīchi* (The 'special privileges for *Zainichi* Koreans' fiction: hate speech created by net spaces), Tokyo: Kawade Shobō Shinsha.

Norris, Pippa, 2005, *Radical Right: Voters and Parties in the Electoral Market*, Cambridge: Cambridge University Press.

Oberschall, Anthony, 1972, *Social Conflict and Social Movements*, New Jersey: Prentice Hall.

————, 1993, *Social Movements: Ideologies, Interests, and Identities*, New Brunswick: Transaction.

Oegema, Dirk and Bert Klandermans, 1994, 'Why social movement sympathizers don't participate: erosion and nonconversion of support,' *American Sociological Review*, 59 (5): pp. 703–22.

Oesch, Daniel, 2008, 'Explaining workers' support for right-wing populist parties in Western Europe: evidence from Austria, Belgium, France, Norway, and Switzerland,' *International Political Science Review*, 29: pp. 349–73.

————, 2012, 'The class basis of the cleavage between the new left and the radical right: an analysis for Austria, Denmark, Norway and Switzerland,' in Jens Rydgren (ed.), in *Class Politics and the Radical Right*, London: Routledge.

Oguma, Eiji, 1995, *Tanitsu minzoku shinwa no kigen: 'Nihonjin' no jigazō no keifu* (The origins of the myth of racial homogeneity: a genealogy of 'Japanese' self images), Tokyo: Shinyōsha.

———, 1998, *'Nihonjin' no kyōkai: Okinawa, Ainu, Taiwan, Chōsen – shokuminchi shihai kara fukki undō made* (The borders of 'Japanese': Okinawa, Ainu, Taiwan, Korea – from colonial rule to the reversion movement), Tokyo: Shinyosha.

——— and Yōko Ueno, 2003, *'Iyashi' no nashonarizumu: kusa no ne hoshu undō no jisshō kenkyū* ('Comforting' nationalism: an empirical study of the grass roots conservative movement), Tokyo: Keiō Gijuku Daigaku Shuppankai.

Oh, Ingyu, 2012, 'From nationalistic diaspora to transnational diaspora: the evolution of identity crisis among the Korean-Japanese,' *Journal of Ethnic and Migration Studies*, 38 (4): pp. 651–69.

Okamura, Tadao, 1971, 'Gendai Nihon ni okeru seijiteki shakaika: seiji ishiki no baiyō to seijika zō (Political socialization in contemporary Japan: the cultivation of political consciousness and the image of politicians),' in Nihon Seiji Gakkai (ed.), *Nenpō seijigaku: gendai Nihon ni okeru seiji taido no keisei to kōzō* (Annual Review of Political Science: the creation and structure of political attitudes in contemporary Japan), Tokyo: Iwanami Shoten.

Oliver, Pamela E. and Gerald Marwell, 1992, 'Mobilizing technologies for collective action,' in Aldon D. Morris and Carol M. Mueller (eds.), *Frontiers in Social Movement Theory*, New Haven: Yale University Press.

Olson, Mancur, 1965, *The Logic of Collective Action*, Cambridge, MA: Harvard University Press.

Olzak, Suzan, 1992, *The Dynamics of Ethnic Competition and Conflict*, Stanford: Stanford University Press.

——— and Joane Nagel (eds.), 1986, *Competitive Ethnic Relations*, Orlando: Academic Press.

Omagari, Yukiko, Sachi Takaya, Itaru Kaji, Nanako Inaba and Naoto Higuchi, 2011, 'Zainichi gaikokujin no shigoto: 2000 nen kokusei chōsa dēta no bunseki kara' (Jobs held by foreigners in Japan: an analysis of the 2000 census data), *Ibaraki Daigaku Chiiki Sōgō Kenkyūjo Nenpō*, 44.

Ōnuma, Yasuaki, 1979a, 'Zainichi Chōsenjin no hōteki chii ni kansuru ichi kōsatsu (1)' (Examining the legal status of *Zainichi* Koreans (1)), *Hōgaku Kyōkai Zasshi* (Legal Society Journal), 96 (3).

———, 1979b, 'Zainichi Chōsenjin no hōteki chii ni kansuru ichi kōsatsu (2),' *Hōgaku Kyōkai Zasshi*, 96 (5).

———, 1979c, 'Zainichi Chōsenjin no hōteki chii ni kansuru ichi kōsatsu (3),' *Hōgaku Kyōkai Zasshi*, 96 (8).

———, 1980a, 'Zainichi Chōsenjin no hōteki chii ni kansuru ichi kōsatsu (4),' *Hōgaku Kyōkai Zasshi*, 97 (2).

———, 1980b, 'Zainichi Chōsenjin no hōteki chii ni kansuru ichi kōsatsu (5),' *Hōgaku Kyōkai Zasshi*, 96 (3).

————, 1980c, 'Zainichi Chōsenjin no hōteki chii ni kansuru ichi kōsatsu (6),' *Hōgaku Kyōkai Zasshi*, 96 (4).

————, 1993, *Shinpan – tanitsu minzoku shakai no shinwa o koete* (Overcoming the myth of a racially homogeneous society), (new edition), Tokyo: Toshindō.

Opp, Karl-Dieter, 1988, 'Grievances and participation in social movements,' *American Sociological Review*, 53: pp. 853–64.

———— and Wolfgang Roehl, 1990, 'Repression, micromobilization, and political protest,' *Social Forces*, 69 (2): pp. 521–47.

————, Peter Voss and Christiane Gern, 1995, *Origins of a Spontaneous Revolution: East Germany, 1989*, Ann Arbor: University of Michigan Press.

Ōsawa, Masachi, 2008, *Fukanōsei no jidai* (The age of impossibility), Tokyo: Iwanami Shoten.

————, 2011, *Kindai Nihon no nashonarizumu*, (Nationalism in modern Japan), Tokyo: Kodansha.

Ōta, Osamu et al., 2006, *'Manga kenkanryū' no koko ga detarame* (This aspect of Korea hatred manga is nonsense), Tokyo: Commons.

Ōtake, Hideo, 1996, *Sengo Nihon no ideorogī tairitsu* (Ideological conflict in post-war Japan), Tokyo: Sanichi Shobō.

Ōtsuki, Takahiro, 2005, '"Kenkanryū" wa "gōsen" yori sugoin desu ("Korea hatred" is more amazing than "Gomanism Sengen"),' *Shokun!*, 37 (10).

Ozawa, Yūsaku, 1974, 'Minzoku sabetsu no kyōiku o kokuhatsu suru mono: Chōsen kōkōsei bōkō jiken ni okeru seiji to kyōiku' (Factors that expose racially discriminatory education: politics and education in incidents of violence against Korean high school students), in Katsumi Sato (ed.), *Zainichi Chōsenjin no shomondai* (The various problems of *Zainichi* Koreans), Tokyo: Dōseisha.

Pak, Katherine Tagtmayer, 2000a, 'Living in harmony: prospects for cooperative local responses to foreign migrants,' in Sheila A. Smith (ed.), *Local Voices, National Issues: The Impact of Local Initiative in Japanese Policy-Making*, Ann Arbor: Center for Japanese Studies, the University of Michigan.

————, 2000b, 'Foreigners are local citizens too: local governments respond to international migration in Japan,' in Mike Douglass and Glenda S. Roberts (eds.), *Japan and Global Migration: Foreign Workers and the Advent of a Multicultural Society*, London: Routledge.

Park, Il, 1999, *'Zainichi' toiu ikikata: sai to byōdō no jirenma* (The *'zainichi'* way of life: the dilemma between difference and equality), Tokyo: Kodansha.

————, 2005, 'Zainichi Korian no keizai jijō' (The economic conditions of *Zainichi* Koreans), in Fujiwara Shoten Henshūbu (ed.), *Rekishi no naka no 'zainichi'* (*'Zainichi'* in history), Tokyo: Fujiwara Shoten.

————, 2011, '"Uchi e no kaikoku" o kitai suru (Anticipating the "internal opening up of Japan"),' *Buraku Kaihō*, 644.

Park, Kyong-sik, 1989, *Kaihōgo – Zainichi Chōsenjin undōshi* (After liberation – history of the *Zainichi* Korean movement), Tokyo: Sanichi Shobō.

Pedroza, Luicy, forthcoming, 'The democratic potential of enfranchising resident migrants,' *International Migration*, (doi: 10.1111/imig.12162).

Pelinka, Anton, 2013, 'Right-wing populism: concept and typology,' in Ruth Wodak, Majid KhosraviNik and Brigitte Mral (eds.), *Right-Wing Populism in Europe: Politics and Discourse*, London: Bloomsbury.

Peterson, Ruth, Lauren J. Krivo and John Hagan (eds.), 2006, *The Many Colors of Crime: Inequalities of Race, Ethnicity, and Crime in America*, New York: New York University Press.

Quassoli, Fabio, 2001, 'Migrant as criminal: the judicial treatment of migrant criminality,' in Christian Joppke and Virginia Guiraudon (eds.), *Controlling a New Migration World*, London: Routledge.

————, 'Making the neighborhood safer: social alarm, police practices and immigrant exclusion in Italy,' *Journal of Ethnic and Migration Studies*, 30 (6): pp. 1,163–81.

Rainie, Lee and Barry Wellman, 2012, *Networked: The New Social Operating System*, Cambridge, MA: MIT Press.

Rath, Jan, 1990, 'Voting rights,' in Zig Layton-Henry (ed.), *The Political Rights of Migrant Workers in Western Europe*, London: Sage.

Ray, Beverley and George Marsh E., 2001, 'Recruitment by extremist groups on the internet,' *First Monday*, 6 (2): pp. 1–26.

Reid, Edna and Hsinchen Chen, 2007, 'Internet-savvy U.S. and Middle Eastern extremist groups,' *Mobilization*, 12 (2): pp. 177–92.

Rikihisa, Masayuki, 2006, 'Teikoku no henyō to "gaikokujin" sanseiken: Igirisu ni okeru shiminken hensen to sanseiken no kanren ni chūmoku shite (The altered appearance of empire and voting rights for "foreigners": a focus on the link between changes in citizenship in the United Kingdom and voting rights),' in Yuma Kawahara and Kazuhide Uekusa (eds.), *Gaikokujin sanseiken mondai no kokusai hikaku* (An international comparison of the voting rights for foreign residents issue), Kyoto: Shōwadō.

Rink, Nathalie, Karen Phalet and Marc Swyngedouw, 2009, 'The effect of immigrant population size, unemployment and individual characteristics on voting for Vlaams Blok in Flanders 1991–1999,' *European Sociological Review*, 25 (4): pp. 411–24.

Rippl, Susanne and Christian Seipel, 1999, 'Gender differences in right-wing extremism: intergroup validity of a second-order construct,' *Social Psychology Quarterly*, 62 (4): pp. 381–93.

Roh, Kiyong, 2011, 'Zainichi mindan no hongoku shikō rōsen to Nikkan kōshō' (The homeland-oriented alignment of *Mindan* and Japan–South Korean neogtiations), in Jongwon Yi, Masafumi Kimiya and Toyomi Asano (eds.), *Rekishi toshite no Nikkan kokkyō seijōka II – datsushokuminchika hen* (The normalization of Japan–South Korea diplomatic relations as history II: decolonization volume), Tokyo: Hōsei Daigaku Shuppankyoku.

Robinson, Vaughan, 1998, 'Security, migration, and refugees,' in Nana Poku and David T. Graham (eds.), *Redefining Security: Population Movements and National Security*, Westport: Praeger.

Rubio-Marín, R., 2000, *Immigration as a Democratic Challenge: Citizenship and Inclusion in Germany and the United States*, Cambridge: Cambridge University Press.

Rucht, Dieter and Thomas Ohlemacher, 1992, 'Protest event data: collection, uses and perspectives,' in Mario Diani and Ron Eyerman (eds.), *Studying Collective Action*, London: Sage.

Rucht, Dieter, Ruud Koopmans and Friedlich Neidhardt (eds.), 1998, *Acts of Dissent: New Developments in the Study of Protest*, Berlin: Sigma.

Ryang, Sonia, 1997, *North Koreans in Japan: Language, Ideology, and Identity*, Boulder: Westview Press.

————, 2000, 'The North Korean homeland of Koreans in Japan,' in Sonia Ryang (ed.), *Koreans in Japan: Critical Voices from the Margin*, New York: Routledge.

———— and John Lie, 2009, *Diaspora without Homeland: Being Korean in Japan*, Berkeley: University of California Press.

Rydgren, Jens, 2003, 'Meso-level reasons for racism and xenophobia: some converging and diverging effects of radical right populism in France and Sweden,' *European Journal of Social Theory*, 6 (1): pp. 45–68.

————, 2007, 'The sociology of the radical right,' *Annual Review of Sociology*, 33: pp. 241–62.

————, 2008, 'Immigration sceptics, xenophobes or racists? Radical right-wing voting in six West European countries,' *European Journal of Political Research*, 47: pp. 737–65.

————, 2009, 'Social isolation? Social capital and radical right-wing voting in Western Europe,' *Journal of Civil Society*, 5 (2): pp. 129–50.

Ryu, Kwangsu, 1996, 'Dōka ni tsunagaru sanseiken ni hantaisuru (Opposing voting rights that are linked to assimilation),' *Dōhō no jinken to seikatsu* (Human rights and the lives of Koreans), 3.

Saaler, Sven, 2005, *Politics, Memory and Public Opinion: The History Textbook Controversy and Japanese Society*, Munich: IUDICIUM.

Sado, Akihiro, 2012, 'Nansei shotō ni okeru jieitai haibi mondai (The issue of the deployment of the Self-Defense Forces in the Ryūkyū Islands),' *Bessatsu kan*, 19.

Sakaki, Alessandra, 2013, *Japan and Germany as Regional Actors*, London: Routledge.

Sakamoto, Haruya, 2012, 'Ōsaka daburu senkyo no bunseki: yūkensha no sentaku to Ōsaka ishin no kai shiji kiban no kaimei (Analysis of the Osaka double election: the voters' choices and an elucidation of the support base for the Osaka Restoration Party),' *Kansai Daigaku Hōgaku Ronshū* (Kansai University legal essays collection), 62 (3).

Sakanaka, Hidenori, 1999, *Zainichi Kankoku Chōsenjin seisakuron no tenkai* (The development of *Zainichi* South and North Korean policy arguments), Tokyo: Nihon Kajo Shuppan.

————, 2006, 'Zainichi wa "Chōsenkei Nihon kokumin" e no michi o (*Zainichi* Koerans should become "Korean-Japanese citizens"),' in Zainichi Korian no Nihon kokuseki shutokuken kakuritsu kyōgikai (Committee for the establishment of the right of *Zainichi* Koreans to acquire Japanese Citizenship) (ed.), *Zainichi Korian ni kenri toshite no Nihon kokuseki o* (Granting rights-based Japanese nationality for *Zainichi* Koreans), Tokyo: Akashi Shoten.

Sakurai, Makoto, 2006, *Kenkanryū jissen handobukku: Hannichi bōgen gekitai manyuaru* (A handbook for implementing the Korea hatred wave: a manual for repulsing abusive anti-Japanese language), Tokyo: Shinyūsha.

————, 2010, *Nihon shinshoku: Nihonjin no 'teki' ga takuramu bōkoku* (Encroaching on Japan: the ruined country that the enemies of the Japanese people are plotting), Tokyo: Shinyūsha.

————, 2013, *Zaitokukai towa 'Zainichi tokken o yurusanai shimin no kai' no ryakushō desu!* (*Zaitokukai* is an abbreviation of 'Association of Citizens against the Special Privileges of the *zainichi*'!), Tokyo: Seirindō.

Sakurai, Yoshiko, 2000, 'Nonaka-san, kuni o uru ki desuka! (Mr Nonaka, are you for selling Japan!),' *Shokun!*, 32 (11).

Salter, Lee, 2003, 'Democracy, new social movements, and the internet: a Habermasian analysis,' in Martha McCaughey and Michael D. Ayers (eds.), *Cyberactivism: Online Activism in Theory and Practice*, London: Routledge.

Samuels, Richard J., 2007, *Securing Japan: Tokyo's Grand Strategy and the Future of East Asia*, Ithaca: Cornell University Press.

Sanami, Yuko, 2013, *Joshi to aikoku* (Women and patriotism), Tokyo: Shōdensha.

Sato, Rei, 2008, 'Gaikokujin sanseiken o meguru ronten (The main points concerning voting rights for foreign residents),' *Jinkō genshō shakai no gaikokujin mondai* (The foreigner issue in a society in population decline), Tokyo: Kokuritsu Kokkai Toshokan Chōsa Shiryō.

Sato, Shigeki, 2008, *Nashonaru aidentiti to ryōdo: sengo Doitsu no tōhō kokkyō o meguru ronsō* (National identity and territory: disputes over post-war Germany's eastern national border), Tokyo: Shinyōsha.

Schain, Martin A., Aristide Zolberg and Patric Hossay, 2002, 'The development of radical right parties in Western Europe,' in Martin Schain, Aristide Zolberg and Patrick Hossay (eds.), *Shadows over Europe: The Development and Impact of the Extreme Right in Western Europe*, London: Palgrave.

Schgal, Meera, 2007, 'Manufacturing a feminized siege mentality: Hindu nationalist paramilitary camps for women in India,' *Journal of Contemporary Ethnography*, 36 (2): pp. 165–83.

Schiebel, Martina, 2000, 'Extreme right attitudes in the biographies of West German youth,' in Prue Chamberlayne, Joanna Bornat and Tom Wengraf (eds.), *The Turn to Biographical Methods in Social Science: Comparative issues and examples*, London: Routledge.

Sejersen, Tanja Brøndsted, 2008, ''I vow to thee my countries': the expansion of dual citizenship in the 21st century,' *International Migration Review*, 42 (3): pp. 523–49.

Selznick, Philip, 1970, 'Institutional vulnerability in mass society,' in Joseph R. Gusfield (ed.), *Protest, Reform, and Revolt: A Reader in Social Movements*, New York: John Wiley and Sons.

Semyonov, Moshe, Rebeca Raijman, Anat Yom-Tov, 2002, 'Labor market competition, perceived threat, and endorsement of economic discrimination against foreign workers in Israel,' *Social Problems*, 49 (3): 416–31.

Seto, Hiroyuki, 2000, *Gaikokujin hanzai* (Foreigner crimes), Tokyo: Central Shuppan.

———, 2007, *Netto ga kaeru Nihon no seiji* (Japanese politics as altered by the net), Tokyo: Iwasaki Kikaku.

Shakai Mondai Kenkyūkai (ed.), 1976, *Uyoku, minzokuha jiten* (Dictionary of the right wing and nationalists), Tokyo: Kokusho Kankōkai.

Sharp, Joanne P., 2000, *Condensing the Cold War: Reader's Digest and American Identity*, Minneapolis: University of Minnesota Press.

Shirai, Satoshi, 2013, *Eizoku haisen ron: sengo Nihon no kakushin* (A theory of eternal war defeat: the crux of post-war Japan), Tokyo: Ōta Shuppan.

Shorter, Edward and Charles Tilly, 1974, *Strikes in France 1830–1968*, New York: Cambridge University Press.

Simi, Pete and Robert Futrell, 2010, *American Swastika: Inside the White Power Movement's Hidden Spaces of Hate*, Lanham: Rowman and Littlefield.

Simon, Rita J. and Keri W. Sikich, 2007, 'Public attitudes toward immigrants and immigration policies across seven nations,' *International Migration Review*, 41 (4): 956–62.

Smelser, Neil J., 1963, *Theory of Collective Behavior*, New York: MacMillan.

Smith, David J., 2002, 'Framing the national question in Central and Eastern Europe: a quadratic nexus?' *Global Review of Ethnopolitics*, 2 (1): pp. 3–16.

Snow, David, 2000, 'Clarifying the relationship between framing and ideology,' *Mobilization*, 5 (1): pp. 55–60.

———, Louis A. Zurcher, Jr., Sheldon Ekland-Olson, 1980, 'Social networks and social movements: a microstructural approach to differential recruitment,' *American Sociological Review*, 45: pp. 787–801.

——— et al., 1986, 'Frame alignment processes, micromobilization and movement participation,' *American Sociological Review*, 51: pp. 464–81.

——— and Robert D. Benford, 1988, 'Ideology, frame resonance, and participant mobilization,' *International Social Movement Research*, 1: pp. 197–217.

———, 1992, 'Master frames and cycles of protest,' in Aldon D. Morris and Carol M. Muller (eds.), *Frontiers in Social Movement Theory*, New Haven: Yale University Press.

Snyder, David and Charles Tilly, 1972, 'Hardship and collective violence in France, 1830 to 1960,' *American Sociological Review*, 37: 520–32.

So, Kyongsik, 1997, *Bundan o ikiru: 'Zainichi' o koete* (Living separation: beyond *'zainichi'*), Tokyo: Kage Shobō.

So, Ryongdal, 1987, 'Zainichi Kankoku, Chōsenjin no jinken yōgo undō (The movement to protect the human rights of *Zainichi* South and North Koreans),' in Ryongdal So (ed.), *Kankoku, Chōsenjin no genjō to shōrai: 'jinken senshinkoku Nihon' e no teigen* (The present conditions and future for *Zainichi* South and North Koreans: proposals for turning Japan into an 'advanced country in terms of human rights'), Tokyo: Shakai Hyōronsha.

———, 2010, 'Ajia shimin shakai e no michi (The road to Asian citizen society), *Sekai*, 803.

——— (ed.), 1992, *Teijū gaikokujin no chihō sanseiken* (Municipal voting rights for permanent resident foreigners), Tokyo: Nihon Hyōronsha.

———— (ed.), 1995, *Kyōsei shakai e no chihō sanseiken* (Municipal voting rights for a symbiosis society), Tokyo: Nihon Hyōronsha.

Soh, Woncheol, 2010, 'Jūmin toshite no kenri hoshō o mezasu gaikokujin sanseiken (Municipal voting rights for foreigners aimed at assuring residents' rights), *Toshi mondai* (Municipal problems), 101 (4).

————, 2011a, 'Genten ni tachikaeri, chiiki kara no undō o: eijū gaikokujin no chihō sanseiken o motomeru (Returning to the starting point, movements from the local: seeking municipal voting rights for permanent resident foreigners), *Buraku Kaihō*, 644.

————, 2011b, 'Eijū gaikokujin no chihō sanseiken o kangaeru (Considering municipal voting rights for permanent resident foreigners), *Heiwa undō* (Pece movement), 483.

Söderberg, Marie, 2011a, 'Introduction: Japan–South Korea relations at a crossroads,' in Marie Söderberg (ed.), *Changing Power Relations in Northeast Asia: Implications for Relations between Japan and South Korea*, London: Routledge.

————, 2011b, 'The struggle for a decent life in Japan: the Korean minority adapting to changing legal and political conditions,' in Marie Söderberg (ed.), *Changing Power Relations in Northeast Asia: Implications for Relations between Japan and South Korea*, London, Routledge.

Sōmushō Tōkeikyoku, 2004, *Heisei 12 nen kokusei chōsa hōkoku dai 8 kan: Gaikokujin ni kan suru tokubetsu shūkei kekka* (2000 National census report, part 8: results of special aggregation with regard to foreigners), Tokyo: National Printing Office.

Song, Sarah, 2009, 'Democracy and noncitizen voting rights,' *Citizenship Studies*, 13 (6): pp. 607–20.

Soysal, Yasemin N., 1994, *Limits of Citizenship: Migrants and Postnational Membership in Europe*, Chicago: University of Chicago Press.

Stalker, Glenn J. and Lesley J. Wood, 2013, 'Reaching beyond the net: political circuits and participation in Toronto's G20 protests,' *Social Movement Studies*, 12 (2): pp. 178–98.

Steinberg, Marc W., 1999, 'The talk and back talk of collective action: a dialogic analysis of repertoires of discourse among nineteenth-century English cotton spinners,' *American Journal of Sociology*, 105: pp. 736–80.

Sugawara, Taku, 2009, *Yoron no kyokkai: naze Jimintō wa taihai shita no ka* (A distortion of public opinion: Why did the LDP suffer a crushing defeat?), Tokyo: Kōbunsha.

Sugimoto, Yoshio, 1981, *Popular Disturbance in Postwar Japan*, Hong Kong: Asian Research Service.

Sunier, Thijl and Rob van Ginkel, 2006, '"At your service!" Reflections on the rise of neo-nationalism in the Netherlands,' in Andre Gingrich and Marcus Banks (eds.), *Neo-Nationalism in Europe and Beyond: Perspectives from Social Anthropology*, New York: Berghahn Books.

Sunstein, Cass R., 2001, *Republic.com*, Princeton: Princeton University Press.

Suzuki, Ayaka, 2011, 'Shufutachi no jendā furī bakkurasshu: hoshukei zasshi kiji no bunseki kara (Housewives' gender equality backlash: from an analysis of articles in conservative magazines),' *Soshioroji* (Sociology), 171.

————, 2013, 'Kusa no ne hoshu no danjo kyōdō sankaku shakai hantai undō: Ehime ken ni okeru jendā furī o meguru kōbō (Grass roots conservatives' anti-gender equality movement: struggles around gender equality in Ehime Prefecture),' *Nenpō Ningen Kagaku* (Annual review of human sciences), 34.

Suzuki, Kensuke, 2005, 'Wakamono wa 'ukeika' shite iru ka: saha no yuganda utsushi sugata (Are young people drifting to the right?: a distorted image of the left),' *Sekai*, 741.

Swidler, Ann, 1986, 'Culture in action: symbols and strategies,' *American Sociological Review*, 51 (2): pp. 273–86.

Swyngedouw, Marc, 1998, 'The extreme right in Belgium: of a non-existent Front National and an omnipresent Vlaams Blok,' in Hans-Georg Betz and Stefan Immerfall (eds.), *The New Politics of the Right: Neo-Populist Parties and Movements in Established Democracies*, New York: St. Martin's Press.

———, 2001, 'The subjective cognitive and affective map of extreme right voters: using open-ended questions in exit polls,' *Electoral Studies*, 20: pp. 217–41.

Szymkowiak, Kenneth and Patricia G. Steinhoff, 1995, 'Wrapping up in something long: intimidation and violence by right-wing groups in postwar Japan,' in Tore Bjørgo (ed.), *Terror from the Extreme Right*, London: Frank Cass.

Taggart, Paul, 1996, *The New Populism and the New Politics: New Protest Parties in Sweden in a Comparative Perspective*, Basingstoke: Macmillan.

Takahara, Motoaki, 2006, *Fuangata nashonarizumu no jidai* (The age of anxiety-driven nationalism), Tokyo: Yōsensha.

Takahashi, Masami, 1969, 'Haisengo no Nihon ni okeru Chōsenjin no hanzai (Crimes by Koreans in Japan after defeat),' in Koyu Iwai et al. (eds.), *Nihon no hanzaigaku 1: Genin I* (Japanese criminology 1: Causes I), Tokyo: Tokyo Daigaku Shuppankai.

Takaichi, Sanae, 2010, 'Gaikokujin sanseiken fuyo wa bōkoku e no michi (The granting of voting rights for foreign residents is the road to a a ruined country),' *Seiron*, 457.

——— and Akira Momochi, 2000, 'Rippōfu ga okasu kenpō ihan no gu (Unconstitutional foolishness committed by the legislature), *Shokun!* 32 (11).

Takasaki, Soji, 2014, *'Bōgen' no genkei: Nihonjin no Chōsenkan* (Prototype of 'abusive language': Japanese view of Koreans), Matsumoto: Mokuseisha.

Takaya, Sachi, 2007, '"Gaikokujin" ni taisuru shokumu shitsumon to chian seisaku (Police questioning of and public order policies with regard to "foreigners"),' in Gaikokujin Jinkenhō Renrakukai (ed.), *'Gaikokujin', minzokuteki mainoriti to jinken hakusho* ('Foreigners, ethnic minorities and human rights white paper), Tokyo: Akashi Shoten.

———, Yukiko Omagiri, Naoto Higuchi and Itaru Kaji, 2013, '2005 nen kokusei chōsa ni miru zainichi gaikokujin no shigoto (Jobs held by Japan's foreign residents: views from the 2005 census data),' *Okayama Daigaku Daigakuin Shakai Bunka Kagaku Kenkyūka Kiyō* (Bulletin of the Okayama University Graduate School of Social and Cultural Sciences), 35.

Takaya, Sachi, Yukiko Omagiri, Naoto Higuchi, Itaru Kaji and Nanako Inaba, 2013, '1995 nen kokusei chōsa ni miru zainichi gaikokujin no shigoto,' *Okayama Daigaku Daigakuin Shakai Bunka Kagaku Kenkyūka Kiyō,* 36.

———, 2014a, '1990 nen kokusei chōsa ni miru zainichi gaikokujin no shigoto,' *Bunka kyōseigaku kenkyū* (Studies in cultural symbiosis), 13.

———, 2014b, '1980 nen kokusei chōsa ni miru zainichi gaikokujin no shigoto,' *Okayama Daigaku Daigakuin Shakai Bunka Kagaku Kenkyūka Kiyō,* 37.

———, 2015, '2010 nen kokusei chōsa ni miru zainichi gaikokujin no shigoto,' *Okayama Daigaku Daigakuin Shakai Bunka Kagaku Kenkyūka Kiyō,* 38.

Takigawa, Hirode, 2002, 'Kokumin to minzoku no setsudan: gaikokujin no sanseiken mondai o megutte (The severance of nationality and ethnicity: the voting rights for foreign residents issue),' Ōsaka Shiritsu Daigaku Hōgaku Zasshi (Osaka City University Law Journal), 49 (1).

Takubo, Chūbei, 2001, *'Kokka' o miushinatta Nihonjin: gaikokujin sanseiken mondai no honshitsu* (Japanese who have lost sight of the state: the essence of the voting rights for foreign residents issue), Tokyo: Shōgakukan.

Tanaka, Aiji, 1995, ' "55 nen taisei" hōkai to shisutemu sapōto no keizoku (The collapse of the "1955 regime" and ongoing system support),' *Leviathan,* 17.

———, 1996, 'Kokumin ishiki ni okeru "55 nen taisei" no henyō to hōkai: seitō hensei hōkai to shisutemu sapōto no renzoku to henka (The altered appearance and collapse of the "1955 regime" in the national consciousness: the collapse of political party organization and the continuation of and changes in continuing system support),' in Nihon Seiji Gakkai (ed.), *Nenpō seijigaku 55 nen taisei no hōkai* (Annual review of political science, the collapse of the 1955 regime), Tokyo: Iwanami Shoten.

Tanaka, Hiroshi, 1990, *Kyomō no kokusai kokka, Nihon: Ajia no shiten kara* (Deluded international state, Japan: from an Asian perspective), Nagoya: Fubaisha.

———, 1995, *Shinpan zainichi gaikokujin: hō no kabe, kokoro no mizo* (Foreigners in Japan: a legal wall and a gulf between minds), (new edition), Tokyo: Iwanami Shoten.

———, 2005, ' "Zainichi" no kenri tōsō no 50 nen (Fifty years of *"zainichi"* civil rights struggles),' in Fujiwara Shoten Henshubu (ed.), *Rekishi no naka no 'zainichi'* (*'Zainichi'* in History), Tokyo: Fujiwara Shoten.

———, 2010, 'Sogai no shakai ka, kyōsei no shakai ka (An alienated society or a symbiotic society?),' *Sekai,* 803.

——— and Ryūta Itagaki (eds.), 2007, *Nikkan aratana hajimari no tame no 20 shō* (20 chapters on a new beginning for Japan and South Korea), Tokyo: Iwanami Shoten.

Tani, Tomio, (ed.), 2002, *Minzoku kankei ni okeru ketsugō to bunri: shakaigakuteki mekanizumu o kaimei suru* (Unity and division in ethnic relations: elucidating sociological mechanisms), Kyoto: Minerva Shobō.

Tarde, Gabriel, 1901, *L'Opinion et la Foule,* Paris: Alcan.

Tarrow, Sidney, 1989, *Democracy and Disorder: Protest and Politics in Italy, 1965–1975*, Oxford: Clarendon Press.

————, 1998, *Power in Movement: Social Movements and Contentious Politics*, (second edition), Cambridge: Cambridge University Press.

Tateo, Luca, 2005, 'The Italian extreme right on-line network: an exploratory study using an integrated social network analysis and content analysis approach,' *Journal of Computer-Mediated Communication*, 10 (2): article 10.

Tawara, Yoshifumi, 2001, '"Tsukurukai" undō towa nandatta ka (What was the *"Tusukurukai"* movement?),' *Sekai*, 696.

Tei, Taikin, 2010a, 'Naze saha wa gaikokujin sanseiken o yōkyū suru no ka: "kagaisha kokka, Nihon" no ikishōnin toshite riyō sareru zainichi Korian (Why does the left wing demand voting rights for foreigners?: *Zainichi* Koreans being used as living witnesses of "Japan, the aggressor nation"),' *Sokoku to Seinen* (Fatherland and youth), 376.

————, 2010b, 'Mindan no sanseiken undō wa zainichi no tame ni naranai (*Mindan*'s voting rights for foreigners movement will not benefit the *zainichi*),' *Seiron*, 456.

————, 2010c, 'Gaikokujin sanseiken ni hantai no kore dake no riyū' (This many reasons for opposing voting rights for foreign residents),' *Chūō kōron*, 125 (1).

————, 2010d, 'Kankoku Mindan ni towarete iru koto (Questions being asked of South Korean *Mindan*),' *Chūō kōron*, 125 (4).

Teiju Gaikokujin no Chihō Sanseiken wo Mezasu Shimin no Kai (ed.), 1998, *Teijū gaikokujin no chihō sanseiken* (Municipal voting rights for permanent resident foreigners), Kyoto: Kamogawa Shuppan.

Terriff, Terry et al., 1999, *Security Studies Today*, London: Routledge.

Tilly, Charles, 1978, *From Mobilization to Revolution*, Reading: Addison-Wesley.

Tokairin, Satoshi, 2013, *15 sai kara no rōdō kumiai nyūmon* (Introduction to labor unions from the age of 15), Tokyo: Mainichi Shuppansha.

Tonomura, Masaru, 2013, 'Sengo Nihon no hoshu seiji seiryoku to zainichi Chōsenjin: tanitsu minzoku shakai shiko no teichaku made (Post-war Japanese conservative political force and *Zainichi* Koreans: a way toward monoethnic orientation),' *Nihongaku* (Japanology), 36.

Tonry, Michael (ed.), 1997, *Ethnicity, Crime, and Immigration: Comparative and Cross-National Perspective*, Chicago: University of Chicago Press.

Toyoshita, Naohiko, 2012, *'Senkaku mondai' towa nanika* (What is the 'Senkaku issue'?), Tokyo: Iwanami Shoten.

Traugott, Mark (ed.), 1995, *Repertoires and Cycles of Collective Action*, Durham: Duke University Press.

Tsuji, Daisuke, 2008, 'Intānetto ni okeru "ukeika" genshō ni kansuru jisshō kenkyū chōsa kekka gaiyō hōkokusho (Report on the outline of findings from empirical research surveys on the phenomenon of a "drift to the right" on the internet),' Nihon Shōken Shōgaku Zaidan Kenkyū Chōsa Joseikin Hōkokusho.

————, 2009, 'Chōsa dēta ni miru netto uyoku jittai (The realities of the net right as seen in survey data),' *Journalism*, 226.

————, 2011, '"Netto uyoku" teki naru mono no kyojitsu: chōsa dēta kara no jisshōteki kentō (Truths and lies about those who become "internet right wingers'": an empirical examination based on research data),' in Satoshi Kotani et al. (eds.), *Wakamono no genzai* (Young people's present), Tokyo: Nihon Tosho Centre.

Tsoukala, Anastassia, 2005, 'Looking at migrants as enemies,' in Didier Bigo and Elspeth Guild (eds.), *Controlling Frontiers: Free Movement into and within Europe*, Aldershot: Ashgate.

Tuathail, Gearóid Ó., 1996, *Critical Geopolitics*, Minneapolis: University of Minnesota Press.

Turner, Ralph H. and Lewis M. Killian, 1972, *Collective Behavior*, (second edition), Englewood Cliffs, NJ: Princeton-Hall.

Turunen, Marti, 2011, 'Kika o joken ni sezu, chihō sanseiken o fuyo subeki (Municipal voting rights should be granted without the precondition of naturalization),' *Buraku kaihō*, 644.

van de Donk, Wim, Brian D. Loader, Paul G. Nixon and Dieter Rucht, 2004, 'Introduction: social movements and ICTs,' in Wim van de Donk, Brian D. Loader, Paul G. Nixon and Dieter Rucht (eds.), *Cyberprotest: New Media, Citizens and Social Movements*, London: Routledge.

Van der Brug, Wouter, 2003, 'How the LPF fuelled discontent: empirical test of explanations of LPF support,' *Acta Politica*, 38: pp. 89–106.

————— and Meindert Fennema, 2003, 'Protest or Mainstream? How the European Anti-Immigrant Parties Developed into Two Separate Groups by 1999,' *European Journal of Political Research*, 42: 55–76.

————— and Meindert Fennema, 2007, 'What causes people to vote for a radical right party? A review of recent works,' *International Journal of Public Opinion Research*, 19: pp. 474–87.

—————, Meindert Fennema and Jan Tillie, 2000, 'Anti-immigrant parties in Europe: ideological or protest vote?' *European Journal of Political Research*, 37: pp. 77–102.

—————, Meindert Fennema and Jan Tillie, 2005, 'Why some anti-immigrant parties fail and others succeed: a two-step model of aggregate electoral support,' *Comparative Political Studies*, 38: pp. 537–73.

————— and Anthony Mughan, 2007, 'Charisma, leader effects and support for right-wing populist parties,' *Party Politics*, 13 (1): pp. 29–51.

Van Dyke, Nella and Sarah H. Soule, 2002, 'Structural social change and the mobilizing effect of threat: explaining levels of patriot and militia organizing in the United States,' *Social Problems*, 49 (4): pp. 497–520.

Van Laer, Jeroen, 2010, 'Activists online and offline: the internet as an information channel for protest demonstrations,' *Mobilization*, 15 (3): pp. 347–66.

————— and Peter Van Aelst, 2010, 'Internet and social movement action repertoires: opportunities and limitations,' *Information, Communication & Society*, 13 (8): pp. 1,146–71.

Van Spanje, Joost and Wouter Van der Brug, 2007, 'The party as pariah: the exclusion of anti-immigration parties and its effect on their ideological positions,' *West European Politics*, 30 (5): pp. 1,022–40.

—————, 'Being intolerant of the intolerant: the exclusion of Western European anti-immigration parties and its consequences for party choice,' *Acta Politica*, 44 (4): pp. 353–84.

Varga, Mihai, 2008, 'How political opportunities strengthen the far right:

understanding the rise in far-right militancy in Russia,' *Europe-Asia Studies*, 60 (4): pp. 561–79.

Vasilevich, Hanna, 2013, 'Majority as minority: a comparative case of autochthonous Slavs in Lithuania and Hungarians in Slovakia after the Second World War,' in Julien Danero Iglesias, Nenad Stojanović and Sharon Weinblum (eds.), *New Nation-States and National Minorities*, Colchester: ECPR Press.

Virchow, Fabian, 2007, 'Performance, emotion, and ideology: on the creation of "collectives of emotion" and worldview in the contemporary German far right,' *Journal of Contemporary Ethnography*, 36 (2): pp. 147–64.

Vuori, Juha, 2011, 'Religion bites: Falungong, securitization/desecuritization in the People's Republic of China,' in Thierry Balzacq (ed.), *Securitization Theory: How Security Problems Emerge and Dissolve*, London: Routledge.

Wada Haruki, 2004, '"Rachi sareta" kokuron o dasshite: Nikkan kokkō seijōka to tōhoku Ajia no heiwa (Getting away from "the kidnapped" national opinion: the normalization of Japan–South Korea diplomatic relations and peace in Northeast Asia),' *Sekai*, 722.

Wæver, Ole, 1995, 'Securitization and desecuritization,' in Ronnie D. Lipschutz (ed.), *On Security*, New York: Columbia University Press.

———— et al., 1993, *Identity, Migration and the New Security Agenda in Europe*, London: Pinter.

Wakamiya Yoshifumi, 2006, *Wakai to nashonarizumu: shinpan, sengo hoshu no Ajia kan* (Rapprochement and nationalism: post-war conservatives' view of Asia), (new edition), Tokyo: Asahi Shinbunsha.

Wakatsuki, Yasuo, 1991, *Sengo hikiage no kiroku* (Record of post-war repatriation), Tokyo: Jiji Tsūshinsha.

Walsh, Edward, 1983, 'Resource mobilization and citizen protest in communities around Three Mile Island,' *Social Problems*, 29 (1): pp. 1–21.

Watado, Ichirō (ed.), 1995, *Jichitai seisaku no tenkai to NGO* (Municipal policies and NGOs), Tokyo: Akashi Shoten.

Waters, Tony, 1999, *Crime & Immigrant Youth*, Thousand Oaks: Sage.

Waters, William, 2010, 'Migration and security,' in J. Peter Burgess (ed.), *The Routledge Handbook of New Security Studies*, London: Routledge.

Weatherby, Georgie Ann and Brian Scoggins, 2005, 'A content analysis of persuasion techniques used on white supremacist websites,' *Journal of Hate Studies*, 4: pp. 9–31.

Weeber, Stan and Daniel G. Rodeheaver, 2003, 'Militias at the millennium: a test of Smelser's theory of collective behavior,' *Sociological Quarterly*, 44 (2): pp. 181–204.

————, 2004, *Militias in the New Millennium: A Test of Smelser's Theory of Collective Behavior*, Dallas: University Press of America.

Weerdt, Yves De et al., 2007, 'Perceived socio-economic change and right-wing extremism: results of the SIREN – survey among European workers,' in Jörg Flecker (ed.), *Changing Working Life and the Appeal of the Extreme Right*, Aldershot: Ashgate.

Wellman, Barry, 1979, 'The community question,' *American Journal of Sociology*, 99: pp. 1,201–31.

———— and Milena Gulia, 1999, 'Net-surfers don't ride alone: virtual communities as communities,' in Barry Wellman (ed.), *Networks in the Global Village*, Boulder: Westview Press.

Wender, Melissa L., 2005, *Lamentation as History: Narratives by Koreans in Japan, 1965–2000*, Stanford: Stanford University Press.

Widfeldt, Anders, 2004, 'The diversified approach: Swedish responses to the extreme right,' in Roger Eatwell and Cas Mudde (eds.), *Western Democracies and the New Extreme Right Challenge*, London: Routledge.

Willems, Helmut, 1995, 'Development, patterns and causes of violence against foreigners in Germany: social and biographical characteristics of perpetrators and the process of escalation,' in Tore Bjørgo (ed.), *Terror from the Extreme Right*, London: Frank Cass.

Williams, Brad and Eric Mobrand, 2010, 'Explaining divergent responses to the North Korean abductions issue in Japan and South Korea,' *Journal of Asian Studies*, 69(2): pp.507–36.

Wiltfang, Gregory L. and Doug McAdam, 1991, 'The costs and risks of social activism: a study of sanctuary movement activism,' *Social Forces*, 69 (4): 987–1,010.

Wintrobe, Ronald, 2006, *Rational Extremism: The Political Economy of Radicalism*, Cambridge: Cambridge University Press.

Witte, Rob, 1996, *Racist Violence and State: A Comparative Analysis of Britain, France and the Netherlands*, London: Routledge.

Yagi, Hidetsugu, 1999, 'Gaikokujin sanseiken toiu ninki tori seiji no keisotsu (The rashness of publicity stunt politics such as voting rights for foreign residents),' *Seiron*, 328.

Yakahi, Osamu, 2005, 'Kengen suru "kokkyō": Okinawa Yonaguni no mitsu bōeki shūsoku no haikei (Salience of "national borders": background to the ending of Okinawa and Yonaguni's smuggling),' in Minoru Iwasaki et al., (eds.), *Keizoku suru shokuminchishugi: jendā/minzoku/jinshu/kaikyū* (Enduring colonialism: gender/ethnicity/race/class), Tokyo: Seikyūsha.

Yamaguchi, Tomomi, Masami Saito and Chiki Ogiue, 2012, *Shakai undō no tomadoi: feminizumu no 'ushinawareta jidai' to kusa no ne hoshu undō* (The embarassments of social movements: feminism's 'lost era' and the grassroots conservative movement), Tokyo: Keisō Shobō.

Yamamoto, Kōichi, 2010, *Kokkyō no shima ga abunai!* (The islands on our national borders are in danger!), Tokyo: Asuka Shinsha.

Yamano, Sharin, 2005, *Manga kenkanryū* (Korea hatred manga wave), Tokyo: Shinyūsha.

————, 2006a, *Manga kenkanryū 2*, Tokyo: Shinyūsha.

————, 2006b, 'Yamano Sharin rongu intabyū (Yamano Sharin long interview),' *Manga kenkanryū kōshiki gaidobukku* (Manga Korea hatred wave official guidebook), Tokyo: Shinyūsha.

————, 2007, *Manga kenkanryū 3*, Tokyo: Shinyūsha.

————, 2009, *Manga kenkanryū 4*, Tokyo: Shinyūsha.

————, 2010, *Gaikokujin sanseiken wa iranai* (Voting rights for foreign residents are not needed), Tokyo: Shinyūsha.

Yang, Taeho, 1985, 'Jijitsu toshite no "zainichi": Kan sanjung shi e no gimon

("*Zainichi*" as reality: doubts about Mr Kang sang-jung),' *Kikan sanzenri*, 43.

————, 1986, 'Kyōzon, kyōsei, kyōkan (Coexistence, symbiosis, empathy),' *Kikan sanzenri*, 45.

Yasuda, Kōichi, 2011, 'Heito supīchi no genba kara (From the site of hate speech),' *Gendai haigaishugi to sabetsu hyōgen kisei: jinshu sabetsu kinshihō to heito kuraimu no kentō* (Present-day nativism and the regulation of discriminatory expressions: an examination of laws prohibiting racial discrimination and hate crime laws), Tokyo: Daini Tokyo Bengoshikai Jinken Yōgo Iinkai.

————, 2012a, *Netto to aikoku: Zaitokukai no 'yami' o oikakete* (The net and patriotism: pursuing *Zaitokukai*'s 'darkness'), Tokyo: Kodansha.

————, 2012b, 'Nechizumu (netto fashizumu) wa kakusan suru (Nettism (net fascism) is spreading),' *G2*, 10.

————, 2012c, 'Zaitokukai wa "ima no Nihon no kibun" o wakariyasuku hyō shita mono nan desu (*Zaitokukai* is a body that readily expresses "the mood in Japan today"),' *Voice*, 419.

————, 2012d, 'Futtōsuru nashonarizumu (Seething nationalism),' *Shuppan nyūsu*, 2,288.

Yi, Jongwon, 1996, *Higashi Ajia reisen to Kanbeinichi kankei* (East Asian Cold War and South Korea–US–Japan relations), Tokyo: Tokyo Daigaku Shuppankai.

————, Masafumi Kimiya and Toyomi Asano (eds.), 2011, *Rekishi toshite no Nikkan kokkō sejōka II: Datsushokuminchika hen* (The normalization of diplomatic relations between Japan and South Korea as history II: decolonization volume), Tokyo: Hōsei Daigaku Shuppankyoku.

Yi, Yonghwa, 1993, *Zainichi Kankoku, Chōsenjin to sanseiken*, Tokyo: Akashi Shoten.

Yoshimi, Shunya, 2003, *Karuchuraru tān: bunka no seijigaku e* (Cultural turn: toward a politics of culture), Kyoto: Jinbun Shoin.

Yoshino, Kosaku, 1992, *Cultural Nationalism in Contemporary Japan: A Sociological Enquiry*, London: Routledge.

Yun, Koncha, 1992, *'Zainichi' o ikiru towa* (Living as a '*zainichi*'), Tokyo: Iwanami Shoten.

Zainichi Chosenjin no Jinken o Mamoru Kai, 1977, *Zainichi Chōsenjin no kihonteki jinken* (The basic human rights of *Zainichi* Koreans), Tokyo: Nigatsusha.

Zainichi Kankoku Seinen Dōmei Chūō Honbu (ed.), 1970, *Zainichi Kankokujin no rekishi to genjitsu* (History and reality for *Zainichi* Koreans), Tokyo: Yōyōsha.

Zainichi Korian no Nihon Kokuseki Shutokuken Kakuritsu Kyōgikai (ed.), 2006, *Zainichi korian ni kenri toshite no Nihon kokuseki o* (Rights-based Japanese nationality for *Zainichi* Koreans), Tokyo: Akashi Shoten.

Zainihon Daikan Minkoku Kyoryū Mindan Chūō Honbu (The Association of Koreans in Japan), 1982, *Sabetsu hakusho dai 6 shū: seichi sagyō o kakujitsu ni* (6th Discrimination white paper: reliably preparing the groundwork).

Zdravomyslova, Elena, 1996, 'Opportunities and framing in the transition to democracy: the case of Russia,' in Doug McAdam, John D. McCarthy and Mayer N. Zald (eds.), *Comparative Perspectives on Social Movements: Political Opportunities, Mobilizing Structures, and Cultural Framings*, Cambridge: Cambridge University Press.

Zhirkov, Kirill, 2014, 'Nativist but not alienated: a comparative perspective on the radical right vote in Western Europe,' *Party Politics*, 20 (2): pp. 286–96.

Index

www.ingramcontent.com/pod-product-compliance
Lightning Source LLC
Chambersburg PA
CBHW071839270326

41929CB00013B/2045